Studies in Literary Types
in
Seventeenth Century America
(1607-1710)

By
JOSEPHINE K. PIERCY

SECOND EDITION

ARCHON BOOKS
1969

Reprinted 1969 with permission of Yale University Press

[*Yale Studies in English, Vol. 91*]

SBN: 208 00783 0
Library of Congress Catalog Card Number: 69-15689
Printed in the United States of America

To

M. K. P. and J. W. P.,

To whom I need write no flourishing "Epistle Dedicatory," but to whom I am nevertheless grateful for moments of encouragement and hours of tedious proof-reading.

TABLE OF CONTENTS

PART I

LITERARY TYPES

	PAGE
PREFACE	ix
PREFACE, 1968	xiii
"THE TIMES OPINIONISTS"	1
"THE LATEST NEWES"	8
1. The "Pamphlets of Newes"	8
2. Witchcraft Papers	18
3. Miscellaneous Papers	27
THE ALMANAC	32
THE SCIENTIFIC ESSAY	37
1. Astronomy and Astrology	41
2. Meteorology	51
3. Agriculture	53
4. Botany	55
5. Zoölogy, Ornithology, etc.	57
6. Medicine	64
7. Mineralogy, Geology, Seismology	67
8. Anthroponomics	70
PERSONAL RECORDS	78
1. Journals, Diaries, Autobiographies	78
2. The Letter	82
DEDICATIONS, PREFACES, INTRODUCTIONS	92
1. The Familiar Spirit	93
2. The Didactic Spirit	96
3. Analysis of a Problem	100
4. Critical Estimates of Literature	101
5. The Literary Biography	127
SATIRE AND INVECTIVE	132
MEDITATIONS	147
THE SERMON AND RELIGIOUS DISCOURSE	155
THE BEGINNINGS OF BIOGRAPHY	168
COTTON MATHER	176

Part II

INFLUENCES

	PAGE
Literary Forms	203
1. Travel Books	203
2. Science	204
3. The Almanac	209
4. Histories	210
5. *Exempla* and Courtesy Books	215
Seventeenth Century Prose Style	226
The Classical Inheritance	245
"The Times Opinionists" Answered	263
Poetry	271
Appendix A	281
Almanacs (in chronological order)	281
Appendix B	331
S. Danforth, *An Astronomical Description of the Late Comet* (1665)	331
Appendix C	346
Cotton Mather, *Of Poetry and Of Style*	346
Samuel Sewall, *On Slavery*	352
Thomas Thacher, *A Brief Rule against Small Pocks*	357

PREFACE

"Among the many customs of the world, which it is become almost necessary to comply withal, it seems this is one, that a book must not appear without a Preface. And this little book willingly submits unto the customary ceremony." Thus did Cotton Mather, in 1710, introduce his *Essays to Do Good.* In 1939, his humble admirer, the author of this piece, willingly submits to the same ceremony.

Studies in Literary Types in Seventeenth Century America is derived from a dissertation originally submitted in 1937 for the degree of Doctor of Philosophy. It proposes to be a critical analysis of prose writings to determine what forms of literature were established in America before 1710. And, since American literature of this period must necessarily find its origins in established models, it proposes, also, to trace the background and influences upon these types of our earliest literature.

There is a wealth of material in the beginnings of our literature from the time that Captain John Smith landed upon the shores of America in 1607 until Cotton Mather published his little volume *Essays to Do Good* in 1710. The appearance of this book is a kind of milestone that ends the first period of our literature and looks toward another. Until then most of our literature, in spite of creative and individual touches, had been occasional. *Essays to Do Good* is a collection of short prose pieces of a wholly creative nature. Although it is written for instruction, its lessons are hardly more obtrusive than those in the essays of Addison and Steele and Dr. Johnson or in the *Do Good Papers* of Dr. Franklin whom it inspired. It closes our youngest period of literature and prepares the way for our eighteenth century.

There have always been two attitudes toward our Colonial literature: the inquisitive one of the historian who looks to it for valuable source material, and the defensive one of the critic toward those who suggest curtly that there was then no American literature. This paper does not examine this period to gather material for the history of America, nor does its author attempt to defend all its publications as literature, however prejudiced she may have grown in its study. There were no *belles-lettres* at that period. But times, rather than the character of the men, prevented their creation. Leisure, so necessary to the conscious production of creative literature, was not a part of the lives of the colonists.

There had been no study at all, previous to this one, of the literary types of early America. Coincidentally with the writing of this paper, however, there has been a growing interest in the seventeenth century, as manifest in the careful attention in scholarly anthologies given to this period[1] and in a recent revaluation of the Puritan period by Professors Perry Miller and Thomas H. Johnson in their new book *The Puritans.*[2]

Another study, a dissertation submitted to Brown University in 1933, is directly related to this subject. It is Winthrop Tilley's *The Literature of Natural and Physical Science in the American Colonies from the Beginnings to 1765.* This thesis strengthened my belief in the early interest in scientific study. I am not otherwise indebted to it. I am, however, indebted to Mr. Damon Foster of Brown University for his suggestion that I read Mr. Tilley's dissertation.

In order to make my study complete I have investigated rare books and pamphlets in the libraries of Yale and Harvard Universities, the American Antiquarian Society, the Massachusetts Historical Society, the John Carter Brown Library, and others. Where I have been unable to make personal investigation of the originals, as the material in the Huntington Library, I have examined photostat copies. The pamphlets of early sermons are now in most instances rare, and in the case of the almanacs many are extant only in

[1] E.g., *The American Mind*, edited by Harry R. Warfel, Ralph H. Gabriel, and Stanley T. Williams (New York, 1937), and *The Oxford Anthology of American Literature*, edited by William Rose Benét and Norman Holmes Pearson (1938).

[2] New York, 1938.

single copies and these are in the possession of the societies and libraries that I have just mentioned.

In an appendix to this thesis, I have incorporated a representative collection of the prose from the almanacs. In another I have included an excerpt from Cotton Mather's *Manuductio ad Ministerium,* which, though published after 1710, is undoubtedly expressive of his theories on style before that date. In this appendix, also, I have included a few rare publications.

To the librarians in the libraries and societies which I have mentioned, I am indeed grateful for their courtesy in helping me find my material. I am deeply appreciative of some suggestions and encouragement from Professor George L. Kittredge. I wish to thank Professor Kenneth B. Murdock for his permission to quote from his paper on the reading of Cotton Mather which he presented at the Modern Language Meeting at Richmond. I am indebted to Professor Vernon Schumann of Indiana University for his courtesy in translating from a difficult text the encomiums of Menander, Rhetor. My thanks are due Professor Norman H. Pearson for his thoughtful criticisms. And I am most deeply grateful to Professor Stanley T. Williams, whose wisdom and infinite patience is appreciated by his students.

PREFACE, 1968

When *Studies in Literary Types in Seventeenth Century America* was published in 1939, my efforts had been directed to the study of prose of that period with only occasional related references to poetry. Since then a greater interest in early American poetry has been developing, along with a growing recognition of early American literature as a whole. To be sure, poetry had received passing mention by several students of the period, but not even Moses Coit Tyler had given it the study that was due it.

The full extent of the colonists' interest in poetry was realized—at least for a section of the country—in Harold Jantz's *The First Century of New England Verse.* In the 1962 edition of his book, his bibliography lists some one hundred sixty poets who were born before 1670, a date he chose in order to confine his study to the seventeenth century. His book does not include the poets in the southern colonies, which could very well raise the figure of colonial poets to two hundred or more. As has been evident from our study of types, New England, the real center of colonial culture, was much more productive than the South. Nevertheless, it, too, showed considerable literary endeavor in poetry as well as prose.

It seems imperative, therefore, that my study in literary types should now include a chapter on poetry.

ABBREVIATIONS

AAS—American Antiquarian Society.

Col. Conn. Hist. Soc.—Collections of the Connecticut Historical Society.

LC—Library of Congress.

MHS—Massachusetts Historical Society.

MHSC—Massachusetts Historical Society Collections.

Narr. Pub.—Publications of the Narragansett Club.

Pub. Col. Soc. of Mass.—Publication of the Colonial Society of Massachusetts.

Part I

LITERARY TYPES

THE TIMES OPINIONISTS

Seeing the deedes of the most iust, and the writings of the most wise, not onely of men, but of God himselfe, haue beene diuersly traduced by variable iudgements of the Times opinionists; what shall such an ignorant as I expect? Yet reposing my selfe on your fauours, I present this rude discourse to the worldes construction.[1]

The "Times opinionists," to whom Captain John Smith so aptly refers, have traduced among the writings of the wise the literary endeavours of the early colonists. They have traduced, particularly, the character and the writings of the northern colonists, and, except for Smith's works, they have almost ignored the writings of the southern. In recent years, eminent writers have defended the character of the Puritan[2] and, to some extent, the character of the captain;[3] but they have done little to analyze, in the mass of material at hand, the creative processes of our forefathers' literary endeavours. If Smith was proved to be other than a glorious liar, if the Puritan was portrayed as a romanticist, the books of early America were still left unread, except by a few specialists, on the shelves of our antiquarian libraries. The reason was simple: we were among the "Times opinionists"; we had formulated our biased judgments. We had the indiscriminate notion that all these writings were theological in nature, and we feared to read moral sentiments. If we thought further, we were sure that books written in a wilderness must be necessarily crude, and we would have none of them. If we did, we chose hastily a few examples for their historical significance and deposited them in our new anthologies of American literature.

[1] Captain John Smith, *Works* (Westminster, 1895), Arber edition, Epistle Dedicatory, "A Description of New England," I, 178.

[2] E.g., Stuart Sherman in *What Is a Puritan?*

[3] E.g., Edward Arber in Smith's *Works.*

But our forefathers' writings, though composed in a wilderness, were not without form and interest. As we peruse their work, we are impressed by their persistent sense of the creative process and their zealous following of literary models already established. We discover their easy acquaintance with the literature of the classical past and contemporary England. We find emerging from the supposed "chaos," certain definite types of literature.

The colonists did not, of course, produce drama or the short-story or the novel, all of which compose the larger part of our *belles-lettres.* Drama in the seventeenth century would seem curiously inappropriate. In the South the population was too shifting to produce it; in New England, the Puritan, like the Puritans of England, would not have sanctioned it. The novel and the short-story existed neither in England nor America, but the romance found its expression in the narrative adventures. Of poetry the colonists had a fair amount. For lack of *belles-lettres* there was a prodigious amount of what we might now call non-fictional literature, ranging from a paragraph or two of the almanac to the long chronicle histories.

The shorter prose writings with which our study is concerned form themselves into definite literary types: the "pamphlet of newes," describing the new country; other papers of timely interest expressing opinion on witchcraft and matters of immediate concern; the almanac, concerning itself not only with tabular data but also with short prose pieces of moral or scientific nature; the introductions and prefaces disclosing our first attempts at literary criticism; satirical writings scattered among the almanacs and polemical works and existing, also, individually; and, finally, the sermon and its related form, the meditation, showing the most prolific and perhaps the most creative prose of the time.

Together these completely refute our indifferent conception of our early literature as wholly dry and uninteresting, as wholly factual or dogmatic. It might well have been either. Our forefathers, with so many new responsibilities, might have been content with a few factual reports on colonization and a few dull sermons. But colonial writing is neither wholly factual nor dogmatic, though at times it may have either of these qualities. It is not only informative; it is also creative. It is not only a "literature of knowledge," but also a "literature of power."

That the prose of our first American ancestors should have been prolific or creative is not at all strange if one considers the cultural background from which the authors sprang and their early endeavours to perpetuate their traditions of learning. The laws of Harvard, for instance, begin auspiciously:

> Every one competent to read Cicero or any other classic author of that kind extemporaneously, and also to speak and write Latin prose and verse with tolerable skill and without assistance, and of declining the Greek nouns and verbs, may expect to be admitted to the College: if deficient in any of these qualifications, he cannot under any circumstances be admitted.[4]

These are the first words, rendered originally in Latin, that greeted a prospective college student who might have turned to the "college catalogue" of early New England. If he was entered—and no ambitious youth of that day thought of these requirements as extraordinary—he continued with the standard set at his entrance. He must read and explain Scripture not only for the good it would do, but for the proficiency it might give him in language and logic. He must be well grounded in logic, in astronomy, and in natural and moral philosophy. He must be able to deliver and stand trial to debates and orations in English and Latin. This is the background and this the education of the youth of the New England states.

From this state of affairs, we might well make two assumptions, if we did not know them as facts already: first, that the founders of Harvard and the colonists of Massachusetts Bay were educated men; and second, that, in order to perpetuate their own standards of education, they would have libraries to educate their youth to their own standards. But

[4] *Magnalia,* II, 24.

we know that most of these men were educated in Oxford or Cambridge before they came over, and that they brought with them a surprising number of books for their own libraries.

Professor Thomas Goddard Wright ably demonstrated the intellectual background of New England in his *Literary Culture in Early New England*, 1620-1730.[5] A remarkable number of university men of recognized ability in England settled the Colony of Massachusetts Bay.[6] That is the reason why, dissatisfied with the informal education by individual tutoring first given to their youth, these men established our first university only six years after they had landed in America. They named their college "Harvard" after the man who helped to make it possible by willing them not only an estate, but a respectable personal library.[7] In planning their course of instruction, they followed the models that they had known in Oxford and Cambridge. Not satisfied with the provision merely for higher education, they made way in Massachusetts, as early as 1647, for the education of children.

The libraries of these early people are a credit to our history. Although theological works predominated, there was, nevertheless, a surprising number of books that might be classed as literary or historical. The libraries of Brewster, Bradford, Winthrop, Harvard, the Mathers, who may be taken to be the leaders of the colonies, were large in number and varied in content, and yet theirs, though perhaps larger than most, were indicative of the libraries of other citizens who could afford them. Even in Plymouth, whose first settlers were not university graduates,

> Very few of the Pilgrims were without books. The inventories of estates filed among the Wills in the Plymouth Colony Records give proof of this. Of over seventy inventories examined in the first two volumes of the Wills, only a dozen failed to make specific mention of books, and among these were some whose entire estates, including house and land, clothes and tools,

[5] Yale University Press, 1920.

[6] Cf. *ibid.*, pp. 16 & 17.

[7] For some of the books in his library see Wright, p. 18.

> amounted to only twenty-five or thirty pounds. Such people . . . would not be likely to possess books . . . even today.[8]

The libraries of these settlers did not remain stationary, but were constantly added to by shipments from England. Records are available to show orders sent by the Winthrops, the Mathers, Samuel Sewall and many other citizens as prominent or less prominent than these.[9] Presently there were booksellers. And about the middle of the seventeenth century a public library was established at Boston. Nor did the interest in books and education die with the period of the first settlers. For one thing, another university was founded in 1700, and for another "the flow of books to the New England colonies increased rather than diminished during the second period.[10] Gifts and shipments to individuals continued to come from England; booksellers became numerous; and both the Public Library and Harvard Library grew in size."[11]

The books of history, literature, science, and the classics were numerous. Among the booklists of private and public libraries and of booksellers, these authors and titles—by no means the complete list—may be picked at random: of history, Raleigh, Camden, Guicciardini, Bacon, and, if we may include authors of "natural history" here, Pliny and Bacon; of science, Robert Boyle, several books on "physicke" and "chymistry" and mathematics; of literature, Bacon (mentioned many times, with "Complete Works" and "Advancement of Learning" predominating), Sir Thomas Browne, George Wither, Erasmus, Bunyan, Feltham, Sir Thomas More, Robert Burton, Samuel Butler, Sir William Cornwallis, Quarles, Abraham Cowley, Montaigne, Milton (prose), Lilly, Taylor. Of the classics, there are the names of Cicero, Caesar, Homer, Virgil, Aesop, Demosthenes, Epicte-

[8] *Ibid.*, p. 27.
[9] *Ibid.*, cf. chaps. II and VII.
[10] 1670-1700, the period of the first American born.
[11] Wright, *op. cit.*, p. 110.

tus, Plutarch (North's translation), Plautus, Tully and others.

Perhaps the most surprising list of books is that of a consignment sent to John Usher, a Boston bookseller, in 1682. No merchant orders goods that his customers do not want. John Usher received, among other things,

> 4 esops in english, 2 felthams resolves, 16 Cap of gray haires, 9 argalus and parthenia, 1 pembrooks arcadia, 1 Bacons works, 1 Cambdens Elizabeth, 1 Miltons history, 6 Guy of Warwick, 6 Reynard fox, 12 dr. Faustus, 6 Garland of delight, 8 Soggins jests, 4 Mandeville travells, 4 pack cards.[12]

Now while Scoggings Jests and Mandeville's Travels and Reynard the Fox and Dr. Faustus do not particularly concern us here, they serve to indicate in contrast to our more limited conception of Puritan reading, the broadmindedness of the early New England readers. Perhaps in some subtle way, these books also influenced the character, point-of-view, or style of the writers of the New England Colonies.

Indeed the persistent appearance of certain literary types in our early literature, as well as in our libraries, is evidence of a lively interest not only in what men were thinking but how they were writing. We find, to be sure, a spirit of didacticism and morality pervading almost the whole of our colonial literature, whether it was purportedly scientific or admittedly didactic; but we find, also, that dogmatism did not obscure a certain literary *esprit de corps*—at least a fair beginning and one which must inevitably have paved the way for our literary men of the eighteenth century. When we look at New England before 1710 and consider the English cultural background of its inhabitants—their early founding of schools and colleges, their establishment of libraries, the activity of their booksellers, and the versatility of their reading,—we must concede that here was a fertile field for the beginning of a literature in the New World.

Captain Smith's apology for his "rude discourse" is mis-

[12] *Ibid.*, p. 121.

leading to one who does not remember the customary seventeenth century apologetic preface or who does not know the actual zest with which Smith and others wrote. Such an apology was frequent, but it betrayed less crudeness than an actual awareness of composition. Far different from the picture of crude and painful endeavour are those rather remarkable pictures of Sandys, in a wilderness, translating Ovid; of Bradford, in the midst of official burdens, recording a daily chronicle of New England's history; of Mrs. Bradstreet, while attending a busy household, producing an octavo volume of poems; of Cotton Mather, industrious Puritan, formulating his ideas on poetry and style.

THE LATEST NEWES

1. The "Pamphlets of Newes"

There can be no doubt that the active mind of Captain John Smith was at work recording what he saw from the moment that he landed upon the shores of Virginia in 1607. In 1608, he published in London "A True Relation of Such occurences and accidents of note, as hath hapned in Virginia, since the first planting of that Collony, which is now resident in the South part thereof, till the last returne." It is one of a long line of "pamphlets of newes" about the new country, published for the benefit of prospective residents there and for the delight of all good Englishmen who read with extreme eagerness these tales of adventure for which their country was responsible.

From these, there emerged two trends of development: on the one hand, the long and detailed narrative accounts and histories of the early settlers' adventures; on the other hand, the shorter and more objective descriptions and expository writings on the new land. It is with the latter that we are here concerned.

The most natural medium for these pamphlets was, of course, descriptive writing; but the ultimate object of each was exposition, in that they were written for the dissemination of information. A great part of literature has been produced to suit a given purpose and to follow a certain fashion of the age; but here, where so very much depended solely upon what the author saw, heard, and experienced in unknown territory, the element of personal reaction was quite likely to enter into the subject. In proportion, therefore, as the personality of the author and his enthusiasm for his subject colored his writing, so appeared a literary flavor in his account. Upon this depended whether the "pamphlet of newes" and its kindred accounts were merely expository records or those touched with something more; whether they belonged only to the "literature of knowledge" or approached the "literature of power"; whether in manner or attitude they were only analytical; or whether they had the contagious enthusiasm of the creative artist.

In spite of this very real difference within the "accounts" of America, most of them bore a resemblance to each other in outward form. As one looks over many of these pieces, one is impressed by the same orderly plan in their development. They are so similar in outline that one can be almost sure of some classification like the following: first, an account of the "commodities" of the new country—that is, a description of the "four elements" of medieval science: earth, air, water, and fire; second, the country's natural resources—its trees, fruits, birds, and beasts; third, its "natural inhabitants" and their strange customs; and then, perhaps, some reference to the advantages to be gained by England in the possession of such a rich and fertile land, or the advantages that are to be gained by the prospective colonist.

Sometimes these chapters and sections are distinctly separate treatments of each subject—trees, birds, air, Indians. Although each chapter is related to the subject of America, each really stands by itself in separate treatment. Except for transitional sentences obviously made to join one chapter to another, they have no internal relationship. "Thus," says Francis Higginson, "you have heard of the Earth, Water and Air of New-England. Now it may be you expect something to be said of the Fire, proportionable to the rest of the elements."[13] The Encyclopaedia Britannica is regarded as a whole, as a book of knowledge; yet each chapter of that book is a unit in itself. In a much smaller way and in a limited field, these accounts are similarly written.

When such accounts as these subordinate the personal element to the information given, we may treat them as early scientific essays and as such shall consider them in another chapter.[14] Suffice it to say here, that Captain John Smith,

[13] Alexander Young, *Chronicles of the First Planters of the Colony of Massachusetts Bay* (Boston, 1846), "New England's Plantation," p. 253.

[14] See Chap. III, "The Scientific Essay."

who is thought of as lending an atmosphere of personal adventure to all that he writes, represents very well in his *Map of Virginia*[15] the impersonal and objective point-of-view. Here, in his record of natural resources, is the literature of information gathered together and classified under marginal notes. For the moment, at least, he is a scientist and a collector of facts. Though not devoid of personal enthusiasms and individual manner, Francis Higginson in *New England's Plantation,* William Wood in *New England's Prospect,* and John Josselyn in *New England's Rareties* collect under chapter headings their findings in the new country.

In the literature of exploitation there are, indeed, many degrees of formality of style. In William Penn's accounts there is no attempt at literary expression, no purpose other than to state facts. His first pamphlet, written before he reached America, is an expository advertisement. His second is sheer exposition of the country and "advice to adventurers how to imploy their estates, with fair profit." Another example of unadorned exposition is Captain Holme's *A Short Advertisement upon the Scituation and Extent of the City of Philadelphia and the Ensuing Plat-form there of, by the Surveyor General.*[16]

Higginson, on the other hand, has a charm that these writers lack. Entranced with the new country, he records his impressions in a simple, naive manner. Without rhetorical device or conscious style, he reveals his enthusiasm and his personality. When we have finished reading his book,

[15] Full title: *A Map of Virginia. With a Description of the Country, the Commodities, People, Government and Religion.* See Captain John Smith, *op. cit.*, pp. 41 ff.

[16] *Original Narratives of Early American History* (New York, 1912) XIII, 242 f. Similar impersonal expositions may be found in accounts of other parts of the country, as in Robert Horne's "Brief Description of the Province of Carolina," *Orig. Narr.* XII, 63 ff. John Hammond wrote "Leah and Rachell, or the two fruitfull Sisters Virginia and Maryland" to give advice to those coming over and to refute derogatory accounts that had got abroad. It is bluntly written, without pretense at literary flavor. See *Orig. Narr.* XI, 277 ff.

we have a definite impression of the writer. The new land is everything, has everything, that one can wish. Milk can be bought at one cent a quart. "The form of the earth here, in the superfices of it, is neither too flat in plainnesse, nor too high in hills, but partakes of both in mediocrity, and fit for pasture or plough or meadow ground, as man pleases to employ it." The earth is whatever one wishes to find: black earth, clay, gravel, sand. There are hills and plains, wooded lands and cleared. Corn and milk are plentiful. The waters provide fish in abundance. In fact, though there be such "discommodities as little flies called mosquitoes" in summer and snow in winter, the "commodities" far outweigh them. Even a "discommodity" cannot threaten too evilly, and he tells in an engaging way about rattlesnakes:

> . . . this country being very full of woods and wildernesses, doth also much abound with snakes and serpents, of strange colors and huge greatness. Yea, there are some serpents, called rattlesnakes, that have rattles in their tails, that will not fly from a man as others will, but will fly upon him and sting him so mortally that he will die within a quarter of an hour after, except the party stinged have about him some of the root of an herb called snake-weed to bite on, and then he shall receive no harm. But yet seldom falls it out that any hurt is done by these. About three years since an Indian was stung to death by one of them; but we heard of none since that time.[17]

Daniel Denton in *A Brief Description of New York,* sees with the eyes of a naturalist and of a pastoral artist. People enter into his landscape and make it alive. Here, for instance, is the picture of an American Arcadia:

> The Fruits natural to the Island are Mulberries, Posimons, Grapes great and small, Huckelberries, Cramberries, Plums of several sorts, Rosberries and Strawberries, of which last is such abundance in June, that the Fields and Woods are died red: Which the Countrey-people perceiving, instantly arm themselves with bottles of Wine, Cream, and Sugar and in stead of a Coat

[17] Young, *op. cit.,* p. 255.

> of Male, every one takes a Female upon his Horse behind him, and so rushing violently into the fields, never leave till they have disrob'd them of their red colours, and turned them into the old habit.[18]

He had the naturalist's and the poet's interpretation of common things in nature:

> There is also the red Bird, with divers sorts of singing birds, whose chirping notes salute the ears of Travellers with an harmonious discord, and in every pond and brook green silken Frogs, who warbling forth their untun'd tunes strive to bear a part in this musick.[19]

One of the qualities of a nature essayist is his ability not only to make his landscape alive but to give his "brute neighbors" personality. "The Porcupine," says William Wood, "is a small thing not much unlike a Hedgehog; something bigger, who stands upon his guard and proclaims a Noli me tangere, to man and beast, that shall approach too neare him, darting his quills into their legges, and hides."[20]

In William Wood's account is a curious mingling of factual information and whimsicality of style. The title page of his book tells the reader it is "A true, lively, and experimental[21] description of that part of America, commonly called New England." And, indeed, it is lively, though perhaps not true, when he suspects that lions exist in the natural life of America. Some of the most "lively" parts of these chapters are original poetry which he introduces into some of his chapters, whenever he feels so inclined:

> The kingly Lyon, and the strong arm'd Beare
> The large limbed Mooses, with the tripping Deare,
> Quill darting Porcupines, and Rackcoones bee,
> Castelld in the hollow of an aged tree;
> The skipping Squerrell, Rabbet, purblinde Hare,

[18] Daniel Denton, *A Brief Description of New York* (London, 1670). Reprint, Gawan's Bibliotheca Americana (New York, 1845), p. 3 f.

[19] *Ibid.*, p. 6.

[20] *New England's Prospect* (London, 1634), p. 23.

[21] i.e., description written from experience.

Immured in the selfesame Castle are,
Least red-eyed Ferrets, wily Foxes should
Them undermine, if rampird but with mould.
The grim fac't Ounce, and ravenous howling Woolfe,
Whose meagre paunch suckes like a swallowing gulfe.[22]
Blacke glistering Otters, and rich coated Bever,
The Civet sented Musquash smelling ever.[23]

The introduction of poetry into a prose piece has been used by a few essayists from time to time.[24] It adds a touch of intimacy and poetic interpretation to the composition. As in Wood's account, it gives a personal and whimsical character to the writing.

This is manifest, also, in the writings of George Alsop of Virginia, although his work, on the whole, does not attain the refinement and ideality of the "literature of power." His *A Character of Maryland* (1666) is at the opposite pole from the strictly informative account of William Penn. He not only introduces poetry into his work to make it "lively," but he assumes an attitude of familiarity with his reader that at times amounts to pertness. We may call him literally the most familiar spirit in early American letters.[25] Alsop is not motivated, like Penn or Higginson, in giving solemn advice to those coming to live here. He seems, at least, to be writing for the fun of it. He is on intimate terms with his reader, and he feels it his privilege to handle his subject in whatever whimsical manner his mood dictates. However accurately he may present his subject, he cannot be altogether

[22] In the rather terrifying character of some of the beasts in these accounts the remote influence of animals described in fables and bestiaries is suggested. The influence, if there is any, is entirely unconscious. It is rather remarkable that, in a time when moral lessons were so very frequently pointed to, these American writers made little use of natural life for this purpose—an omission hardly to be overlooked by Christian writers well acquainted with bestiaries or fables.

[23] *Op. cit.,* p. 20.

[24] Cf. Abraham Cowley, Alexander Wilson, and Izaak Walton.

[25] Thomas Morton in his *New English Canaan* is sometimes impudent, but he thumbs his nose at the Puritan, not at the reader.

serious. The full title of his account seems staid enough and it promises the usual division of subject matter. But the contents from the three impudent prefaces to the end are written with amazing good humour. Sometimes his taste is inexcusably coarse; but, on the whole, his manner is refreshing in contrast to that of others. If he tells that Maryland cannot raise sheep because of the wolves—a serious subject enough—he must tell it in his own way:

> Mary-Land (I must confess) cannot boast of her plenty of Sheep here, as other Countries; not but that they will thrive and increase here, as well as in any place of the World besides, but few desire them, because they commonly draw down the Wolves among the Plantations, as well by the sweetness of their flesh, as by the humility of their nature, in not making a defensive resistance against the rough dealing of a ravenous Enemy. They who for curiosity will keep Sheep, may expect that after the Wolves have breathed themselves all day in the Woods to sharpen their stomachs, they will come without fail and sup with them at night, though many times they surfeit themselves with the sawce that's dish'd out of the muzzle of a Gun, and so in the midst of their banquet (poor Animals) they often sleep with their Ancestors.[26]

The separate essay-like quality of his chapters is enhanced by his trick of closing a chapter with an original poem. For instance, his first chapter "Of the situation and plenty of the Province of Mary-Land" concludes with this didactic apostrophe to Earth:

> Could'st thou (O Earth) live thus obscure, and now
> Within an Age, shew forth thy plentious brow
> Of rich variety, gilded with fruitful Fame,
> That (Trumpet-like) doth Heraldize thy Name,
> And tells the World there is a Land now found,
> That all Earth's Globe can't parallel its Ground?
> Dwell, and be prosperous, and with thy plenty feed
> The craving Carkesses of those Souls that need.[27]

[26] *Orig. Narr.*, XI, 347.
[27] *Ibid.*, p. 348.

With one exception, the nearest approach to a complete essay in the "pamphlet of newes" lies in the well-rounded chapters of such writers as Wood and Alsop. The one pleasing example of the seventeenth century essay in the "pamphlet of newes", is contributed by Captain John Smith, who can be the romantic narrator, the collector of scientific data, or the essayist. It appears in *A Description of New-England* which, on the whole, is more informally written than the work on Virginia. The author is evidently quite interested in telling people in England "of the goodnesse and greatnesse of those spacious Tracts of land." Anyone reading it might, indeed, be tempted to come over to experience for himself the healthful climate, the excellent "soyle" so amenable to agriculture, and the untold possibilities for developing a fishing industry. The account is full of the personal element; the attitude of the author is subjective. We know that it is he who has found the new country thus and so. Moreover, like the familiar essayist, he digresses from time to time. For instance, in the midst of things, he gives an autobiographical paragraph or two to show that he has no purpose but to give what is true in this account. In another place, he stops to give a bit of his own philosophy. And it is at this point that we become aware of the development of an essay. It is to be noted that the author is conscious of what he is doing, for there is a distinct break before and after this digression, and he labels it: "A note for men that haue great spirits, and smal meanes."

> Who can desire more content, that hath small meanes; or but only his merit to aduance his fortune, then to tread, and plant that ground hee hath purchased by the hazard of his life? If he haue but the taste of virtue and magnanimitie, what to such a minde can bee more pleasant, then planting and building a foundation for his Posteritie, gotte from the rude earth, by Gods blessing and his owne industrie, without preiudice to any? If hee haue any graine of faith or zeale in Religion, what can hee doe lesse hurtfull to any: or more agreeable to God, then to seeke to conuert those poore Saluages to know Christ, and humanitie, whose labors with discretion will triple requite thy charge and paines?

What so truely su[i]tes with honour and honestie, as the discouering things vnknowne? erecting Townes, peopling Countries, informing the ignorant, reforming things vniust, teaching virtue; and gaine to our Natiue mother-countrie a kingdom to attend her; finde imployment for those that are idle, because they know not what to doe: so farre from wronging any, as to cause Posteritie to remember thee; and remembring thee, euer honour that remembrance with praise?

Consider: What were the beginnings and endings of the Monarkies of the *Chaldeans*, the *Syrians*, the *Grecians*, and *Romanes*, but this one rule: What was it they would not doe, for the good of the commonwealth, or their Mother-citie? For example: *Rome*, What made her such a Monarchesse, but onely the aduentures of her youth, not in riots at home; but in dangers abroade? and the iustice and iudgement out of their experience, when they grewe aged. What was their ruine and hurt, but this; The excesse of idlenesse, the fondnesse of Parents, the want of experience in Magistrates, the admiration of their vndeserued honours, the contempt of true merit, their vniust iealo[u]sies, their politicke incredulities, their hypocriticall seeming goodnesse, and their deeds of secret lewdnesse? finally, in fine, growing onely formall temporists, all that their predecessors got in many years, they lost in few daies. Those by their pain and vertues became Lords of the world; they by their ease and vices became slaues to their seruants. This is the difference betwixt the vse of Armes in the field, and on the monuments of stones; the golden age and the leaden age, prosperity and miserie, iustice and corruption, substance and shadowes, words and deeds, experience and imagination, making Commonwealths and marring Commonwealths, the fruits of vertue and the conclusions of vice.

Then, who would liue at home idly (or thinke in himselfe any worth to liue) onely to eate, drink, and sleepe, and so die? Or by consuming that carelesly, his friends got worthily? Or by vsing that miserably, that maintained vertue honestly? Or for being descended nobly, pine with the vaine vaunt of great kindred, in penurie? Or (to maintaine a silly shewe of brauery) toyle out thy heart, soule, and time, basely; by shifts, tricks, cards, and dice? Or by relating newes of others actions, sharke here or there for a dinner, or supper; deceiue thy friends, by faire promises and dissimulation, in borrow-

> ing where thou neuer intendest to pay; offend the lawes, surfeit with excesse, burden thy Country, abuse thy selfe, despaire in want, and then couzen thy kindred, yea euen thine owne brother, and wish thy parents death (I will not say damnation) to haue their estates? though thou seest what honours, and rewards, the world yet hath for them [who] will seeke them and worthily deserue them.
>
> I would be sor[r]y to offend, or that any should mistake my honest meaning: for I wish good to all, hurt to none. But rich men for the most part are growne to that dotage, through their pride in their wealth, as though there were no accident could end it, or their life.[28]

Put bluntly Smith's text is: "America is the land of opportunity for those who have little material means, but plenty of courage." Obviously, such a paraphrase as this has the same effect upon the author's title as transcribing poetry into literal prose. How much more effective than this paraphrase and how much in the manner of the essayist is the marginal title: "A note for men that have great spirits, and small meanes." His epigrammatic first sentence, too, is worthy of an essayist. His means of developing his theme are those most popularly used by the seventeenth century essayist: the rhetorical question; the sentences, as in the first paragraph, in parallel and rhythmic structure; the examples from popular figures and episodes in history to illustrate his point, as in the second paragraph; the balanced sentence structure, as in the last sentence of that paragraph; the return to moralistic contemplation in the third; the personal reference as in the fourth.* In its rhetorical devices, its subject, its moral application, its unity of form, it is an essay. Among the "pamphlets of newes," this essay by Captain Smith is the exception. It seems to be a conscious interpretation of a form already being established, for it combines most of the

[28] Smith, *op. cit.*, I, 208 ff.

* There are four more paragraphs in this digression, but these are sufficient for illustration. The whole "note for men that have good spirits, and smal meanes" is a complete essay.

devices of the seventeenth century essayist within this digression.

On the whole, the literature of exploitation is the beginning of our informative literature. It is, in fact, well named the "pamphlet of newes," for its purpose is to inform the world of the latest news about America. It varies, somewhat like our news, and feature stories, in manner of approach, and it resembles on the one hand the "literature of knowledge" and, on the other, the "literature of power." William Penn's letters and a small part of Smith's writings are representative of the one; Higginson, Wood, Alsop, and Smith, representative of the other.

2. Witchcraft Papers

Toward the end of the seventeenth century, witchcraft was the subject of most vital interest in New England. The existence of workers in the black art and the evidence of their machinations with the devil were as unquestioned as the existence of our public enemies to-day and their machinations with the underworld. The defenders of the Puritans have proved that the witchcraft delusion was a product neither of the people of New England nor yet of religious fanatics; that it was consistent with the times and with the whole world, and that it existed in the minds of the civilized and the uncivilized, the learned as well as the ignorant.[29] The trial and punishment of a witch were merely the trial and punishment of a criminal as truly as the procedure with our lawbreakers to-day. If there had been flourishing newspapers and magazines then, they would have contained many articles on the subject by New England's most eminent men. In lieu of magazines, there appeared letters and pamphlets and books on the subject by those who were the spokesmen and writers of the day. Of all the "timely articles" that

[29] See Barrett Wendell, *Cotton Mather* (New York, 1891), Chap. VI; Kenneth Murdock, *Increase Mather* (Cambridge, 1925), Chap. XVII; G. L. Kittredge, *Witchcraft in Old and New England* (Cambridge, 1929), Chap. XVIII.

engaged the attention of the people of New England, those on witchcraft held the most excited attention.

Although the usual magazine article may be somewhat argumentative, it is meant on the whole to be impersonal, objective, analytical, and critical. However wrong an opinion expressed in it may prove to be, the author is nevertheless sincere in the presentation of his opinions. His reader's respect is enhanced by his tone of sincerity and also by the apparent authoritativeness of his opinions and his reputation for veracity.

The seventeenth century writer on witchcraft thought he was right and a great many others thought he was. There were, however, a few intellectual skeptics and several among the mildly dubious. For these the writer attempted to clarify his ideas and to prove the actual presence of workers in the black art.

On no other subject was the use of authority and illustration quite so necessary or so effective. The most obvious use of the latter was case history of the past and of contemporary times. All the papers on witchcraft,[30] whether written by believers or skeptics, were full of these. The direct evidence of eye witnesses and even of the "practitioners" themselves was the source of these "cases" and was, therefore, the most important and most often used for illustration. The quoting of authority from individuals and from history was also effective in quelling the thoughts of the doubtful. Cotton Mather, as usual, had done the most reading on the history of witchcraft. In *Enchantments Encountered,* he reminds the reader that "the Kingdoms of *Sweden, Denmark, Scotland,* yea and *England* it self, as well as the

[30] The "cases," considered individually, belong to the beginnings of narrative in America.

The most famous witchcraft papers are *An Essay for the Recording of Illustrious Providences* (1684) by Increase Mather; *Memorable Providences* (1689) and *The Wonders of the Invisible World* (1693) by Cotton Mather; *More Wonders of the Invisible World* (1700) by Robert Calef; and *A Modest Inquiry into the Nature of Witchcraft* (1702) by John Hale. See *Orig. Narr.,* XVI.

Province of *New-England,* have had their Storms of *Witchcrafts* breaking upon them . . ."[31] When about to publish his *Memorable Providences,* he remembers the work of notable English writers,

> I can with a Contentment beyond meer Patience give these rescinded Sheets unto the Stationer, when I see what pains Mr. Baxter, Mr. Glanvil, Dr. More and several other Great Names have taken to publish Histories of Witchcrafts and Possessions unto the World.[32]

Authority also rested upon the reputation for veracity of the authors of witchcraft papers. Even with his character already established, an author could command more respect if other eminent people vouched for the truth and importance of his work in its introduction. At the same time, it gave the authors of such a preface an opportunity to add their word to the subject. Four respected Boston ministers, for instance, wrote a preface to Cotton Mather's *Memorable Providences*[33] in which they discussed witchcraft, rebuked unbelievers, and recommended for the moral good of the reader a perusal of this book written by a worthy and respected author.

The fact that educated leaders of the community knew witchcraft to exist, that other countries had been affected by the same curse, and that there were eye witnesses to cases might have been sufficient evidence to make an unbeliever reconsider. But the logical manner in which the writers explained their subject and refuted arguments of skeptics was, indeed, the most convincing proof of all. As we have said before, the modern critical essay on current topics is analytical and, as far as possible, impersonal. The conviction in the reader's mind that the author is right depends upon the clarity and force with which the latter presents his subject. A logical manner, even in opinions in error, is sometimes convincing

[31] "Enchantments Encountered," *The Wonders of the Invisible World* (London, 1862), p. 17.

[32] *Orig. Narr.,* XVI, 98.

[33] Charles Morton, James Allen, Joshua Moodey, Samuel Willard. See *Orig. Narr.,* XVI, 97.

to those not too skeptically minded or critically acute. That does not mean that either the author or the reader is totally ignorant or uneducated. The arguments to prove the existence of witchcraft and the proposals for dealing with the problem were perfectly in keeping with seventeenth century thought, even among the most educated. Satan was a living force for evil, and so were his cohorts and agents, such as witches. Cotton Mather explains in his "Introduction" to *Memorable Providences* that Devils are sent "to reprove the Madness of ungodly men" and that it must be the effort of godly men "to leave no stroke untouch't that may conduce to bring men from the power of Satan unto God."[34]

Cotton Mather's little "essay" "Enchantments Encountered"[35] might interest a seventeenth century reader and lead him to believe in witchcraft by virtue of its coherent, logical, and convincing manner: In the first place, the author shows that, while the people of New England are assuredly a godly people, the appearance of Satan in their midst is not a paradox: "*If any are Scandalized, that* New-England, *a place of as serious Piety, as any I can hear of, under Heaven, should be troubled so much with Witches; I think, 'tis no wonder: Where will the Devil show most Malice, but where he is hated, and hateth most . . .*"[36] In the second place, "it may easily be supposed that the *Devil* was exceedingly disturbed, when he perceived such a People here accomplishing the Promise of old made unto our Blessed Jesus, *That He should have the Utmost parts of the Earth for his Possession.*"[37] In the third place, Mather meets a criticism against New-England—for the number of persons who have been accused or suspected—by pointing to the fact that other Kingdoms "have had their Storms of Witchcrafts."[38] He admits that a few innocent persons may have been executed, but his answer is indisputable to the man of the seventeenth

[34] *Orig. Narr.*, XVI, 98.
[35] *The Wonders of the Invisible World* (London, 1862), pp. 9 ff.
[36] *Ibid.*, p. 10.
[37] *Ibid.*, p. 13.
[38] *Ibid.*, p. 17.

century; "The best man that ever lived has been called a *Witch*: and why may not this too usual and unhappy Symptom of *A Witch*, even a Spectral Representation, befall a person that shall be none of the worst?"[39] In the fourth place, lest anyone think the Devil is present solely because of the presence of witches, other things point to his presence: "The design of the Devil . . . to sink that Happy Settlement of Government, wherewith Almighty God has graciously enclined Their Majesties to favour us."[40] And he would have us remember that the affairs of the colonists are now in the hands of men of integrity, the Governour (Phipps) and the Lieutenant Governour (Stoughton), and, also, Councellours of most Eminent Persons. "All which Things are by the Devil exceedingly *Envy'd* unto us."[41] Under these circumstances, he would

> entreat every Man to maintain an holy Jealousie over his Soul at this time, and think; May not the Devil make me, though ignorantly and unwillingly, to be an Instrument of doing something that he would have to be done? . . . let us more generally agree to maintain a kind Opinion one of another.[42]

There are worthy Men, who . . . earnestly desire to have witchcraft "sifted unto the bottom of it."[43] On the other hand, there are other worthy men who are in error in their dissatisfaction with the witchcraft proceedings though acting "by a noble Principle of Conscience."[44] But in order "to succeed in our Endeavours to deliver our distressed Neighbours, from the horrible Annoyances and Molestations with which a dreadful Witchcraft is now persecuting them," he declares that "'Tis necessary [for the people] to unite in everything."[45]

[39] *Ibid.*, p. 18.
[40] *Ibid.*, p. 21.
[41] *Ibid.*, p. 21.
[42] *Ibid.*, p. 23.
[43] *Ibid.*, p. 23.
[44] *Ibid.*, p. 24 f.
[45] *Ibid.*, p. 27.

This, in brief, is Cotton Mather's essay on "Enchantments Encountered." Supposing ourselves, for the moment, to be citizens of the seventeenth century New-England with an eager interest in this current problem, what could we find more sensible and more convincing than this?

The most "convincing" part of these discussions is their apparent impersonal analysis and, conversely, their lack of impassioned and emotional argument that one might expect as the natural product of superstition and fanaticism. Even the Mathers, whom posterity has wrongfully blamed for most of the Salem outrages, were, rather, among those of comparatively cool judgment. The impartial historian has discovered that the judges, rather than the divines, were mostly responsible for the actual suffering of the "witches." In accordance with this, Cotton Mather wrote a letter of caution in 1692 to John Richards, a judge who was about to take the bench in the witchcraft trials. It is a warning against too much credence in "spectre testimony." The fact that it is written in the year of greatest hysteria and that it questions the most frequently accepted evidence is, indeed, a credit to Mather's judgment. The letter itself turns out to be an exposition of his theories on "spectre evidence," developed in an orderly, progressive, and analytical fashion. Its theme is that such evidence is not reliable since it is possible for the Devil for his own ends to represent the shapes of persons "not onely innocent, but also very vertuous."[46]

If there had been more healthy skepticism in 1692-3, suggested by this timely discussion, the witchcraft persecutions might have died out before they had really gained momentum. The fact that the hysteria did die in a comparatively short time may be due to a few New England gentlemen—and we may include Increase Mather among those on the testimony of Brattle—who questioned the too zealous action of the courts at that time. One of these was Thomas Brattle who wrote a letter in October, 1692, to an unidentified min-

[46] For this letter, see *MHSC*, Ser. 4, VIII, 391 ff.

ister concerning the Salem witchcraft. It is not merely a passionate denunciation of the belief in witchcraft, but it is a writing in skepticism on the proceedings at Salem. He questions the methods of examinations and of the "inditements" and trials. Of the former he says,

> I would fain know of these Salem Gentlemen, but as yet could never know, how it comes about, that if these apprehended persons are witches, and, by a look of their eye, do cast the afflicted into their fitts by poisoning them, how it comes about, I say, that, by a look of their eye, they do not cast others into fitts, and poison others by their looks; and in particular, tender, fearfull women, who often are beheld by them, and as likely as any in the whole world to receive an ill impression from them. This Salem philosophy, some men may call the new philosophy; but I think it rather deserves the name of Salem superstition and sorcery, and it is not fitt to be named in a land of such light as New-England is.[47]

With respect to the confessors of witchcraft he says, "These confessours, (as they are called,) do very often contradict themselves, as inconsistently as is usual for any crazed, distempered person to do."[48]

His remarks about "inditements" and trials are equally skeptical. We need quote only a few sentences to illustrate:

> In the next place, I proceed to the form of their inditements, and the Trials thereupon . . . .
>
> This consulting of these afflicted children, as abovesaid, seems to me to be a very grosse evill, a real abomination, not fitt to be known in N. E. and yet is a thing practised, not only by Tom and John—I mean the ruder and more ignorant sort—but by many who professe high, and passe among us for some of the better sort . . . .
>
> The chief Judge is very zealous in these proceedings, and says, he is very clear as to all that hath as yet been acted by this Court, and, as far as ever I could perceive, is very impatient in hearing any thing that looks another

[47] *Orig. Narr.*, XVI, 171 f.

[48] *Ibid.*, p. 173.

> way. I very highly honour and reverence the wisdome and integrity of the said Judge, and hope that this matter shall not diminish my veneration for his honour; however, I cannot but say, my great fear is, that wisdome and counsell are withheld from his honour as to this matter, which yet I look upon not so much as a Judgment to his honour as to this poor land.
>
> But altho' the Chief Judge, and some of the other Judges, be very zealous in these proceedings, yet this you may take for a truth, that there are several about the Bay, men for understanding, Judgment, and Piety, inferiour to few, (if any,) in N. E. that do utterly condemn the said proceedings, and do freely deliver their Judgment in the case to be this, *viz.* that these methods will utterly ruine and undoe poor N. E. I shall nominate some of these to you, *viz.* The hon'ble Simon Bradstreet, Esq. (our late Governor); the hon'ble Thomas Danforth, Esq. (our late Deputy Governor); the Rev'd Mr. Increase Mather, and the Rev'd Samuel Willard.[49]

These are a few of the major points in Brattle's criticism on the witchcraft persecutions at Salem. His points are neatly made and logically reasoned. His rationalization seems to be, indeed, an anticipation of the eighteenth century and the age of reason.

The use of data, authority, and illustration and the procedure of analyses are in keeping with the critical method. This is true of the two letters from which we have just quoted: the one is a criticism of "spectre evidence"; the other, of witchcraft court proceedings. It is true, also, of the individual parts of Cotton Mather's *The Wonders of the Invisible World.* "Enchantments Encountered" is a critical exposition of witchcraft, and "The Devil Discovered" is a serious revelation of "the methods with which the Powers of Darkness do assault the Children of men." These qualities are also true of some of the prefaces written to the works on witchcraft; for instance, the preface to the "Christian Reader," to Increase Mather's Cases of *Conscience Concern-*

[49] *Ibid.*, p. 174 ff.

ing Witchcraft,[50] and the two prefaces introducing Reverand John Hale's *A Modest Inquiry Into the Nature of Witchcraft* (1702).[51] The first of these three is a short discussion of witchcraft as it then concerned the people. The second, by the Reverend John Higginson, is a commentary on witchcraft, and the last by Hale himself is a discussion of the "Mysteries of the Lord" and the "Mysteries of the Devil."

The witchcraft papers were written by men moved to express their opinions on a vital contemporary problem. One can hardly call them consciously formulated prose essays; neither can one conclude that they were written without some ideas of literary form and style, for they have certain characteristics repeated too often to be accidental. The qualities of logic and of quoting authority were true of all those papers. Frequently, but less consistently, certain seventeenth century tricks of style are obvious. For instance, the Baconian manner of opening an essay with an epigrammatic sentence was used by many of the writers on witchcraft and other contemporary problems. The Rev. John Higginson begins his epistle to Hale's *Modest Inquiry . . .*[52] with a proverb: "It hath been said of Old, That Time is the Mother of Truth, and Truth is the Daughter of Time." The four ministers introduce their preface[53] with, "The old Heresy of the sensual Sadducees, denying the Being of Angels either good or evil, died not with them; nor will it, whiles [sic] men (abandoning both Faith and Reason) count it their wisdom to credit nothing but what they see and feel . . . ."[54] Cotton Mather, particularly happy at this sort of thing, begins his introduction to *Memorable Providences* with, "It was once the Mistake of one gone to the Congregation of the

[50] Published in the same volume with Cotton Mather's *Wonders of the Invisible World,* pp. 221 ff. The preface is signed by fourteen prominent men, including William Hubbard, Charles Morton, Michael Wigglesworth and Samuel Willard.

[51] *Orig. Narr.,* XVI, 395.

[52] See above.

[53] *Supra,* p. 20.

[54] *Orig. Narr.,* XVI, 95.

Dead, concerning Survivers, *If one went unto them from the dead, they will repent.*"[55]

Besides these occasional introductory sentences so very characteristic of the seventeenth century essay, one finds among the witchcraft papers of the Mathers a few interesting uses of the term *essay* itself. "An Essay for the Recording of Illustrious Providences" may be taken in the old sense of the term as "An Attempt to Record . . . ." On the other hand, Cotton Mather closes the introduction to his *Memorable Providences* with, "Go then, my little Book, as a Lackey to the more elaborate Essayes of those learned men . . . ."[56] I very much question whether "Essayes" as used here could be interpreted strictly in the old meaning of "attempt." That sense, it seems to me, has been used heretofore subjectively—the application of the term by an author to his own book as a modest gesture before his reading public. I have not found it used in this sense as a term applied to a class of writing. It seems to me that, as Cotton Mather uses it here, he has a growing conception of it as a form of writing that anticipates its later history.

The term occurs again in the endorsement to his letter written to John Richards.[57] "Mr. Cotton Mather, an Essay Concerning Witchcraft." This, certainly, cannot be termed as an "attempt" or a "trial" concerning witchcraft, but an *essay* concerning witchcraft.

The arresting epigram at the beginning of these discussions and the use of the term "essay" do not occur with sufficient frequency to be called characteristic. Nevertheless, they do indicate an awareness of literary form and style.

3. Miscellaneous Papers

Although the subject of witchcraft consumed the greater part of the writings on contemporary problems, there were critical writings on other current questions, such as: exhorta-

[55] *Ibid.*, p. 97.
[56] *Ibid.*, p. 98 f.
[57] *Supra*, p. 23.

tions to the people concerning "the peril of the times,"[58] an exposé of the wickedness of the "stage-player,"[59] timely "articles" on "things that young people should think upon,"[60] Bacon's Rebellion, the wars with the Indians, and innumerable political questions in the election sermons. These obviously are contemporary problems open to criticism and analysis.

Winthrop's "little speech on liberty"[61] (1645), an oration delivered before a court, is, when stripped of personal and provincial references, an admirable exposition on the meaning of liberty.

The principles of personal liberty were expressed in another way later by George Keith and Samuel Sewall. In 1693, in Pennsylvania, George Keith issued from the Philadelphia Press our first printed protest against slavery, *An Exhortation & Caution to Friends Concerning Buying or Keeping of Negroes*[62]—an essay on the fact that "the buying of the souls and bodies of men for money" is not consistent with Christianity—especially that of the "Christian Quakers."

In New England, Samuel Sewall expresses his ideas on slavery in *The Selling of Joseph* in 1700[63] and in *The Athenian Oracle* in 1705.[64] Although both of these are broken by "Question" or "Objection" and "Answer," they are nevertheless critical commentaries on a current problem. The theme of the first, and for that matter of the second, is *"Forasmuch as Liberty is in real value next unto*

[58] Cf. Samuel Willard, *The Peril of the Times Displayed* (Boston, 1700).

[59] Cf. Cotton Mather, "The stage-player unmasked" in *Batteries Upon the Kingdom* of the Devil (London, 1695).

[60] Cotton Mather, *Things that Young People Should Think Upon* (Boston, 1700), For further mention of these, see the chapter on "The Sermon . . . ," p. 155.

[61] *Orig. Narr.*, IX, 237.

[62] Reprint in *The Pennsylvania Magazine of History and Biography* (Phila., 1889).

[63] Anti-slavery tract published in Boston, June 24, 1700. Reprinted in footnote in *Diary of Samuel Sewall*, MHSC, Ser. 5, VI, 16-20.

[64] Boston, 1705. Massachusetts Broadside. See Appendix C.

Life: None ought to part with it themselves, or deprive others of it, but upon most mature Consideration." Its timeliness is suggested by the first sentence,

> The Numerousness of Slaves at this day in the Province, and the Uneasiness of them under their Slavery, both put many upon thinking whether the Foundation of it be firmly and well laid; so as to sustain the Vast Weight that is built upon it.

His chief consideration is that there can be no real slavery since all men are the sons of Adam. But he also touches economic principles. In his letter published in the *Athenian Oracle* he destroys the rationalization that negroes are not stolen, but are taken as prisoners of war. After all who makes these wars? is his pertinent question.

On war itself, we find an expression in a protest written by William Hooke. His definition of war and his vivid picture of it is one, calculated like many others, to influence his hearers and readers against it. It is a bit too alliterative and rhetorical for our day of realism, but in its own day it must have been an effective condemnation of war. It is eloquent despite its fine writing:

> If you should but see Warre described to you in a Map, especially in a Countrey, well knowne to you, nay dearely beloved of you, where you drew your first breath, where once, yea where lately you dwelt, where you have received ten thousand mercies, and have many a deare friend and Countrey-man and kinsman abiding, how could you but lament and mourne?
>
> Warre is the conflict of enemies enraged with bloody revenge, wherein the parties opposite carry their lives in their hands, every man turning prodigall of his very heart blood, and willing to be killed to kill. The instruments are clashing swords, ratling speares, skul-dividing Holberds, murthering pieces, and thundering Cannons, from whose mouthes proceed the fire, and smell, and smoake, and terrour, death, as it were, of the very bottomlesse pit. Wee wonder now and then at the sudden death of a man: alas, you might there see a thousand men not onely healthy, but stout and strong, struck dead in the twinckling of an eye, their breath exhales without so much as, *Lord have mercy upon us.* Death heweth

its way thorow a wood of men in a minute of time from the mouth of a murderer, turning a forest into a Champion suddenly; and when it hath used these to slay their opposites, they are recompenced with the like death themselves. *O, the shrill eare-piercing clangs of the Trumpets, noise of Drums, the animating voyces of Horse Captaines, and Commanders, learned and learning to destroy! There is the undaunted Horse whose neck is clothed with thunder, and the glory of whose nostrills is terrible; how doth hee lye pawing and praunsing in the valley, going forth to meete the armed men? he mocks at feare, swallowing the ground with fiercenesse and rage, and saying among the trumpets, Ha, Ha, hee smels the battell a far off, the thunder of the Captaines and the shouting.* Here ride some dead men swagging in their deepe saddles; there fall others alive upon their dead Horses; death sends a message to those from the mouth of the Muskets, these it talkes with face to face, and stabs them in the fift rib: In yonder file there is a man hath his arme struck off from his shoulder, another by him hath lost his leg; here stands a Soldier with halfe a face, there fights another upon his stumps, and at once both kils and is killed; not far off lies a company wallowing in their sweat and goare; such a man whilst he chargeth his Musket is discharg'd of his life, and falls upon his dead fellow. Every battell of the warriour is with confused noise and garments rouled in blood. Death reignes in the field, and is sure to have the day which side soever falls. In the meanewhile (O formidable!) the infernall fiends follow the Campe to catch after the soules of rude nefarous souldiers (such as are commonly men of that calling) who fight themselves fearlesly into the mouth of hell for revenge, a booty or a little revenue. How thicke and three-fole doe they speed one another to destruction? A day of battell is a day of harvest for the devill.

All this while, the poore wife and tender children sit weeping together at home . . .[65]

The most often quoted of timely criticisms are those from Nathaniel Ward's "Simple Cobler of Aggawam in Amer-

[65] Quotation in Hon. Francis Baylies, *The Ministry of Taunton* (London, 1853). For a defense of the soldier and of justifiable war, see Benjamin Wadsworth, *Good Soldiers a Great Blessing* (Boston, 1700).

ica." Here one has satirical comment on anything from Ireland to women's styles. There is spice in the reading as there is spice in the "Spectator" and the "Tatler," but a good deal more of malice. This curious tract is a critical protest against the sins of Old and New England. The author sees the need for reform and he assumes the role of adviser. "I am the unablest adviser of a thousand, the unworthiest of ten thousand; yet I hope I may presume to assert what follows without just offence."[66] His heart detests a number of things, but the greatest of these is toleration. Upon this basis, he analyzes the weaknesses of his contemporaries. His garrulous, biting satires anticipate, in a less tolerant and happy way, the social criticism of the eighteenth century. With less genius, they anticipate the misanthropy of Swift. Ward is utterly fearless: he may criticize a king and his counsellors; he would recommend an expedition against the Irish; he would institute a reform in woman's dress, which he thinks is undoubtedly the source of most evil.

These "essays" of Ward's together with the literature of exploitation and of contemporary problems, belong to informative rather than creative literature. They deal with the news of the day, with subjects of current interest. In their separate ways, they anticipate the expression of opinion which must eventually give birth to newspapers and magazines.

[66] Nathaniel Ward, "The Simple Cobler of Aggawam in America." London, 1647. Boston, 1713. Reprinted in Peter Force, *Historical Tracts* (Washington, 1844), Vol. III, No. 8, p. 6.

THE ALMANAC

The almanacs of early America are a rich and interesting source in the beginnings of the essay. Their purpose was primarily to disseminate astronomical and astrological information. This gave rise to short explanations or expository essays on heavenly phenomena, and, also, on their influence on the lives of human beings. The latter included not only the influence of heavenly bodies upon individual lives, but also upon everything from the letting of blood to the planting of crops. The majority of these short expositions were not, however, merely superstitious in point-of-view. They showed, rather, an honest questioning of natural phenomena and an effort at reasonable explanation, attitudes that are fundamental to scientific investigation. But the almanac was not devoted wholly to a discussion of natural phenomena. A purely mechanical circumstance gave opportunity for the composer of the almanac to make personal comment on sundry matters; for, when the table of computations was completed, space was left at the bottom of the last page or on the last page or two for odd bits of information; or for didactic instruction; or, as was frequently the case, for satirical comments on rival almanac-makers.

The almanacs were not compendia of ill-gotten information. They were written by well-educated men of whom Brattle, Chauncy, Dudley, and Flint were only a few. Even the names of Nathaniel and Cotton Mather dignified a few numbers. The usual author of the almanac had to be educated in mathematics and general science. It was no wonder, then, that these well-informed men should find their almanacs media for other than tabular information. Occasionally, indeed, they invaded the realm of pure literature so far as to add bits of poetry to these small pamphlets, sometimes giving in these scientific information, sometimes indulging in moral or philosophic comment.[67]

Cotton Mather and John Sherman found the almanac a proper place for religious instruction. "J. S." introduced his almanac for 1677 by "A brief Essay to promote a religious improvement of this preceding Calendar,"[68] and in it instructs its reader to look to the heavens for inspiration of the Divine Maker. Cotton Mather declares that the "advancement of *Scripture-Knowledge,* and *Christian Piety*" was "no unsuitable Service for an Almanack,"[69] and therefore takes the opportunity to deliver a short sermon beseeching the Readers of the Almanacs to become Christian Men.

Josiah Flint, in 1666, writes a short moral discourse on "The Worlds Eternity is an Impossibility."[70] John Tulley, in 1695, writes "An Account of the Cruelty of the Papists acted upon the Bodies of some of the Godly Martyrs,"[71] which is a short history of Protestant martyrs like John Wickleif [sic], Thomas Cranmer, and other familiar figures of the Reformation. The moral is implied by example. There is always something inspiring in the contemplation of the stars, and it is not to be wondered at that such men as these found the almanac a convenient place for moral preachments.

Other odd bits of information were put into the almanac to fill up space. Clough, for 1706, adds short expositions of "the difference between Troy & Averdupoize weights: As

[67] Wars beget Poverty, Poverty Peace,
Peace maketh Riches flow (fate ne'er doth erase)
Riches produceth Pride, Pride is Wars ground
War begets Pov'rty, and so th' World goes round.
Daniel Leeds, *The American Almanack for 1710.*

[68] Cambridge. Here, it seems to me, is another instance of that mingling of *essay* meaning "attempt" and *essay* meaning a brief form of literature. It could mean either in this instance. Such ambiguity may be indicative of a transition period from the time that the word indicated only the apologetic *attitude* of the writer to the time that it indicated a *form* of literature.

[69] Cambridge, 1683.

[70] Cambridge. See Appendix A.

[71] Boston.

also an Account of the Jewish Coins, Weights and Measures mentioned in the Scripture; Carefully Collected from a Learned & Judicious Author, and reduced to our English Standards, which (though not Astronomical yet) may be of great use for the better understanding many places in the Bible."[72]

"An Account of the Christian Era" was a favorite subject. William Brattle in 1682[73] and Clough in 1707[74] include it in their almanacs. Brattle writes only a few sentences, but Clough writes more elaborately in his endeavor to show that "the incomparable Mr. William Whiston, Professor of the Mathematiks in the University of Cambridge, in an Exquisite Work of his, about the Chronology of the Bible, but lately Published, has now brought the matter under such a Demonstration, that it is no longer to be disputed of." And he gives "the Sum of the matter" in a short explanation.

In William Brattle's almanac there are several short expository compositions besides the one "Of the Christian Era"—some only of a paragraph—on "the notation of the word, Ephemeris," "Of the Julian Year, and Bissextile or Leap-Year," "Of the Gregorian Calendar," and some paragraphs on astronomical matters in the usual manner. But his introduction to this almanac is, in our study, the most interesting of all, for it has the subject, the wisdom, the philosophic comment, the personal quality, and the style of the seventeenth century essay:

> Reading without Understanding, is one way to introduce the tongue of a Parrat into the head of a Rational creature:
>
> This heedless reading is that, that hath caused many men Parrat-like [sic] to talk of things so by Roat, and so absurdly, that one would be ready to think, that man might properly suffer the distribution of Animal *in genere*, into Rationall and Irrationall Beings. I remember a Learned man being about to prove that Brutes

[72] Boston, 1705.
[73] Cambridge.
[74] Boston.

were Irrationall, or beings without Reason among the rest of his *gravia argumenta* (weighty arguments) to this end, doth lay down this viz. (*quod nec causas, nec effecta rerum intelligunt,*) their not understanding of the causes or effects of things; and truely, if this argument doth sufficiently prove the thing intended, (as I suppose no man that doth understand it aright will deny) then I think I should not be guilty of a weak, or false argumentation, if from its being so with many men, I should inferr the Irrationallity of many who bear the title of Rational creatures. They are such who perhaps have attained to the perfect knowledge of the *oti* of these and those things, (a knowledge where of even bruit beasts may attain unto) but as fot[?] a right understanding of the *dioti* of them, their Pates truly are so shallow, that it is (if not impossible yet) very improbable, that it should ever harbour there.

In a word, many men there are, who though they are potentially Rational, yet actually are they not Irrational beings? But seeing that they are arrived at a Port so near to that of Rationality as that they are potentially (yet should be actually) there, I think it would not be amisse, if every one would endeavour (as opportunity does serve) the turning this *Potentia* in *actum*; Having respect to the verity of that Philosophical axiome, *Frustra est potentia quae non traducitur in actum.*

This indeed is the end, which I have proposed to my self in making that improvement of the vacant piece of paper which you see I have; That men might not only know the *oti* of things made mention of in the *Ephemeris,* as that there will be an *Eclipse* of the Sun or Moon or such a Configuration on this or that day, and the like, but that they may also know the *dioti* of them, what the Reason of an Eclipse of the Sun or Moon is; and whence it comes to pass that there is said to be a Trine, Quar iie and the like of these and those Planets at such times, etc.

And that I might attain my end, I have (not having over much regard to concisenesse or propriety of words) spoke to things so largely and so plainly, that even men of mean capacities may come to know a Reason for, and the meaning of many things here made mention of, which before (perhaps) they were wholly ignorant of.[75]

[75] William Brattle, *An Ephemeris of Celestial Motions* (Cambridge, 1682).

No other almanac writer does so well as this by the seventeenth century essay. A promise from Leeds in the two titles "Of Swearing" and "Of Enthusiasm" turns out to be a criticism of religious forms among the Quakers.[76] He gives better promise of essay-writing in such poetic commentary as one finds on his title-pages:

> Death *is a Fisher-man,* the World, *we see*
> *His* Fish-Pond is, *and* we *the Fishes be*:
> He sometimes, Angler-like, doth with us play,
> *And slyly takes us One by One away*;
> *At other times he brings his Net, and then*
> *At once sweeps up whole Cities full of them.*[77]

With occasional exceptions like these of Brattle and Leeds, most of these short pieces to be found in the almanacs are merely prose paragraphs in instruction and miscellaneous information. By far the greatest number, however, deal with scientific subjects. These, together with other papers, deserve special attention and are discussed in the next chapter.

[76] Daniel Leeds, *Almanack* (New York, 1706).

[77] Daniel Leeds, *The American Almanack* . . . for 1705. Such use of epigram in rhyming couplet, which equals the axiom of prose essays, suggests that Pope used the term "essay," not only in application to thought, but also to epigrammatic prose.

THE SCIENTIFIC ESSAY

The subjects for scientific comment in colonial America were by no means limited to astronomical observations, although these formed the major part of them. In the almanacs, travel journals, letters and elsewhere there are scientific essays on various branches of science: in agriculture, zoölogy, botany, mineralogy, medicine, and meteorology. In New England, particularly, this was not at all unnatural since the divines were, as we have said, broadly educated. Charles Morton was not only minister of Charlestown, but teacher of physics as well. The Reverend Edward Taylor of Westfield, Connecticut, found time to transcribe Riviere's "Principles of Physic" for his own use, particularly to satisfy his own curiosity in "metallographia."[78] He found time, also, to compile a kind of encyclopedia of four hundred twenty-six quarto pages, carefully indexed and with a glossary of terms, on sundry scientific matters: mineralogy, entomology, ornithology, medicinal "recipes" and, mostly, botany.[79] Apparently there were no religious scruples against scientific study among the divines. The reconciliation of the two studies, since then so very often in conflict, may be explained by the preface to Charles Morton's textbook on physics:

> The usuall Proem of Physicks shews it to be a propper science in y^t it hath all ye Requisites which to science do belong: viz. ye End, *Contemplation*, and y^e *object*, a reall and necessary being. The End, Contemplation; ye end indeed of science or that which puts a man upon ye study of nature, both may be, and should be, both practice and operation; and y^t in many ways: as medicine, Husbandry and all Handye Crafts, and Trades

[78] See manuscript formerly owned by Ezra Stiles and now in the possession of Yale University.

[79] See manuscript copy in the possession of Yale University.

wch can never be well Handled, without some understanding of ye nature of those things, which we have in Hand. Yet ye End and Last Design of ye science itselfe is to enable a man to contemplate; and meditate upon ye nature of bodies, and ye like may be said of all other sciences.

The scient meditates for Operation
The science hath its end in Contemplation.

Of scientific method and discovery he has this to say:

. . . Now because of ye necessity which is scientificall, there are *many* things in nature most certain and demonstrable; and yet it must be acknowledged y^{t} the Doctrine of Bodyes admitts of *more disputes* y^{n} any other part of Philosophy; so y^{t} ye gratest part of it is made up of opinions and conjectures, how that comes to pass wch appears to be; this they call ye solving ye Phainomina of Nature.

You may remember in Logick, The Rule of settling Probable opinions, is by—*sense, Observations, Experience,* and *Induction.* Now because somethings, fall out in some Place or Age more observable than in another and because men also in severall Places and times are born of more y^{n} ordinary Reach, Sagacity, Opportunityes, Encouragements etc.: and Lastly because there is a mutuall subserviency of Arts and sciences (Like stones in an arch which support each other) and some of these have been at several seasons, and by degrees improved (as for instance printing, optick Glasses, Chymistry, Anatomie, Bitumen [?] etc.) hence it is that Latter [*sic*] observations do contradict ye former Hypotheses [or suppositions] and therefore these new Discoveries do beget new Suppositions which after observations will be again Regulating, so that in this matter we can't say certainly which is the very truth, but what seems most probable according to ye discoveries already made.

And hence grows a distinction of ye old and new Philosophy: and y will never be still, (in all Likelyhood as to some particulars) even unto the End of the World.

Where new appearance is before ye Eyes,
New suppositions thereupon arise.

And yet, (notwithstanding this uncertainty) it is not impertinent for men to be inquisitive into ye mystery of *nature natured* (ye Creation) which is ye worke of

> *nature naturing* (ye Creator) because it makes for his Glory and our own good: yea it is his command y^{t} wee should meditate upon all his works both of Creation and Providence. Hence David's practice, (Ps^{m}: 4. 3 & 5) I meditate on all thy works, *I muse on ye works of thy Hands. This is ye travel God hath given to ye sons of men to be exercised in it* (Eccle: 3: 10) yea tho it be Perfectly unconquerable by y^{m}, *he hath made everything beautifull in its Time*: also he hath set ye world [word?] in their hearts, so that no man can find out ye work that God maketh from the beginning to ye End: (verse 11) (see also Job: 11: 3 [?]) *yet hath he set it in their hearts*: He hath given y^{m} an instinct for inquiry: & Pleasures—concomitant, to encourage y^{m}. The works of the Lord are great, sought out of all them y^{t} have pleasure therein; *Psalm*: *111*: *27*. And hence it is said (Pro: 18) Thro' Desire a man having seperated himselfe, seeketh and intermedleth with all Wisdom. A fool hath no Delight in understanding etc.: so y^{t} you see it is naturall theology y^{t} men should be industrious in naturall Phylosophy.
>
> Tho' man can't fully know w^{t} God hath done,
> Yet tis his duty still to think thereon.[80]

This preface is, in brief, an exposition of the seventeenth century approach to the study of science.

"Though man can't fully know what God hath done, yet it is his duty still to think thereon." The end of science is Contemplation. This was at least the intelligence and understanding of the clergy. If there was doubt and distrust of science, it existed among the laymen. Daniel Leeds in his "Postscript" to his anthology, "the Temple of Wisdom" expresses his uneasiness concerning too much inquisitiveness on man's part concerning "Mysteries" that penetrate even to "the Celestial Seats of the blessed":

> . . . I . . . do verily believe, that there is nothing more pernitious, nothing more destructive to the well-being of men, or to the Salvation of our Souls than the Arts & Sciences themselves. All Sciences are as well

[80] *Philosophia Naturalis Ex Authoribus Extracta* per Dominum Carolum Mortonum (Cambridge, 1707), MS copy in the possession of Harvard University. Used here by permission of the librarian.

> evil as good, & they bring no other advantage to excel as *Deities,* more than what the Serpent promised of Old, when he said, *Ye shall be as Gods, knowing Good* and *Evil.* . . But if God and just men be the professors of Knowledge, than [*sic*] Arts and Sciences may probably become useful to the publick-weal, though they render their professors nothing more happy. Nor doth it follow that the Sciences themselves have any thing of Virtue, any thing of Truth in them, but what they reap and borrow from the Inventors and Professors thereof; for if they light upon an evil Person, they are hurtful, as a perferse *Grammarian,* an ostentatious *Poet,* a lying *Historian,* a flattering *Rhetoritian,* a litigious *Logician,* a turbulent *Sophister,* . . . a heretical & seducing *Divine.*[81]

This, he said, in spite of his own excursions into astronomy.

Many of the most eminent among the clergy carried on scientific investigations to such purpose that they were made members of the Royal Society of London and were in constant communication with such notable persons as Sir Robert Boyle and Sir Robert Moray. John Winthrop, Jr., and Cotton Mather were two of the most respected members of the Society who resided in America.

The treatment of scientific subjects, however, and their place of writing and publication, were not limited on the one hand to the clergy nor, on the other, to such a medium as the almanac. Explorers and promoters wrote their scientific findings in their journals, and the letters of corresponding members of the Royal Society conveyed such information abroad as they found of scientific interest. We find, then, among the letters, journals, and almanacs written before 1710 in America, a prolific and varied writing on such branches as astronomy and its questionable ally, astrology; agriculture; botany; zoölogy and ornithology; mineralogy, geology and seismology; meteorology; anthroponomics; and medicine.

One does not find here merely the coldly scientific. The kind of contemplation of heavenly bodies of which Charles Morton

[81] Daniel Leeds, *The Temple of Wisdom for the Little World* (Philadelphia, 1688), p. 117 f.

spoke so enthusiastically would naturally give rise to moral applications, so that frequently a prose piece that promised, or was intended to be a scientific writing is really a little sermon in disguise.

We can therefore anticipate certain conclusions concerning these beginnings in scientific writings: their authors attempted to disseminate knowledge concerning natural phenomena. In this, their work was analytical and instructive. But since their authors' real end was a contemplation of the universe as a manifestation of its Divine Maker, they would naturally have a tendency to moral interpretation. We need not expect here such objectively scientific essays as a Huxley would write, nor such entertaining nature essays for laymen as our American naturalists have since written; but, however groping and unenlightened in comparison they may seem at times, they were trying to arrive at truth concerning natural phenomena in a creditably scientific spirit. Although the authors of these "essays" were not living in the scientific age of the nineteenth and twentieth century, we should remember that they were not unenlightened. Aristotle had lived before them, and Galileo had been their contemporary.

1. Astronomy and Astrology

Astronomy was the most popular subject of discussion among the scientists of early America. Of course, a study of the stars had always fascinated civilized man in every part of the world, whether they appeared to him with scientific or divine significance; and speculation concerning them had been perennially stimulated by fresh discoveries. In the seventeenth and early eighteenth centuries, the Copernican theory of the universe, although propounded a century before, was not sufficiently old to be commonplace; and the telescope had only recently opened up a new and exciting universe. "Astronomy," says Jacob Taylor in his almanac for 1709, "of all the Arts and Sciences that are known (that of Money Getting excepted) has through all Ages been the most admired, the most studied & followed with the greatest Application . . ."[82]

"S. C.," in his almanac for 1661 writes "A breif [*sic*] Discourse of the Rise and Progress of Astronomy." It is a short historical account more discursively moral than plainly factual:

> Man at his First Creation, being endued w^{t} an immortal soul, no less enflamed with an insatiable desire after, then active in the eager attainment of all knowledg [*sic*], was no sooner set by out of the hands of his Maker, upon the Theatre of this Terrestrial world, against those Celestial Lights, (though to enamour his soul not to incrustate his body as some fabulous Jewish Doctours have fondly conceited,) but being of an upright countenance, an Emblem of his Soveraignty over the Creatures, he quickly fixed his eyes upon those glorious objects then presented to his view, and was as quickly acquainted with their regular harmonious motions, But man now since the lapse, is fallen at so great a distance, that his dim Intellectualley [*sic*] by reason likewise or the dark *medium* of body can at first give but a probable conjecture, not get a distinct perception of any object whatsoever, so that its [*sic*] no wonder if this as all other sciences in every age do receive but by degrees some small addition. . .[83]

The compiler only mentions historical facts: the rôles of Egypt and Greece in the study of astronomy, and the development of the science by Aristarchus, Pythagoras, "Ptolomens," Copernicus, "Keplerus" and others.

"Thus," he concludes, "after many sore and tedious throwes time obstetricating, at length

> *"Experientia Scientiam, Scientia veritatem,*
> *sed veritas odium peperit."*[84]

In this instance, and in others, the essay that to all appearances proposes to be a scientific discussion is, after all, a

[82] Jacob Taylor, *An Almanack for the Year of Christian Account 1709*, Philadelphia.

[83] Cambridg [*sic*].

[84] Cambridg [*sic*].

moral lesson in disguise. Others, however, were limited to a more factual treatment.

The Galilean and Gregorian telescopes, of 1609 and 1663 respectively, were sufficiently new to be exciting novelties. N. Mather, quite frankly wishing to fill up a page in the "Boston Ephemeris" for 1685, remarks, "It will not be unpleasant in this Page, which would otherwise be vacant; to take a short view of the Discoveries that have been made in the Heavens with, and since the invention of the Telescope." His "short view" does not resemble an essay so much as an expanded catalogue of things. Similar is the short expository paragraph by Newman in his almanac for 1691. Other dryly expository paragraphs of this nature are those written on the signs of the Zodiack such as Jeremiah Shepard's for 1672[85] and Jacob Taylor's for 1706.[86]

More completely developed are those short expositions such as N. Chauncy writes on the "Primum Mobile" for 1662;[87] I. Chauncy, on "The Theory of Planetary Orbs" for 1663;[88] Alexander Nowell, on "The Suns Prerogative Vindicated" for 1665;[89] J. Foster, on a "Brief Description of the Coelestial Orbs according to the Opinion of that Ancient Philosopher Pythagoras, and of all latter Astronomers," for 1675;[90] N. Mather, "Concerning some late discoveries respecting the Fixed Stars," for 1686;[91] and Danforth's,[92] Foster's,[93] C. Mather's,[94] and Clough's[95] essays on the comets. And there are innumerable short essays on the eclipses of the moon and the sun and on the tides. These and the others

[85] Cambridge.
[86] Philadelphia.
[87] Cambridge.
[88] Cambridge.
[89] Cambridge.
[90] Cambridge.
[91] Boston.
[92] Cambridge, 1665.
[93] Boston, 1681.
[94] Boston, 1683.
[95] Boston, 1703.

mentioned above vary in length from a reasonably short paragraph to two or three pages of the almanac.

An example of the former is Daniel Travis's explanation "Of The Eclipses of the Sun":

> THe Sun is said to be Eclipsed either in whole or in part, when the Moon interposeth between the Sun and our Sight. Tho' it may more properly be called an Eclipse of the Earth, for the Sun loseth not its light, as many foolishly imagine, but only is hid from our Sight for a time. The Eclipse of the Sun happens always when the Moon is in Conjunction with him, she being in the dragons head or tail, or near unto them, this Eclipse may be total in some Places, when partial in others, and not at all in other places. The Sun also may be Eclipsed centrally, and it is not total, the reason is, because sometimes in a central Eclipse, the apparent diameter of the Moon is less than the apparent diameter of the Sun; so that it cannot totally Eclipse it: but the Moon being between our Sight and the center of the Sun, there will still be a ring of light around the circumference of the Moon.[96]

An example of the longer scientific "essay" is that "Postscript" to the almanac of H. Newman "Exhibiting somewhat Touching the Earth's Motion."

> The Familiarity of Discourse upon this Hypothesis, one would think might have given it an Universall receipt, er'e now, s[in]ce it is generally Observed, that Reiteration inculcate's [*sic*] the Credit of a Thing, and *Imprints* it so Strongly in the fancie of the accustomed Hearer, that he'l not receive the contrary without a Reason, and in the mean while can give no more for his own Opinion than for the other, but only that it is the generall voice and that every wise man Beleives [*sic*] it;—*This is all the Argument some men have for their Differing in Religion.*
>
> The *Tenet* of the earths Rotundity not very long since was Look'd on as a Damnable Haeresie, and the *Hypothesis* of Solid Orbs was then in Fashion: And had the Supposition before us been alike Embrac'd by our Predecessours (tho' it would not well have Harmoniz'd with the Notion of the Earths being Flat, yet without

[96] Boston, 1707.

doubt) it would have been so Naturall to us to have Beleiv'd it, that Arguments for that end would have been needless. As for the Common *Hypothesis* it hath no Argument to defend itself, but what hath been already mentioned, and the Suggestions of mens Fancies that we must needs be sensible of it, if it were so, thinking it less Credible and more unlikely for the Earth of Mean bigness compared with the other Planets (the Moon excepted) to be turned on it's Center once in 24 hours, then to Beleive that the Vast SUN (by judicious Observers accounted no less then [*sic*] A Hundred & Fourty times bigger then the Earth) hath been Hurled about all Ages past with a Swiftness unutterable, exceeding Seventeen Thousand Four Hundred Eighty-Nine Miles in a minute: for so much as even each point of the *Superfices* of the Earth it self, if supposed to move by Just allowance, most [*sic*] Run Seven times faster then any *Bullet,*: These things laid together. He must have a Larger Faith and be more Credulous then any Female, that Beleives the Diurnall motion of the Sun and Immobility of the Earth. Further for Experimentall Reason the exquisite Observations of the Industrious *Monsieur Auzout,* in the motion of a First & Second Comet hath (it's thought) Discovered an Indisputable Argument for it, tho too Large to be related here.

That most abstruse Subject in Philosophy *the Ebbing and Flowing of the Seas,* that hath so in all Ages perplexed the minds of the best of *Naturalists,* is now most Ingeniously Described necessarily to have the Earths motion for it's principall cause, by that Eminent *Mathematician* Dr. *John Wallis.*

As for her Resembling other *Planets* and Shining at a distance with the like Splendor to her Neighbours, it is apparent, by her Illuminating the Darker part of the Moon's lower *Hemisphere,* as it is Commonly discerned a Little before, or after the Change, for then to the reputed Inhabitants of the Moon the Earths light is neer the Full.

And for further Demonstration of the Earth's Affinity with the other Planets, it might be instanced how by the *Telescope* invention true forms of Seas and Land have been perceived in the Moon, which hath also been Observed to have (as the well as the Earth) her *Atmosphere,* or a thick vaporous Air, encompassing her body, and Refracting the Sun's Rays in *Solar Eclipses*; from

> which with other Considerations it may be Rationally concluded that all the Planets have the like.
>
> In fine the Air, Clouds, a Bird Flying, a Stone falling from any height, an Arrow or Bullet Shot or driven any way, and all things else within the Sphear of the Earth's *Activity* (whether other-wise moved or not) do naturally and exactly follow, her Annuall and Diurnall motion, so that we the Earth's Inhabitants cannot possibly perceive or be made sensible thereof, any other way then by such Demonstrations as here (and by after Discovery may,) be given.—Whence we may see the Harmony of the Creation both in this, & the Placing of the SUN, and fix'd STARS in Convenient Distance, the Admirable Concinnity and Immense Vastitude of the Universe, and in all things the Infinite Wisdom, Power, and Excellency of the TRI-UNE-BEING their Eternall Author.[97]

Among the most scientific of these essays on astronomy are those on comets. However in error their conclusions sometimes were, the authors' approach to their problems was scientific. For instance, some confusion existed as to the real nature of the comet: whether it was a meteor or a peculiar kind of star. The growing consensus of opinion was in the right direction. S. Danforth writes, in 1665, "An Astronomical Description of the Late Comet As it appeared in New-England"[98] in which he explains, among other things, that "This Comet is no sublunary Meteor or sulphureous Exhalation, but a Celestial Luminary, moving in the starry Heavens." Increase Mather writes a full *Discourse Concerning Comets* and he, too, believes that "Comets are not in the Air, but in the Starry Heaven."[99] Other problems of study concerning this subject were the origin, substance, and motion of the comets. These, also, Mather, Danforth, and others discuss.[100]

Matters related to the planetary system were often the subjects of these essays. "D. R.," in 1671, writes "A brief

[97] N. Newman, *Harvard Ephemeris* (Cambridge, 1690).

[98] Cambridge, 1665.

[99] Boston, 1683.

[100] E.g., William Williams in his *Cambridge Ephemeris* (Cambridge, 1685).

Geographicall Description of the World."[101] "S. C." in 1660[102] and Joseph Dudley in 1668[103] write on the calculation of time.

Heavenly phenomena, particularly as revealed through the new telescope, were sufficiently awe-inspiring, on the one hand, to keep alive the idea that the stars must have some influence on man's destiny; and, paradoxically, on the other, to promote a growing skepticism that the stars had very little to do with him.

By the time that Daniel Leeds compiled his "Temple of Wisdom" in 1688, he had discovered that it was "impossible for an Astrologer, by the Rules of Art (though founded upon the truest ground) to give any certain Judgment of their Effects, but only in a general way." He had found that his own predictions had not always been true. And he observes ironically that "Mars and other Accidents" had overthrown predictions as to the length of life and manner of death of those killed on the battlefield. He gives, in short, his own opinions on the subject. Like most seventeenth century writings, this one is moral in conclusion; for the author ends this short prose piece called "Of Astrology" with the following preachments:

But now since it is so difficult a Road to travel in, and no end of the Journey to be yet found, so hard a work to labour in, and no profit doth thereby acrew, And that the best use we can make of it, brings no advantage to us, neither in divine nor human things, therefore I'll take leave to wave it; And

Let them whose Brains are sick of that Disease,
Be Slaves unto an Ephemerides;
Search Constellations, and themselves apply
To find the Fate of their Nativity.
I'll seek within me, and if there I find
Those Stars that should give Light unto my mind,
Rise fair and timely in me, and affect
Each other with a natural Aspect,

[101] Cambridge.
[102] Cambridge.
[103] Cambridge.

If in Conjunction there perceive I may,
True Vertue and Religion every day;
I fear no Fortunes whatsoever they be,
Nor care I what my Stars do threaten me.

Lastly. To this pure heavenly certain and exceeding advantagious *Astrology,* I shall rather, yea, much rather recommend my self, and all those that desire to be made Inhabitants successively of the twelve heavenly Houses thereof, which are these,

The *first* is the House of Judgment and Fearfulness.
The *second,* Humility and Lowliness.
The *third,* Meekness and Mercifulness.
The *fourth,* Temperance and Savouriness.
The *fifth,* Patience and Settledness.
The *sixth,* Hope and Resolvedness.
The *seventh,* Faith and Perseverance.
The *eighth,* Peace and Quietness.
The *ninth,* Thanksgiving and Remembrance.
The *tenth,* Prayer and Watchfulness.
The *eleventh,* Glorification and Praises.
The *twelfth,* Content and Fulness.

Of which twelve Houses of the Heavens, that we may be all learned Experiencers, and true Witnessers, but above all, that we may look well into that House, in which we are made Inhabitants, which by vertue of covenant is ours, as a proper Possession, that we may see the Glory of the Sign thereof, which shews us the Signs of the Times; even that is the desire of

D. L. Amen[104]

Holding still to the belief in signs and portents, J. S., in 1676, writes an admonition to serious-minded people. His is an essay of warning to show that the unusual signs in the heavens must predict calamity and misfortune. His purpose, therefore, is moral: "The Christian had need to be furnished and well provided, and be laying in for a winter voyage,

[104] D[aniel] L[eeds], *The Temple of Wisdom,* p. 124. This is not an almanac, but an anthology.

nothing but Faith, Patience, and a good Conscience can secure us from a shipwrack, and bring us safe to our desired Port, the longed for shore of blessed Eternity." The whole is, in fact, a sermon: "A Monitory Advertisement To all who desire to approve themselves Serious and seeing; under dark Dispensations, Prov. 22.3."[105]

The almanac-makers who seriously predicted dire events, were sometimes ridiculed by their fellow almanac-makers. In this manner does John Tulley write his little "essays" for his almanac of 1688.[106]

March

Now if thy Body be not well,
This month for Physick doth excel;
But choose a Doctor skill'd in Art,
Not *Quacks* growing rich by others smart.

If some great Person do not die this month, either in *Europe, Asia, Africa,* or *America,* let them light Tobacco, or make Bum-Fodder with our Observations.

. . . .

September

Now Landlords they prick up their ears,
Because St. Michael's *day appeares.*—

Now the Farmers barns are full, and a full barn makes a full Purse & a joyful heart; it makes the Bakers bread heavier, and the Brewers Ale stronger: All you that love Toast & Ale, pray for full barns.

After such monthly prognostications, he writes:

We shall now give you our judgement of such things as without the help of any *Lapland* Devil we may safely prognosticate will assuredly come to pass. We find then by the position of *Mercury,* a great plenty of such people who are thus described by the Poet,

Who in the day do mark
Those houses which they plunder in the dark.

Venus is a full square with *Mars*; therefore those that

[105] J[ohn] S[herman], *An Almanack* (Cambridge, 1676).
[106] Boston.

marry Widows must bear with all their bad qualities, and allow her alwaies to carry with her the Inventory of her Goods and the Summ of her Dowry perpetually in her mouth, and alwayes to be arm'd with the praise of the Deceased:

And he who is with such a widow matcht,
He in the marriage noose is finely catcht,
Then may he sing the *hen-peckt* husbands song,
Like a dog with a bottle ty'd close to his tail,
Like a Tory *'n a Bog, or a thief in a Jayl.*

Now *Mars* & *Mercury* are in a friendly Conjunction with *Venus,* which may invite many young people to enter into the marriage-state: and indeed a wife is no *Curse* when she brings the blessings of a *good estate* with her; but to marry a *Town-flurt* with a *painted face,* a *rotten reputation,* & a *brasie fortune,* that man had better go to *hanging* than be so married. But if you will take *my* advice in the choice of a wife, I will give it you freely; and that you may the better keep it in *memory,* take it *Alphabetically*: Let her be *Amiable, Beautful, Chast, Delicate, Excellent, Fair, Gracious, Honest, Industrious, Kind, Loving, Merry, Neat, Obedient, Pittiful, Quiet, Rich, Shamefac'd, Temperate, Vertuous, Witty, Youthful,* and *Zealous.*
And those who with these properties are sped,
You shall not need to fear with them to wed. . .[107]

Whether the paragraphs of the almanacs were astronomical or astrological in point-of-view, there were two tendencies in their ultimate purpose: the scientific and the moralistic. As long as these colonial scientists approached their subject with the attitude of impartial investigation, as those, for instance, who wrote on comets, then their work was truly a beginning in scientific writing in America. Then, too, the growing skepticism toward astrology aided and abetted this scientific spirit. There still existed, however, among the pseudo-scientific almanack-makers a religious awe in regard to the relationship of man and the stars. When this was the author's attitude of mind, then the short prose piece became

[107] John Tulley, *An Almanac . . . 1688,* Boston.

moral and didactic, rather than scientific. This, as we have seen, was true not only of those who wrote on astrology, but also of those who attempted to keep to the subject of pure astronomy.

2. Meteorology

The greater number of prognostications written for the almanac were not of man's personal destiny, but of weather conditions. This was reasonable and scientific, however inadequate or inaccurate in comparison with the predictions by our present means of information. Like the essays on astronomy and astrology, on the other hand, they were frequently moral in purpose. These and other subjects pertaining to meteorology took the form of short pseudo-scientific essays with such titles as "Of Winds," "Of Rain," "Of Hail," "Of Snow," "Of Frost and Dew," "Signs of Storms," "Signs of Cold Weather," "Concerning a Rainbow," "Concerning Lightning," *et cetera.*

John Tulley, in giving "scientific" information to his readers, attains a curiously poetic quality.

> *Of Fair Weather*
>
> If the Moon look bright and fair, look for Fair Weather. Also the appearing of one Rainbow, after a Storm, is a known sign of Fair Weather. If Mists come down from the Hills, or descend from the heavens, and settle in the valleys, they promise fair hot weather: Mists in the Evening shew a fair, hot day, on the morrow. The like when mists rise from the waters in the evening. Much more might be added, but I would not tire the Reader, craving but what the Poet doth,
>
> ————[*sic*] *Si quid novisti rectius istis*
> *Cundidus imperti, sinon, his utere mecum.*[108]

and another:

> *Of Frost and Dew*
>
> When in the day time through the faint heat of the Sun, there is a cold & moist vapour drawn up a little from the earth, presently at night it descendeth again

[108] *Almanack,* Boston, 1687.

> upon the earth, and is called dew, and in the Spring or Harvest, it is a sign of fair weather, but if by means of cold it be congeal'd, it is called Frost, and therefore Dews come not so often in hot seasons, neither when winds be up, but after a calm and clear night, Frosts dry up wet and moisture: for when (as *Pliny* saith) the ice is melted, the like quantity of water in proportion is not found.[109]

The phenomena of lightning and rainbows were favorite subjects for the almanac. Tulley's information concerning the former is quaint, though it is meant to be scientific:

> *Of Thunder and Lightning*
>
> When an Exhalation, hot and dry, mixt with moisture, is carried up into the middle Region, and there in the body of a Cloud, now these two Contraries being thus shut or pent in one room together, they fall at variance, whereby the water and fire agree not, until they have broken the Prison wherein they were pent, so that fire and water flie out of the cloud, the breaking whereof maketh a noise like the renting of Cloth, which they call Thunder, and the Fire Lightning, first seen, in respect the Light is before the hearing, and of Lightning there be many sorts.[110]

William Williams "Concerning the Rainbow"[111] writes in curious mixture of the scientific and the superstitious. Indeed, he says himself that "There is a twofold final cause of Rainbows, Natural and Supernatural." The one is a sign of rain; the other, of "God's mercy to the world in never destroying it again by a Deluge." He discusses both and concludes: "According to Syr. look upon the Rainbow, and praise [H]im that made it."

If these interpretations of meteorological phenomena were as often superstitious as scientific, as often moral as analytical, that was as it should be, for the seventeenth century mind

[109] John Tulley, *Almanack*, Boston, 1693.

[110] *Ibid.*

[111] *Cambridge Ephemeris*, 1685.

took its Bible literally and it still contemplated with awe these manifestations of the Divine will.

3. Agriculture

When John Tulley wrote his "Prognostica Georgica" for his almanac of 1687,[112] he was showing deference to the farmer for he gave it the half-title, "Or the Country-mans Weather-Glass." His information concerning the wind and the rain, fair weather and foul, was written for the benefit of the man on the plantation. This was frequently the case. Samuel Clough, in 1702,[113] says:

> I have at the desire of several Country People, added the *Anatomy*, with the *Moons* place, and parts of mans Body she governs, as she passeth through the 12 Signs (a thing omitted the last year) which is of use to them in cutting their Creatures: though I would advise them to mind the Weather as well as the Sign: *viz.* to do it when the Weather is Warm and Clear, the Wind at West or N. West.

Daniel Leeds, who styled himself "student of Agriculture" in his almanac of 1687, wrote some directions for planting trees.[114] In this case, his directions have the added interest, other than mere exposition, of closing with a poetic address to the reader:

> Mend, Modest Reader, what thou findst amiss,
> But let the Author know what fault it is.
> All men have err'd since *Adam* first transgrest.
> If I commit no Faults I'm one o' th' best.
> But here my Comfort is, though I offend
> I to my Faults can quickly put an END.[115]

The descriptive accounts, as well as the almanacs, showed an interest in problems of agriculture—very naturally, of course, since they were to be read by prospective planters in

[112] *Op. cit., supra*, p. 51.

[113] Boston.

[114] See Appendix A.

[115] Daniel Leeds, *Almanack*, Broadside (Philadelphia, 1687), See Appendix A.

the new colonies. On the whole, the discussion of agricultural matters was included in the general account of the country. The Letter of Doctor Nicholas More,[116] for instance, contains a paragraph on his own experiences with the planting of crops. Such excerpts show the scientific tendency, but not the scientific essay in itself. However, William Wood treats each subject in his book separately. The fourth chapter of his *New England's Prospect* is a complete discussion "Of the nature of the Soyle." The first paragraph of this is sufficient to illustrate his attack of his problem:

> The Soyle is for the generall a warme kinde of earth, there being little cold-spewing land, no Morish Fennes, no Quagmires, the lowest grounds be the Marshes, over which every full and change the Sea flowes: these Marshes be rich ground, and bring plenty of Hay, of which the Cattle feed and like, as if they were fed with the best up-land Hay in New England; of which likewise there is great store which growes commonly between the Marshes and the Woods. This Medow ground lies higher than the Marshes, whereby it is freed from the over-flowing of the Seas; and besides this, in many places where the Tres grow thinne, there is good fodder to be got amongst the Woods. There be likewise in divers places neare the plantations great broad Medowes, wherein grow neither shrub nor Tree, lying low, in which Plaines growes as much grasse, as may be throwne out with a Sithe, thicke and long, as high as a mans middle; some as high as the shoulders, so that a good mower may cut three loads in a day. But many object, this is but a course fodder: True it is, that it is not so fine to the eye as English grasse, but it is not sowre, though it grow thus ranke; but being made into Hay, the Cattle eate it as well as it were Lea-hay and like as well with it; I doe not thinke England can shew, fairer Cattle either in Winter, or

[116] The last year I did plant about twelve Acres of Indian Corn, and when it came off the Ground, I did only cause the Ground to be Harrowed, and upon that I did sow both Wheat and Rye, at which many Laughed, saying, That I could not expect any Corn from what I had sowed, the Land wanting more Labour; yet I had this Year as good Wheat and Rye upon it, as was to be found in any other place, and that very bright Corn. I have had a good Crop of Barley and Oats . . . 1687. *Orig. Narr.*, XIII, 285.

> Summer, than is in those parts both Winter and Summer; being generally larger and better of milch, and bring forth young as ordinarily as Cattle doe in England, and have hitherto beene free from many diseases that are incident to Cattle in England.[117]

4. Botany

The interest in science did not stop with things related in one way or another to the stars, nor was scientific writing confined to the almanac. It will be remembered that one of the chief interests of those descriptive pamphlets on the new country was its "natural resources," its plants, animals, birds, *et cetera.*

Of these, the most important was the study of botany. In that section of Captain John Smith's *Description of Virginia* headed *Of such things which are naturall in Virginia and how they use them*[118] he describes under marginal topics the "Elme," "Walnuts," "supposed Cypres," "mulberries," "chestnuts," "cherries," "vines," *et cetera.* The whole section is an essay on *natura rerum* of Virginia, including not only those plants, but others, and not only things botanical but also zoölogical. Robert Beverley, in his *History of Virginia* devotes chapter IV to a discussion "Of the wild Fruits of the Country." His chapters, like William Woods', are really component rather than composite parts of the whole work, so that each is really a separate treatment in itself. In the latter's *New England's Prospect,* Chapter V is devoted to the subject "Of the Hearbes, Fruits, Woods, Waters and Mineralls," the most important natural resources.

One can find any number of examples like these among other descriptive pamphlets. The most precious contribution to botany and allied subjects, other than Woods' book, is *New Englands Rareties Discovered* by John Josselyn, Gent. His short explanations of the plants of New-England are not only accurate in word description, but also in drawing. Here, indeed, are real contributions to scientific writing, for

[117] William Wood, *New Englands Prospect* (London, 1634), Chap. III. Reprint edition, E. M. Boynton (Boston, 1898), p. 11.

[118] *Op. cit.*, I, 56 ff.

they are of sufficient accuracy to merit Josselyn a recognized place among our early botanists.

A Branch of the Humming Bird Tree

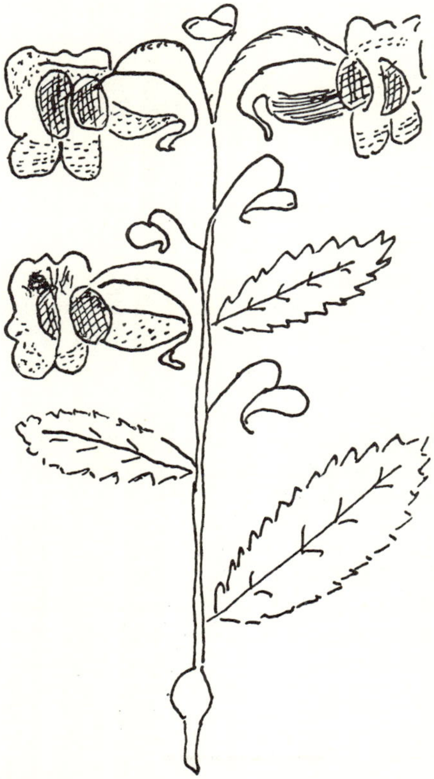

This Plant the *Humming Bird* feedeth upon, it groweth likewise in wet grounds, and is not at its full growth till *July*, and then it is two Cubits high and better, the Leaves are thin, and of a pale green Colour, some of them as big as a Nettle Leaf, it spreads into many Branches, knotty at the setting on, and of a purple Colour, and garnished on the top with many hollow dangling Flowers of a bright yellow Colour, speckled with a deeper yellow as it were shadowed, the Stalkes are as hollow as a Kix, and so are the Roots, which are transparent, very tender, and full of a yellowish juice.[119]

[119] John Josselyn, *New England's Rarities*, ed. Edward Tuckerman (Boston, 1865), pp. 126-8.

5. Zoölogy, Ornithology, etc.

In the descriptive pamphlets, also, are short essays of like nature on animals, fish, and birds. The information is sometimes accurate and sometimes curious.

William Wood writes several chapters on the wild life of New England: Chapter VI, "Of the Beasts that live on Land"; Chapter VII, "Beasts living in the water"; Chapter VIII, "Of the Birds and Fowles both of land and water"; Chapter IX, "Of Fish." In treatment he resembles what we now call the "nature essayist"—his handling of the subject is informal and full of anecdote, and as we have already seen, he even treats the subject in poetry.[120] Of bears he says:

> For Beares they be common, being a great black kind of Beare, which be most fierce in Strawberry time, at which time they have young ones; at this time likewise they will goe upright like a man, and clime trees, and swimme to the Islands; which if the Indians see, they will be more sportfull Beare bayting than Paris Garden can affoard. For seeing the Beares take water, an Indian will leape after him, where they goe to water cuffes for bloody noses, and scratched sides; in the end the man gets the victory, riding the Beare over the watery plaine till he can beare him no longer. In the winter they take themselves to the clifts of rockes, and thicke swamps, to shelter them from the cold; and foode being scant in those cold and hard times, they live onely by sleeping and sucking their pawes, which keepeth them as fat as they are in Summer; there would be more of them if it were not for the Woolves, which devoure them; a kennell of those ravening runnagadoes, setting on a poore single Beare, will teare him as a Dogge will teare a Kid: it would be a good change if the countrey had for every Woolfe a Beare, upon the condition all the woolves were banished; so should the inhabitants be not onely rid of their greatest annoyance, but furnished with more store of provisions, Beares being accounted very good meate, esteemed of all men above Venison: againe they never prey upon the English cattle, or offer to assault the person of any man, unlesse being vexed with a shot, and a man run upon them before they be dead, in which case they will stand in their own defence,

[120] *Supra*, p. 12.

> as may appeare by this instance. Two men going a fowling, appointed at evening to meete at a certaine pond side, to share equally, and to returne home; one of these Gunners having killed a Seale or Sea calfe, brought it to the side of the pond where hee was to meete his comrade, afterwards returning to the Sea side for more gaine; and having loaded himselfe with more Geese and Duckes, he repaired to the pond, where hee saw a great Beare feeding on his Seale, which caused him to throw downe his loade, and give the Beare a salute; which though it was but with Goose shot, yet tumbled him over and over, whereupon the man supposing him to be in a manner dead, ran and beate him with the hand of his Gunne; The Beare perceiving him to be such a coward to strike him when he was down, scrambled up, standing at defiance with him, scratching his legges, tearing his cloathes and face, who stood it out till his six foot Gunne was broken in the middle, then being deprived of his weapon, he ran up to the shoulders into the pond, where hee remained till the Beare was gone, and his mate come in, who accompanied him home.[121]

Although John Josselyn is at his best concerning botanical information, he sometimes writes fairly accurate descriptions of animals and birds. At other times he succumbs to certain superstitions of his day. However, he is always a delightful naturalist, as these examples will show:

The Humming Bird

> The *Humming Bird*, the least of all Birds, little bigger than a *Dor*, of variable glittering Colours, they feed upon Honey, which they suck out of Blossoms and Flowers with their long Needle-like Bills; they sleep all Winter, and are not to be seen till the Spring, at which time they breed in little Nests, made up like a bottom of soft, Silk-like matter, their Eggs no bigger than a white Pease, they hatch three or four at a time, and are proper to this Country.

The Troculus

> The *Troculus*, a small Bird, black and white, no bigger than a Swallow, the points of whose Feathers

[121] *Op. cit.*, pp. 20-22.

> are sharp, which they stick into the sides of the Chymney (to rest themselves, their Legs being exceeding short) where they breed in Nests made like a Swallows Nest, but of a glewy substance, and which is not fastened to the Chymney as a Swallows Nest, but hangs down the Chymney by a clew-like string a yard long. They commonly have four or five young ones, and when they go away, which is much about the time that Swallows use to depart, they never fail to throw down one of their young Birds into the room by way of Gratitude. I have more than once observed, that against the ruin of the Family these Birds will suddenly forsake the house and come no more.[122]

John Lawson, in his account of *A New Voyage to Carolina,* writes paragraphs on the wild life there. The vivid quality of his style, his informal manner, his personal anecdotes, and the human quality that he gives the animals together with the actual information that he records put him distinctly in the class of those popular scientists whom we call nature writers.

> The *Raccoon* is of a dark-gray Colour; if taken young, is easily made tame, but is the drunkenest Creature living, if he can get any Liquor that is sweet and strong. They are rather more unlucky than a Monkey. When wild, they are very subtle in catching their Prey. Those that live in the Salt-Water, feed much on Oysters which they love. They watch the Oyster when it opens, and nimbly put in their Paw, and pluck out the Fish. Sometimes the Oyster shuts, and holds fast their Paw till the Tide comes in, that they are drown'd, tho' they swim very well. The way that this Animal catches Crabs, which he greatly admires, and which are plenty in *Carolina,* is worthy of Remark. When he intends to make a Prey of these Fish, he goes to a Marsh, where standing on the Land, he lets his Tail hang in the Water. This the Crab takes for a Bait, and fastens his Claws therein, which as soon as the *Raccoon* perceives, he, of a sudden, springs forward, a considerable way, on the Land, and brings the Crab along with him. As soon as the Fish finds himself out of his Element, he presently lets go his hold; and then the *Raccoon* encounters him,

[122] *Op. cit.*, pp. 39, 40.

> by getting him cross-wise in his Mouth, and devours him. There is a sort of small Land-Crab, which we call a *Fiddler*, that runs into a Hole when any thing pursues him. This Crab the *Raccoon* takes by putting his Fore-Foot in the Hole, and pulling him out. With a tame *Raccoon*, this Sport is very diverting. The Chief of his other Food is all sorts of wild Fruits, green Corn, and such as the Bear delights in. This and the *Possum* are much of a Bigness. The Fur makes good Hats and Linings. The Skin dress'd makes fine Womens Shooes. . .
>
> Green Lizards are very harmless and beautiful, having a little Bladder under their Throat, which they fill with Wind, and evacuate the same at Pleasure. They are of a most glorious Green, and very tame. They resort to the Walls of Houses in the Summer Season, and stand gazing on a Man, without any Concern or Fear. There are several other Colours of these Lizards; but none so beautiful as the green ones are.[123]

Charles Morton's interest in science covered a broad field. We have already noted his active participation in the teaching of physics.[124] We have noted here, too, his suggestion that in contemplating natural phenomena, one contemplates the wonders of their Creator. In 1703, there was published in London his delightful "Essay[125] Towards the Probable Solution of this Question. Whence come the Stork and the Turtle,[126] the Crane and the Swallow, when they Know and Observe the appointed Time of their Coming. Or Where those Birds do probably make their Recess and Abode, which are absent from our Climate at some certain Times and Seasons of the Year."[127] Although the work is based on a Biblical text,[128] although it digresses frequently for a moral,

[123] John Lawson, *A New Voyage to Carolina* (London, 1709), p. 121.

[124] *Supra*, p. 37 f.

[125] Meaning here *attempt.*

[126] Turtledove.

[127] The author's identity is not given, except as "a Person of Learning and Piety."

[128] *The stork in the Heaven Knoweth her Appointed Times, and the Turtle, and the Crane, and the Swallow observe the Time of their Coming,* etc. Jer. 8. 7.

and although its conclusions are all wrong, Morton treats the whole work scientifically as completely as he and his contemporaries understood how to do so.[129]

In a truly admirable manner, he reconciles theology and the processes of scientific investigation in his prolegomena:

> Before I do propose a direct *Answer* to the *Question, Whither these* Fowls *do probably make their Recess,* I must lay down some *Postulata* or *Prolegomena*: Such as,
>
> 1. That the Creator made the Universe for the Manifestation of his own Glory.
>
> 2. That in order thereunto, he has endowd the Rational Creature (Man) with a Capacity to observe, search out, and celebrate his Power, Wisdom and Goodness in his Works.
>
> 3. That (since the Fall) the Ordinary Method of Man's Understanding any thing of the Works of God, is by Industry in Sense, Observation, Experience, Induction, and the Communication of these things from one Man to another.
>
> 4. That must be acknowledged as true, or at least most probable, that is most easily deducible from Man's Experience and Observation of the *Phenomena* of Nature.
>
> 5. That those *Phenomena* do yeild [*sic*] Ground for Opinions more strange, weak or variable, not so much from the Diversity of Appearances, as of Observation from whence principally they derive their denomination of *Phenomena*; therefore when Men speak of new ones, upon which they ground new Argumentations and Opinions, they are not (for the most part) *New Things* in Nature, but *Old Things* newly taken notice of.
>
> 6. *New Observations* may be made in one Age, that are not in another, by the hints that one Age gives to another, whereby human Reason (being still the same in all Ages) works on upon [*sic*] former Observations, so as what is begun in one Age, may be perfected in another; and the same may hint some Things imperfectly to the next, that may be left to them to perfect, and so onwards. *Ita res accendunt lumina rebus.*

[129] That this essay was regarded as scientific is suggested by the fact that it is incorporated many years later in one volume with "An Account of English Ants . . ." by Rev. William Gould of Exeter College, Oxford, originally published in 1747. Both are in the British Museum, 976, f. 6.

> 7. When it follows, there may be a sober sense of that Saying (*Senescente Mundo Adolescunt ingenia*) the older the World, the wiser; not that new Opinions arise from Affectation of Novelty, or proud Contempt of the Ancients; but granting their Wit and Industry to be equal, yet we may soberly say, their Opportunities were not so; for latter [*sic*] Ages have the Observations of the former, and their own to boot.
>
> 8. That all manner of Sciences have improved, and are still improving, is manifest enough to any that are not over-weening of their own entertained *Conceits*, or impertinently superstitious toward dead *Heroes*, and from hence are Enemies to all Reformation; as if envying that any thing should be done well, that was not by them and their Ancestors; or as if this must needs reflect upon them, as carless or unskilful.
>
> 9. That many little Things in Nature are of great Importance, and become the most admirable (and God's Wisdom therein) when their End and Use come better to be discerned. One would admire to think, Why God should create *Eclipses* to appear only at certain Times: the Thing in itself is a very *Toy*, a *Nonentity*, a *Privation*, a *Shadow of Short Duration*, and no more in Nature than the putting my Hand between my Eye and the Candle, and yet this little Darkness gives Light to all *Astronomy* and *Chronology*; for by this Men only are sure that their Hypotheses in the Main are more than doubtful Conjectures, God making use of this contemptible Mote (*as a Fescue*) to teach Men to read the Heavens, and enables Man (that little Pigmy on a Mole-hill) to measure and comprehend at such a distance such vast Magnitudes and Motions.[130]

What more could one ask of a scientist of this religious age than the composition of this prolegomena?—his definition of the scientific approach as observation, experience, and induction; his statement that new things in nature are but old things newly taken notice of; his suggestion that a new age can profit from the experience of a former age, for human reason is always the same; his warning against the superstitious, who are enemies to progress. Finally, how admirably written, in the didactic manner, is the conclusion

[130] Pp. 13-19.

to his prolegomena! But as far as our interest here is concerned, this introduction to his subject on whence come the dove and the turtle, indicates a beginning in the scientific spirit in America.[131]

This statement is true even though his interesting explanation of the migration of birds is inaccurate. Even here his method is scientific, for he treats first the species; second, the birds' instinct for seasons; third, the appointment of their time to go; and fourth "The Place whence they come, and whither they go." At this point we can say with him that the opportunities of a former age are not like ours. His explanation of whence the birds come and whither they go is now merely laughable: Birds could not venture so far as across the sea. They must go to the heavens across to the moon, for "The moon goes nearer round the earth every day."[132] If the moon is not their habitation, perhaps there are some concrete bodies at less distance from the moon.[133]

Nevertheless, however inaccurate his observations, experiences, and inductions concerning this subject, he has written here a scientific essay of the seventeenth century.

Among the most accurate of the scientists in New England was John Winthrop, Jr., governor of Connecticut, who was a member of the Royal Society of London. In 1670 he contributed to the editor of the Philosophical Transactions two letters on the "rarities and novelties of New England." In one, after a few brief but informative paragraphs on botanical matters, he gives an account of the "stellar" or "basket-fish" (the star-fish). His description is accurate, detailed, and scientific:

> *We omit the other particulars here, that we may reflect a little upon this elaborate piece of Nature, the Fish, which, since it is yet nameless, we may call* Piscis

[131] The philosophy of Charles Morton and his contemporaries that natural phenomena are the manifestations of a Divine and never ending order of the Universe may be compared to the philosophy of the Transcendentalists. In fact these men of the seventeenth century may be said to have prepared the way for Emerson and his contemporaries.

[132] *Ibid.*, p. 45.

[133] *Ibid.*, p. 48.

> Echino-Stellaris Visciformis; *its Body (as was noted by M. Hook) resembling an* Echinus *or* Egg-Fish, *the main Branches a Star, and the dividing of the branches the Plant* Missel-toe. *This Fish spreads itself from a* Pentagonal *Root, which incompasseth the Mouth (being in the middle . . .) into 5 main Limbs or branches, each of which, Just at issuing out from the Body, sub divides it self into two . . ., and each of those 10 branches do again . . . divide into two parts, making* 20 *lesser branches: Each of which again divide . . . into 2 smaller branches, making in all,* 40. *These again . . . into 80, and those . . . into 160; and they . . . into 320: they . . . into 640; . . . into 1280; . . . into 2560; . . . into 5120; . . . into 10240; . . . into 20480; . . . into 40960; . . . into 81920; beyond which the farther expanding of the Fish could not be certainly trac'd, though possibly each of those 81920 small sprouts or threds, in which the branches of this Fish seem'd to terminate, might, if it could have been examined when living, have been found to subdivide yet farther. The Branches between the Joynts were not equally of a length, though, for the most part pretty near: But those branches, which were on that side of the Joynt, on which the preceding Joynt was placed, were always about a 4th or 5th part longer than those on the other side. Every of these branchings seemed to have, from the very mouth to the smallest twiggs or threds, in which it ended, a double chain or rank of pores. . . The Body of the Fish was on the other side, and seemed to have been protuberant, much like an* Echinus (Egg-Fish *or* Button-Fish), *and, like that, divided into 5 ribbs or ridges, and each of these seemed to be kept out by two small bony ribbs.*[134]

6. Medicine

The subject of medicine was of considerable interest in early America not only among those "trained in physic" for the profession, but also among the laymen.[135]

[134] *Philosophical Transactions* (London, 1670), IV, No. 57, 1152 f.

[135] Indeed, it fell upon such leaders of the community as the New-England divines to perform not only ministrations of the spirit, but of the flesh. The most notable scientific dispute comes shortly after 1710 when Cotton Mather championed the cause of inoculation for smallpox against Dr. Douglass.

The forerunner of the patent medicine almanac is to be found in the early almanacs in which advice is given for treatments according to astrological signs. The authors, however, were not charlatans as those of to-day. They were educated men and their theories were consistent with the times. Leeds, in his almanac for 1697,[136] writes a short essay, "Of gathering Herbs," in which he reviews the opinions of "astrological physicians" on the best time to gather them, and then sets "down the Planetary Time of gathering Herbs" for 1697. His theories are quaint. For instance,

> We are generally too subject to pleasure the Palate, and therefore do not take enough of the *bitter Quality*, especially in Drinks; the said *bitter Quality* being moderately taken, is a nourisher of the central fire, the Original of Life, and all Persons that are in Health, or retain their strength, may take liberally thereof Spring and Fall, 'tis a purifier and cleanier of the Blood. But if any who have weak Eyes do fear offending by the *bitter Plants* of *Mars*, let them add an Herb of the Sun therewith, as *Raw*, . . . or the like.
>
> I've no intent the skillful to conduct,
> Or teach the learned, but the weak instruct.[137]

For general information on herbs, he refers the reader to Culpepper's "English Physician."

John Tulley, in his almanac for 1701,[138] gives advice on blood-letting by the sign of the moon.

Medical information was to be found in other than the almanacs. In 1677, Thomas Thacher wrote for a Massachusetts Broadside a complete digest of the symptoms and treatment of smallpox. Its purpose is manifest in its title: "A Brief Rule to Guide the Common-People of New England How to Order themselves and theirs in the Small Pocks, or Measels."[139]

[136] New York.
[137] The rhyming couplets state the purpose of the didactic essayist.
[138] Boston.
[139] Boston, 1677. For the complete broadside, see Appendix C.

The botanist, through his study of herbs, was frequently physician, too. John Josselyn's chief interest to the historians and scientists is as a botanist. Not so well respected are his recipes for aches and pains, which are scattered throughout his "New-England's Rarities," not only in the section on plants, but also on animals and fish. His information concerning cures is many times hardly more than a recipe and in form not an essay; but its purpose of information and its pseudo-scientific attitude suggest a kind of popular scientific essay written for the layman. For instance,

> *Achariston is an excellent Medicine for stopping Lungs upon Cold, Ptisick, &c.*
>
> *Oak of Cappadocia,* both much of a nature, but Oak of Hierusalem is stronger in operation; excellent for stuffing of the Lungs upon Colds, shortness of Wind, and the Ptisick; maladies that the Natives are often troubled with: I helped several of the *Indians* with a Drink made of two Gallons of *Molosses wort,* (for in that part of the Country where I abode, we made our Beer of Molosses, Water, Bran, chips of *Sassafras* Root, and a little Wormwood, well boiled,) into which I put of Oak of *Hierusalem,* Catmint, Sowthistle, of each one handful, of *Enula Campana* Root one Ounce, Liquorice scrap'd brused and cut in pieces, one Ounce, Sassafras Root cut into thin chips, one Ounce, Anny-seed and sweet Fennel-seed, of each one Spoonful bruised; boil these in a close Pot, upon a soft Fire to the consumption of one Gallon, then take it off, and strein it gently; you may if you will (47) boil the streined liquor with Sugar to a Syrup, then when it is Cold, put it up into Glass Bottles, and take thereof three or four spoonfuls at a time, letting it run down your throat as leasurely as possibly you can; do thus in the morning, in the Afternoon, and at Night going to Bed.
>
> *To ripen any Impostume or Swelling. For sore Mouths, The New-Englands standing Dish.*
>
> *Indian* Wheat, of which there is three sorts, yellow, red, and blew; the blew is commonly Ripe before the other a Month: Five or Six Grains of *Indian* Wheat hath produced in one year 600. It is hotter than our

> Wheat and clammy; excellent in *Cataplasms* to ripen any Swelling or impostume. The decoction of the blew Corn, is good to wash sore Mouths with: It is light of digestion, and the *English* make a kind of Loblolly of it (53) to eat with Milk, which they call *Sampe*; they beat it in a Morter, and sift the flower out of it: the remainder they call *Homminey*, which they put into a Pot of two or three Gallons, with Water, and boyl it upon a gentle Fire till it be like a Hasty Pudden; they put of this into Milk, and so eat it. Their Bread also they make of the *Homminey* so boiled, and mix their Flower with it, cast it into a deep Bason in which they form the Loaf, and then turn it out upon the Peel, and presently put it into the Oven before it spreads abroad; the Flower makes excellent Puddens.[140]

These "essays" on medicine now are of no scientific value; they are merely curious. Yet the interest in these matters planted the seed for later results. Even in this period Thacher's broadside on smallpox is meritorious in his consideration of its symptoms and his suggestions on how to treat it. It is meritorious because it is scientifically analytical. The growing interest in this very serious problem, in fact, was soon to lead to the subject of inoculation for its prevention. It is soon after the period of our study that Cotton Mather and Dr. Douglass waged a battle on the advisability of inoculation as a preventive.

7. Mineralogy, Geology, Seismology

Less frequently treated than these foregoing subjects were geology and its related subjects. John Winthrop, Jr., is one whose broad interest in science includes these. Two letters from him to Sir Robert Moray are worthy of note. In the letter for August 18, 1668, and its postscript he treats the subject of mineralogy only casually; but in the letter of 1671 he writes in more detail.[141] In it are some interesting pro-

[140] *Op. cit.*, pp. 90, 101.

[141] An endorsement on a copy of the letter suggests that it was copied for the use of the Royal Society: "Copy to Sir Robt. Moray, 1671."

phesies concerning the use of steel, just recently made from iron. Winthrop gives information concerning the iron of Massachusetts and also a sulphurous marcasite to be found in that state. The fact that he was writing formally an exact bit of information on a scientific subject for the benefit of a learned society, is evidence of our early and genuine interest in scientific writing. All that was lacking for a unified report was the elimination of extraneous matters, which were excusable here in view of the fact that he was writing a letter rather than an article.

Wood treats the subject of mineralogy in his chapter on "Of the Hearbes, Fruites, Woods, Waters and Mineralls."[142]

The least scientifically treated of all subjects was that of the phenomenon of the earthquake, because it was least understood. It was, however, a subject of great interest and of terror.[143]

The Mathers were men of intelligence and education. They were keenly interested in science. Yet Increase Mather's "A Discourse Concerning Earthquakes" may be taken as a typical example of the theories of this phenomenon presented during the seventeenth century. From our own standards, it is mostly an unscientific discussion, because we do not mix the scientific explanation of phenomena with tributes to miracles. It is to be noted, however, that while Mather attributes an earthquake to an act of God, he does suggest its true scientific cause when he describes the changes in the earth's formations. He reconciles the religious and the scientific elements when he says, "Prodigious Storms have Natural causes, yet these Stormy winds fulfill the Word of the Lord." We may quote "Proposition I" as an essay on earthquakes. The rest of the discourse is mostly one of moral exhortation to hear the voice of God and mend our lives. The result is a paradoxical combination, unheard of

[142] *Op. cit.*, chap. V.

[143] It was sufficiently interesting for a Massachusetts Broadside to reprint on February 21, 1695, an account of a recent earthquake in far off Naples.

and impossible in our own day, of the scientific and the didactic:

> *An Earthquake is the Work of God.* There is not the least thing comes to pass without His Providence. Christ said to the Disciples, *Not a Sparrow falls to the Ground without your Father,* Mat. 10. 29. Then we may be sure so great a thing as an Earthquake is not without His Providence. The Earth cannot shake it self; and it is beyond all the Power of all the men in the world to make an Earthquake. But God who made the Earth, can make it tremble when and where He pleaseth: Job 9. 6. *He shakes the Earth out of its place, and the Pillars thereof tremble.* There have been Earthquakes which were Supernatural Miraculous Works of God: So was that on Mount *Sinai,* when the Lord Descended upon it in Fire, and the *whole Mount Quaked greatly*; Exod. 19. 18. And that which swallowed up *Corah* and his Company with all their Houses, Numb. 16. 32. And that which hapned in the days of *Uzziah,* which put the People of *Jerusalem* into a great Consternation. Of this the Prophet *Zechary* takes notice Zec. 14. 5. *Ye shall flee like as you fled from before the Earthquake in the dayes of Uzziah King of Judah.* The *Jewish* Historian reports, that a great Mountain before *Jerusalem* was removed and broken in pieces by that Earthquake, and that all the High-ways were stopped by the fall of it, and the Kings Gardens of pleasure ruined thereby. Some interpreters conceive that then *Amos* his Prophecy was fulfilled: Amos 3. 15. *I will smite the Winter house with the Summer house, and the house of ivory shall perish.* And those *Earthquakes* which were at our Saviours Passion and Resurrection, were Supernatural. So was that which hapned when *Paul* and *Silas* Prayed and sang Praises unto God, when they were in Prison: *Suddenly there was a great Earthquake, so that the Foundations of the Prison were shaken, and all the Doors were opened, and every ones Bands were loosened*; Act. 16. 26. This was Miraculous. Not only Christian, but some Heathen writers, inform us that when *Julian* the Apostate, out of his hatred of Christ, Encouraged the Jews to Rebuild the Temple, an Earthquake overturned what they had began to Build, and Fire breaking out of the Ground consumed all the Work-mens tools, which caused them to desist from that Enterprize. Supernatural Earthquakes are

> Effected either by the Almighty Power of God alone, or, by Angels as the Instruments of His Providence; Mat. 28. 2. *There was a great Earthquake*; *for the Angel of the Lord descended from Heaven.* But many times, Earthquakes proceed from Natural causes. This Earth on which we stand, is not a continued substance of Earth; for then it would be impossible that ever there should be an Earthquake, without a Miracle. But there are in the bowels of the Earth great Caverns or hollow places, and mighty Lakes and Rivers, which wash away the Earth, and sometimes wash it away so far as that it sinks with its own weight; and then both Men and Houses are swallowed up: and from thence it is that great Rains and Floods do sometimes produce Earthquakes, and that which before was dry Land, is turned into a Lake of Water. There are also subterraneous Fires, and bituminous, sulphurous Exhalations, which are like fired Gun-powder within the Earth, causing it to shake and tremble. But notwithstanding there are Natural causes of some Earthquakes, nevertheless, they are awful Works of God. Prodigious Storms have Natural causes, yet *those Stormy winds fulfill the Word of the Lord,* Psal. 148. 8. As we have formerly from that Scripture largely Discoursed. Thunder and Lightning proceeds from Natural causes, yet is it the Lords voice, Psal. 29. 3. 4. *The Voice of the Lord is upon many Waters, the God of Glory Thundreth, the Voice of the Lord is Powerful, the Voice of the Lord is full of Majesty.* So an Earthquake is the *Voice of the Lord,* Ver. 8. *The Voice of the Lord shakes the Wilderness, the Lord shakes the Wilderness of Kadesh.* There never happens an Earthquake but God speaks to men on the Earth by it: And they are very stupid, if they do not hear His Voice therein.[144]

The curious combination of the religious and the scientific, the didactic and the informative is, as we have seen, typical of early writings on science in America.

8. Anthroponomics.

In the study of "things naturall to America," the colonial writers, of course, included the "naturall inhabitants." No

[144] Increase Mather, *A Discourse Concerning Earthquakes* (Boston, 1706), p. 5 f.

account of America, whether written for historical or exploitative purposes, was complete without descriptions of the lives, habits, and customs of these strange native people. The whole of Captain John Smith's "Description of Virginia," of some forty pages in length, is in reality a study of the Indian, for even when he speaks of the natural resources of the country he relates them to their use as he has found them among the inhabitants. The whole is sufficiently correct in the observation to call it a scientific study of a people.

In spite of the picturesque element of such incidents as the Pocahontas story, even romantic stories from such gentlemen as the gallant captain have extreme value to the student; for instance, note the following paragraph with its informative detail:

> For their musicke they vse a thicke cane, on which they pipe as on a Recorder. For thier warres, they haue a great deepe platter of wood. They cover their mouth thereof with a skin, at each corner they tie a walnut, which meeting on the backside neere the bottome, with a small rope they twitch them togither till it be so tought and stiffe, that they may beat vpon it as vpon a drumme. But their chiefe instruments are Rattels made of small gourds or Pumpion shels. Of these they haue Base, Tenor, Counter-tenor, Meane and Trible. These mingled with their voices sometimes 20 or 30 togither, make such a terrible noise as would rather affright then delight any man.[145]

The second part of William Wood's *New England's Prospect* is similarly a study of the Indians as he finds them: of the different tribes, of their dress, their cookery, their physique, their religion, their marriages, their languages, their arts, *et cetera.*

John Josselyn departs from the usual discursive and detailed account of the Indian when he writes a quaint portrait of an Indian squaw and puts her among his New-England's rarities. By way of an introductory remark, he addresses

[145] *Op. cit.*, I, 73.

the "gentle Reader" and he hopes to make amends for his "rude Observations"—that is to say his short excursions into science—by entertaining the reader with:

A Description of an Indian Squa.

Now (gentle Reader) having trespassed upon your patience a long while in the perusing of these rude Observations, I shall, to make you amends, present you by way of Divertisement, or Recreation, with a Coppy of Verses made sometime since upon the Picture of a young and handsome Gypsie, not improperly transferred upon the *Indian* SQUA, or Female *Indian,* trick'd up in all her bravery.

The Men are somewhat Horse Fac'd, and generally Faucious, *i.e.* without Beards; but the Women many of them [100] have very good Features; seldome without a *Come to me*, or *Cos Amoris,* in their Countenance; all of them black Eyed, having even short Teeth, and very white; their Hair black, thick and long, broad Breasted; handsome streight Bodies, and slender, considering their constant loose habit: Their limbs cleanly, straight, and of a convenient stature, generally, as plump as Partridges, and saving here and there one, of a modest deportment.

Their Garments are a pair of Sleeves of Deer, or Moose skin drest, and drawn with lines of several Colours into Asiatick Works, with Buskins of the same, a short Mantle of Trading Cloath, either Blew or Red, fastened with a knot under the Chin, and girt about the middle with a Zone, wrought with white and blew Beads into pretty Works: of these Beads they have Bracelets for their Neck and Arms, and Links to hang in their Ears, and a fair Table curiously made up with Beads likewise, to wear before their Breast; their Hair they Combe backward, and tye it up short with a Border, about two handfulls broad, wrought in Works as the other with their Beads: But enough of this.

The POEM

Whether White or Black be best
Call your Senses to the quest;
And your touch shall quickly tell
The Black in softness doth excel,

And in smoothness; but the Ear,
What, can that a Colour hear?
No, but 'tis your Black ones Wit
That doth catch, and captive it.
And if Slut and Fair be one,
Sweet and Fair, there can be none:
Nor can ought so please the tast
As what's brown and lovely drest:
And who'll say, that that is best
To please ones Sense, displease the rest?
Maugre then all that can be sed
In flattery of White and Red:
Those flatterers themselves must say
That darkness was before the Day:
And such perfection here appears
It neither Wind nor Sun-shine fears.[146]

Roger Williams' information on the Indian departs from the usual procedure of the "pamphlet of newes." Ostensibly his book is, as he says, *A Key Unto the Language of America.* But it is more than that; it is a study in the life of the Indian, each chapter revolving about certain related words in the Indian vocabulary. The chapter is interspersed with the author's own comments on Indian life and his personal account of his experiences. Having done with these, he points a moral and then closes the chapter with several lines of verse of a didactic nature. In these chapters there seems to be a mixture of scientific information, of personal anecdotes and treatment, and of didactic purpose. There is a curious mixture of the informative and the creative writing, as if the scientist were struggling with the creative artist.

If we are seeking information on a topic, Williams suggests that we turn to the table that he has arranged for our help, at the end of the "Key." This sounds like a mere index, but when we turn to it, we find such suggestively essay-like titles as: "Of Salutation," "Of Sleep," "Of Discourse and Newes," "Of the Earth and Fruits thereof," *et cetera.*

[146] *Op. cit.,* pp. 156-158.

The chapter "Of Sleep" is typical:

Concerning Sleepe *and* Lodging

Nsowwushkâwmen	*I am weary.*
Nkàtaquaum.	*I am sleepie.*
Kukkovetoùs.	*Shall I lodge here?*
Yo nickowémen?	*Shall I sleepe here?*
Kukkowéti.	*Will you sleepe here?*
Wunnégin, cówish.	*Welcome, sleepe here.*
Nummouaquômen.	*I will lodge abroad.*
Puckquátchick nickouêmen.	*I will sleepe without the the* doores,*

Which I have knowne them contentedly doe, by a fire under a tree, when sometimes some *English* have (for want of familiaritie and language with them) been fearefull to entertaine them.

In Summer-time I have knowne them lye abroad often themselves, to make roome for stranger, *English, or* others. [An appropriate vocabulary and comment follows. Then he continues:]

Matannauke, or Mattannàukanash	*A finer sort of mats to sleep on.*
Maskítuash	*Straw to ly on.*
Wuddtúckqunash ponamâuta	*Let us lay on wood*

This they doe plentifully when they lie down to sleep winter and summer, abundance they have and abundance they lay on: their Fire is instead of our bedcloaths. And so, themselves and any that have occasion to lodge with them, must be content to turne often to the Fire, if the night be cold, and they who first wake must repaire the Fire. [Here follows the appropriate vocabulary.]

When they have a bad Dreame, which they conceive to be a threatning from God, they fall to prayer at all times of the night, especially early before day: So *Davids* zealous heart to the true and living God: *At midnight will I rise,* &c. *I prevented the dawning of the day,* &c. Psal. 119. &c.

Wunnakúkkussaquaùm	*You sleep much.*
Peeyaûntam	*He prayes.*
Peeyâuntamwock	*They pray.*
Túnna kukkowémis	*Where slept you?*
Awaun wé[k]ick kukkouémis	*At whose house did you sleep?*

* Repetitions and inconsistencies in spelling and punctuation are in the original.

I once travailed to an Iland of the wildest in our parts, where in the night an Indian (as he said) had a vision or dream of the Sun (whom they worship for a God) darting a Beame into his Breast which he conceived to be the Messenger of his Death: this poore Native call'd his Friends and neighbours, and prepared some little refreshing for them, but himselfe was kept waking and Fasting in great Humiliations and Invocations for 10. dayes and nights: I was alone (having travailed from my Barke, the wind being contrary) and little could I speake to them to their understandings, especially because of the change of their Dialect, or manner of Speech from our neighbours: yet so much (through the help of God) I did speake, of the *True* and *living only Wise God*, of the Creation: of Man, and his *fall* from God, &c. that at parting many burst forth, *Oh when will you come againe, to bring us some more newes of this God?*

From their Sleeping: The Observation generall.

Sweet rest is not confind to soft Beds, for, not only God gives his beloved sleep on hard lodgings: but also Nature and Custome gives sound sleep to these Americans on the Earth, on a Boord or Mat. Yet how is *Europe* bound to God for better lodging, &c.

More particular.

1. *God gives them sleep on Ground, on Straw,*
on Sedgie Mats or Board:
When English softest Beds of Downe,
sometimes no sleep affoord.

2. *I have knowne them leave their House and Mat*
to lodge a Friend or stranger,
When Jewes and Christians oft have sent
Christ Jesus *to the Manger.*

3. *'Fore day they invocate their Gods,*
though Many, False and New:
O how should that God worshipt be,
who is but One and True?[147]

In looking over this quoted chapter we can observe the following: the informative quality of the first part of the chapter; the personal observation as, "In summer-time I have

[147] Publications of the Narragansett Club (Providence, 1866), I, 46.

knowne . . ."; the personal anecdote, as that part beginning, "I once travailed . . ."; the philosophic comment, "Sweet rest is not confin'd to soft Beds . . ."; the moral poetic ending. Roger Williams' "Key Unto the Language of America" is really a collection of incipient essays on the different phases of Indian life. There is much more in each chapter than a mere lesson in vocabulary, for each is a development out of a vocabulary on a particular subject related to the Indian. It is, however, not purely informative. There is the lesson of the didactic essay as well and there are the personal anecdotes and observations of the author. The chapter ends, moreover, not only with a moral or philosophic comment, but with this conclusion expressed in a short poem. Roger Williams' original treatment of his subject is an interesting example of the creative process and, as such, is of value to our literary history. It is also noteworthy that his experiments in composition in no wise obscure the book's exact information nor detract from its scientific value.

Other examples of such studies of a people one may find in Daniel Denton's "A Brief Description of New York,"[148] C. W[ooley's] "A Two Years Journal in New York,"[149] John Lawson's "A New Voyage to Carolina,[150] Robert Beverley's "History of Virginia,"[151] or in John Josselyn's "Account of Two Voyages to New-England."[152]

All of these are of scientific value to the historian of early America. Although they vary in the degree of their scientific approach, they are on the whole surprisingly exact.

The scientific essay in America had its beginnings in these humble origins. In these examples we have found varied subject matter, and at least the effort toward scientific approach. Since the end of "scientific" observation, however, was the contemplation of the universe as a manifestation of Deity, the authors of these short prose pieces fre-

[148] *Supra*, p. 11.
[149] London, 1701.
[150] London, 1709.
[151] London, 1722.
[152] Boston, 1685.

quently turned from a purely objective explanation to a moral application, so that at times these "scientific essays" were metamorphosed into didactic "essays." The fact, however, that these early Americans were beginning to recognize the importance of the inductive method of reasoning; the fact that they saw an amazing number of things to write about, not only in the heavens but upon their new earth; the fact that they wished to put their findings in writing and print for the information of others; the fact that they sometimes contributed their observations and conclusions to such important learned bodies as the Royal Society of London; and the fact that some of their records are of sufficient accuracy to be valuable sources of information to-day are sufficient evidence to show that in these early writings were beginnings of the scientific spirit in America.

In these scientific pieces is a happy mingling of factual information and original composition giving them literary as well as historical interest. And these qualities, it might be well pointed out, make a logical background for the Age of Franklin. Contrary to popular belief, the Puritan Age was not a hindrance but an impetus toward America's eighteenth century and her Age of Reason.

PERSONAL RECORDS

The letter, the journal, and the diary are frequently compared to the familiar essay in their personal content, their egoistic point-of-view, their informal manner, their discursive style, their varied and unordered subject matter. For instance, in the running commentary of everyday life in the diary of Samuel Pepys, in the well-rounded discussion of abstract subjects in the letters of Cicero and Seneca, and in the literary artistry and familiar quality of the letters of William Cowper and Charles Lamb, are to be found the stuff of which essays are made. And, indeed, when Cicero writes a letter on old age or Seneca on the happy life, the letter becomes in fact an essay.

The diary and letters of America contain much less evidence than these of literary aplomb, for the colonists, as a rule, had little time for leisurely commentaries. And yet, we find certain trends in their writings of this kind and occasionally some characteristics suggestive of the essay.

1. Journals, Diaries, Autobiographies

Most of the journals before 1710 took their places purposefully in the literature of exploitation or in chronicle history. Except for that of Madame Sarah K. Knight,[153] the journal of familiar character was unknown, because it was out of keeping with the times.

The diary of Samuel Sewall lacks the knowing manner and romantic eagerness of Madame Knight, but it is fre-

[153] *The Journals of Madam Knight and Rev. Mr. Buckingham. From the Original Manuscripts, Written in 1704 and 1710* (New York, 1825). Madame Knight's amusing account of Mr. Devill's habitation and her sprightly observations on the people and customs of New Haven and New York seem, indeed, to have little in common with Puritan writings.

quently unconsciously amusing. This is because he found life less adventurous than Madame Knight, and more serious as a good Christian would. In his comments on small incidents of life and in his unconscious humour[154] he resembles the famous English diarist and, indeed, has been called the "American Samuel Pepys."

It is characteristic of him that he records small incidents of life and then applies a moral. At times he is almost as gossipy as Pepys. Of this quality he is totally unaware, because he is thinking not so much about what happened as about the moral good to be derived from it, as these examples will show:

> June 16, [1707]. My House was broken open in two places, and about Twenty pounds worth of Plate stolen away, and some Linen; My Spoon, and Knife, and Neckcloth was taken: I said, Is not this an Answer of Prayer? Jane came up, and gave us the Alarm betime in the morn. I was helped to submit to Christ's stroke, and say, Wellcome CHRIST![155]

When Josiah Willard shamefully cuts off his hair, Sewall writes a short moral discourse on the text that hair was put on man's head to teach him patience:

> Tuesday, June 10, [1701]. Having last night heard that Josiah Willard had cut off his hair (a very full head of hair) and put on a Wigg, I went to him this morning. Told his Mother what I came about, and she call'd him. I enquired of him what Extremity had forced him to put off his own hair, and put on a Wigg? He answered, none at all. But said that his Hair was streight, and that it parted behinde. Seem'd to argue that men might as well shave their hair off their head, as off their face. I answered men were men before they had hair on their faces, (half of mankind have never any). God seems to have ordain'd our Hair as a Test, to see whether we can bring our minds to be content to be at his finding: or whether we would be our own

[154] He is not wholly devoid of a sense of humour, as some of his letters show.

[155] "Diary of Samuel Sewall," *MHSC*; series 5, VI, 189.

> Carvers, Lords, and come no more at Him. If disliked our Skin, or Nails; 'tis no Thanks to us, that for all that, we cut them not off: Pain and danger restrain us. Your Calling is to teach men self Denial. Twill be displeasing and burdensom to good men: And they that care not what men think of them care not what God thinks of them. Father, Bror Simon, Mr. Pemberton, Mr. Wigglesworth, Oakes, Noyes (Oliver), Brattle of Cambridge their example. Allow me to be so far a *Censor Morum* for this end of the Town. Pray'd him to read the Tenth Chapter of the Third book of Calvins Institutions. I read it this morning in course, not of choice. Told him that it was condemn'd by a Meeting of Ministers at Northampton in Mr. Stoddards house, when the said Josiah was there. Told him of the Solemnity of the Covenant which he and I had lately enterd into, which put me upon discoursing to him. He seem'd to say would leave off his Wigg when his hair was grown. I spake to his Father of it a day or two after: He thank'd me that had discoursed his Son, and told me that when his hair was grown to cover his ears, he promis'd to leave off his Wigg. If he had known of it, would have forbidden him. His Mother heard him talk of it; but was afraid positively to forbid him; lest he should do it, and so be more faulty.[156]

The diary was usually serious in tone and moral in point-of-view. It was mostly devoid of the gossipy character of Sewall's *Diary* or of the humour of Madame Knight's *Journal.* Cotton Mather's diary, for instance, is the record of a soul's direct and constant communication with God; and it lacks, in consequence, the contact with human beings that is characteristic of the other two.

The short autobiographies written before 1710 were very much like the diary in its serious character. They are chronological narrative, to be sure, but the purpose and general content are in the same religious mood. The purpose is the glorification of God; the subject matter is everything that will prove His goodness and show His wisdom, and the particular lesson, to live the good life. So obvious is this that their content, however individual it might be expected

[156] *Ibid.*, p. 36 f.

to be, is almost wholly to be anticipated. Each author professes to have been wicked in his youth, to have been punished for his sins and shown the Way, to have been put to trial again and again throughout his life as a Divine test of his faith, and to have borne whatever was visited upon him with patience and humility, and to have achieved a reward in the victory of the soul over the temptations of Satan. The purpose of revealing these conversions from sin and resolutions for a better life are obviously for the moral one of warning others what to avoid and how better to live. The emphasis is not on the chronological narrative of a life, but on all in that life which tends to illustrate this double moral thesis.[157]

"As I grew vp to bee about 14 or 15," says Anne Bradstreet, in her diary written for the benefit of her children, "I fovnd my heart more carnall, and sitting loose from God, vanity and the follyes of youth take hold of me." In punishment, "the Lord layd his hand sore vpon me and smott mee with the small pox. When I was in my affliction, I besovght the Lord, and confessed my Pride and Vanity and he was entreated of me, and again restored me."[158] Since, according to her own conscience, she "rendered not to him according to the benefitt received" other punishments followed with like results, *ad infinitum*.

Such trials the Lord put upon Michael Wigglesworth and his family. His autobiography is a similar testimony to inscrutable Providence, and only incidentally, an interesting account of their settling in New-England, his early youth, and his education. In his case, the Lord showed him the way out of his evil life by sending him to college.

Governor Winthrop, in his youth, "was very lewdly disposed, inclining unto and attempting (so far as my yeares enabled me) all kind of wickednesse, except swearing and scorning religion, which I had no temptation unto in regard to my education." The name given to this autobiography is

[157] Cf. Bunyan in *Grace Abounding*.
[158] Anne Bradstreet, *The Works of . . .*, ed. by J. H. Ellis (Charlestown, 1867), p. 4 f.

significantly "Governor John Winthrop's (the elder) Christian Experience." The account of his life is more complete than Mrs. Bradstreet's or Wigglesworth's, but it, too, is all tribute to Divine Providence and right living.

According to his own account, Thomas Shepard was one constantly meeting the temptations of Satan, in his youth, in college, and in the ministry. It was necessary for him to turn constantly to meditation and prayer.

Roger Clap's *Memoirs* have the insistent theme of the goodness of God and are as much about God's remarkable providence to the inhabitants as to himself. His account is the dramatic struggle between God, as represented in his agents, and Satan, as represented in his,—the Indians, the witches, and the "Antinomians."

And the ultimate moral of all of these autobiographies is that the struggle is worth while, for the godly life is the best life and full of reward. This does not mean that these writers say, "I have led the good life"; rather, they have said, "I am weak and I have fallen. But I have tried. Lead thou a better life, for God is just and good."

These autobiographies and diaries of high moralistic nature may be thought of as a part of that class of literature known as "wisdom literature," which is expressive of advice and the knowledge of good that has been reaped from experience. To this belong also the stories of the Bible and the didactic essay.

2. The Letter

The letters of American literature before 1710 were not so persistently moralistic. The colonist wrote a voluminous correspondence on varied subjects and with individual manner: the country, the "naturall inhabitants," the neighbors, the government, literature,[159] life, death, and the hereafter. Sometimes they wrote only to give information; sometimes they discussed personal matters.

[159] For informal discussion of literature see the quarrel between Roger Williams and Mrs. Anne Sadleir in the letters of Roger Williams, *Pub. Narr. Club*, VI, 237-252.

First of all, the most interesting subject for letters in those days was news about the lately settled country. Accordingly, a goodly number of letters belonged to the informative class of literature, although these, like the "pamphlet of newes" and kindred writings, were modified and suggestive of the creative type in proportion as the writer knew his correspondent or intruded his own personality within his writing.

Governor Dudley, in 1630, turns aside from "publick" and "domestick" affairs to write his famous letter to the Countess of Lincoln and whoever is interested in hearing about New England.[160] His manner of composing it is unorthodox: he has as yet no table to write upon, and in lieu of it, sits by the fireside and writes upon his knee. He reviews the circumstances attendant upon the founding of New-Plymouth in 1620, and his own in 1630, and then he turns to a description of the country: its resources, its natural inhabitants, and the vicissitudes of the settlers. The contents of the letter are informative as one would expect from one friend writing to another about a strange country.

There were many letters of this sort: John Pory, the first secretary of Virginia, wrote in 1619 on the "Infant Commonwealth";[161] Thomas Pascall, in 1683, on Pennsylvania;[162] and Dr. More[163] and William Penn[164] on the same province. With these, also, may be mentioned that particular group of letters by John Eliot and his colleagues on the Indians, the "sunshine" series.[165] These were not only of informative but of scientific interest and value, most of them being sent to the Royal Society of London.

The letters of Dudley and the rest are like the "pamphlet of newes," whose purpose is informative and whose method is largely descriptive. Like them they vary in the quality of formality depending upon the author's personality and his degree of acquaintance with his correspondent.

[160] *MHSC*, series 1, VIII, p. 63 ff.
[161] *Orig. Narr.*, V, 279.
[162] *Ibid.*, XIII, 245.
[163] *Ibid.*, p. 279.
[164] *Ibid.*, p. 255.
[165] See *MHSC*, series 3, vol. IV.

Letters of this kind—on the country and its inhabitants—had a timely quality, for they pertained to the vital news of the day. Of particularly timely interest, too, were those subjects that initiated some dispute or that stimulated critical comment. For instance, James Cudworth, in 1658, writes a letter on the persecution of the Quakers;[166] Thomas Hooker, though in an extremely religious and moral manner, gives his point-of-view on the first movement for a confederation of the colonies.[167]

Although the subject of news of the day filled a goodly number of these early letters, it was not the only subject of interest. The letters of personal correspondence between friends and the members of a family were more informal, discursive, and full of casual comment of homely matters. The author could let his pen wander as it would. These letters are frequently full of the news of friends and neighbors. They are sometimes "gossipy," as when the American Samuel Pepys, Chief Justice Samuel Sewall, writes to Daniel Gookin: Mr. Wheelwright preaches a sermon; there is news of Sir Bayly and Sir Gerrish; there have been births and deaths and robberies; little Betty has read the Book of Martyrs in "three Moneths space." This letter is full of good humour and amusing metaphors: the auditors of Mr. Wheelwright's sermons "maybe as some are; the pines on the beach will give more attention than they." It is sprinkled with homely wisdom: "For you know that Prosperity is too fullsom a diet for any man, especially a student; unless seasond [*sic*] with some grains of Adversity." It indulges in quotation and illustration from classical learning. It opens with a quotation from Ovid and elaborates it in application:

> *Parve (nec Invideo) sine me, liber, ibis* [*in urbem*];
> *Hei mihi, quod domino non licet ire tuo.*
> . . . Neither may it seem altogether strange; if you consider that Rome, in all her Pomp and Glory; (though

[166] *America. Great Crises in Our History Told by Its Makers* (Chicago, 1925), pp. 175-180.

[167] *Coll. Conn. Hist. Soc.* (Hartford, 1860), vol. I.

> she might brag of her Julius and Augustus) could not be so much to so Noble a Man, and Poet; as that Town [Cambridge] must needs be to me.[168]

Sewall indulges frequently in Latin phraseology—sometimes, one suspects, with a touch of humour: Little Betty "can Read, and Spin passing well; Things (mesaltem Judice) very desirable in a Woman."[169]

The most familiar spirit of all these letter writers is that of George Alsop of Maryland. As the time approaches for him to place himself in servitude and embark for Maryland he begins to write letters to his friends and family. The first of a published series is sent to his friend "T. B." "From the Chimney-corner upon a low Cricket, where i write in the noise of some six women, Aug. 19 Anno," (1658). He writes entertainingly of his disagreeable trip on shipboard and, when it is over, remarks with assurance, "I am now upon land, and there I'll keep myself if I can . . ."

In a letter to his father, he describes his passage to America and his first impressions of the country in picturesque manner. If his humour is not gentle and refined or his style polished, nevertheless his droll comments are whimsical and entertaining:

> To give you the particulars of the several accidents that happened in our Voyage by Sea, it would swell a Journal of some sheets, and therefore too large and tedious for a Letter: I think it therefore necessary to bind up the relation in Octavo, and give it you in short.
>
> We had a blowing and dangerous passage of it, and for some dayes after I arrived, I was an absolute Copernicus, it being one main point of my moral Creed, to believe the World had a pair of long legs, and walked with the burthen of the Creation upon her back. For to tell you the very truth of it, for some dayes upon Land, after so long and tossing a passage, I was so giddy that I could hardly tread an even step; so that all things both above and below (that was in view) appeared to me like the Kentish Britains to William the Conqueror, in a moving posture.

[168] *MHSC*, series 6, I, 17 f.
[169] *Ibid.*

> Those few number of weeks since my arrival, has given me but little experience to write any thing large of the Country; only thus much I can say, and that not from any imaginary conjectures, but from an occular observation, That this Country of Mary-land abounds in a flourishing variety of delightful Woods, pleasant Groves, lovely Springs, together with spacious Navigable Rivers and Creeks, it being a most healthful and pleasant situation, so far as my knowledge has yet had any view in it.
>
> Herds of Deer are as numerous in this Province of Mary-land, as Cuckolds can be in London, only their horns are not so well drest and tipt with silver as theirs are.
>
> Here if the Devil had such a Vagary in his head as he had once among the Gadareans, he might drown a thousand head of Hogs and they'd ne're be miss'd, for the very Woods of this Province swarms with them...[170]

His rollicking humour and his droll comments merit him a place among our early creative writers.

These informal, chatty letters are, in a way, the stuff of which the familiar essay is made, for their authors talk engagingly to their readers; they indulge in the autobiographical and the egoistic; they reveal their own personalities, their philosophy, and their eccentricities; they write on the commonplace; they digress from one subject to another as their whims dictate; and if it suits their purpose, they may enliven their discussion by anecdote and illustration. On the other hand, these letters, unlike those of classical literature, are too haphazard to be considered as essays in themselves.

There are other letters that contain the advice of "wisdom literature" and much of the axiomatic expression of the didactic essay. Jonathan Mitchel, at Harvard College in 1649, writes a letter to his brother, whose mind, apparently, had been assailed by doubt and whose spiritual welfare, therefore, was in need of advice and direction: "salvation is worth all our Labour, be it what it will: Is it a Trifle to be

[170] *Orig. Narr.,* XI, 377 f.

saved eternally? Do we think to get to Heaven by a good Wish? Or to go thither in a Feather Bed?"

Another example is Josiah Flint's letter of consolation to his aunt, Mrs. Bridget Usher, which introduces his "Sting of Death." From his "Study" he writes, in brief:

> Its good for your self, with all other Relations that yet survive, to look at the supream Disposer; when the rongs of the wheels are high and dreadful to eye him that sits upon the Throne: . . .[171]

After such counsel growing out of experience, he adds, "There is no Staff of indignation in the hand of Providence, but it is grounded in the eternal Decree."

A most natural source of "wisdom literature" in colonial America will be seen, therefore, to be letters written to the members of the author's family. To them, of course, is he most prone to give advice. For instance, Samuel Sewall advises his daughter on marriage. She must think carefully before she refuses one so desirable as Mr. Hirst:

> When persons come toward us, we are apt to look upon their Undesirable Circumstances mostly; and thereupon to shun them. But when persons retire from us for good and all, we are in danger of looking only on that which is desirable in them, to our wofull Disquiet. Whereas tis the property of a good Balance to turn where the most weight is, though there be some also in the other Scale.[172]

John Winthrop, Jr., on September 9, 1658, advises his son, who had just left the shelter of his home:

> Be carefull to avoid all evill and vaine company, wch are so great instrumets of Sathan to draw and intice to evill, and to allure the simple into the snares of destruction, as the bird is taken in the evill nett; who so is wise will beware of them.[173]

[171] Written from Dorchester in 1680.
[172] *MHSC*, series 6, I, 213 (Boston, 1699).
[173] *MHSC*, series 5, VIII, 45 f.

Thomas Shepard also writes his son, in a long letter on the occasion of the latter's "admission into college." His advice on study and reading seems to be an echo of Bacon:

> VI. Remember that in ordering your Studies you make them as pleasant as may be, and as fruitfull as possibly you are able, that so you may not be weary in the work God setts you about: and for this End remember these Rules, viz. . .
>
> 3. Lett your studies be so ordered as to have variety of Studies before you, that when you are weary of one book, you may take pleasure (through this variety) in another: and for this End read some Histories often, which (they Say) make men wise, as Poets make witty; bothe which are pleasant things in the midst of more difficult studies.[174]

One complete type of the seventeenth century essay may be found in John Dunton's *Letters from New-England.* The author was interested in telling his correspondents about some of the eminent and good people of New England, and therefore wrote "characters" of them. His letters do not, like others, unconsciously bear qualities of the essay, but they consciously imitate this form. Examples of these are the "characters" of Samuel Willard briefly drawn; of Mrs. Green, the example of a good wife; and of Charles Morton, the great and good man. It is to be noted that Dunton uses the term *character* a number of times. The portrait of Mrs. Green reads:

> A Wife is the next Change that a Virgin can lawfully make, and draws many other Relations after it. Which Mrs. Green was sensible of; For I have heard her say, "That when she married Mr. Green, she espous'd his Obligations also! and where-ever her Husband, either by Tyes of Nature or squeezing of Wax, owed either Money or Love, she esteem'd herself to be no less a Debtor." She knew her Marriage was an adoption into his Family, and therefore paid to every Branch of it what their respective Stations requir'd. She is sensible that the Duty of her place has several Aspects. First

[174] *Pub. Col. Soc. of Mass.* (Boston, 1913), XIV, 193 f. Cf. Bacon, *Of Studies* "Histories make men wise; poets witty. . ."

As it relates to her Husbands Person, and next to his Relations, and thirdly to his Fortune. . .

Another thing that was very remarkable in Mrs. Green was her Obedience to her Husband; to whose will she was so exactly observant, that he cou'd not be more ready to Command, than she was to obey; and when some of his Commands seem'd not to be so kind as she might have expected, she wou'd not only obey 'em, but wisely dissemble the Unkindness of them, as knowing where Men have not wholly put off humanity, there is a native Compassion to a meek sufferer. She was also extreamly tender of her Husbands Reputation, setting his Worth in the clearest Light, putting his Infirmities (for where is the Man that lives without 'em?) in the Shade. And as she was this way tender of his Reputation, so she was also in another respect more particularly relating to herself; for, knowing that the misbehaviour of the Wife reflects upon the Husband, she took care to abstain even from all appearance of evil, and resolved to be (what Caesar desir'd of his Wife) not only free from Fault, but from all suspicion of it.

But Mrs. Green was not only a Loving, a Faithful, and an Obedient Wife, but an Industrious Wife too; managing that part of his Business which he had deputed to her, with so much Application and Dexterity as if she had never come into the House; and yet so manag'd her House as if she had never gone into the Ware-house. The Emperour Augustus himself scarce wore anything but what was the Manufacture of his Wife, his Sister, his Daughter, or his Nieces. Should our gay English Ladies, those Lilies of our Fields, which neither sow nor spin, nor gather into Barns, be exempted from furnishing others, and only left to Cloath themselves, 'tis to be doubted they wou'd reverse Our Saviour's Parallel of Solomon's Glories, and no Beggar in all his Rags, wou'd be array'd like one of these.

But Mrs. Green follow'd the Example of Solomon's Vertuous Wife, who riseth while it is yet Night, giving Meat to her Houshold, and a Portion to her Maidens; and as she is a good Wife to her Husband, so she is also a good Mother to her Children, whom she brings up with that sweetness and Facility as is admirable, not keeping them at too great a distance, (as some do) thereby Discouraging their good Parts; nor by an Over-Fondness (a fault most Mothers are guilty of) betraying 'em into a thousand Inconveniences, which oftentimes proves fatal to 'em.

> In brief, she takes care of their Education, and whatever else belongs to 'em; so that Mr. Green enjoys the comfort of his Children, without knowing anything of the trouble of 'em.
>
> Nor is she less a Good Mistress than a good Mother; Treating her Servants with that Love and Gentleness as if she were their Mother; taking care both of their Souls and Bodies, and not letting them want any thing necessary for either. I one Day told her, That I believ'd she was an extraordinary Wife; but Mr. Green was so good a Man, she cou'd not well be otherwise. To which she answer'd "That she had so good a Husband, was her Mercy; but had her Husband been as bad a Man as any in the World, her Duty wou'd have been the same, and so she hop'd her Practice shou'd have been too." Which, as it is a great Truth, it wants to be more known and Practic'd.[175]

This "character" of Mrs. Green is deliberately planned after established models: first, he defines a good wife and then he shows how Mrs. Green is an example of this "character." In conclusion, he says, "And thus, Reader, I have given you the Character of another of my Female Friends in Boston, and in her, the Character of a good Wife."

The personality of Samuel Willard must have been overwhelming, since one who had drawn Mrs. Green with such enthusiasm was almost powerless to "write his Character":

> He's a Man of Profound Notions: Can say what he will, and prove what he says: I darken his Merits if I call him less than a Walking Library. The Civilities I receiv'd from him, both at his House, and in other places, might (had I any Gratitude) engage me further to write his Character; but he's too great a Man for me to Attempt it; . . . So I shall leave his House, with only admiring what I cann't Describe.[176]

Charles Morton, however, seemed more adaptable to character writing, although Dunton apologizes for his attempt: "I know it would be Presumption in me to draw his character; and yet I cannot but say something of him, as an

[175] "John Dunton's Letters from New-England," *Publications of the Prince Society* (Boston, 1867), p. 102 ff.

[176] *Ibid.*, p. 75 f.

Essay towards it.[177] He proceeds with enthusiasm to write a character of this Great Man of Charlestown:

> His Conversation shews him a Gentleman: For he has sense Enough for a Privy Counsellour, and Soul Great Enough for a King: And whoever has the honour of his Company, will quickly be satisfy'd that he is not only the Repository of all Arts and Sciences, but of the Graces too; and Will find that for matter, Words, and Manner, he is all that is delightful in Conversation: His matter is not stale and studied, but always resent, and occasional: for whatever subject is at any time started, he has still some pleasant and pat story for it; nor is he stiff and morose, but ductile and plyable to the Company; his Discourse is high, but not Soaring; familiar, but not low; profound, but not obscure; and the more sublime, the more Intelligible and Conspicuous.
>
> His Memory is as vast as his Knowledge, which is so great, that in the Firmament of Learning, the Name of Morton will shine like a Bright Star of the first Magnitude to all Posterity: and as tho' he were the Epitomy both of Aristotle and Descartes, he is the very Soul of philosophy. Yet tho' he be a very Panaretus, or Magazine of all the vertues, so great is his Humility he knows it least of any; and is as far from Pride as Ignorance: And if we may judge of a Mans Religion by his Charity, (and can we go by a surer Rule) he is a truly Pious and Religious Man: and being thus qualify'd, he must certainly be the fittest to bring up young Men to the Ministry, of any Man in England: And that is matter of Fact, the many Eminent and Learned Divines, now Preachers in England, of his bringing up, is a convincing Testimony.[178]

In this manner does Dunton draw the character of a great and learned man in the person of Charles Morton.

Examples of the letters of advice with the aphoristic tendency, or of the "character" are not usual. The letters of information like Governor Dudley's or of news and gossip like Sewall's were more characteristic of seventeenth century America.

[177] Here, obviously, "Essay" is used to mean attempt.
[178] *Ibid.*, p. 296.

DEDICATIONS, PREFACES, INTRODUCTIONS[179]

When Montaigne said to his reader, "Lecteur, je suis moy mesme la matière de mon livre,"[180] he not only established the character of the essay, but he also expressed the content of all prefaces, introductions, and dedications of the seventeenth century—je suis moy mesme la matière de ma préface.

The preface of the twentieth century is usually an explanation of the purpose of a book or the history of its writing, or a brief explanation of what is to follow. Only occasionally does a writer become informal and address his reader in the manner of a familiar essayist, and only rarely does a writer, other than the author, compose an introduction to a book. Either of these things may be done; but, as a rule, the preface or introduction is merely an explanation. And the dedication of a book has at last dwindled to a mere line or two of tribute to a friend or a member of one's family, because an author no longer seeks a patron to launch his book by writing him an elaborate compliment.

There are two reasons for this change in introductory matter: in the first place, the impersonal agent known as the "publisher" has taken the place of the patron. One cannot pay him a compliment with the purpose of expecting a favor. Also, the publisher's advertisements of one's book take the place of the enthusiastic introductions formerly written by friends to launch a book. In the second place, the periodical has become the medium for other people's reception of the book. Here the critic, more or less profes-

[179] In my discussion I shall not as a rule distinguish one of these from another, for their difference, so far as their bearing on this subject is concerned, is negligible.

[180] "L'Aucteur au Lecteur," *Essais de Montaigne*. Nouvelle Edition, par M. J.—V. LeClerc, I., Paris, n. d.

sional, keeps to his subject. On the other hand, the seventeenth century introducer, whether the author or his friend, having no organ for personal comment, sometimes found the introduction a splendid medium for indulgence of personal commentaries in his own manner. Here, the authors, feeling more at ease than in their longer work in hand, unconsciously reveal their own personalities and opinions, and discourse informally on varied subjects. Even the learned divines, with the weight of theological matters on their minds, address the reader no less revealingly. Their informality is evident in the actual address in the prefaces "To the Courteous Reader," "Kind Reader," *et cetera* which are to be compared at once to such expressions as "Gentle Reader," so very dear to the heart of familiar essayists. As far back as 1603 Florio set the style for these when, in his publication of Montaigne's essays, he caught the spirit of the great essayist and translated the simple "Lecteur" into "Gentle Reader."

1. The Familiar Spirit

Though in its early history the South was not prolific in literary men or scholars, the familiar spirit had an auspicious beginning in the prefatory "epistles" to such works as those of Captain John Smith. T. Abbay, who accompanied Smith to Virginia, wrote a dedication "To the Hand" as an introduction to the first part of "A Map of Virginia" (1612).[181] He is Elizabeth in spirit and in style. Loving the far-fetched and the unusual he addresses "the hand" rather than the reader, and he attracts our amused attention to his euphuistic flourishes: the balanced sentence like his first one, the more elaborate parallelism as in his last, the repetition of a key word as "a Hand," the historical allusion as that to Queen Izabell:

> *Least I should wrong any in dedicating this Booke to one: I have concluded it shal be particular to none. I found it only dedicated to a Hand, and to that hand I*

[181] *Op. cit.*, I, 43.

> *addresse it. Now for that this businesse is common to the world, this booke may best satisfie the world, because it was penned in the Land it treateth of. If it bee disliked of men, then I would recommend it to women, for being dearely bought and farre sought, it should be good for Ladies. When all men rejected* Christopher Collumbus: *that ever renowned Queene Izabell of Spaine, could pawne her Jewels to supply his wants; whom all the wise men (as they thought themselues) of that age contemned. I need not say what was his worthinesse, her noblenesse, and their ignorance, that so scornefully did spit at his wants, seeing the whole world is enriched with his golden fortunes. Cannot this successfull example moue the incredulous of this time, to consider, to conceaue, and apprehend* Virginia, *which might be, or breed vs a second India? hath not England an Izabell, as well as Spaine, nor yet a* Collumbus *as well as* Geneua? *yes surely it hath. whose desires are no lesse then was worthy* Collumbus, *their certainties more, their experiences no way wanting, only there wants but an Izabell, so it were not from Spaine.*—T.A.[182]

Captain John Smith himself was a much more successful writer in the familiar style than Abbay because he held this euphuistic spirit in restraint. Yet he uses all the established devices that Abbay does and one other, too: the comparison of other things to "natural phenomena." But he uses his tools much more gracefully. He has not assumed a merely clever attitude; on the contrary, he introduces a note of the didactic and philosophic. The first three sentences of his preface express the thoughts of the familiar essayist who muses on the world about him, and would give the reader the benefit of his conclusions:

> If the little Ant, and the sillie Bee seek by their diligence the good of their Commonwealth; much more ought Man. If they punish the drones and sting them [that] steales their labour; then blame not Man. Little hony hath that hiue, where there are more Drones then Bees: and miserable is that Land, where more are idle then well imployed.[183]

[182] *Ibid.*

[183] *Ibid.*, "A Description of New England," I, 179.

The rest of the preface is autobiographical in character, being the comments on his own experiences. Here, also, he speaks in figurative language:

> But because I speake so much of fishing, if any take mee for such a deuote *devoted* fisher, as I dreame of nought else, they mistake mee. I know a ring of golde from a graine of barley, aswell as a goldsmith: and nothing is there to bee had which fishing doth hinder, but furder vs to obtaine.[184]

Similarly written is Smith's epistle to the "Honest Reader" introducing him to his *Pathway to Experience to erect a Plantation.*[185] But the preface from which we have just quoted and his "note for men that have great spirits and smal meanes," to which we alluded in another chapter,[186] are sufficient to show in Captain John Smith a style that is graceful and a charm that is Elizabethan.

From Maryland, 1666, comes the familiar figure of George Alsop, with his "A Character of Maryland." His title instantly reminds one of the seventeenth century's use of the term "character"; and perhaps, since he was a bit of a wag, he used it with intent to parody the character writers. That Alsop was familiar with contemporary essayists is apparent from his not infrequent references to their names and works.[187] His three prefaces to his "Character of Maryland" are written with the mannerisms of the seventeenth century writer of euphuistic leaning. Like Abbay he carries these to excess so that one becomes more aware of his impertinent manner than of the thing he has to say:

> If I have wrote or composed any thing that's wilde and confused, it is because I am so my self, and the world, as far as I can perceive, is not much out of the same trim![188]

[184] *Ibid.*, I, 180.

[185] *Ibid.*, II, 917.

[186] *Supra*, p. 15 f.

[187] E.g., Bacon and Felltham. See George Alsop, "A Character of the Province of Maryland," *Orig. Narr.*, XI, 341.

[188] *Ibid.*, p. 341.

Like his more learned contemporaries, he uses Latin phrases, but the depth of his learning may be doubtful since these amount to such simple and commonplace phrases as *non compos mentis.* He is extremely fond of using maxims, frequently of his own making, though as frequently not: "There is no Globe like the occular and experimental view of a Countrey,"[189] or "There is an old Saying in English, He must rise betimes that would please every one."[190] His language is figurative and frequently effective: addressing the "Merchant Adventurers for Maryland" and the "Commander of Ships that saile into that Province," he says, "You are both Adventurers, the one of estate, the other of Life." His humour is never refined, yet it is frequently acceptable. He had addressed his first preface to Lord Baltimore and the second to the merchant adventurers and commanders. To these latter he remarks drolly, "This dish of Discourse was intended for you at first, but it was manners to let my Lord have the first cut, the Pye being his own."[191] And he concludes with a remark to the reader, "But I am affraid I have kept you too long in the Entry, I shall desire you therefore to come in and sit down."[192]

2. The Didactic Spirit

Our differences in character and temperament between the North and the South began even with the settlement of the first colonies, and it is nowhere more apparent than in the introductions and prefaces where every writer was at liberty to express himself as he chose. Men like Abbay, Smith, and Alsop were familiar in style, and in spirit sometimes irreverent,—always worldly and distinctly Elizabethan. These lived still in the world of the Renaissance with its love of life. The Puritans, imbued with the spirit of the Reformation, with their eyes not upon a present but a future world, used

[189] *Ibid.*, p. 340.
[190] *Ibid.*, p. 341.
[191] *Ibid.*, p. 341.
[192] *Ibid.*, p. 342.

their introductions to discourse on matters of conduct and Christian living. And the thought and style of their introductions characterized by the moral purpose, the contemplative manner, the philosophic comment, the tendency to aphoristic sentence were in the true seventeenth century manner.

William Morton's address "To the Reader" introducing John Cotton's *The Way of Life* (1641) begins:

> *Hee resolved well that said,* Books and friends would I have few and choice; *He advised well that wisht,* Be courteous to all, familiar with few; *Many there are both books and men that meet us in our journey to heaven, whom, a man that knowes what he hath to doe, would not once deigne to salute; others, whom he would grudge any more then a courteous salutation at most: Amid all that almost infinite variety of Bookes that offer themselves to our view, (wherein it is both an easie and an ordinary thing for a man, while he travels after knowledge, to wander and lose himselfe) it is not the least part of a mans wisdome to cull out such, as he may most familiarly converse withall; . . .*[193]

Here are the typical aphorisms and the typical advice. Even the subject matter of books and friendship is in the manner of his seventeenth century contemporaries. The parallel sentences do not follow the more tortuous path of euphuistic pattern, but the clean cut statement of truths as Bacon would have said them.

Samuel Willard's preface to the "Christian Reader" introducing his sermon, "The Child's Portion" (1684), might be called an embryo essay "Of Faith"—of man's faith in times of peril. The nature of it is not merely theological or religious; it is philosophical and meditative. Its style is felicitous in metaphorical language and rhythmical structure, deeply influenced, as one might suspect, by the Bible:

> . . . *There are times when the Churches have rest, are edified, and multiplied: and there are times when iniquity abounds, and Persecution ariseth, and Gods people are scattered. What these times are into which we are now fallen is obvious to him that will not shut*

[193] John Cotton, *The Way of Life* (London, 1641).

> *his eyes. It is the happiness of the true fearers of God, that he hath provided them consolations strong enough to hold up their heads above water when the waves rise highest, and the raging billows make the greatest noise. When the Earth and all in it will afford us no comfort, then heaven can. And as it is our wisdom to be laying up treasures beyond Death and the Grave, out of the reach of time and change, so it is our interest to be strengthening our faith, and corroborating our hope by such things as all the malice of Men and Devils cannot pluck away from us. The time is coming when every mans foundation shall be tryed, he only that is built upon the Rock shall then stand. To be able in an evil day to sit still with an undaunted courage and calm serenity upon our spirit, is a great felicity: the only way to do this is to be able to trust in the Lord, and with all grounded confidence to rely upon his Power, goodness, and fidelity: . . . Could we draw all the water out of this Well, it could make us to think our selves in Heaven before we come there. But the Well is deep, and our line too short, and bucket too shallow, whence they are but sips and small draughts we here obtain.*[194]

A close examination of these sentences will show that almost every one is in the nature of an aphorism, for each is capable of standing by itself as a truth. This, as we have noted, is the chief characteristic of the essays of Bacon. This parallel is discernible even though the axiomatic statements of Willard are limited to the religious point-of-view.

Occasionally, the religious import in the prefaces to the sermons is less evident, though its application is implied. The discussion of Christian precepts is left to the sermon that follows it. William Davis, writing on "Jesus the Crucified Man," answers, in points of doctrine, a paper by one John Wats [*sic*]. The "Preface to the Reader," however, does not indulge in theological dispute, but becomes a simple essay on truth:

> Friendly Reader;
>
> It is a Maxim that is granted, not only by all Reformed Christians, but also by the very Heathen Philosophers themselves, *That Truth is the brightest Gem in*

[194] Samuel Willard, *The Child's Portion* (Boston, 1684).

> *the Regal Diadem, and that she sets herself off in her own Attire, with a far more shining Luster than all the Praises of Poets, or the extravagant and mis-applyed Commendations of dissembling and hypocritical Parasites.* And I could heartily wish it was the Genius of every mans Disposition to thirst after Truth & Knowledge more & more, and to place a more than ordinary felicity in the enjoyment of it. It is indeed a noble Prize, and always rewards its adorers with lasting and inestimable blessings. And although so few are found to be Possessors hereof, yet the want of it stains & sullies the Dignity of humane nature, but in whomsoever it doth predominate it restrains all evil Passions of the Soul, that promp [*sic*] him to unreasonable actions, bridles and curbs those Appetites that solicite him to Injustice, banishes all that inordinate fear that enslaves the Soul: It encourages all those noble seeds of Justice and Fortitude that lead a man on to an entire conquest over his Lusts and distempered Affections; and it instructs a man to discharge his Function, and exercise his Power in a due and regular way. It is that that dignifies mans Nature, and enables to a degree of Hononr [*sic*] much above the inferior Creatures. This doth illustrate a mans Name more than the Trophies of his Ancestors, or the Success of his indisputable Courage and Bravery, or what ever other brave qualifications in famous humane Arts and Sciences, as Tongues and Languages he may or hath attained unto.[195]

It is to be noted that Davis begins this preface with the conscious use of a maxim. Although his sentences are longer than the usual epigram, each is a declarative statement sufficient unto itself. Along with this similarity to the Baconian essay are two others: the use of the abstract subject, as this on truth, and the obvious didactic impulse that motivates his writing.

These prefaces are like many that introduce the reader to a religious discourse. The authors frequently talk upon an abstract or moral subject in epigrammatic fashion, and their purpose is more often didactic than otherwise.

[195] William Davis, *Jesus, the Crucified Man* (Printed for the Author, 1700).

3. Analysis of a Problem

The analysis of problems in these early prefaces dealt chiefly with theological questions, because the majority of published works were on doctrinal matters and the majority of those who introduced the author were themselves divines. Not content with introducing the work or the author, the writer of the preface who was not the author of the piece seized the opportunity to voice his own opinion. Sometimes the authors themselves outlined and summarized the work to follow in such detail that they merely presented the longer work in miniature. Winslow's "A Short Story of the Rise, reign, and ruine of the *Antinomians, Familists & Libertines*"[196] is prefaced by himself in such detail that a short analysis and a treatise on the same subject occur side by side. It seemed impossible for a colleague to introduce a work without expressing himself, also, on the subject. Urian Oakes, for instance, in introducing the "Christian Reader" to Increase Mather's *The Divine Right of Infant Baptism*, must explain how Divine Truth is the ultimate authority for infant baptism.[197]

Thomas Hooker's preface to his treatise, *A Survey of the Summe of Church-Discipline*, is written "by way of Introduction . . . wherein the attentive Reader may understand the scope, the matter and method thereof, and how far there is a joint concurrence of most of the Elders of New-England." It is not, however, like "The Short Story of the Antinomians," a mere detailed review and outline of what is to follow, but an historical review of the struggles of the early church, the Reformation, and the events that necessitated a church discipline. He develops his subject in his individual way: he introduces his theme in a metaphor on Truth, and he re-introduces his figure again whenever necessary to give his preface the sense of a unified whole. He begins with a proverb and then applies it to his subject.

[196] First published anonymously, 1644.
[197] Boston, 1680.

> Truth is the Daughter of time, *was the saying of old, and our daily experience gives in evidence and proof hereof, to ever mans ordinary observation. Only as in other births, so here, the barrennesse and fruitfulness of severall ages, depend meerly upon Gods good pleasure; who opens and shuts the womb of truth from bearing, as he sees fit, according to the counsell of his own will.*[198]

Then he traces the eclipse of truth and the usurpation of falsehood and sin during the supremacy of what these New England fathers liked to call "Popery," until the time of such men as Wickliff and Luther and the period of the Reformation; and he concludes this part of his preface with a return to his metaphor, with the safe delivery of Truth through such of her ministers as have come to New-England. Only toward the end does he devote some space to a sketch of what is to follow.

4. Critical Estimates of Literature

Whatever there was in the nature of literary criticism before 1710 was contained almost entirely in prefatory remarks to a published work. On the whole, these introductions are a revelation of the literary criteria of the times, especially as they pertain to the writing of history. We do not pretend, however, to find in these prefaces complete critical essays. We are interested, rather, in the critical opinions that they express. We can say, as Professor Smith said of his collection of Elizabethan writings that pertained to English literary criticism, "In no other way can we find the historical perspective of what appears to be a 'mingl-mangle' of ill-considered, off-hand sayings, or better appreciate the fact that in these we have the true beginnings of [American Criticism] as a separate literary 'kind.' "[199]

198 Thomas Hooker, *A Survey of the Summe of Church-Discipline* (London, 1648). First copy of the original edition, from the library of J. Hammond Trumbull, with his book label. Sabin, 328600.

199 Gregory G. Smith, *Elizabethan Critical Essays* (Oxford, Clarendon Press, 1904), preface, p. v. f.

The most remote beginning of the critical essay may be said to be the apologetic preface, written to justify the publication of a work. Perhaps it was because the printing-press and the writing of books in the vulgar tongue had broadened the reading pubiic until writing and publishing were no longer aristocratic or even respectable, or perhaps it was because a writer, in order to obtain a livelihood, had to dedicate his creation with proper humility to a patron, that the apologetic preface became a necessary part of a printed work. At any rate, the usual seventeenth century writer professed to be somewhat bold and indelicate (to borrow an eighteenth century term) in appearing in print. We have, therefore, those addresses of the writer to the reader which, whether they appear in England or America, are very much the same: "Forgive the temerity of publication. . . I wrote for my own and my family's gratification. . . I was led to publish the work by some friend who felt it might do the world some good or I was forced to publish it because of pirated editions of the work. . . Overlook the style, for it is done by one who does not know the art of expression. . . I give it to you for what it is worth. . . Goe, little booke, with my apologies."[200]

Examples of prefaces with these characteristics are almost too obvious and too numerous to require illustration. Rather, it is more difficult to find a preface that does not contain some element of the apologetic, or at least some detailed explanation of how and why the work was created. Said the writer of "New-England's Crisis" to the reader:

> I never thought this Babe of my weak Phantasie worthy of an Imprimatur; but being an Abortive, it was b[e]g'd in these perplexing Times to be cherished by the Charity of others. If its Lineaments please not the Reader better than the Writer, I shall be glad to see it

[200] Montaigne had said, "Reader, Loe here a well-meaning Booke" and "I have proposed unto my selfe no other than a familiar end." The resemblance of the apologetic preface to the informal essay lies in this humble attitude. In this very spirit was created the type of literature called by Montaigne *essais* with its apologetic meaning of *attempt*. The author's frequent declaration, too, that he publishes with the hope of doing good is an obvious parallel to the didactic essay.

> prest to death: but if it displease not many and satisfie any, its to me a glorious Reward, who am more willing than able to any Service to my Countrey and Friend.[201]

Daniel Gookin humbly addresses Charles II, when he presents to him and the English world some matters concerning the work of the missionaries among the Indians. He hopes, of course, not to attain his own glory thereby but to promote a worthy cause:

> Royal Sir,
> I have read that Artaxerxes Mnemon, king of Persia, going his progress, the people used to present him with their several gifts in the way; and among the rest a countryman, having nothing else to present him with, ran to the river, and taking up his hands full of water, presented him with that. Artaxerxes was so taken therewith, that he gave the fellow a considerable beneficence.
> So have I, dread Sovereign, presumed to offer this poor mite, as a testimony of my affection. I must acknowledge it is most unworthy to kiss your royal hands, being so meanly apparelled in an Indian garb. But the matter therein contained, being a true account of the progress of the Gospel among the poor Indians, within your dominions, and that under the influence of your royal favor, this, as I conceive, is not unmeet for your Majesty's knowledge. Therefore let it please your Majesty graciously to accept and peruse these Collections, and especially that humble proposal made in Chap. 12. Sect. 5. as a necessary expedient to promote this great work, and which must have its life, under God, from the rays of your Majesty's favor.[202]

Samuel Willard, following the custom of his colleagues, apologizes for the publication of his sermon and declares that his only purpose in "committing it to the World in Print" is to do good.[203]

[201] *New England Crisis* . . . By a Well Wisher to his Countrey (Boston, 1676).

[202] Daniel Gookin, *Historical Collections of the Indians.* Published by the Massachusetts Historical Society in 1792. Reprinted in Trent and Wells, *Colonial Literature* (New York, 1903), p. 78.

[203] Samuel Willard, "The Character of a Good Ruler" (Boston, 1694).

An apology for a printed work is not only personal in character, but by its very insistence on a *raison d'etre* for the writing, it turns its attention, in a sense, to how that work was created and why. This is the foundation of literary criticism. In England, to be sure, the notable development of literary criticism found its patterns in Renaissance Italy and classical learning. The emphasis here was on the writing of poetry and drama. In America before 1710, poetry for the most part and drama altogether found barren soil. There were no really defined theories of poetry and no theories at all of drama.[204] If there was any talent for poetry or drama, it found no encouragement, not only because literature of the imagination might be an instrument of the devil, but because life itself found no time nor place for it. There were no salons where groups of people might have engaged in literary disputes. There was no occasion for Sidneys, or Jonsons, or Drydens.

It is not to be assumed, however, that these English-Americans were ignorant of theories of verse. If they wrote verse at all, they wrote in some accepted fashion of the mother country without the ado of a literary preface. A few words of introduction concerning his Muse in traditional fashion, such as William Morrell's in his *Nova Anglia* (1625),[205] was all that was necessary. They wrote mostly,

[204] It was not until the late eighteenth century that Crèvecoeur wrote a little play called "Landscapes." See *Sketches of Eighteenth Century America*. By St. John de Crèvecoeur, edited by Henri L. Bourdin, Ralph H. Gabriel, and Stanley T. Williams (New Haven, 1925), pp. 250-332.

[205] If thou Apollo hold'st Thy scepter forth,
To these harsh numbers, that's thy royall worth.
Vaine is all search in these to search that vaine,
Whose stately style is great Apolloe's straine.
Minerva ne're distil'd into my muse
Her sacred droppes, my pumesse wants all juce.
My muse is plaine, concise, her fam's to tell
In truth, and method, love or leave: Farewell.

MHSC, series 1, I, 125. This, addressed to "Lectori," and the rest of the poem is written in Latin and English.

as a great many of their fellow Englishmen did, in rhymed couplets; and they enjoyed, particularly in their elegies, the composition of conceits in the manner of Quarles and others.[206]

The preface of Anne Bradstreet's poems is written by her brother-in-law, John Woodbridge, who put them into the hands of the publisher. It is not a literary criticism, but an eulogy on the author and a rhapsodic wonder that the poems are the "Work of Woman."[207] Nathaniel Ward writes an introduction in doggerel to them and while he pays obvious acknowledgment of her debt to Du Bartas, his theme is "Let Men look to it, least Women wear the Spurs.[208] Anne Bradstreet herself, except for her particular acknowledgment to Du Bartas, writes nothing but the apologetic preface in her introductory remarks in poetry.[209] In her "In Honour of Du Bartas," she praises his eloquence and his learning, but proposes no real literary theories.[210]

In 1610, Richard Rich writes a preface to his "Newes from Virginia." Like Abbay and Alsop he is euphuistic and familiar in style, and he plays the jester with the reader.

[206] The concluding stanza of Joseph Caper's "A Funeral Elegy upon . . . John Foster," the first Boston printer, runs:

> "Yea, though with dust thy body Soiled be,
> Yet at the Resurrection We Shall See
> A fair Edition & of matchless worth,
> Free from Errata, new in Heav'n set forth:
> Tis but a word from God the great Creatour,
> It shall be done When he Saith *Imprimatur*."

Harper's Literary Museum, ed. O. E. Wilson (New York, 1927), I, 97.

[207] See Anne Bradstreet, *The Works of . . .* ed. John Harvard Ellis (Charlestown, 1867), p. 83 f.

[208] *Ibid.*, p. 85.

[209] "But when my wondring eyes and envious heart
> Great *Bartas* sugar'd lines, do but read o're
> Fool I do grudg the Muses did not part
> Twixt him and me that overfluent store;
> A *Bartas* can, do what a *Bartas* will
> But simple I according to my skill."

From the Prologue, *Works of Anne Bradstreet*, p. 100.

[210] *Ibid.*, p. 353.

He includes, however, some suggestion of literary criticism. He despises those poets who write, in flattery, for mercenary reasons: "Reader, thou dost peradventure imagine that I am mercenarie in this business, and write for money (as your moderne Poets used to do) hired by some of those ever to be admired adventurers to flatter the world." He composes out of his own experience: "I have knowne the voyage, past the danger, seene that honorable work of Virginia, and I thanke God am arrived here to tell thee what I have seene, done and past." He tells the truth bluntly: "I am a soldier, blunt and plaine, and so is the phrase of my newes; and I protest it is true." Nevertheless, he writes in poetry rather than in prose apparently for the greater challenge in it: "had I not debared myselfe of that large scope which to the writing of prose is allowed, I should have much easd myselfe, and given thee better content." He aims another thrust at his contemporaries who get "any newes by the tayle" in any manner convenient to themselves: "I did feare prevention by some of your writers, if they should have gotten but some part of the newes by the tayle." On the whole, the criticism, suggested rather than stated, is that poetry is more difficult writing than prose, and that poets who write for mercenary reasons are beneath his own standards of poetic composition.

In Virginia, too, there resided for a time a real poet, George Sandys. His translation of "Ovid's *Metamorphosis*," 1621-1626, deserved the praise of Pope and Dryden and Thomas Fuller; but his poetry is as uninfluenced by the New World as if he had been still residing in England. His dedication to King Charles is written almost entirely as if he had never left his native shores. His only statement in regard to the composition of his work is untrue: "Sprung from the Stocke of the ancient Romanes; but bred in the New-World, of the rudeness whereof it cannot but participate; especially having Warres and Tumults to bring it to light instead of the Muses." If there is any rudeness, it is not from his surroundings. So untouched is he by his environment that one is rather surprised that he was aware of "Warres and Tumults."

In New England, Calvinistic doctrine, somehow, was extremely discouraging to the artistic temperament and literary output. Poetry must be free and unhampered by dogma. *The Day of Doom* is an example of doctrine mixed with rhyme. *The Bay Psalm Book,* with verse little better than this, yielded however, a preface worth noting. At first glance, it seems to promise little in the way of literary criticism, for its author, Richard Mather, is chiefly concerned with the giving good reasons for the singing of psalms in the church. But he is aware of literary expression. He takes pains to explain away the shortcomings of the verse. However crude these psalms are, he excuses them on the score that the writers are following an exact translation from the Hebrew into the English tongue. Although it is to be suspected that the translators were not over-burdened with poetic talent, they have, nevertheless, at least as the author of the preface reveals it—an awareness of English metre and rhyme. In these introductory remarks are the expression of real literary principles:

In the first place, he meets the objection which some will inevitably make against putting the psalms of David into metre:

> As for the scruple that some take at the translatiō of the book of psalmes into meeter, because Davids psalms were sung in his owne words without meeter: wee answer—First. There are many verses together in several psalmes of David which run into rithmes. . .[211]

In the second place, no one will deny the need of having psalms in the vernacular of every nation, and so it follows in England. And since they are to be sung in English, like other songs in that language, they will be in metre. And

> . . . men might as well stumble at singing the hebrew psalms in our english tunes (and not in the hebrew tunes) as at singing them in english meeter, (which are our verses) and not in such verses as are generally used

[211] *The Bay Psalm Book,* Facsimile Reprint (New York, 1905), The Preface, by [Richard Mather].

> by David according to the poetry of the hebrew language: but the truth is, as the Lord hath hid from us the hebrew tunes, lest wee should think ourselves bound to imitate them; soe also the course and frame (for the most part) of their hebrew poetry, that wee might not think ourselves bound to imitate that, but that every nation without scruple might follow as the graver sort of tunes of their owne country songs, soe the graver sort of verses of their owne country poetry.[212]

The question of exact translation or paraphrase was a bone of contention in seventeenth century England. Since the Puritans had a rooted suspicion of art for art's sake, it is not to be wondered at that the authors of the "Bay Psalm Book" favoured exact translation over the poetic license of paraphrasing:

> Neither let any think, that for the meetre sake wee have taken liberty or poeticall licence to depart from the true and proper sence of Davids words in the hebrew verses, noe; but it hath beene one part of our religious care and faithfull indeavor, to keepe close to the originall text.[213]

The author of the preface objects, in fact, to previous free translations of the psalms of David on the score that they were mere paraphrasing, a thing easily detected and abhorred by the "Godly learned." He objects to "alterations of the sacred text" on the moral ground that they bring grief and offence to those who really know—the grief and offence, one suspects, not so much of the scholar's love for exact knowledge, as the Puritan's distrust of creative impulse, the "material detractions from words" and "sence":

> As for other objections taken from the difficulty of *Ainsworths* tunes, and the corruptions in our common psalme booke, wee hope they are answered in this new edition of psalmes which wee here present to God and his Churches. For although wee have cause to blesse God in many respects for the religious indeavours of the

[212] *Idem.*
[213] *Idem.*

translaters of the psalmes into meetre usually annexed to our Bibles, yet it is not unknowne to the godly learned that they have rather presented a paraphrase then the words of David translated according to the rule *2 chron. 29.30.* and that their addition to the words, detractions from the words are not seldome and rare, but very frequent and many times needles, (which we suppose would not be approved of if the psalmes were so translated into prose) and that their variations of the sense, and alterations of the sacred text too frequently, may iustly minister matter of offence to them that are able to compare the translation with the text; of which failings, some iudicious have oft complained, others have been grieved, wherupon it hath bin generally desired, that as wee doe inioye other, soe (if it were the Lords will) wee might inioye this ordinance also in its native purity: wee have therefore done our indeavour to make a plaine and familiar translation of the psalmes and words of David into english metre, and have not soe much as presumed to paraphrase to give the sense of his meaning in other words; we have therefore attended heerin as our chief guide the originall, shuñing all additions, except such as even the best translators of them in prose supply, avoiding all materiall detractions from words or sence. The word ו· which wee translate *and* as it is redundant sometime in the Hebrew, soe sometimes (though not very often) it hath been left out and yet not then, if the sence were not faire without it.[214]

The most conscientious cannot follow exact translations all the time. These exceptions Mather explains with painstaking care. It is noteworthy that at this point, as in the method of criticism when it has become an art, he makes his statements exact by illustrating them with specific example:

As for our translations, wee have with our english Bibles (to which next to the Originall wee have had respect) used the Idioms of our owne tongue in stead of Hebraismes, lest they might seeme english barbarismes. Synonimaes wee use indifferently: as *folk* for *people,* and *Lord* for *Iehovah*, and sometimes (though seldome) *God* for *Iehovah*; for which (as for some other interpretations of places cited in the new Testament) we

[214] *Idem.*

> have the scriptures authority ps. 14. with 53 Heb. 1. 6. with psalme 97. 7. Where a phrase is doubtfull wee have followed that which (in our owne apprehensiõ) is most genuine & edifying:[215]

As for other changes in translation, Mather makes the blanket excuse of necessity, but reiterates that the sense has not been changed. He is perfectly well aware that exact translation of the psalms into the English that must fit a tune will be crude. His excuse, in the final paragraph, is the Puritanical one of scruples of conscience, but the fact is nevertheless significant that the excuses which he has carefully given in defence of exact translation are, in effect, literary criticism. Perhaps, after all, the authors' failure to write good verse came not from a lack of knowledge or of literary background, but from a too conscientious purpose.[216]

Except for the suggestion of criticism in Rich's preface and the more definite contribution in the "Bay Psalm Book," the poetry in America before 1710 yields practically nothing in the way of literary criticism.[217]

[215] *Idem.*

[216] Cf. Dr. William Everett who aptly remarks that the fault lay largely in the "excess of reverence for the subject." "Introduction," *The Bay Psalm Book,* facsimile edition (New York, 1905), p. vii.

[217] In the *Manuductio ad Ministerium,* printed in 1726, Cotton Mather expresses his opinions on poetry and style. His ideas were formulated, doubtless, many years before the publication date and are therefore worthy of mention here. Although he sees not always the best moral examples in the writings of classical poets; nevertheless, he recommends to the young poet the reading of Homer and Virgil. He thinks the reading of epics particularly beneficial, and he urges, also, the writing of epigram as a means toward effective expression. At the same time he would recommend to the young candidates of the ministry, to whom he is really speaking, to be "not so set upon *Poetry,* as to be always poring on the *Passionate* and *Measured* Pages," but to let it be Sauce rather than Food, and a Recreation "in the midst of more painful Studies."

In his paragraph on style, he is particularly interested in defending the individual styles of authors against the harping critics who would mould them all into standard patterns. (See the Appendix for his complete discussion.)

If the colonist thought at all of Aristotle's principle that "poetry tends to express the universal; history the particular," it was with his eye on the latter. Our people were making history; and some, realizing the fact, were writing it down. Their attitude toward their work was typically humble and apologetic, and their stated purposes were at bottom the same. Their writing was motivated by a sense of moral obligation: to present an honest account for the instruction and information of their contemporaries and of posterity. In so far as this consisted of a chronicle of good men, it was also didactic in purpose in that it set them up for examples. Out of these conscientious purposes evolved two critical principles: the first was truth of statement; the second was the plain and simple telling of it. These are certainly the bases of historical writing.

There were usually two reasons given for publication: in the southern colonies, one wrote to advertise the country for the glory of their majesties and for further settlement. Hence came the "true accounts"—true in proportion to the author's purpose and imagination. In the north, one published mostly for the glory of God and for posterity. In either case, one was writing history. In the South, the "accounts" took on the qualities of the descriptive and expository "pamphlet of newes"; in the North, the quality of longer historical writings. There appeared to be a sense of this difference among the writers themselves. Virginia and other southern colonies considered themselves integral parts of England. New England inhabitants, having come here for religious principles, were in effect in exile. Their historians seemed to sense the need of permanence for future records in all that they wrote, in contrast to those in the South who wrote for immediate reading.

The prefaces of expository and descriptive accounts of the southern colonies yielded little more in the way of critical standards than did the prefaces to their poetry. The reason is obvious: no advertisement needs a preface; no account of the glory of a new country needs anything but the insistence that it is true. Thoughts on the manner of writing had better be left unsaid or in the background. In the first place, they would be a superfluity, something standing in the way of an immediate reading of a description of America. Every Englishman was interested in adventure and travel, and he read accounts of them avidly. The virtue of such writing and its seeming truth came from its spontaneity, its apparent lack of literary artistry. The only thing, then, that the writer needed to stress was the truth of the telling, and, if he indulged in any reference to composition, an insistence on its humble origin and crudity of style.

Even in the work of Captain John Smith one is struck with a note of sincerity and Montaigne-like explanation of his *True Travels* in his dedication of the book to the Earle of Pembroke. If we can believe him,* he has composed his account not for any personal aggrandizement but for the satisfaction of a few intimate friends; and only now has he been persuaded to publish it by the insistence of Sir Robert Cotton and by the fact that he wishes to prevent "future misprisons." It all sounds like the traditional apology, but the ring of sincerity is there:

> Envie hath taxed me to have writ too much, and done too little: but that such should know, how little I esteeme them, I have writ this; more for the satisfaction of my friends, and all generous and well disposed Readers.[218]

George Alsop, in his dedication to Lord Baltimore, insists he is writing out of experience:

> What I present I know to be true, *Experientia docet*; It being an infallible Maxim, That there is no Globe like the occular and experimental view of a Countrey. And had not Fate by a necessary imployment, confin'd me within the narrow walks of a four years Servitude, and by degrees led me through the most intricate and dubious paths of this Countrey. By a commanding and

* It has been customary to question the veracity of the hero of the Pocahontas legend. E. Arber, in his edition of Smith's works, rather explains away Smith's discrepancies and suggests, if we read Smith more closely, we may find there not merely a glorious adventurer but a true and honest Elizabethan gentleman.

[218] *Op. cit.*, II, 809.

> undeniable Enjoynment, I could not, nor should I ever have undertaken to have written a line of this nature.[219]

And again he assures the merchant adventurers that he writes from "an experimental knowledge of the Countrey, and not from any imaginary supposition."

It is obvious, however, that an adventurer's mind does not merely catalogue accurate details. There is too much fun in the telling: the bigger the experience, the more glory to oneself. This has been posterity's criticism of the captain of Virginia legend; but, if Smith was guilty, he was not the only one. Those who read or heard the growing tales of America or who listened to derogatory propaganda became skeptical, so that presently there is not only the insistence on telling the truth, but on telling it in order to clear this country of "infamous lies." In 1656, John Hammond wrote his "Leah and Rachel, or the Two Fruitfull Sisters of Virginia and Mary-land; *Their Present Condition Impartially stated and related.*"[220] He writes two dedications: one to two creditable and prominent men of the two provinces, and the second to the commander of two ships then bound for the two provinces. Both insist on its truth, and seek to add authoritative weight to his declarations by their direct address to reputable persons known to England and to the colonies. In the second, he says:

> Sirs,
>
> As I have made choice of two Honourable Gentlemen, the one belonging to Virginia, the other to Mary-land; So I thought it not impertinent equally with them to Dedicate this to you two living in England, and using the Trade of Virginia and Mary-land, that yourselves may judge and testifie, who well know the Country, that I have not added to their worths, but rather been sparing of what is justly their dues: For it is a received errour amongst the many slanders cast on these places, that we are sworn neither to Speak nor Write but glossingly of them; If we are so sworn, they cannot believe yee are; and therefore will credite your Affirmations.[221]

[219] *Orig. Narr.*, XI, 340.
[220] Italics mine.
[221] *Orig. Narr.*, XI, 282.

At the very end of the seventeenth century, Daniel Denton published his *A Brief Description of New York* in which he proposed to tell without fabrication about the part of New York that he knew from his own experiences, and to leave the unknown part until "a better discovery shall make way for such a Relation":

> READER,—I Have here thorough the Instigation of divers Persons in England, and elsewhere, presented you with a brief but true Relation of a known unknown part of America. The known part which is either inhabited, or lieth near the Sea, I have described to you, and have writ nothing, but what I have been an eye witness to all or the greatest part of it: Neither can I safely say, was I willing to exceed, but was rather willing the place it self should exceed by Commendation, which I question not but will be owned by those that shall travel thither: For the unknown part, which is either some places lying to the Northward yet undiscovered by any English, or the Bowels of the earth not yet opened, though the Natives tell us of Glittering Stones, Diamonds, or Pearl in the one, and the Dutch hath boasted of Gold and Silver in the other; yet I shall not feed your expectation with any thing of that nature; but leave it till a better discovery shall make way for such a Relation. In the mean time accept of this from him who desireth to deal impartially with every one.
>
> DANIEL DENTON.[222]

In so far as a man was faced by the responsibility of establishing a new community, or had any hand in it, his seriousness of purpose was proportionately manifest in his accounts and in his prefaces to them. William Penn and Gabriel Thomas wrote no mere standard apologetic prefaces. The former, in his first account of Pennsylvania, in 1681, says,

> Since (by the good providence of God) a Country in America is fallen to my lot, I thought it not less my Duty than my honest Interest to give some publick notice of it to the World.[223]

[222] *Op. cit.*

[223] *Orig. Narr.*, XIII, 202.

And Gabriel Thomas, nearly twenty years after, declared,

> There never having been any fair or full Account given to the World of Pensilvania, I thought the Curious wou'd be gratified with an ample Description thereof.[224]

But consciousness of writing and the first real sense of permanency in it came from New England, as did our literary criticism in the *Bay Psalm Book*. Men like Bradford were inspired with the thought that they were founding a new country and that historical accounts might be of interest to generations to come. There is, therefore, a sense of duty and a feeling for writing the truth.

At first their prefaces began humbly enough in the traditional apologetic manner. "G. Mourt" wrote nothing original, but, as a kind of amateur editor, adapted the Journals of Bradford and Winslow. His purpose is to promote the kingdom of Christ and of King James, too:

> COURTEOUS READER,
>
> Be entreated to make a favorable construction of my forwardness in publishing these ensuing discourses. . .
> These Relations coming to my hand from my both known and faithful friends, on whose writings I do much rely, I thought it not amiss to make them more general, hoping of a cheerful proceeding both of adventurers and planters. . . My hearty Prayer to God is that the event of this and all other honorable and honest undertakings, may be for the furtherance of the kingdom of Christ, the enlarging of the bounds of our sovereign lord King James. . .[225]

Although all that he puts before the public may be true, he has not followed historical truth to the letter: he emphasizes the good and the glory, but he omits, when necessary, unpleasant details. For instance, he fails to mention that a large number of the first Plymouth contingent perished under the hardships endured there. He does not suppress the fact, however, that there were hardships. He remembers

[224] *Ibid.*, p. 314.
[225] See Young, *Chronicles of the Pilgrim Fathers*, p. 111 f.

the good examples set by the Virginia and Bermuda Companies: their "unwearied resolution" in spite of many disasters, and he wishes his own "no less hopeful country"[226] to be likewise.

Robert Cushman, in the introduction to "Mourt's Relation," makes a specific comment on style. He apologizes to the "courteous reader" for the publication of these papers, not because it is unbecoming, but because the account is "writ by the several actors themselves, after their plain and rude manner. Therefore doubt nothing of the truth thereof. If it be defective in any thing, it is their ignorance, that are better acquainted with planting than writing."[227]

The writings of Bradford made the occasion for a number of prefaces by other people. Nathaniel Morton, in his preface to Bradford's *Dialogue*, explains that the purpose of the *Dialogue* is to disentangle the true religion from the false. On the whole, he is writing an expository analysis on the late religious disputes; but he makes the true critical comment that the dialogue is "plain, well composed, and useful."[228] Bradford's style is always plain and well-composed: the simplicity and nobility of his character shine through all his work. The fact that Morton, in spite of his own self-conscious and rather elaborate style, is able to see this is a significant step in our literary criticism.[229]

In 1669, Morton himself published a history called *New-England's Memorial*, based upon Bradford's *History*. The foreword "To the Reader" is written by his contemporaries, John Higginson and Thomas Thacher. The purpose of his memorial, they state, is to present an "ebenezer," a record of the Lord's remarkable providences; and to give a true account of the colonies of New-England for posterity's sake. While this sounds familiar enough, a truer purpose in historical

[226] *Ibid.*, p. 111 f.

[227] *Ibid.*, p. 115.

[228] *Ibid.*, p. 412.

[229] Compare the part of the History, confessedly worked over by Morton himself, with the last part in which Morton quotes directly from the original manuscript. The change of style is apparent.

writing is found in their recognition of the fact that it was imperative to make a history of these earliest days while the oldest inhabitants, the eye-witnesses of its making, were still living, so that it might be an *accurate* account for future generations:

TO THE READER

> It is much to be desired there might be extant *A Compleat History of the United Colonies of New-England*, that God may have the praise of his goodness to his People here, and that the present and future Generations may have the benefit thereof. This being not attainable for the present, nor suddenly to be expected, it is very expedient, that (while sundry of the Eldest Planters are yet living) *Records* and *Memorials of Remarkable Providences* be preserved and published, that the true Originals of these Plantations may not be lost, that *New-England*, in all times to come, may remember the day of her smallest things, and that there may be a furniture of *Materials* for a true and full History in after-times.
>
> For these and such-like Reasons we are willing to Recommend unto the Reader this present *Narrative* as a Useful Piece.[230]

This is an important step toward the historical truth finally to be attained by Thomas Prince in the eighteenth century. Even though it is questionable how accurate these oldest inhabitants might have been, since the accounts of these early days might be distorted in the memory of old age or of religious prejudice, the history must be fairly accurate, since most of it was based on history by Bradford—Bradford who was wise enough to look into the future and record for it in his journal things as they happened. Neither is this introduction without its comment on style: "The work itself is compiled with Modesty of Spirit, Simplicity of Style, and Truth of Matter."[231] There is also in this preface the real desire of the careful historian for information à propos of his subject from other sources so that "what is wanting in

[230] Nathaniel Morton, *New-England's Memorial* (Boston, 1855), p. iv.
[231] *Ibid.*

this Narrative may be supplied by some others."[232] And, finally, pervading the criticism and motivating the whole is the seventeenth century moral purpose: to build an "Ebenezer, that Hitherto the Lord hath helped us."[233] The last quality, however, is not critical. On the contrary the religious purpose always suggests a bias that contradicts the real spirit of criticism. But the moral and the didactic motifs were, as we have seen, an integral part of seventeenth century prose; and their absence can hardly be expected in the Colonial writings. In spite of a suggested religious bias, Morton's preface to *New-England's Memorial* has taken a long step toward critical standards in historical writing.

But these comments are not all that *New-England's Memorial* contributes to the beginnings in criticism. In his own dedicatory letter, Morton not only stresses the importance of an accurate history for the same reasons that Higginson and Thacher do, but he actually acknowledges the sources from which he has taken his material:

> . . . the greatest part of my intelligence hath been borrowed from my much honored uncle, Mr. William Bradford, and such manuscripts as he left in his study, from the year 1620 unto 1646.[234]

Also, he sees no necessity of going into matters already adequately handled by his contemporaries:

> I shall not insist upon the clime nor soil of the country, its commodities, or discommodities; nor at large on the natives, or their customs and manners, all of which have been already declared by Captain Smith, Mr. Higginson, Mr. Williams, Mr. Wood, and others.[235]

He dedicates the book to the people who can vouch for its truth. And he composes it with a fine sense of its importance:

> Were it so, that any other had travelled in this kind in such a way as might have conduced to a brief and

[232] *Ibid.*

[233] *Ibid.*

[234] *Ibid.*, "Epistle Dedicatory," p. 2.

[235] *Ibid.*, p. 2 f.

> satisfactory intelligence in particulars relating to the premises, I would have spared this labor, and have satisfied myself in perusal of their works, rather than to have set pen to paper about the same; but having never seen nor heard of any, especially respecting this our plantation of New Plimouth, which God hath honored to be the first in this land, I have made bold to present your Worships with, and to publish to the world, something of the very first beginnings of the great actions of God in New England, begun at New Plimouth.[236]

There is a curious difference, which serves to emphasize the literary aspect of the work, between this dedication to men who are eminent in the colony and well-educated and the second preface, also by Morton, to the "Christian Reader." The reason given for writing the history in this case is entirely the religious one that God may have his true praise. The only reference to literary matters occurs at the end of the preface, but it is immediately linked with the religious element:

> Let not the harshness of my style, prejudice thy tast or appetite to the dish I present thee with. Accept it as freely as I give it. Carp not at what thou dost not approve, but use it as a remembrance of the Lord's goodness. . .[237]

In 1736, Thomas Prince found Captain John Mason's history, *Some Grounds of War Against the Pequots*[238] sufficiently important and accurate to write an introduction to a new edition of it. The Pequots were among the most vicious of Indian tribes. They had planned to destroy the English, and Mason was put in charge of the English forces against them.[239] After his efficient work, he was made major general

[236] *Ibid.*, p. 2.

[237] *Ibid.*, p. 7.

[238] First published in Increase Mather's *Relations of the Troubles which have hapned in New-England*, and attributed by him to John Allyn. Reprint, *MHSC*, series 2, VIII, 120-151.

[239] The nation of the Pequots extended from the Powcatuck River "thence Westward to Connecticut River, and over it, as far as Branford, if not Quinnepiack. . ."—Thomas Prince in his introduction to his edition of Mason's history. *MHSC,* series 2, VIII, 122 f.

of all their forces by the government of Connecticut; and later, reaping greater honor, was made Deputy Governor. As an active participant in the wars he knew his subject at first hand. Recognized as an authority, he was asked to write the history of these events. His own effort and purpose was to write an exact account. In his preface, it is to be noted that he aims at accuracy and actually seeks correction from his readers:

> . . . though I could heartily have wished that some other who had been less interested and better qualified might have undertaken the Task, for I am not unacquainted with my own Weakness; yet I shall endeavor in plainness and faithfulness impartially to declare the Matter, not taking the Crown from the Head of one and putting it upon another. There are several who have Wrote and also Printed at random on this Subject, greatly missing the Mark in many Things as I conceive. I shall not exempt myself from frailties, yet from material Faults I presume you may pronounce it not Guilty, and do assure you that if I should see or by any be convinced of an Error, I shall at once confess and amend it.[240]

No man had yet written a general history of the Pequot War; therefore Mason is attempting to fulfill a need. In so doing, he is aware of an important criterion in historical writing: "If Truth be wanting in History, it proves but a fruitless Discourse." History, he would define as an account, in an honest and plain manner, of the actions and doings of men:

> I shall therefore, God helping, endeavour not so much to stir up the Affections of Men, as to declare in Truth and Plainness the Actions and Doings of Men; I shall therefore set down Matter in order as they Began and were carried on and Issued; that so I may not deceive the Reader in Confounding of Things, but the Discourse may be both Plain and Easy.[241]

[240] *Ibid.*, p. 126.
[241] *Ibid.*, p. 129. ("To the Judicious Reader.")

And this leads him to comment on style. Some have written in "high stile," but not always with absolute truth, for truth demands plain telling:

> And although some may think they have Wrote in a high Stile, and done some notable Things, yet in my Opinion they have not spoken truly in some Particulars, and in general to little Purpose: For how can History find Credit, if in the Beginning you do not deliver plainly and clearly from whence and how you do come to the Relation which you presently intend to make of Actions?[242]

Then, to make his point quite plain, he uses the seventeenth century writer's device of metaphorical parallel:

> As a Rule, although it hath less length and breadth, yet notwithstanding it retains the Name if it hath that which is proper to a Rule. When the Bones are Separated from a living Creature, it becomes unserviceable: So a History, if you take away Order and Truth, the rest will prove to be but a Vain Narration.[243]

Of his own style, he says he will not use a "multitude of words" nor burden the reader with conceits. With such gloss he has little patience:

> I shall not make a long Discourse, nor labour to hold the Reader in doubt, using a multitude of Words, which is no sure Way to find out the Truth; as if one should seek for Verity in the Current of Pratling, having nothing but a conceit worthy to hold the Reader in suspence.[244]

John Mason's style is plain, in that it is composed of clear cut statements. It is not crudely plain, however, nor inappropriately adorned: "I shall only draw the Curtain and open

[242] *Ibid.*
[243] *Ibid.*, p. 129 f.
[244] *Ibid.*, p. 130.

my little Casement, that so others of larger Hearts and Abilities may let in a bigger Light."[245] Thus far we have been concerned only with the critical ideas that have been expressed without much conscious literary art. Here Mason catches something more: something of the *esprit* of the true literary critic.

In connection with this history is also another preface that is critically significant. It is addressed "To the American Reader" and is written apparently by the publishers,[246] who take pleasure in printing something a little different from the usual run of pamphlets, in presenting something that is worthy of attention, something that is a tribute to Divine Providence and that is in itself accurate history. At this point they define history as "a Declaration of Things that are done by those that were present at the doing of them. . . ." and they point with pride to the fact that the present historiographer was one of the principal actors in the Pequot War, which he has here recorded:

[245] In his letter to the "Judicious Reader" his apology for his style, although reminiscent of the usual humble manner of the apologetic preface, is couched in expressions of a literary flavor.

Gentlemen,

I never had thought that this should have come to the Press, until of late: If I had, I should have endeavoured to have put a little more Varnish upon it: But being over perswaded by some friends, I thought it not altogether amiss to present it to your courteous Disposition, hoping it might find your favourable Entertainment and Acceptance, though rude and impolished. I wish it had fallen into some better Hands that might have performed it to the life; I shall only draw the Curtain and open my little Casement, that so others of larger Hearts and Abilities may let in a bigger Light; that so at least some small Glimmering may be left to Posterity what Difficulties and Obstructions their Forefathers met with in their first settling these desart Parts of America; how God was pleased to prove them, and how by his wise Providence he ordered and disposed all their Occasions and Affairs for them in regard to both their Civils and Ecclesiasticals. *Ibid.*, p. 128 f.

[246] "N.B. This Epistle to the American Reader appears to have been written by another Hand than Major Mason's." Prince's note, p. 128.

Judicious Reader,

Although it be too true indeed that the Press labours under, and the World doth too much abound with pamphleting Papers; yet know that this Piece cannot or at least ought not to be disaccepted by thee; For by the help of this thou mayest look backward and interpret how God hath been working, and that very wonderfully for thy Safety and Comfort: And it being the Lord's doing, it should be marvellous in thine Eyes.

And when thou shalt have viewed over this Paper, thou wilt say the Printers of this Edition have done well to prevent the possible Imputation of Posterity; in that they have consulted the exhibition at least to the American World, of the remarkable Providencies of God, which thou mayest at thy leisure read, consider and affect thy self with, in the Sequel.

History most properly is a Declaration of Things that are done by those that were present at the doing of them: Therefore this here presented to thee may in that respect plead for liking and acceptance with thee: The Historiographer being one of the principal Actors, by whom those English Engagements were under God carried on and so successfully effected. And for a President for him in this his Publication of his own, in Parte Rei Bellicae, he hath that great Man at arms the first of the noble Caesars, being the Manager and Inditer of his martial Exploits.

He has also that necessary Ingredient in an Historian; Ut nequid falsi dicere, et nequid veri non dicere audeat; That he will tell the Truth and will not say a jot of Falsehood.

And Memorandum that those divine Over-rulings, their Recollection, as they ought to be Quickeners of us up to a Theological Reformation, and Awakeners of us from a lethargilike Security, least the Lord should yet again make them more afflicting Thorns in our Eyes and slashing Scourges in our Sides: so also they may well be Pledges or Earnests to us of his future saving Mercies; and that if we by our Declensions from him in his ways do not provoke him, he will not forsake us, but have respect to us in our Dwellings, and lend us the desirable Providence of his perpetual Salvation.[247]

[247] *Ibid.*, p. 127 f. The didactic purpose is here, as in most of these early writings, an integral part of their emphasis on accuracy: a *true* history of America is all to the glory of God; its actors are His champions in His cause in the new country.

Mason's history appeared in 1677, and also William Hubbard's "*The Present State of New-England*—Being a Narrative of the Troubles with the Indians."[248]

In the author's "Advertisement to the Reader," he makes the familiar statement that "the following historical Essay, was, when first drawn up, intended only for the Satisfaction of a private Friend."[249] Although he makes this casual origin the excuse for possible errors, he has, nevertheless, some definite ideas on the composition of history:

> *The Compiler of an History can challenge little to himself but methodizing the Work, the Materials being found ready to his Hand: Diligence in gathering them together, and Faithfulness in improving them, is all that is upon point required of him; in both which I have endeavoured to make good what the Profession I have now taken up obliges me unto.*[250]

Just what these sources are and how authoritative, he is quite frank in telling the reader:

> *The Matter of Fact therein related (being rather Massacres, barbarous inhumane Outrages, than Acts of Hostility, or valiant Atchievements) no more deserve the Name of a War than the Report of them the Title of an History, therefore I contented myself with a Narrative. Much of what is therein mentioned, depending on the single Authority of particular Persons, an exact Description of every Occurrent was hardly to be obtained; All Soldiers are not like Caesar, able to describe with their Pens, what they have done with their Swords: But the most material Passages inserted, were either gathered out of the Letters, or taken from the Mouths of such as were eye or ear Witnesses of the things themselves; and*

[248] The dedicatory letter by the author to John Leveret and others has many of the characteristics of the familiar essay: abundant illustration from the classics and the Bible, anecdote, maxims, digressions, the declaration that it was written as a "Private essay," and the final endorsement "From my Study Window." The style is discursive.

[249] Rev. William Hubbard, *The History of the Indian Wars in New England*, ed. by Samuel G. Drake (Roxbury, Mass., 1865). Reprint of Boston, 1677.

[250] *Ibid.*, p. 15.

> *those also Persons worthy of Credit. In such Passages as were variously reported by the Actors, or Spectators, that which seemed most probable is only inserted. If any Errour be committed about the Scituation or Distance of Places, it may deserve an Excuse rather than a Censure: For our Soldiers in the Pursuit of their Enemies being drawn into many desert Places, inaccessible Woods, and unknown Paths, which no Geographer's Hand ever measured, scarce any vultures Eye had ever seen, there was a Necessity to take up many Things in Reference thereunto upon no better Credit sometimes than common Report.*[251]

Hubbard has the real historian's desire to illuminate statements that may be puzzling to the reader. He, therefore, devotes a good part of his preface to an explanation of particular passages and he does so with facts in his hand:

> *One or two passages need a more particular Excuse, or at least Explication: As where it is said,* p. 2. That the first Colony was sent hither *Anno* 1605, *The Mistake is easily helped, by minding the Reader that the Patent or Commission was that Year granted, when also Capt.* Henry Challons *was sent over upon some further Discovery of the Country, before the Adventurers would hazard a greater Charge.*[252]

Increase Mather, inspired by Hubbard, wrote his *Early History of New England.* He acknowledged his sources to

[251] *Ibid.*, p. 15 f.

[252] *Ibid.*, p. 16.

One other thing in Hubbard's preface needs particular mention. He calls his account of the Indian wars an "Historical essay." Although we do not usually consider an account, which is necessarily chronological narrative, as an essay, his use of the term is nevertheless of interest. The meaning of it in his mind must have been taking some definite literary form, although it probably still retained some of the apologetic sense of "attempt," since he states characteristically that it was "first drawn up, intended only for the Satisfaction of a private Friend, and not for the Use of the Publick." But the adjective in this phrase "Historical essay" limits the meaning to one of form. One can hardly say "Historical attempt." Moreover, in the sense that his history is written for the purpose of explaining the Indian war to the reader, it can be called in fact an "historical essay."

the satisfaction of an historical writer. This fact is significant, even when we are aware that in the true Matherian, and, for that matter, in the true seventeenth century manner, he is impressing his reader with his learning. His comments abound with Latin quotations and he adds a few in Greek. After a page or more of citations of sources, he explains the purpose of his history: to supplement the work already done by Hubbard. He makes the critical comment that Hubbard's history has been "truely and impartially" told, but that he has omitted certain matters which he, Increase Mather, now undertakes to write about:

> If this endeavor shall contribute any Light or Help in writing an *History of New-England*, I hope they whose Hearts are upon seeking out and declaring the Works of God in the Generation which he cast them into, will accept my Labour, however mean and inconsiderable.

Occasionally the criticism of high flown style becomes specific. Mason, after his own declaration of purpose, questions whether those who have written elaborately have always written truthfully.

The fault of the "high Stile" was occasionally apparent in the historical accounts, but it was certainly not characteristic: Historical writing *is* a challenge to truth and simplicity. Its related form, the descriptive account, was a greater temptation to write with euphuistic flourish. Indeed, one purpose in the writing of true history was to counteract the false reports of the too enthusiastic descriptive accounts. There is always the person who can dress an untruth in deceiving garb. Captain John Smith implies that an "army of conceits" can turn the trick. In his preface to his "Pathway to Experience" he finds that many have passed judgment on things of which they are practically ignorant and their works "passe currant" because they are hidden by an "army of conceits." He proposes to write honestly and to make his work vivid by example, "Now because examples give a quicker impression than argument, I have writ this discourse to satisfie understanding."[253]

[253] *Op. cit.*, II, 921. "The Pathway . . ."

Many of the writers of these historical prefaces had observed or intimated quite truly that truth of content is most effectively garbed in simple style.[254] In the old country, there had been some reaction to elaborate writing and a growing insistence on simplicity of style and a condemnation of such specific ornamentations as the conceit. A distaste for these eccentricities was, on the whole, implied rather than stated in the prefaces to our historical writing by the authors' very insistence on truth and simplicity. This had led, no doubt, to Nathaniel Morton's accurate observation that Bradford's style was "plain, well composed, and useful"; to Higginson's comment on "New England's Memorial" that "the Work itself is Compiled with Modesty of Spirit, Simplicity of Style, and Truth of Matter"; and to Mason's declaration, "I shall . . . endeavour in Truth and Plainness the Actions and Doings of Men . . . that so I may not deceive the Reader in Confounding of Things."

At least in the writing of the chronicles of America, the writers arrived at the high principles of truth of content and simplicity of style however influenced they were in their writings by mannerisms already established. The prefaces to histories and the preface to the *Bay Psalm Book* are our first real expressions of literary criticism.

5. The Literary Biography

Truth, as we have seen, was, theoretically at least, the guiding light for Colonial writings, whether they were psalm book, history, or sermon. It is self-evident that one whose written word must be accepted for the truth must be one whose reputation for veracity is unquestioned. This fact must have been the impetus for a well-known citizen to write a few words of biography about the author of a book. It may have motivated the first literary biography.

[254] This applies, of course, only to such chronicle histories as we have mentioned. The Mathers are notable exceptions. Sermons and theological works gave writers a splendid opportunity for sophistic flourish. See above, p. 96 ff.

In New England, such beginnings were indeed very meagre but they were nevertheless evident. The autobiographical element had prepared the way when such men as Smith, Alsop, and Wood had declared that they wrote plainly and out of their own experiences. The literary biography, however, is not autobiography, because it has to be less personal, less prejudiced. Some one else attests the author's veracity, his ability to write, his knowledge of his subject, the relation of his life or character to his writings. Such analysis in completed form did not exist in these Colonial writings, unless, perhaps, in Cotton Mather's *Magnalia.*[255] The real beginnings were a sentence here or there, or perhaps a paragraph or two, but these, however slight, were the impetus for a later and fuller development.

In one small sentence, John Higginson vouched for the veracity and knowledge of Nathaniel Morton: "The Author is an approved godly man, and one of the first Planters at Plimouth."[256]

Samuel Mather demonstrated that Samuel Stone was the one most fit to write upon "the nature of a Catholike visible Church."

> *The Author hereof is one who sees about him, understands the Principles and grounds he goes upon, and therefore knowes what he saith. His relation to* M. Hooker (*being Teacher of the same church*) *together with his personal abilities, caused many to judge him most meet to do this office of love to him and truth. . .*[257]

The prefaces to the witchcraft papers, of grave necessity, had to declare the authors men of truth and eye-witnesses to the crimes. To give weight to their words, four divines told the reader that Cotton Mather and others who contributed to "Memorable Providences" were men of integrity and eye-witnesses to the incidents recorded. Cotton Mather, for instance,

[255] See chapter on Cotton Mather.

[256] *New England's Memorial,* p. iv.

[257] Samuel Stone, *A Congregational Church is a Catholike Visible Church* (London, 1652). "To the Reader."

> the Reverend Author of this short History, was spirited to be more than ordinarily engaged in attending, and making particular Remarks upon the several passages occurring therein, and hath accordingly written very little besides what Himself was an eye-witness of, together with others, and the rest was gathered up with much Accuracy and Caution.
>
> It is needless for us to insist upon the Commendation either of the Author or the Work. . .[258]

The biographical data here are very slight but the reminder is given that Cotton Mather was a man of integrity and conscientious purpose, well known among colonial readers. That no other information given is simply due to the fact that Cotton Mather *was* well known and his reading public was limited and more or less intimate.

Increase Mather was particularly adept at introducing a reader to a writer. Writing a preface to Samuel Willard's *The Peril of the Times Displayed,*[259] he reaffirms the author's excellent reputation and assures the reader that he writes on a subject of utmost importance in language that everyone can understand.

> Concerning the Reverend Author of these *Sermons,* it is needless to say any thing. Many of those *Discourses,* which he has formerly written, discover him to be one of rare Accomplishments in respect of the Gifts and Graces of the Spirit of Christ richly adorning him. The subject here treated on, is of the greatest importance. It is *The Present Truth,* . . . The manner of delivering the Truth, is with such clearness and plainess, as that ordinary Capacities may understand, and be edified by what is here presented to them.

Here is another suggestion of literary biography. The author has a growing reputation as a writer from other discourses already familiar to the public. He is a man of rare accomplishments. He writes upon subjects of importance. His veracity can be relied upon. And he delivers what he has to say "with such clearness and plainness . . . that ordi-

[258] *Orig. Narr.,* XVI, 96.
[259] Boston, 1700.

nary" minds can understand him. The lack of more detail of biographical nature is due only to the fact, as in the other cases, that he is too well known for it to be necessary.

In 1704, Increase Mather adds the more personal touch of literary biography by giving an account of the author, Jeremy Dummer, when he knew him as a student in college. Dummer is less well known than Cotton Mather or Samuel Willard. Therefore, a little biographical data given by one who is well known becomes effective:

> I had a great respect for this Ingenious Author, when he was a Student in the Colledge. For I observed that he was diligent, and by far the best Scholar in the Colledge when he left that Society. He having been since that, several years in the *Acadamies* in *Holland,* where he had the happiness of a free Conversation with as Learned Men as are in the World, has been very advantageous to him. That Man of Renown Dr. *Witsius* the present Professor of *Theology* in the University of *Leyden,* then whom I know not a man on the face of the Earth at this Day, more deservedly famous for Learning and Piety, after much acquaintance with him, has commended his industry, and blameless Conversation during his abode in that Celebrious *University,* withal acknowledging his good accomplishments as to knowledge in *Divinity* as well as in *Philosophy.* And as that great man declares his hopes concerning him that he will *Cresere in virum Dei,* Increase until he becomes a man of God, so I cannot but have the same hope concerning him. Nor will it be for the honour of *New-England* that one so qualified should for want of due Encouragement, after his return to his Country, be constrained to leave it again. As God has blessed him with an Eminency (considering his years) of Acquired as well as Natural abilities, so I Pray the Lord to go on to bless him, to make and keep him humble, and to give him as an heart, so an Opportunity to use those Talents for the Service of *Christ,* and his Church.
> *November, 7th.*
>
> INCREASE MATHER.[260]

[260] Jeremy Dummer, *Discourse on The Holiness of the Sabbath Day* (Boston, 1704). "To the Reader," p. vi.

Such beginnings as these are, indeed, very meagre. The remarks concerning the author are frequently buried in the introducer's own eager discussion of the subject or in his display of eulogistic rhetoric; but the seed of the literary biography is there, for as soon as the author's competence and character are given as introduction to his work, the literary biography has begun.

SATIRE AND INVECTIVE

The interest in current problems and the desire to give expression to them in vigorous criticism frequently gave rise to satire and invective. These forms of expression are to be found in the prefaces to almanacs which give vent to the personal animosities of rival almanac makers or in the controversial letters and pamphlets which deal with theological questions.

Satire at its best is objective. It is usually directed against a class of people or against some bad practice of society. Its wit, usually the expression of disillusionment, is sharp and sometimes brilliant, and these qualities frequently secure for it a permanent place in the world's literature.

The Puritan of the seventeenth century, when writing satire or invective, was not wholly disillusioned. He was filled with the zeal for reform, and reform presupposes the possibility of change for the better. The passionate wish to change people for the better is the motivating force of the whole Puritan movement.[261] It pins its attention not only upon groups but upon individuals, and it finds satire an effective instrument to accomplish its purpose. Satire, which is most effective against a group, does not maintain its high level of wit when it focuses upon the individual. At that moment it begins to indulge in personal animosities and subjective point-of-view, and presently it is metamorphosed into its less worthy counterpart, invective.

America before 1710 presents several types of satire and invective, which are not original to America but which happen to be a part of its literature: the satire of classes and current problems in the work of Nathaniel Ward, the satire on

[261] For this discussion, cf. Raymond MacDonald Alden, *The Rise of Formal Satire in England* (Phil., 1899), Pub. Univ. Penn., VII, No. 2, and Stuart Sherman, "What is a Puritan?", *The Genius of America* (New York, 1923).

political problems in the *Political Fables* of Cotton Mather, the satire and invective of religious controversy as exemplified in the Quaker dispute and in the quarrel between John Cotton and Roger Williams, and the invective of rival almanac makers.

Since the Puritan is a reformer he is in a sense, a mender of society. Allegorically he may be a "cooper," who mends barrels[262] or a cobbler, who mends shoes. Accordingly Nathaniel Ward, in 1647, becomes "the Simple Cobler of Aggawam in America," who is "willing to help mend his Native Country, lamentably tattered, both in the upper-leather and sole, with all the honest stitches he can take . . . It is his trade," he assures us, "to patch all the year long, gratis. Therefore I Pray Gentlemen," he says, "keep your Purses."[263]

Having introduced himself in this manner, he proceeds with a prose satire on the evils of society.[264] Here he does not let his allegory of the cobbler get in his way but, introducing it only now and then, goes about his direct attack upon unorthodox religion, the liberty of conscience, women's fashions, civil liberties, and the Irish. His personal intolerance does not defeat the effectiveness of his prose:

> these *Irish* anciently called *Antropophagi*, man eaters: Have a Tradition among them, that when the Devil shewed our Savior all the Kingdoms of the Earth and their glory, that he would not shew him Ireland, but reserved it for himself: it is probably true, for he hath kept it ever since for his own peculiar . . .[265]

Ward is capable of epigrammatic prose which is characteristic of much satirical composition. This is true of his "most

[262] Cf., "Hay any worke for Cooper?" a pamphlet of the Martin Marprelate Controversy.

[263] The title page. (London, 1647, Boston, 1713.)

[264] A vigorous example of poetical satire written in this period is Ebenezer Cook's *The Sot-Weed Factor,* 1708.

[265] See *Tracts and Other Papers,* collected by Peter Force (Washington, 1844), III, No. 8, 50.

humble heel-piece" to his tract which he addresses to "the most Honourable Head-piece the Parliament of England":

> I Might excuse my self in Part, with a speech *Lycurgus* used in the like exigent of State, *senectute fio audacior, publica necessitate loquacior*, but it much better becomes me with all lowliness and uprightness, wherein I have failed to pray pardon on both my knees, which I most humbly and willingly do; only, before I rise, I crave leave to present this six-fold Petition.
>
> That you would be pleased,
>
> To preserve the Sacred reputation of Parliaments, or, we shall have no common-wealth.
>
> To uphold the due estimation of good Ministers, else, we shall have no Church.
>
> To heal the sad dislocation of our Head, throughly, perfectly, or, we shall have no King.
>
> To oppugne the bold violation of divine Truths, else we shall have no God.[266]

Among the most cryptic utterances of this man's work are those contained at the end of his pamphlet under "Errata At Non Corrigenda":

> Now I come to rub over my work, I find five or six things like faults, which would be mended or commended, I know not well which, nor greatly care.
>
> 1. For *Levity*, read *Lepidity*,—and that a very little, and that very necessary, if not unavoidable.
>
> *Misce stultitiam Consilijs breven*
> —*Dulce est desipere in loco.* Horat.
>
> To speak to light heads with heavy words, were to break their Necks; to cloathe Summer matter, with Winter Rugg, would make the Reader sweat. It is Musick to me, to hear every Dity speak its spirit in its apt tune: every breast, to sing its proper part, and every Creature, to express it self in its natural Note: should I hear a Mouse roar like a Bear, a Cat lowgh

[266] *Ibid.*, p. 52.

like an Ox, or a Horse whistle like a Red-breast, it would scare—me.

The World's a well strung fidle, mans tongue the quill,
That fills the World with fumble for want of skill,
When things and words in tune and tone do meet,
The universal Song goes smooth and sweet.

* * * * * *

For, *all my other faults, which may be more and greater than I see*; read, *I am heartily sorry for them,* before I know them, least I should forget it after; and humbly crave pardon at adventure, having nothing that I can think of, to plead but this,

Quisquis inops peccat, minor est reus. Petron.

Poor Coblers well may fault it now and then,
They'r ever mending faults for other men.
And if I work for nought, why is it said,
This bungling Cobler would be soundly paid?

So farewell England *old*
If evil times ensue,
Let good men come to us,
Wee'l welcome them to New.
And farewell Honor'd Friends,
If happy dayes ensue,
You'l have some Guests from hence.
Pray Welcome us to you.
And farewell simple World,
If thou'lt thy Cranium mend,
There is my Last and All.
And a Shoem-Akers[267]

These examples serve to show the quality of Ward's satire, which is equally effective in his attack on the other problems that annoy him, whether they be the unorthodoxy of the church or the sinfulness of women's clothes. It is vigorous, effective, amusing; and it anticipates, in such work as that against the Irish, the sharp sabre thrusts of later prose satire.

Another effective prose satire is that of *The Political Fables* of Cotton Mather. Here the allegory is sustained throughout. He chooses a different medium—that of the

[267] *Ibid.*, pp. 54, 57.

once popular beast fable. This allegory, unlike most allegories in literature, is simply and effectively written and the identification of characters even in this day, if one knows the historical background,[268] is comparatively easy. The author discusses "The New Settlement of Birds" in America and his characters represent appropriate people:

The Birds	The New Englanders
Jupiter	The King of England
The Eagle	Increase Mather
The Goldfinch	Sir Henry Ashurst
The Harpies (or Locusts)	The foes of New England
The King's-fisher	Sir William Phips[269]

His fables are as simply told as the fables of Aesop.

> The birds had maintained good order among themselves for several years, under the shelter of charters by Jupiter granted to several flocks among them: but heaven, to chastise many faults too observable in its birds, left them to be deprived of their ancient settlements. There were birds of all sorts in their several flocks; for some catched fish, some lived upon grains; the woodpeckers also made a great figure among them; some of them scraped for their living with their claws; and many supplied their nests, from beyond sea. Geese you may be sure there were good store, as there are everywhere. Moreover, when they had lost their charters, those poetical birds called harpies became really existent, and visited these flocks, not so much that they might build nests of their own, as plunder and pull down the nests of others.[270]

Here is a political fable told without obscurity of meaning or structure.

[268] The revoking of the Massachusetts charter, the selection of Sir Edmund Andros for governor, the sending of Increase Mather to England to plead the colonists' cause, the "capture" of Andros headed by Cotton Mather, the granting of a new charter, and the selection of Sir William Phips as the new governor.

[269] Table contributed by Kenneth B. Murdock in his "Introduction" to *Selections from Cotton Mather* (New York, 1926), p. lv.

[270] *Ibid.*, p. 363. The fables were not printed during Mather's life, but supposedly were circulated in manuscript.

Much less artistic than either Ward or Mather are the writers of personal invective in the almanacs and in the papers of Quaker controversy. The first was occasioned by the rivalry of almanac makers; the second, by religious disagreement. We have already seen the satirical prognostications of John Tulley.[271]

> For all Predictions do to this belong,
> That Either they are right, or they are wrong.[272]

The best way to force a rival out of a field of endeavour is to pick flaws in the quality of his work. "N. W.," "a Lover of Astronomy," and Samuel Clough devote a part of their almanacs in the first decade of the eighteenth century to the lively game of finding errors in each other's almanacs. In 1703 the "Lover of Astronomy" had attacked his contemporaries. Samuel Clough in his *New-England Almanack* for 1704 replies in kind by finding the errors in the calendar of his accuser, and the "Lover of Astronomy," publishing his new work in the same year but after Clough's, returns with, "I remember he told us in his Preface we should find something not usual in his *Almanack* which (to speak like an Astrologer) perhaps was this great number of Errors." The next time a new kind of attack was needed and the "Lover of Astronomy" turns not so much upon his rival's errors as upon the rival, "N. W.," himself.

> THe World has evermore been greatly abused by bold and Ignorant pretenders to Arts and Sciences; and even now in our days there is nothing more common than to see Almanacks publisht by those who can scarce either tell the difference between a Sphere and a Cube, or know any of the Planets except the Sun and Moon. One of this Tribe is N. W. that has publisht an Almanack for this year; who is not only guilty of affronting the World with Nonsence and rude and intolerable Calculations, but also of profaning and contaminating the Divine and Heavenly Science of Astronomy. It came too late to my hand to give thee now a particular account of the

271 *Supra*, p. 49.
272 John Tulley, *Almanack for 1688* (Boston).

> Erroniousness of it, but the next oppertunity thou mayst expect from me the true Longitude and Latitude of this new and amazing appearance.[273]

Clough, in the same year, writes in the same language:

> *AS the World has been greatly abused by bold and ignorant pretenders* to *Arts* and *Sciences*; so it has on the other hand been equally affronted by aspiring *Pedants*, who have no other arts to raise their own fame and reputation, but by building it on the ruins of others. Not unlike the Princes of the *Ottoman* blood (if I may compare little things with great) who never think themselves safe, till they have strangled all their brethren: there are many vain & ignorant *Sciolists,* [*sic*] who looking through the Tube of censure, imagine they descry spots in the Sun, when alas it is but a fly on the glass of envy: One of this Kidney is a late Almanack well willer among us, who assumes to himself every year a liberty in quarrelling with my Calculations, tho' hitherto with no other success than the Spider in the Fable, which broke its own teeth by fastening on the File.[274]

"N. W.," the third in this quarrel, attacks both Clough and the "Lover of Astronomy."

> THere was an *Almanack* Emitted the last year, viz. 1705, by N. W. who was willing to Serve his Country, which has been so well accepted as to Encourage another for 1706. But there is one who goes by the name of a *Lover of Astronomy,* was pleas'd to term it a New & Amazing Appearance, who Perhaps was so much amaz'd at it, as himself became an *Erratic*; for this N. W. could have informed him of some in his to be inserted: & tho' his last years Reflections took up so much room, that there was none left for an *Errata,* yet we hope his Modesty will this year leave room for one; unless his thoughts are too much taken up about the true Longitude & Latitude he threaten'd to give us.
>
> As for Mr. *Clough,* he said but little to me the last year, so I shall say the less to him this, but in what he did say, he bit hard, however since it was not with his own teeth, I shall give him a grain of allowance. I must

[273] "Lover of Astronomy," *The New England Kalendar,* 1705 (Boston).

[274] Samuel Clough, *Kalendarium Nov-Anglicanum,* 1705 (Boston).

confess it is an undervaluing of that Noble Science of *Astronomy*, to fill up Pages with Reflections, therefore for the future I'm resolved not to follow their Example, tho' they may have occasion to Copy after my Calculation. *Saturn* shall make two Revolutions, (and it shall be Three-score years) before I will submit unto his Influences, & be Envious, or unto *Mars's* and be quarrelsome.

I can give a good Reason why One should be Excused from the Wars for one year at least, & why the other should be for Joyning matters in the best manner. Certainly the Country-Roads are wide enough: Two may go a breast, & if they were good condition'd, I don't know why three may not Jog on together, in endeavouring to Serve their Country-men without Jostling at one another: for my part I shall endeavour it. Who am

YOUR WELL-WISHER, N. W.[275]

With the exception of the last example, the wit displayed in these arguments is not very subtle nor is it very forceful. And the disputes among these three almanac makers are not so vigorous as one between Daniel Leeds and Jacob Taylor. Here, also, these two suffer by comparison. Taylor defends himself against Leed's charges of inaccuracy and plagiarism in the manner of those whom we have examined. Daniel Leeds, however, by virtue of his polemical experience during the Quaker disagreement in Pennsylvania,[276] could write lengthily and effectively. There is, in the following quotation, a curious absence of personal hatred. With a shrug of the shoulders, expressive of a man of long and tried experience, he seems to say "What nonsense these petty wranglings are":

Yet friend *Taylor* would have the world believe that what he publishes is new. This is his Pride. Whenas I could produce a Book, that is not 60 Miles from him,

[275] N. W. Whittemore, *Almanack for 1706* (Boston).

[276] The polemical war among the Quakers raged from 1696-1706. George Keith, the leader of a revolt, denied, among other things, the sufficiency of "inner light." Leeds was one of his followers and the most prolific writer in the cause. Keith and Leeds had returned to the Anglican church. Caleb Pusey, another prominent disputant, remained with the original Quaker church.

> wherein those prophane Verses in his Almanack 1707, were printed before he was born (unless he be above 50 years old) they were first writ against the Papists, but friend *Taylor* has curtail'd some of them and made 'em fit to throw at the *Church of England.* If I did not grudge to blot Paper with such Contention as this, I could give Mr. *Taylor* more examples of this kind. But while we thus Clash, the World may say, one of us twain are both Lyars, or at least full of Errors, For,
>
> *No place but is of Errors rife,*
> *In Labours, Lectures, Leaves, Lines, Life.*
> *Then* Taylors Almanack, *as Ill as* Mine
> *Has* Errors *in it. Yet he Contends,*
> *And so do I, whenas a Glass of Wine,*
> *If we should meet, and drink, might make us* Friends.[277]

The Quaker controversy produced many polemical writings, and it shows two definite periods: the first, before 1696 when Keith was defending the Quakers against the accusations of the Boston church voiced by such men as Cotton Mather and Samuel Willard; and the second, after that date, when there occurred a schism in the Quaker church and when Keith and Leeds were on the side of revolt and Caleb Pusey kept the Quaker faith.

It seems usually true that when a point-of-view finds little logic to help it, it then resorts to personal invective. The Quaker religion preached the religion of Christ and its arguments against the Anglican faith were reasonable. The Church of New England would have nothing to do with it except to express its disapproval. Its representatives, having tried rather unsuccessfully to find flaws in its creed, turned upon the rhetoric of George Keith, its chief spokesman.

> . . . For however he expresseth a right spirit of a *Quaker,* in his nonsense, fallacious way of declaring himself, and bitter Reviling of the Orthodox, which is enough to proclaim him one of that Society; yet might any Credit be given to his words, and the commonly-received Sense put upon his Expressions, it is apparent that he hath mightily betrayed the Cause he undertook to

[277] Daniel Leeds, *The American Almanack for . . . 1710* (New York).

> patronize, and (setting aside his *Billingsgate*-Rhetorick, a gift seldome separable from these men) hath said more against *their* received Principles (if they ever had any) than against *ours*: For if he speak the Judgement of the Quakers, it is certain that G. F. and other Rabbi's of that Sect were mistaken, for they speak quite another thing; except he will tell us, we poor Ignorants understand not the Language of their spirit, which regards neither *Grammer* nor *Logick*; and this is the *Hercules's* Club, where-with they are wont to knock all our Reasons in the head, and brain them at once.[278]

With frequent references to the influence of "the Old Serpent" upon George Keith, the authors of this pamphlet make a great deal of fuss, with frequent assurances that this "choak-weed" grows in sandy soil and therefore cannot live long. But he who argues on the side of toleration finds logic where others fail.

"I find," says George Keith in his reply, *Pretended Antidote Proved Poyson*,[279] "ye are not a little vexed at my Book; since it containeth little else but *Non-sence, Tautologies, Nauseous Repetitions, Cavils* and *Sophisms*, as ye alledge, why are ye so angry and fretted? Why should *Non-sence* and *Tautologies, Cavils* and *Sophisms* vex you so very much? what aileth you, that ye come with such a company?" And he charges that their work contains "little else but Railing" and many "gross Mistakes."[280] A part of the cleverness of a satirist in a controversy lies in this ability to fling the words of his enemy back into his face.

The later controversy, during which Keith and Leeds returned to the Anglican church, was also productive of satirical and invective writing. Its media were almanacs and pamphlets and its manner was in kind,—the enemy was

[278] *The Principles of the Protestant Religion Maintained* . . . by the Ministers of the Gospel in Boston (Boston, 1690). The introduction from which this quotation is taken is undoubtedly written by Cotton Mather, since it begins exactly in the style of such other introductions as those in his *Magnalia*.

[279] (Phil., 1690), Introduction.

[280] *Ibid.*

always the maker of "Lyes" and "Forgeries." The work of Daniel Leeds stands out above the rest. In his *Almanack* for 1706[281] he writes an expostulation, "Of Enthusiasm," against the Quakers, which he begins in satirical vein

> I write from Experience, that the life of *Quaker*-Doctrin [*sic*] whether true or false, sense or non-sense, is from the Preachers delivering it in a fiery Zeal antick Posture, wry face, and a Tone suitable. This I shall demonstrate from F. Telner a Dutch-man who (when I was a *Quaker*) preached at *Burlington* in Dutch without an Interpreter and tho' we understood not his Doctrine yet he had such a powerful Testimony (that is, preacht with such fierceness, and a Tone agreeable) that he mightily raised that we called the Life, *viz.* set us generally a weeping and singing, *Hum, hum, ha, ha.* I among the rest was bewitcht with this enthusiasm. . .

This is the attack against a class and it is effectively written. On the other hand, when Daniel Leeds directs his attack at the individual as in the case of Caleb Pusey, he becomes merely abusive. He uses the word "Lyar" frequently and he challenges the man's reputation when he says ". . . as for C. Pusey I have no reason to expect better fruits from him, for he is not honest in Morals, he unjustly withholds part of an Estate from the Executor of Thomas Cross . . . he's a fit Fool to serve the Quakers, because he can lye and abuse men without shame."[282]

A part of the picturesque quality of these controversial writings lay in their titles: *News of a Trumpet Sounding in the Wilderness*[283] and *A Trumpet Sounded*[284] by Daniel Leeds; *The Rebuker Rebuked*, a reply by "D. L. to Caleb Pusey his Scurrilous Pamphlet";[285] a reply to this by Caleb Pusey in *Proteus Ecclesiasticus or George Keith Varied in Fundamentals*.[286]

[281] New York.
[282] Daniel Leeds, *A Challenge to Caleb Pusey* (New York, 1701).
[283] New York, 1697.
[284] New York, 1699.
[285] New York, 1702.
[286] New York, 1703.

Picturesque titles occur also in the series of controversial pamphlets exchanged by Roger Williams and John Cotton: *The Bloody Tenent of Persecution* (1644) by Roger Williams[287] is answered by Cotton's *The Bloody Tenent, Washed, and Made White,* (1652). This, in turn, is answered by Williams' *The Bloody Tenent Yet More Bloody*: By Mr. Cotton's endeavour to wash it white in the Blood of the Lambe (1652). The allegorical turn which these titles take has already been illustrated by Ward's *The Simple Cobler* and Mather's *Political Fables.* The figure of the fox, depicting sly deceitful persons, is familiar in many literatures. Roger Williams, in a pamphlet against the Quakers, neatly combines two puns in *George Fox Digg'd Out of his Burrowes,* with double meaning not only on the name of the founder of Quakerism but also upon another Quaker, George Burrowes.

Roger Williams is perhaps the only person among these early writers who is as skillful in invective as in the more objective satire. He is successful where most of the almanac makers are almost amateurish and where John Cotton, his victim, is too matter-of-fact.

Their dispute begins with *A Letter of Mr. John Cotton to Mr. Williams,* which was published in London in 1643, apparently without the consent or knowledge of either. In this, Cotton is merely the Puritan preacher who wishes to reform an erring brother. The letter is seriously written to refute the arguments of the Separatists. But Williams was not one to ignore a public criticism from one who had driven him into a wilderness. It is in the manner of rebuke, therefore, that he makes a public reply, the first sentence of which shows his spirit:

> Beloved *In Christ.*[288]
>
> *Answer.* Though I humbly desire to acknowledge my selfe unworthy to be beloved and most of all unworthy of the name of Christ, and to be beloved for his sake:

[287] For this controversy see *Narr. Pub.,* Vols. I-IV.
[288] Reference to Cotton's salutation.

> yet since Mr. *Cotton* is pleased to use such an affectionate compellation and testimoniall expression to one so afflicted and persecuted by Himselfe and others (whom for their personall worth and godlinesse I also honour and love.) I desire it may be seriously reviewed by Himselfe and Them, and all men, whether the Lord Jesus be well pleased that one, beloved in him, should (for no other cause, then shall presently appeare) be denyed the common aire to breath in, and a civill cohabitation upon the same common earth; yea and also without mercy and humane compassion be exposed to winter miseries in a howling Wilderness?

His prose, as usual, is logical and incisive. He refutes one by one the arguments of Cotton. The sharpness of his prose is heightened by ironical marginal annotations:

> A monstrous Paradox, that Gods children should persecute Gods children and that they that hope to live eternally together with Christ Jesus in the heavens should not suffer each other to live in this common aire together, etc. I am informed it was the Speech of an honourable Knight of the Parliament: What, Christ persecute Christ in New England?
>
> Mr. Cotton expecting more Light, must (according to his way of persecution) persecute Christ Jesus if he bring it.
>
> Will-worship varnished over with the glittering shew of Humility.
>
> Spirituall pride may swell out of the sence of a mans Humility.
>
> Humility most unseasonable in setting up will-worship, or persecuting others.[289]

The arguments of the two men are renewed in the "bloody tenent" series in "a Conference between Truth and Peace",[290] and here a different type of satire appears: the satire presented dramatically through dialogue. In this first contribution to the series by Williams there is absent the asperity of which he, like Sir Thomas More, was capable when occa-

[289] *Narr. Pub.*, I, 319 ff.

[290] Subtitle to *The Bloody Tenent.* See *Narr. Pub.*, III, 55 *seq.*

sion arose. There is, rather, the sorrowful recognition of Peace and Truth that they are banished from the earth:

> *Truth.* In what *darke corner* of the World (*sweet Peace*) are *we two* met? How hath this present evill *World* banished *Me* from all the Coasts and Quarters of it? and how hath the Righteous *God* in judgement taken *Thee* from the *Earth,* Rev. 6.4.
>
> *Peace.* 'Tis lamentably true (*blessed Truth*) the *foundations* of the *World* have long been out of course: the *Gates* of *Earth* and *Hell* have conspired together to intercept our joyfull *meeting* and our holy *kisses*: With what a wearied, *tyred Wing* have I flowne over *Nations, Kingdomes, Cities, Townes,* to finde out precious *Truth*?[291]

The tone of eloquent pleading is characteristic of *The Bloody Tenent.* Yet, sometimes the tone of asperity occurs in direct references to Mr. Cotton:

> Another while, when Princes crosse Mr. *Cotton's* judgement and practice, then it matters not what the *profession* and *practice* of Princes is; for (saith he) their *profession* and *practice* is no Rule to *Conscience.*[292]

The Bloody Tenent Yet More Bloody is composed with growing impatience. Truth says, "I will not be silent. . . . I shall prevail to scatter and dispell the *mists* and *fogs,* that for a while arise to cloud and choak us."[293]

The change of tone from one pleading a cause to one roused to righteous indignation is apparent in such a passage as the following, in which Williams is examining Chapter 64 of Cotton's book.

> In this Chapter *God* is pleased to leave Mr. *Cotton* to fall into two *Evills,* then which (ordinarily) *greater* cannot be among the *sonnes* of *Men*: I speake not of the *Aggravations* of *malice* and *obstinacie,* which I hope the most gracious *Lord* will keepe him from, but of the *sinnes* themselves in *themselves*: The One is monstrous *Blasphemie* and abominable profanation of the most holy

[291] *Ibid.*
[292] *Ibid.,* p. 177.
[293] *Ibid.,* IV, 51.

> Name of his most *High* and holy *Maker,* etc. The second extremest *Crueltie* and *Tyrannie* against *Men* his fellow *Creatures.*
>
> For the first, after a new *refined fashion* and dress, he projects how to turne this whole *Dunghill* of the corrupt and *rotten World,* into a most sweet and fragrant *Garden* of the *Church,* or *Dove* of *Christ.*
>
> For the second, he contents not Himselfe with the *Severitie* and *Crueltie* of former times exercised by the *Emperours* professing the Name of *Christ,* against such, whom they reputed *Hereticks,* but blames them for applying too favourable and gentle *Medicines* of *Exile* and *Banishment,* and in *plaine tearmes* he sayth, It had been better they had put them to death.[294]

These illustrations are sufficient to show the qualities of seventeenth century satire and invective that had come with the Puritans to America. Their content, manner, and purpose were varied, though their authors were comparatively few. Current problems of women's dress, toleration, civil government and other matters were attacked in amusing satire by *The Simple Cobler of Aggawam.* A satirical picture of a local political episode was depicted in *Political Fables* by Cotton Mather. Rival almanac makers, like Clough, "N. W.," and the anonymous "Lover of Astronomy," attacked their competitors in their almanacs. Polemical battles of the Quakers occurred also in almanacs and pamphlets, in which the two outstanding writers were George Keith and Daniel Leeds. And finally, the most voluminous controversy was that of John Cotton and Roger Williams. All of these show a noteworthy versatility among the writers of satire and invective in seventeenth century America.

[294] *Ibid.,* p. 332 f.

MEDITATIONS

Essays are, according to one familiar definition, "dispersed meditations."[295] The meditation is like the essay in form and substance: both are written out of the intimate personal experience of the writer; both show his interpretation of life; both give the benefit of his experience in his conclusions on how to live. In the didactic essay, such as Bacon wrote, haphazard musings collect themselves into logical prose commentaries on such diverse subjects as truth, beauty, death, friendship, boldness, high place, seeming wise. We may find the same sort of thing in the "Meditations of Marcus Aurelius." His first book is an autobiographical background for his teachings; and the rest, comments, resolutions, and considerations growing out of what he sees, and his resultant philosophy of life. The point-of-view of either man is moral and didactic. Although these meditations have not reached the definite form of Bacon's essays, the whole book is a collection of inspired jottings knitted together by the personality of the author himself.

The didactic essay must, by its own name, teach a lesson, whether it be stated as a moral or merely implied. This, obviously, is for the benefit of those who will read. The meditation, if written for the benefit of readers, will also exhort them to a better life. On the other hand, if it is confined within the covers of a diary, it will not exhort others, but will make personal resolutions that the author intends to follow. In either case, the resemblance of the meditation to the didactic essay is obvious, for, in all circumstances, they are meditations on life completed by a moral (stated or implied), or an exhortation, or a resolve.

In America before 1710, the meditation is to be found in an extremely personal form in the diary, and in a less personal and more broadly conceived form written and published for

[295] Bacon, "Dedication to Prince Henry," *Essays* (1612 edition).

Christian readers. In the latter form, it varies in length and treatment in these respects: some examples are a series of paragraphs on the same text; others are a series of disconnected paragraphs, each a complete unit in itself.

Turning to the diary of Cotton Mather, we find that, on an evening in May, 1683, he

> had much satisfaction of Mind in contriving what *noble Attainments,* I should bee continually pursuing of. And while I was lying on my Couch, in the Dark of the evening, I *extempore* composed the following Hymn, which I then sang unto the Lord.
>
> *High Attainments*
>
> *Lord*, what shall I return unto Him, from Whom all my mercies flow?
> (I) To mee *to live,* it *Christ* shall bee
> For All I do, I'l do for Thee.[296]

One stanza is sufficient. There are nine of them, in the nature of resolves, each explained and enlarged upon by a corresponding paragraph in "Notes" that follow the "poem." Each of these is, in varying degree, a paragraph of meditation and resolve.

> The World, is filled with loud and plain *Preachers,* whose Instructions, it shall bee no lesse a *Pleasure,* than a *Profit* for mee, to yeeld Attention unto. And especially, the little Parcels, Fragments, and Intervals of *Time,* wherein the Generalitie of People, do suffer their minds to ly like the *Field* of the Sluggard, *overgrown with Weeds,* I would have to bee so well-husbanded by mee, as that at all Places of Diversion, I would be at my spiritual *Alchymie.* The candid *Lessons,* thus received, shall not bee *dismissed* without a gainful *Ejaculation,* unto the *God of all Grace.*[297]

Of course, the meditation and the resolve, as illustrated here, are strictly personal. The real essay is personal, but its application is general. Yet these paragraphs of Mather are, in a sense, combined into a kind of didactic essay more

[296] *MHSC.* Series 7, VII, 58 f.
[297] *Ibid.*, p. 61 f.

broadly conceived when he concludes all of them by the sentence, "Surely, *Hee that doeth these Things, shall never bee moved.*"[298]

The form of the meditation was frequently composed of a text, an explication of the text, resolves, and a moral or injunction or "use." This, as we shall see, was also the form of the sermon.[299] Both resemble the didactic essay which, however briefly, presents a striking topic sentence as its text, explicates by further restatements in epigrammatic form, and concludes with a moral stated or implied. The underlying difference is that the sermon does not become subjective, like the meditation, and permit the author to make resolutions for himself.

The meditation was frequently a series of short connected explications, of a paragraph or more, on a chosen text of the Bible. For instance, Charles Morton's *The Spirit of Man* is "Some Meditations (by way of Essay) on the Sense of that Scripture. I Thes. 5.23: 'And the very God of Peace Sanctifie you wholly, and I pray God, your whole Spirit, and Soul, and Body, be Preserved Blameless unto the Coming of our Lord Jesus Christ.'" His phrase "by way of *Essay*" means here the modest *attempt*, but his table of contents to the whole work suggests the subject matter of the essay: "Chearfulness," "Activity," "Courage," "Anger in zeal," et cetera. Unfortunately the lack of positive division of the text into the sections corresponding to these topics makes a consideration of them as units in themselves somewhat confusing. This, however, is rather a question of mechanics than of actual subject-matter. As far as the content of the book is concerned, as these topics above will show, it is also the content of the essay. Morton's style, moreover, with its abundant illustration and quotation, its discursiveness, its philosophic comment, and his curious anatomy of the spirit and mind of man remind one again and again of similar qualities in Robert Burton who, because

[298] *Ibid.*, p. 62.

[299] See the following chapter. The sermon is, in fact, a kind of expanded meditation.

of them, has been classified as a seventeenth century essayist. A paragraph chosen at random will illustrate:

> The *Temperament* of the *Body,* which is (more or less) Different in every Individual Man. As there are scarce Two Pebbles on the Sea Beach, or Two Chips hewen from the same wood, exactly figured alike; Nay, As there are hardly Two Faces, Gestures, or Meenes of Men (which are the outward Indices of their Inward Constitutions) But doe in some things Differ, tho' some are more alike than others: Even so it is with their *Temperaments,* which are a chief Ingredient onto their *Spirits,* whereof we now speak. That saying of Philosophers *Manners of the Mind follow the Temperament of the Body* is true if rightly understood with a due Temper, or (as we say) with a *Grain of Salt*: By *Manners,* we must understand, not the *Vertues,* or *Vices* themselves; But the *Genius and Inclination,* which leads and *Disposes* to them. And that's the same with this our *Spirit.* Otherwise, skilful *Physicians* (who may perhaps have the worst Manners) might be accounted the best *Morallists,* & they could easily mend all the world, who cannot mend themselves.[300]

Samuel Willard composed a series of meditations not on a given text, but on the ceremony of the sacrament. Some of these, by way of illustration, are: "I. *On the* Good Will *of Christ in leaving us* this Sacrament"; "III. *Particularly On the* Bread"; "IV. *On the* Wine"; "XII. *On Eating and Drinking* Unworthily"; "XIII. On *Self Examination*"; *et cetera.* Meditation III, "Particularly on the Bread," though profoundly religious rather than worldly, is like the essay in its comment on Man as a Creature dependent upon nourishment—spiritual nourishment, of course:

> Man is a dependent Creature; as he hath his being from out of himself, so the preservation and continuance of it, must be from abroad, without which he must starve & dye. Man consists of two constituent parts, Soul and Body; nor is this dependence the Bodies condition only, but the Souls too: that can no more live without something to sustein it, than can the other. There is a

[300] Charles Morton, *The Spirit of Man* (Boston, 1693), p. 19.

> *Spiritual* as well as a *Temporal* Death to be avoided, and life to be sought after: yea, it ought to be the great care of all the Children of Men, altho' there be but few that regard it, and hence they labour for the Meat that perisheth, and neglect that which endureth to everlasting Life. Now, as God hath provided and appointed the *Creatures* to be the Mediate Supporters of the *Bodily Life*; so he hath declared *Himself* to be the only immediate, adequate, and sufficient Object of the Life and Happiness of the *Soul*: nor can a whole World supply the want of him, or Save a Soul from Perdition, *Matth.* 16.26. The Communion with God which Man was made for, and in which his blessedness did consist, was broken off by the Fall of our first Parents, and thereupon he lost his Life. Rich Grace hath restored Man again to this Communion by a Mediator, the Lord Jesus Christ, *in whom it hath pleas'd the Father that all fulness should dwell,* and through whom it shall derive to us; and for that reason he is called *our Life, Col.* 3.4. And because we are best acquainted with those things that are adapted to the Life of the Body, he hath chosen to exhibit himself to us under the shadow of such things. Thus hath he represented himself in the Sacrament, under the resemblance of *Bread*.[301]

The quality of these meditations is different from those of Mather and Shepard because they are less subjective and therefore, in general application, more like the essay. "I, in my poor measure," says Willard in Meditation XXVII "On the *Redeeming Love of God* the Son," "contemplate the whole mass of Mankind, fallen into a pit of unconceivable Misery, by an unhappy Apostasy, held fast under an unconceivable Curse, dooming him to suffer the whole weight of Divine indignation eternally, & going, without all hope in himself, or in the whole Creation, to be made a Sacrifice to Revenging Justice."[302] The essayist does not hold himself to such pessimistic thoughts, but he and the writer of meditations, in their respective ways, "contemplate the whole mass

[301] Willard, *Brief Meditations* (Boston, 1711), No. III, p. 9. Published after his death.

[302] *Ibid.*, p. 133.

of Mankind" and moralize, too, in their respective manners. Each makes a philosophic comment on life as he sees it.

This relationship of the meditation to the essay is most evident when we come to the meditation or contemplation of a single paragraph. In Cotton Mather's *Magnalia* we find "Sixty Memorials of a Godly Life. A Covenant" by John Rogers of Dedham.[303] Within this is "A Form for a Minister's Life." Each resolution is a separate paragraph—moral, of course, brief, personal, but sufficiently broad to include its application to all ministers.

> XV. Many *ministers* set their minds much upon *this world,* either profit or preferment, for which they venture dangerously, and some of them are "soon snatched away." Therefore, God keep me ever from setting my foot on such a path as hath no continuance, and is not without much danger in the end.
>
> XVII. When God hedgeth in a man with many mercies, and gives him a comfortable condition, it is good to acknowledge it often, and be highly thankful for it. Else God may soon bring a man so low, as he would think that state happy that he was in before, if now he had it again. Therefore, God make me wise!
>
> XXVI. Innocence is a very good fence and fort against *impatience* in false accusations or great afflictions. Let them that be guilty fret and vex themselves, and shew bitterness of stomach against such as speak ill of them; but they that look carefully to their hearts and ways; (without looking at men's eye) let them be still, and of a "meek and quiet spirit."[304]

The best examples of the meditative paragraph are those of Anne Bradstreet's "Meditations Divine and Moral." They are more compact, more unified, more impersonal, more epigrammatic, more like the Baconian or didactic essay than any of those just quoted:

> XLI. A wise father will not lay a burden on a child of seven yeares old, which he knows is enough for one of twice his strength, much lesse will our heauenly

[303] Cotton Mather, Appendix to "Eulogius; the Life of Mr. Nathaniel Rogers," *Magnalia Christi Americana* (Hartford, 1852), I, 423 ff.
[304] *Ibid.*

father (who knowes our mould), lay such afflictions vpon his weak children as would crush them to the dust, but according to the strength he will proportion the load, as God hath his little children so he hath his strong men, such as are come to a full Stature in Christ; and many times he imposes waighty burdens on their shoulders, and yet they go vpright vnder them, but it matters not whether the load be more or lesse if God afford his help.

LXII. As man is called the little world, so his heart may be cal'd the little Commonwealth: his more fixed and resolued thoughts are like to inhabitants, his slight and flitting thoughts are like passengers that trauell to and fro continvally; here is also the great Court of iustic erected, which is always kept by conscience who is both accuser, excuser, witnes, and Judg, whom no bribes can pervert, nor flattery cause to favour, but as he finds the evidence, so he absolues or condemnes: yea, so Absolute is this court of Judicature, that there is no appeale from it,—no, not to the Court of heaven itself, —for if our conscience condemn vs, he, also, who is greater than our conscience, will do it much more; but he that would haue boldnes to go to the throne of grace to be accepted there, must be sure to carry a certificate from the Court of conscience, that he stands right there.

LXVII. All the works and doings of God are wonderfull, but none more awfull than his great worke of election and Reprobation; when we consider how many good parents haue had bad children, and againe how many bad parents haue had pious children, it should make vs adore the Souerainty of God, who will not be tyed to time nor place, nor yet to persons, but takes and chuses when and where and whom he pleases: it should alsoe teach the children of godly parents to walk with feare and trembling, lest they, through vnbeleif, fall short of a promise: it may also be a support to such as haue or had wicked parents, that, if they abide not in vnbeleif, God is able to graffe them in: the vpshot of all should makes vs, with the Apostle, to admire the iustice and mercy of God, and say, how vnsearchable are his wayes, and his footsteps past finding out.[305]

[305] Anne Bradstreet, *"Meditations Divine and Moral," The Works of Anne Bradstreet,* ed. by John Harvard Ellis (Charlestown, 1867), pp. 57, 65 ff.

> LXX. All men are truly sayd to be tenants at will, and it may as truly be sayd, that all haue a lease of their liues,—some longer, some shorter,—as it pleases our great landlord to let. All haue their bounds set, ouer which they cannot passe, and till the expiration of that time, no dangers, no sicknes, no paines nor troubles, shall put a period to our dayes; the certainty that that time will come, together with the vncertainty how, wher, and when, should make vs so to number our dayes as to apply our hearts to wisedome, that when wee are put out of these houses of clay, we may be sure of an euerlasting habitation that fades not away.

Here, in effect, are qualities of the didactic essay; its aphoristic statement ("As man is called the little world, so his heart may be cal'd the little Commonwealth"); its use of analogy; its expansion of the first striking sentence; its didactic significance.

The meditation and the resolve, one might venture to say, go toward the creation of the essay, particularly the didactic essay, in America, whether they appear in the diary written only for the benefit of oneself or the more extended meditations for Christian readers. The latter, because of their broader application, are more like the essay than the former, and finally attain many of the essentials of the didactic essay in the "Meditations" of Anne Bradstreet.

THE SERMON AND RELIGIOUS DISCOURSE

The sermon is more closely related to the essay than the meditation, because its form is more highly developed. It has the same qualities as the essay: it is didactic in purpose, it discusses the abstract as it pertains to moral virtues and vices of mankind, it portrays character, it is at once discursive and epigrammatic.

We have seen already how the preface to the sermon gives the author or the one who introduces him an opportunity to express himself on a question under discussion or to discourse in a more or less informal manner upon such abstract subjects as *truth* and *happiness*.[306]

The sermon itself, of course, is formal in content and style. It nearly always follows an accepted pattern: a text from the Bible; a minute explication of this, phrase by phrase; a statement of the "Doctrine" involved; its "Use" and "Application." Samuel Willard's *Fiery Tryal*[307] is typical. The text is from I Pet. IV, XII: *Beloved, think it not strange concerning the Fiery Tryal, which is to try you, as though some strange thing hapned to you.* After a few words of introduction, Willard explains in detail the interpretation to be given to each of these phrases: *beloved, fiery tryal, think it not strange, as if some strange thing happned unto you.* Then he states his doctrine, *"It becomes not the people of God to look upon the fiery tryal which befals the Church of Christ in the World, as a strange thing."*[308] In the explication of this, he takes up three points: "1. What is meant by fiery Tryals? 2. What is it to count them strange? 3. The ground of the Doctrine." These points he subdivides and labels. Finally, he applies the "Use" in as

[306] *Supra*, p. 96 f.

[307] *The Fiery Tryal no strange thing* (Boston, 1682).

[308] *Ibid.*, p. 3.

detailed a study as the explication of his "Doctrine." This development of the sermon was quite the usual thing. The minister had been taught to compose it in this manner and his congregation expected it. The delight of the latter lay perhaps not only in the voice of their minister instructing them, but also in knowing anticipation of the manner in which the sermon was going to be developed.

In these characteristics of form and substance are marked similarities of the sermon to the didactic essay, in spite of the obvious difference in their length. The sermon is a kind of expanded form of the other. For instance, to take the standard example, Bacon begins an essay with a striking sentence: "*What is Truth*? said jesting Pilate; and would not stay for an answer." The first step in the composition of the sermon is the choice of an arresting text from the Bible, which is almost inevitably epigrammatic: "Hee that being often reproved, hardneth his neck, shall suddenly be destroyed, and that without remedie."[309] The sermon proper, after the text, frequently opens with an axiomatic sentence: "Tis commonly reckoned a *Curse* to live undesired, and die unlamented; and the contrary is look'd upon as a *Blessing*."[310] After the first sentence is given in the essay, there is a piling up of other sentences, mostly of epigrammatic nature, which explain and define and illustrate the topic of the essay. The author uses metaphor and anecdote in brief form effectively. The sermon, though greatly developed in length, is really an expansion of its topic or text, with an easy use of the epigrammatic sentences or proverbs. It defines and illustrates, with frequent use of metaphor and anecdote. The essay is written briefly and succinctly; the sermon, in elaborate detail. Finally, the sermon ends with its "Use" or "Application"; that is, a statement of the lesson to be learned, the moral to be applied. The didactic essay may baldly state the moral: "For in counsel it is good to see

[309] Prov. 29.1. Text of Thomas Hooker's sermon on *Wilful Hardnesse: or the Means of Grace Abused* (London, 1651).

[310] Benjamin Wadsworth, *King William Lamented in America* (Boston, 1702).

dangers; and in execution not to see them, except they be very great."[311] If the moral is not so plainly and briefly stated as this, it is implied, since the brevity of the didactic essay is sufficient to enable the reader to understand clearly its import.

The subject-matter of the sermon is directly comparable to that of the essay. In the latter, the writer makes his observations on man's follies and his wisdom; in the former, the writer does the same thing although in another way: in the subjects related to the seven deadly sins and the corresponding virtues.

The first sermon that was preached in New England is nothing more than an essay on "Self-Love," a title by which it is frequently called.[312] It has the abstract subject, the felicitous style of the informal essayist, the didactic purpose and moral application, the loving personality of the author. Not the least of its virtues is that it ignores a strict adherence to the outlined form of the sermon, and for that reason is one of the few sermons that can be considered in its complete form as an essay. Its quality of style makes it acceptable as literature and as something that can be read with pleasure.

The abstract subject such as one finds in the essay was most frequently the subject of the sermon. The titles of two of Thomas Hooker's sermons are suggestive: "Culpable Ignorance, Or, the Danger of Ignorance under Meanes,"[313] and "Wilful Hardnesse: or the Means of Grace Abused."[314] And Cotton Mather's "Memoria Wilsoniana"[315] treats the two subjects of hypocrisy and penitence. Mather writes again on hypocrisy in *Batteries Upon the Kingdom of the Devil.*[316] A favorite subject for a preacher—or essayist—is

[311] Bacon, *Of Boldness.*

[312] Robert Cushman, *Self-Love* (New York, 1847). Called also, "Cushman's *Discourse.*" See also Alexander Young, *Chronicles of the Pilgrim Fathers* (New York, 1841), chap. XVII.

[313] London, 1651.

[314] London, 1651.

[315] Boston, 1695.

[316] Boston, 1695.

mortality. It was particularly favored of Cotton Mather, who was in perpetual anticipation of death. For example, he delivered a moral discourse on this subject in "Things that Young People Should Think Upon"[317] and in his funeral sermon for John Winthrop, Jr., Governor of Connecticut.[318] The second part of the title of a sermon by Samuel Willard suggests the essay on an abstract subject: "The Truly Blessed Man; Or, the Way to be Happy here, and For Ever."[319] Under various titles, abstract subjects are treated: Benjamin Colman writes on faith in his sermon "Faith Victorious";[320] and in his "Practical Discourses on the Parable of the Ten Virgins,"[321] on *wisdom* and on *humility*. Benjamin Wadsworth's "Considerations to Prevent Murmuring, and Promote Patience in Christians," is a discourse on *humility*.

The most striking relation of the sermon to the essay is the resemblance to—or, rather, the direct use of—the character essay. The election and funeral sermons found them particularly à propos: the election sermon using mostly the type character—of the good ruler or the good soldier—and the funeral sermon finding the type of the good man or the good minister in the exemplary character of the one whom it is eulogizing. This, in general, was true; but the other sermons used them equally well. In these, the bad as well as the good character was portrayed, for it was sometimes as advantageous to hold up a wicked character for a warning as a good character for a model of Christian behaviour.

Of course, one of the chief qualities of style of the "character" is succinctness: the essay as a whole is brief and the sentences are short and distinct. This quality the sermon never has, for a minister used to turning the hour glass while he preached would not reform his manner when he composed a "character." He adapted it, however, by expansion:

[317] Boston, 1700.
[318] London, 1710.
[319] Boston, 1700.
[320] Boston, 1702.
[321] London, 1707.

that is, he would create a short and vivid sentence descriptive of his "character" and from it develop a paragraph or a page. In "Proposition 1" of Cotton Mather's "The Stage-player unmasked," he portrays the hypocrite. It is quite noticeable that he has observed the short epigrammatic sentence of the "character" and has written in this style, but he has not reduced his thoughts about the hypocrite to a minimum.

> An *Hypocrite* is one who does pretend *Religion,* and *but* pretend it. *Hypocrisie* is properly a *counterfeit* of Religion. The *Greek* word for an *Hypocrite,* signifies a *Stage-player.* As a *Stage-player* will act the part of a *King,* though he be indeed a *Beggar*; so an *Hypocrite* acts the part of a *Saint,* while he is but a *Sinner* still. The word comes from a Theme, that signifies to *compare*; and a diminutive Particle is prefixed unto it; so that *Hypocrisie* is a thing that may be *compared* unto true Religion; it has a *likeness* and a *shadow* of Religion; but it comes very *short* of the reality; the resemblance is a dull, a faint, an empty thing. Accordingly, the *Hebrew* word for an *Hypocrite* comes from a Root that signifies, to *tinge,* or *dye* a thing of another Colour than what is Natural. Thus an *Hypocrite,* is one that appears not in his own *colours*; there are *false colours* that his Religion is disguised and concealed with.[322]

In three long moral paragraphs, he expands from this as many characteristics of the devil: "First, In the Religion of an *Hypocrite* his Graces want an *Ingredient,* essential to the Graces of true Religion . . . [323] Secondly. In the Religion of An *Hypocrite,* his *Duties* want a *Principle* necessary to the Duties of true Religion . . . [324] Thirdly. The Hypocrite is not *secretly,* that which he *openly* seems to be."[325]

[322] Cotton Mather, *Batteries Upon the Kingdom of the Devil* (London, 1695), p. 71.

[323] *Ibid.*, p. 72.

[324] *Ibid.*, p. 73.

[325] *Ibid.*, p. 75.

Benjamin Colman in his *Practical Discourses Upon the Parable of the Ten Virgins* writes at length on the hypocrite. He combines the use of character and moral lesson in such a paragraph as the following:

> But if the Hypocrite believes not a Word of what he professes, then he is a trifling Fool to make any Profession at all. What a Wanton, ludicrous Animal is he! What a ridiculous Figure does he make here at God's Worship! How grave is his Play! How serious a Pageantry! How solemn a Mock! For his Worship is so to him if he do not believe, and worse if he do.[326]

Two paragraphs particularly may be taken to show Colman's use of character. The cryptic sentences, the metaphor, the use of contrast and balanced structure were all in keeping with the best examples:

> And lastly, The Hypocrite is a Fool, for at the best he only proposes to himself to repent hereafter of what he does. Which is but a sorrowful Work at last, and yet the best that he can hope for. That is, he courts one Hour's Sin now, tho' it cost him an Age of Sorrow if he live to be old. This is indeed better than an Eternity of it, but never the less a dear Price for a Minute's Pleasure. Wou'd any Man take a *Bee* into his Mouth, and be content it shou'd leave its Sting in his Tongue, for a Drop of *Honey* in its Body? Much less wou'd a wise Man undergo the Pains of Repentance for all the Pleasures of Sin. Grant it then that *Wickedness be sweet in the Mouth,* yet 'tis like to prove the *Gall of Asps within.* Suppose the Poison be vomited up, and we escape with our Life, yet not without dreadful Convulsions and dying Sickness. But of this piece of Folly more may be said in a more proper Place. Meanwhile let me only add this General Account of a Hypocrite, and I will do no more to paint his egregious Folly.[327]

These two last sentences are as if to say, "But in moralizing I have wandered from my *character* of a type—my *General Account of a Hypocrite.*" Whereupon, he concludes

[326] Benjamin Colman, *Practical Discourses Upon the Parable of the Ten Virgins* (London, 1707), p. 99.

[327] *Ibid.*, p. 101 f.

with the "General Account" in a paragraph that is indeed a character essay:

> He pretends to believe that God is, and to worship him, and to live to him. He professes to think Religion a Reality, and to show forth the Life and Power of it: He says, that God ought to be feared for his Power and Righteousness, loved for his Beauty and Goodness, praised for his Benefits, trusted in for his Truth and Faithfulness, imitated for his Holiness, and obeyed for his Dominion and Authority: but all this while he no more regards God in his Heart, than if he were only a Name, or a stupid Stock. He is the grossest Piece of Self-contradiction in the whole World. He knows the *Judgment* of God and yet incurs it, believes the *Promises* and yet slights 'em; puts on a demure Look as from a reverential Awe of God's Presence, and yet laughs at him in his Heart: disdains him when in secret, says of him—he is not, or he can't see, or he can't strike: takes off his Mask when none but God can see, and puts it on again when he goes out. Surfeits jollily on the Dainties at home, which he has stollen by long Prayers abroad; and uses the Name of Christ only as the *Silver-Smith* did *Diana's*, to maintain his Craft. His Life is Farce and Comedy, but will have a Tragical End. The Play won't last always, the last *Act* will be sad and doleful, when God will terribly revenge the Sport Men make of holy Things.[328]

Here, too, is to be noted a favorite device of "character" writers, the use of the conceit: "Surfeits jollily on the Dainties at home, which he has stollen by long Prayers abroad; and uses the Name of Christ only as the *Silver-Smith* did *Diana's*, to maintain his Craft."

Even if there were not these obvious similarities to the

[328] *Ibid.*, p. 102 f. The subject of hypocrisy or the character of the hypocrite was long a favorite one in depicting "humours" or character. It is suggested in the portraits of "The Dissembler" and "The Flatterer" of Theophrastus, and it appears variously in the writings of Joseph Hall, John Marston, George Wither, Ben Jonson, Thomas Fuller. The adaptability of this subject to satire is shown in Raymond MacDonald Alden's thesis on *The Rise of Formal Satire in England.* See p. 196 n. 1.

character essay, we should be made aware that Colman deliberately made use of these patterns when he says, "Let us then take a Character of a good Man in a few Particulars," and then he develops a portrait of this character as he did for the hypocrite.[329]

Colman was the most skillful in his use of "character." Samuel Willard's "The Truly Blessed Man" promises more than it gives, for his emphasis is on the lesson rather than the portrait.

The election sermons, however, gave such an opportunity for "characters" of the good ruler and of the good soldier, that not even Willard might neglect it.[330] His election sermon for May, 1694, was "'The Character of the Good Ruler."[331] After the usual discursive preliminaries, he makes his portrait. The emphasis, however, is not here on what the good ruler is, but what he must be.[332] "Civil Rulers are all such as are in the exercise of a rightful Authority over others . . . he must be one that respects the Cause, and not the persons in all his Administrations."[333] We should be tempted to say that his patterns were wholly "courtesy books" rather than "character" if we were not sure of his awareness of "character" from such titles of his sermons as the two just mentioned.

Ebenezer Pemberton sums up his qualifications of the good soldier in "Use I" of his artillery election sermon for June 2, 1701.

> *This teaches us, That the good Christian is like to make the best Souldier.* Indeed others may be masters of as great or greater natural strength, courage, and policy; but yet the good Christian, when all other things are equal, is like to prove the best Martialist. For he is the best Souldier that best performs the duties that

[329] *Op. cit.*, pp. 128-141.

[330] There are, of course, other patterns like the courtesy books. See p. 215 ff.

[331] Boston.

[332] Cf. p. 278 ff.

[333] *Op. cit.*, p. 9 f.

> Christianity prescribes the Souldier; and consequently he is most like to prove the best Souldier, who is most like to observe these duties; & the Religious man will in all probability make most Conscience to observe these directions: Hence the Devout Souldier is like to make the greatest proficiency in Military Accomplishments, and so to be best prepared for Service: He is likely to atchieve [*sic*] the greatest Exploits when called to look danger in the face. *Antoninus* the Emperor found this verified in that *Thundering Legion* of Christians under his conduct; who essay'd, and performed *Miracles in Chivalry. And happy is that Prince; happy is that State, who have their quiver filled with these; they shall not be ashamed to speak with the Enemy in the Gate.*[334]

And on election day of May 31, 1710, after defining Civil government, Pemberton considers "The Character & Title put upon Rulers."[335] It is, however, hardly more than a list of characteristics.

In his lecture sermon "for Town Officers" on the "9th 1st Month 1709," Thomas Bridge recommends the seven qualifications recommended in "Jethro's Advice": "wise men," "men of understanding," "men known among your tribes," [men] fearing God," "Men of Truth," "Men hating Covetousness."[336] It resembles character, but it also is hardly more than a tabulated list of qualifications.

The funeral sermon did more than portray the type of character of a good ruler. It gave an opportunity for that second kind of character essay—the portrait of particular persons who exemplify a certain "character" which it is the writer's purpose to portray. The lives of great men, whether they were New England divines or English kings, were excellent *exempla* to be held up before the members of one's community.

[334] Ebenezer Pemberton, *The Souldier Defended & Directed* (Boston, 1701), p. 34.

[335] *The Divine Original and Dignity of Government Asserted* (Boston, 1710).

[336] Thomas Bridge, *Jethro's Advice Recommended to the Inhabitants of Boston* (Boston, 1710), p. 5 ff.

Benjamin Colman says as much in his artillery election sermon of June 1, 1702, entitled "Faith Victorious."

> The Power of Great and Excellent *Examples* is so confessed by all men, that *they have gain'd* the preference to other modes of instruction, both for Facility and Efficacy: they are more easily perceived, and do more powerfully incline to practice, than bare *Precepts*: they insinuate into the minds of men, and leave very strong Impressions there. And as good *Examples* are apt to teach, so do they strictly oblige the *Conscience*: they condemn the Evil practices of others, as *Noah* did the Old World: and bind us to imitate, leaving us steps which we ought to follow. But among all the blessed Patterns which the Christian has before him to govern himself by, none are so commanding as the Illustrious Saints on Sacred Record; the *Patriarchs, Prophets* and *Apostles* of the Church; of whom we ought to be followers as they were of Christ. And of all the *Graces* which adorned those holy men of God, no *one* shone in them more conspicuous than *Faith*, and none more worthy or necessary than *this* to be imitated by us.[337]

This sermon is, in a way, an unofficial funeral sermon as well as an official election sermon, since it holds up before the soldiers the model of King William just dead. After he has discussed his subject—the faith that soldiers must have—he portrays King William as the soldier of martial faith.

> And as an *Illustrious Instance of Martial Faith*, I would crave leave to name our late *Sovereign Lord* KING WILLIAM the Third, of Glorious Memory: than whom as no Prince was ever bolder in Battel, so none ever fought more by Principles. His Belief imbold'ned him in all the Dangers He faced. I am satisfyed, *Gentlemen*, you desire no better Example, and after those on Sacred Record, there is none more agreeable can be presented to you.
>
> And having named this *Royal Person*, I cannot but call to mind the many Salvations and Victories, which Faith has obtained, and the Church of Christ has received *by His Arms*. We our selves have seen the strange, and next to Miraculous, effects of Faith and Prayer in our days. What was it that Sav'd *England*

[337] Benjamin Colman, *Faith Victorious* (Boston, 1702), p. 1 f.

> and routed an *Unhappy Prince* at the head of a vast Army, and yet scarce a drop of blood shed? When Tyranny was trampling on the State, and Popery stood ready to mount the Pulpit, when Law and Religion were forc'd to couch before the *Assumed Absoluteness of the Court,* and were Sold at a Cheap price by Mercenary *Judges,* Dejected *Britain* then call'd for our dutiful Tears and Prayers, under ten thousand Omens of evil, and no door of Deliverance visible. The God *arose, for the Oppression of the Poor, for the sighing of the Needy, to set him in safety from him that puffeth at him.* Then God moved the *Brave and Generous Prince* to attempt our Deliverance: God gave him *Faith and unknown Hopes,* else however Mighty His Mind was, he could not have engaged a Power so Unequal. We stood amaz'd at the Miraculous Salvation: We wonder'd how it was effected, and could only adore the Might and Grace of God our Saviour. Millions of Prayers went up from gracious hearts, and *Faith subdued,* or rather Sav'd, *Three Kingdoms.*
>
> Lo here an Instance of what Courage Faith can inspire, and what Help it can engage from God. By *this* which we have seen at home, and in our day, we may be convinc'd, That *Faith can yet Subdue Kingdoms, escape the Edge of the Sword,* make *Valiant in Fight and put Armies of Aliens* to the Rout.
>
> Let all this strengthen your hands, and encourage your heart in the work wherein you are Engaged. Be always in this Spirit; let Faith animate you, and it will also prosper you.[338]

Solomon Stoddard, on the death of Colonel John Pynchen in 1702, preaches on "Gods Frown in the Death of Usefull Men." Although his theme or doctrine is "There is many times a Great Frown in GODS taking away those that are Eminently Useful," he must, in the course of his discussion, define useful men. Although, as in the manner of all ministers, his portrait is elaborate rather than concise, its pattern is that of the "character." One paragraph of it will illustrate his use of this familiar form:

> Some also by their skill, wisdom and experience do a great deal of good. Some are well skilled in the Law

[338] *Ibid.,* pp. 34-36.

> and able to direct in difficult cases; they are men of ability to discern between right and wrong, to see through cases that have intanglements and perplexity in them: This was that, that he prayed for, 1 King. 3. 9. *Give thy Servant an understanding heart, to judge thy People, that I may discern between good and bad.* They are men of prudence to find out proper means to advance the publick good; to find out expedients in difficult cases, and to discern what is to be done, to advance Religion, to prevent miscarriages, to advance peace, and compose differences. *2 Chron.* 12. 32. *Men that had understanding in the times to know what Israel ought to do*: By their experience they are fitted to take right methods in doubtful cases. But many times when such men are dead, such may arise after them, as are ignorant and unskilful, rash and unexperienced men, who by their precipitate counsels expose a Land to much misery: So the Young men that were bred with *Rehoboam* gave foolish counsel, and laid a foundation of lasting sorrow to *Israel* by their rashness, they opened a gap that let in a flood of misery: 1 *King*. 12. 10, 11.[339]

Benjamin Wadsworth, preaching his sermon on *King William Lamented in America,* interweaves a portrait of this beloved monarch with the character of a good ruler. He uses "character" deliberately, for he says, "I am not able to give his Character, and therefore dare not undertake it, unless in repeating the words of one who has attempted it:

> "A Prince the best qualify'd for a Throne, being great without Pride, true to his word, wise in his deliberations, secret in his Counsils, generous in his Attempts, undaunted in Dangers, Valiant without Cruelty. Who loves Justice with moderation, Government without Tyranny, Religion without Persecution, & Devotion without Hypocrisie or Superstition. A Prince unchanged under all Events, never puffed up with Success, or dishearten'd with hardships and misfortunes; always the same tho' under various circumstances, which is the true symptom of a Great Soul."[340]

[339] Solomon Stoddard, *Gods Frown in the Death of Usefull Men* (Boston, 1703), p. 9f.

[340] *Op. cit.*, p. 7.

Cotton Mather, on the death of Michael Wigglesworth writes a "character" of a faithful minister exemplified in him.[341]

The sermon and the religious discourse were beginnings in the essay in America, for their form, their subject matter, their purpose, and their use of "character" were directly parallel to established models. Like the didactic essay, they were meant not so much to inform as to instruct. Like it, too, they were similar in form: first, a striking thesis; second, its development by anecdote, illustrations, and epigram; and lastly, its moral application. Like the essay, its predilection was for the abstract subject. Finally, it delighted, especially in its form as a funeral or an election sermon, in the use of "character."

[341] See chap. on "Cotton Mather."

The use of "character" in the sermon and elsewhere seems to me to be a most important beginning of the biographical essay, for the portrait of an individual representing a great or a good man—or even a wicked man—emerges really as biography.[342]

For instance, after Pemberton, in his funeral sermon on Willard, has given his character of the true gospel minister, he turns to its example in the life of Willard. He does not use very much biographical data, but this omission was perhaps due to the fact that Willard was too well known in his community for it to be necessary. Almost all that he says is applicable to true "character." In his eulogistic enthusiasm, he undertakes to depict Willard as a man who had *all* the ideal qualities of a man of God:

> In Him Bountiful Heaven was pleased to cause a Concurrence of all those Natural and Acquired, Moral and Spiritual Excellencies, which are necessary to constitute a *Great Man*, a profound *Divine*, a very considerable *Scholar*, and an Heavenly *Christian*. In the light and influence of these Perfections he appeared as a Star of the First Magnitude in the Orb of the Church.[343]

To quote only a few qualities given this excellent man, "*Divinity* was his Favourite Study . . . He was a *Judicious Textuary* . . . His knowledge in *Systematical Divinity* was

[342] That is not to say that *exempla* and courtesy books had not some influence, too; rather, the three were moulded together, with the "character" of the second class (the type exemplified) taking precedence. *Exempla* held up great men; courtesy books held up qualifications; "character" gave the complete portrait combining in itself the qualifications of a type and the illustration of these in a specific example. Cf. p. 215 ff.

[343] Ebenezer Pemberton, *A Funeral Sermon on the Death of That Learned & Excellent Divine The Reverend Mr. Samuel Willard* (Boston, 1707), p. 63.

celebrated by all . . . In *Controversy* he was a Champion, a Worthy of the First Stength [*sic*], Skill, and Courage . . . He was an *Excellent Casuist*." These are topic sentences, and their paragraphs are in kind:

> In *Controversy* he was a Champion, a Worthy of the First St r ngth, Skill, and Courage. He was qualifyed for it by a clear Head, a cool Thought, and Inflexible Principles. He was able to weild [*sic*] the Sword of the Spirit to the Terrour of Gainsayers; to their Confutation, tho' not always to their Conviction: And has once and again sheathed this Sword of the Spirit in the Bowels of Trimphant Errors. And was every way fit to be Set for *the Defence of the Gospel.*[344]

This was a "character"—and a kind of idealized biography—of a man well-known to his community.

Less intimately known to these people was King William. Though the New-Englanders had benefited by some of his good deeds, they did not know him personally as they did Willard. The "character" of King William given by Wadsworth in his sermon, therefore, is more replete with biographical data, and is a nearer approach to the biographical essay. After he had quoted a "character" of a good prince exemplified in the person of King William, he continued with his portrait of the king. It is an enlarged "character" such as we found in the sermons. It is interspersed with "character" sentences: "He was ever ready to deny Himself even of Lawful, Allowable Recreations and Pleasures, for the Good of His People, and that from His very Youth . . . Like another *Nehemiah,* he sought the welfare of his People . . ."[345] And he concludes his portrait:

> He was surely a Prince of such vast Abilities, excellent Endowments, and Notable Atchievements [*sic*]; that all men of worth could not but justly admire him, and count him a good and a great King. And the more good, great and just he was, so much the greater is our loss in his Death, & so much the more it is to be lamented.

[344] *Ibid.*, p. 67.
[345] *Op. cit.*, p. 8 f.

> If *David* wept forth a Funeral *Elegy* on King *Saul's* Death, & told of his good deeds, as, 1 *Sam.* 1 ch. much more reason have we to do the like, with respect to our Deceased Soveraign.[346]

Throughout this "character" are scattered specific biographical data:

> Neither did he seek the welfare of any one Nation only, but the welfare of all Protestant People. When *England, Scotland* and *Ireland,* were in languishing circumstances; almost quite depriv'd of *Liberty* and *Property;* having their *Religion, Laws* and *Lives* in utmost hazard: sinking under *Arbitrary Power* and *Tyranny;* almost overwhelm'd with *Popery* and *Slavery,* (or at least in eminent danger of being so:) I say, when they were in this woful case; This illustrious and Noble Prince, with great Generosity, Valour and Courage, did venture his Person for their relief, and came over the Sea to help them. He Landed in *England, November* 5. 1688. and never ceas'd his prudent Applications, till the Kingdom was quietly possessed of those precious things, which were before so much indangered. The greatness of his *Spirit* and *Action* in this affair, is not easily to be described: 'Twas a pious and noble undertaking, that has but few (if any) parallels in History. Neither did he seek himself in this affair, but the good of our Nation, and the *Protestants* in general; declaring Himself in these Words, "We have nothing before our Eyes in this our undertaking, but the Preservation of the *Protestant Religion,* the covering of all men from Persecution for their Consciences, and the Securing the whole Nation the free enjoyment of all their *Laws, Rights,* and *Liberties,* under a just and legal Government."[347]

The interest of this biographical data is heightened by direct quotation of the noble speeches of the King in the interests of his people.

This portrait completed is the "character" of a good—indeed, of a perfect—king, but in place of the brief character of a type, we have an illustration of it in specific example.

[346] *Ibid.*, p. 15.
[347] *Ibid.*, p. 9 f.

As long as a "character" is merely a type, it needs nothing more but a summation of qualifications. When the ideal is applied specifically to a person, it is only natural to accompany it with abundant illustration from the life of that person, the "character" living. From this, it seems to me, emerges the real biographical essay.

The most obvious uses of the "character" for biography occur in the works of Bradford. His famous "Dialogue" is that of "some young men born in New England" who would ask "sundry ancient men that came out of Holland and Old England" concerning the early history of the Pilgrims. Among other things, they would know about those worthy ministers who accompanied them to Holland. The "ancient men" reply with "characters" of several. The model of true "character" is obvious, even to the first sentence that incorporates the title:

> Mr. Richard Clifton
>
> Was a grave and fatherly old man when he came first into Holland, having a great white beard; and pity it was that such a reverend old man should be forced to leave his country, and at those years to go into exile. But it was his lot; and he bore it patiently. Much good had he done in the country where he lived, and converted many to God by his faithful and painful ministry, both in preaching and catechizing. Sound and orthodox he always was, and so continued to his end. He belonged to the church at Leyden; but being settled at Amsterdam, and thus aged, he was loath to remove any more; and so when they removed, he was dismissed to them there, and there remained until he died. Thus we briefly satisfied your desire.[348]

This is a "character" of a good man. Bereft of its title and its specific data, it might stand for the type "character" of the ideal pastor.

Bradford's "character" of Mr. John Smith, however, presents something more illuminating in the evolution of the

[348] Alexander Young, *Chronicles of the Pilgrim Fathers*, p. 453. See also Bradford's "characters" of "Mr. Henry Ainsworth" and "Mr. John Robinson," pp. 448 f. and 451 f., respectively.

biographical essay out of the "character." He begins "Mr. John Smith [the title] Was an eminent man in his time, and a good preacher, and of other good parts; . . ." This promises a typical "character" essay. But the sentence finishes: "but his inconstancy, and unstable judgment, and being so suddenly carried away with things, did soon overthrow him." The effect of that conclusion is electric upon one who has read a series of these "character" essays. Mr. John Smith is neither god nor devil; he is not a type of a good man or a bad; he is a human being. Here, certainly, is the material of real biography:

> Mr. John Smith
>
> Was an eminent man in his time, and a good preacher, and of other good parts; but his inconstancy, and unstable judgment, and being so suddenly carried away with things, did soon overthrow him. Yet we have some of us heard him use this speech: "Truly," said he, "we being now come into a place of liberty, are in great danger, if we look not well to our ways; for we are like men set upon the ice, and therefore may easily slide and fall." But in this example it appears it is an easier matter to give good counsel than to follow it, to foresee danger than to prevent it: which made the prophet to say, "O Lord, the way of man is not in himself, neither is it in man to walk and to direct his steps." He was some time pastor to a company of honest and godly men which came with him out of England, and pitched at Amsterdam. He first fell into some errors about the Scriptures, and so into some opposition with Mr. Johnson, who had been his tutor, and the church there. But he was convinced of them by the pains and faithfulness of Mr. Johnson and Mr. Ainsworth, and revoked them; but afterwards was drawn away by some of the Dutch Anabaptists, who finding him to be a good scholar and unsettled, they easily misled the most of his people, and other of them scattered away. He lived not many years after, but died there of a consumption, to which he was inclined before he came out of England. His and his people's condition may be an object of pity for after times.[349]

[349] *Ibid.*, p. 450 f.

The hypocrite, as we have noted, was a favorite "character" for sermons.[350] It is really the hypocrite that Bradford is drawing in his portrait of Mr. John Lyford, but he has departed strikingly from the standard pattern of "character" drawing. His description of this man is rather that form of literary biography called the "character sketch." One would have to go far, even in later centuries when the art of writing this literary form was highly developed, to find a character sketch more vivid and more telling than the one of this Uriah Heep of New England:

> The 3d eminente person (which the letters before mention) was the minister which they sent over, by name Mr. John Lyford, of whom and whose doing I must be more large, though I shall abridg things as much as I can. When this man first came a shore, he saluted them with that reverence and humilitie as is seldome to be seen, and indeed made them ashamed, he so bowed and cringed unto them, and would have kissed their hands if they would have suffered him: yea, he wept and shed many tears, blessing God that had brought him to see their faces; and admiring the things they had done in their wants, etc. as if he had been made all of love, and the humblest person in the world. And all the while (if we may judg by his after cariags) he was but like him mentioned in Psa: 10. 10. That croucheth and boweth, that heaps of poore may fall by his might. Or like to that dissembling Ishmaell, who, when he had slaine Gedelia, went out weeping and mette them that were coming to offer incence in the house of the Lord; saing, Come to Gedelia, when he ment to slay them. They gave him the best entertainment they could, (in all simplisitie,) and a larger alowans of food out of the store then any other had, and as the Govr had used in all waightie affairs to consulte with their Elder, Mr. Brewster, (togeither with his assistants,) so now he caled Mr Liford also to counsell with them in their waightiest bussineses. After some short time he desired to joyne himselfe a member to the church hear, and was accordingly received. He made a large confession of his faith, and an acknowledgmente of his former disorderly walking, and his being intangled with many corrup-

[350] *Supra*, p. 159 f.

> tions, which had been a burthen to his conscience, and blessed God for this opportunitie of freedom and libertie to injoye the ordinances of God in puritie among his people, with many more such like expressions.[351]

Bradford could also write the longer biography, as his "Memoir of Elder Brewster" will testify. His subject was a man much beloved by Bradford and all those who knew him—an exemplary elder in a Pilgrim community. He had suffered much for his faith, and he had learned humility. Although Bradford gives a chronological account of the man's life, he is more interested in drawing the portrait of an ideal, an ideal which must inevitably emerge at times into the "character" of a saintly and trusted man:

> After he had attained some learning, viz. the knowledge of the Latin tongue and some insight into the Greek, and spent some small time at Cambridge, and then being first seasoned with the seeds of grace and virtue, he went to the Court, and served that religious and godly gentleman, Mr. Davison, divers years, when he was Secretary of State; who found him so discreet and faithful, as he trusted him above all others that were about him, and only employed him in matters of greatest trust and secrecy. He esteemed him rather as a son than a servant, and for his wisdom and godliness, in private, he would converse with him more like a familiar than a master. He attended his master when he was sent in ambassage by the Queen into the Low Countries, (in the Earl of Leicester's time,) as for other weighty affairs of State, so to receive possession of the cautionary towns; and in token and sign thereof the keys of Flushing being delivered to him in her Majesty's name, he kept them some time, and committed them to his servant, who kept them under his pillow on which he slept, the first night. And, at his return, the States honored him with a gold chain, and his master committed it to him, and commanded him to wear it when they arrived in England, as they rode through the country, until they came to the Court. He afterwards remained with him until his troubles, when he was put from his place about the death of Queen of Scots, and some good time after doing him many offices of service in the time of his

[351] "History of the Plymouth Plantation," *Orig. Narr.*, X, 177 f.

> troubles. Afterwards he went and lived in the country, in good esteem amongst his friends and the good gentlemen of those parts, especially the godly and religious.[352]

We saw in the preceding chapter how the type of a good or bad "character" could be used effectively in a sermon to point out an example and a moral. Presently these types were to be illustrated in the lives of exemplary men, particularly as portrayed in such occasional sermons as the funeral and the election sermons. Here, indeed, was the opportunity to present, in a more effective way than in the portrait of a type, a specific example of a man already known to the community. In proportion as the character was less intimately known, the greater was the need for supplementary biographical data, a circumstance that must inevitably lead into the biographical essay. For after awhile, as the accepted pattern of "character" and the moral import are forgotten, the true biography of a human being must begin. Even this higher form is suggested in our earliest period of American literature, when Bradford shows some skill in the portrait of a man who was both good and bad.[353]

[352] Alexander Young, *Chronicles of the Pilgrim Fathers*, p. 463 f.

[353] Cotton Mather's *Magnalia* and his sermons had a large part in the history of character and biographical essays of early America. See the following chapter on "Cotton Mather."

The biographical note that occurred occasionally in the preface (see p. 127 ff.) doubtless contributed to the development of biography, but it is less distinct in form than the "character."

COTTON MATHER

Cotton Mather's *Essays to Do Good* was published in 1710. It culminates approximately a century in the establishment of our literary background. It is significant in our study of literary types because it is a collection of writings to which we can legitimately give the title of essays, a consciously creative literary form. It is important, too, because it gives inspiration to our first periodical essayist, Benjamin Franklin, for his *Do Good Papers.* It is fitting that we should close this part of our study with an analysis of the man who was the most prolific writer of his time in America; and who had, more than any other, the feeling of a conscious literary artist.[354] His diary, his sermons and his meditations, his ecclesiastical history, and his *Essays to Do Good* are revelations of the man and of the writer. And, by and large, they incorporate nearly all the literary types that have been the subjects of our study.

The diary of the English Samuel Pepys or of the American Samuel Sewall are running commentaries on everyday life, written, naturally, in an intimate style. Yet, despite the fact that the authors were recording their own thought for their own perusing, they maintained in their diaries a lively and objective interest in the world about them. Their material is the stuff of which Addison and Steele created their essays. One turns to Cotton Mather with anticipation, only to find that the material in his diary is, paradoxically, *too* personal even for a personal essay. Cotton Mather, in his personal record, saw the world and the manifestations of Providence only as *they* were related to *him.*

[354] The greatest evidence of Cotton Mather's awareness of literary style is to be found in his *Manuductio ad Ministerium,* published in 1726. Since his theories were formed before that, we reprint in the Appendix the part of the work "On Poetry and Style."

His diary for 1709 begins with a promise of objective commentaries.

> He that has God on his side, does all things, with Ease. A saying of one of the *Greek Poets*.
> "Castitas periclitatur in Delicijs, Humilitas in Divitijs Pietas in Negotijs, Veritas in Multiloquio, Charitas in hoc mundo. *Bern*.
> "Somnium narrare, vigilantis est, et vitia sua confiteri, sanitatis indicium est." *Sen.*[355]

But he does not enlarge upon these moral and philosophic quotations; and, indeed, it is not even his habit in this personal record either to make or quote axiomatic statements. Once, in June, 1681, he quotes a paragraph from Henry Lukin's *The Interest of the Spirit in Prayer*[356] beginning:

> Some men go to Markett only for Company and Curiosity, and such are soon weary of being there; and may come home as soon as they please. But those that are Men of much Business, and great Dealing have many Occasions to take up their Time, which cause them many times to stay late. Formal Christians have little to do with God, when they come to Him only for Company or Custome . . .[357]

His reaction to this is characteristic. He does not make further general applications to the World at large, but he applies his observation to himself *only*:

> These Words were to mee like a Rebuke of Thunder. I thought, they came to mee, as if the Lord from Heaven had intended mee an Admonition for the Slothfulness, the Lukewarmness, the Formality, which I saw was of late grown upon mee, in the Wayes of God. And I hope, not without some Impression![358]

[355] *Epist. Mor.* Lib. VI. Ep. 1. 153.—Editor's note. "Diary of Cotton Mather," *MHSC*, series 7, VIII, 1.

[356] Printed, London, 1674 and 1678.—Editor's note.

[357] *MHSC*, series 7, VII, 14.

[358] *Ibid.*

Even the cold weather of February 1699-1700 is in the nature of special Providence:

> I now sett myself, to recommend these and such Things[359] at the *Lecture*; but the extreme Coldness of the Season, hindred my dispatching of my Design in one Discourse. I beleeve, this was of the Lord, that so, I may with a greater Enlargement, and a greater Assembly and a greater Efficacy, at some other time further proceed upon it. I am verily perswaded, the Lord will be remarkably present with mee in what I have to do.[360]

Contrast this with Sewall's objective comment on the same thing:

> Febr. 6, 7, 8. were reputed to be the coldest days that have been of many years. Some say Brooks were frozen for carts to pass over them, as has not been these Ten years. Ground very dry and dusty by the high wind.[361]

When Mather passes along a street and observes a tall man, a lame man, or children at play, he does not react to the opportunity for "character" or for didactic comment; but he makes "Ejaculations" on these, respectively: "*Lord,* give that Man, *High Attainments* in Christianity: lett him fear God, *above many*"; "*Lord,* help that Man to *walk uprightly*"; "*Lord,* lett not these children always forgett the *Work,* which they came into the World upon."[362] Even the pun does not change the egoistic character of these ejaculations.

His work other than the diary is more amenable to literary types; for here, perforce, as he turned to influence others, he was less egoistic. His sermons and other discourses, in fact, show a wide variety of subject matter and treatment, and some characteristics of the essay. His "Meat Out of the Eater" contains much of this sort. For instance, one "Application" is like a moral essay—an admonition to people to be courteous and loving to their "desirable relatives," while they

[359] Resolutions made in the diary just preceding this.

[360] *MHSC*, series 7, VII, 334.

[361] "Diary of Samuel Sewall," *MHSC*, series 5, VI, 5 f. Cf. Editor's note, *MHSC*, series 7, VII, 334.

[362] *MHSC*, series 7, VII, 83.

may, for death is at hand. "Are the *Children of men* sometimes blessed with *Desirable Relatives*? Tis then a Lamentable Thing, when *Relatives* do not study to render themselves Desirable."[363] Here is the general comment with the moral implication. His concluding paragraph, while directly of religious nature, resembles, nevertheless, the concluding paragraph of a didactic essay:

> In fine; We Encounter many Grievances in *this present Evil World*. Our *Desireable Relatives* have got the Start of us, to the *Blessedness* of a *Better World*! *We* shall shortly see the Period of all our Grievances, as well as they, and in the Society of them, that are got before us. And give me leave, to Conclude my Sermon, with the Words, wherewith the *Desire of my Eyes,* has newly Concluded her Life; Words, which I Pray God, help me to make the Solace of Mine: *Heaven, Heaven will make Amends to all.*[364]

A noteworthy difference between the ego of the diary and the objective value of the sermon is indicated in the subtitle, "A Work accommodated unto the Service of all that are in any Affliction."

His discourses were not always of a wholly religious nature. For instance, his "Unum Necessarium"[365] is really a critical discussion of the current problems of neglect of education; "The *Crime* of *Ingratitude* unto *Publick Servants*"; and "The lamentable want of *Regeneration* in the *Rising Generation*; as well as "the slothful, careless, quarrelsome Delay of *Destitute Churches,* to furnish themselves with Officers appointed by the Lord Jesus Christ, for their Edification." Problems of education, politics, and the younger generation are always subjects for critical comment.

[363] *Meat Out of the Eater,* Or, Funeral-Discourses, Occasioned by the DEATH of several RELATIVES. A Work accommodated unto the Service of all that are in any Affliction (Boston, 1703). "An House of Mourning. The Death of Desirable Relatives, Lamented and Improved . . .", p. 207.

[364] *Ibid.,* p. 222.

[365] (Boston, 1693). "Introduction."

Mather's prefaces frequently show literary acumen. His apologies are affected: "the obscure Author of this *Feeble Discourse*"[366] is surely not what he really thought of himself. Yet he was aware of the affectations in dedications past, when, directing his introductory epistle of "Theopolis Americana" to Judge Sewall, he said,

> Dedications *use* [*sic*] *to be* Adulations. Flattery *has, for the most part, so depraved them, that they are become a trifling and an useless* Formality. *Yea,* the Epistle *sometimes is,* A Troubled Fountain, and a corrupt Spring.[367]

With similar comment, he begins his preface to "Essays to Do Good."

> Among the many customs of the world, which it is become almost necessary to comply withal, it seems this is one, that a book must not appear without a Preface. And this little book willingly submits unto the customary ceremony. It comes with a Preface, however it shall not be one like the gates of Mindus. But there appears a greater difficulty in a compliance with another usage; that of "An Epistle Dedicatory." Dedications are become such foolish and fulsome adulations, that they are now in a manner useless. Oftentimes all the use of them is, to furnish the critics on "The Manners of the Age," with matter of ridicule. The excellent Boyle employed but a just expression in saying, "It is almost as much out of fashion in such addresses, to omit giving praises, (I may say, unjust ones) as it is to believe the praises given on such an occasion." Sometimes the authors themselves live to see their own mistakes, and own them. An Austin makes the flourishes he had once used in a dedication, an article of his "Retractions;" a Calvin does revoke a Dedication, because he finds he had made it unto an unworthy person. I may add, that at other times, every one sees, what the authors would be at, and how much they write for themselves when they flatter other men. Another course must now be steered.[368]

[366] *The Great Physician* (Boston, 1700).
[367] *Theopolis Americana* (Boston, 1710).
[668] *Essays to Do Good* (Boston, 1845).

His "Decennium Luctuosum" was published anonymously in 1699. Concealment of his identity apparently gave free rein to the expression of Cotton Mather as we should like to know him—that other more gracious and less conceited self. At least so it seems in his prefatory letter "To the People of New-England." Here is an introduction, partially critical but chiefly noteworthy for its informal style. As usual he has at his finger tips innumerable illustrations and parallels from history and literature, and an abundance of figures of speech. But, not at all in his usual manner, he descends to a kind of gracious impudence when turning to the reader, and, more remarkably, smiles at himself. After a few short paragraphs devoted to the presentation of his book to the readers, he speaks informally in behalf of the anonymous author:

> All the Favour he desires of you is, That you would not Enquire after him; or ask, who he is? But that as he is at best but an Obscure Person, he may continue in yet more Obscurity: which will be a greater pleasure to him than to be placed among the Great men of Achaia.
>
> For indeed, He hath often thought on a passage written by Holy Mr. Row to his Excellent Son, *I pray that God would make use of my self and you in such a way, as that God only may be seen and we not be taken notice of at all*; *that he may have the Glory, and we may not be seen.*
>
> Could he have invited his Excellency unto such a Glorious Table as that in a certain Cabinet at Florence, which is furnished with Birds and flowers, all consisting of Neatly polished Jewels inlain into it; a work Fifteen years in making, and worth an Hundred Thousand crowns; or could he have written a Book worthy to be laid up in the Cabinet of Darius: the Author might have been under a Temptation to have had his Name Engraved upon his Work. But a little Boiled Indian Corn in a Tray, is as much as our Best History of an Indian War, composed perhaps in fewer Dayes than there were Years in the War, may presume to be compar'd unto. And since our History will not afford such a Diversion unto His Excellency, under the Indispositions of His Health, as those of Livy and Curtius did unto the Princes that Recovered their lost Health by Reading

them; nor can any passage here be so happy, as that which cured Laurentius Medices of a Malady by having it read unto him: it will require no more than a Nameless Writer to Assure that Great Person on this Occasion, That all the good People of New-England make their Fervent Vows unto the Almighty, For His Excellencies Prosperity, and the Welfare of his Excellent Lady, and of his Noble and Hopeful Offspring.

* * * * * * * *

I pray, Sirs, Ask no further; Let this Writing be, like that on the Wall to Belshazzar, where the Hand only was to be seen, and not who'se it was. The History is compiled with Incontestable Veracity; and since there is no Ingenuity in it, but less than what many Pens in the Land might Command, he knows not why his Writing Anonymously may not Shelter him from the Inconveniencies of having any Notice, one way or other, taken of him. Though among his other small Furniture, he hath not left himself unfurnished with skill in the Spanish Language, yet he never could bring himself to the Belief of the Spanish Proverb, *Quien no parece, perece*; *i.e.* He that appears not, perishes; He that Shows not himself to the world is undone. At Milain there is an Academy of Sensible Persons, called The Nascosti, or, Hidden men; at Venice there is one of such persons called, the Incogniti; and at Parma there is one of them, called, The Innominati. If there were nothing else Disagreeable in them, the Author of this History would be glad of an Admission into such an Academy.

The History is indeed of no very Fine Thread; and the Readers, who every where Fish for nothing but Carps, and who Love, like Augustus, to Tax all the World may find Fault enough with it. Nevertheless, while the Fault of an Untruth can't be found in it, the Author pretends that the famous History of the Trojan War it self comes behind our little History of the Indian War; For the best Antiquaries have now confuted Homer; the Walls of Troy were, it seems, all made of Poets Paper; and the Siege of the Town, with the Tragedies of the Wooden Horse, were all but a piece of Poetry.[369]

Mather's "Introduction" to the same work is written more seriously and in the critical manner on the Indian Wars and

[369] *Orig. Narr.*, XIV, 180 ff.

the writing of history. Like our other historians,[370] he aims at truth and accuracy. Having made a declaration of his aims he can ignore the malice of unfriendly critics:

> . . . With all Faithfulness, I say; because tho' there should happen any Circumstantial Mistake in our Story, (for 'tis a rare thing for any Two men concern'd in the same Action, to give the Story of it without some Circumstantial Difference) yet even this also I shall be willing to Retract and Correct, if there be found any just occasion: But for any one Material Error in the whole Composure, I challenge the most Sagacious Malice upon Earth to detect it, while matters are yet so fresh as to allow the Detection of it. I disdain to make the Apology once made by the Roman Historian, *Nemo Historicus non aliquid mentitus, et habiturus sum mendaciorum Comites, quos Historiae et eloquentiae miramur Authores.* No, I will write with an Irreproachable and Incontestable Veracity; and I will write not one Thing but what I am furnished with so good Authority for, that any Reasonable man, who will please to Examine it, shall say, I do well to insert it as I do: And I will hope that my reader hath not been Studying of Godefridus de Valle's book, *De arte nihil Credendi*; About the Art of Believing Nothing. Wherefore having at the very Beginning thus given such a Knock upon thy Head, O Malice, that thou canst never with Reason Hiss at our History, we will proceed unto the several Articles of it.[371]

Thus, in the critical tradition already being established, Mather takes his part. "I will write with an Irreproachable and Incontestable Veracity . . . I will write not one Thing but what I am furnished with so good Authority for, that any Reasonable man . . . shall say, I do well to insert it as I do."

Other examples of critical estimates are to be found in those numerous introductions to the *Magnalia.* For instance, "Section 4" of his introduction to the *Magnalia* explains his attitude toward church histories: "of all History it must be confessed that the palm is to be given unto Church History." Not the histories of Herodotus, Thucydides, Livy, or any of

[370] *Supra,* p. 111 ff.
[371] *Orig. Narr.,* XIV, 185.

the ancients, great as they may be, "hath given us more glorious entertainments than . . . the two short books of Ecclesiastical History, written by the evangelist Luke." Yet, with this prejudiced attitude, Mather believes he has "done the part of an impartial historian" and he writes four pages in proof of his statement. He adds further some critical comments on style, the most interesting of which is his defence of "ornament." Some critics, he says, will find fault because his style is simple. "Whereas others, it may be, will reckon the *style* embellished with too much of *ornament*, by the multiplied references to other and former concerns, closely couched,

> . . . but I must confess, that I am of his mind who said, *Sicuti sal modice cibis aspersus Condit, et gratiam saporis addit, ita si paulum antiquitatis admiscueris, Oratio fit venustior*. And I have seldom seen that way of writing faulted, but by those who, for a certain odd reason, sometimes find fault that "the grapes are not ripe." These embellishments (of which yet I only—*Veniam pro laude peto*) are not the puerile spoils of Polyanthea's; but I should have asserted them to be as choice *flowers* as most that occur in ancient or modern writings, almost unavoidably putting themselves into the author's hand, while about his work, if those words of Ambrose had not a little frighted me, as well as they did Baronius, *Unumquemque Fallunt sua scripta.* I observe that learned men have been so terrified by the reproaches of pedantry, which little smatterers at reading and learning have, by their quoting humours, brought upon themselves, that, for to avoid all approaches towards that which those feeble creatures have gone to imitate, the best way of writing has been most injuriously deserted. But what shall we say? The best way of writing under heaven shall be the worst, when Erasmus, his monosyllable tyrant, will have it so! and if I should have resigned my self wholly to the judgment of *others*, what way of writing to have taken, the story of the two statues made by Policletus tells me what may have been the issue: he contrived one of them according to the rules that best pleased himself, and the other according to the fancy of every one that looked upon his work: the former was afterwards applauded

> by all, and the latter derided by those very persons who had given their directions for it.[372]

From this quotation and almost any other from the works of Cotton Mather, it is quite apparent that his prose is packed with example, anecdote, and quotation from the classics, in quite the accepted manner of the English seventeenth century prose writers. It is evident from this, too, that he was extremely fond of these and other "ornamentations." Indeed, a superabundance of these qualities, even in comparison with such contemporaries as Robert Burton, marks Cotton Mather's style in mannerisms above the rest. He is extremely fond of the conceit and the pun. He loves to unroll his sentences, as it were, out of a maze of phrases and clauses. These sentences are, however, correctly done and understandable.[373]

Other critical estimates may be found in the other introductions to the books of his *Magnalia.* They are alike in style and in critical principles.

Examples of expository and historical essays we may find scattered throughout the *Magnalia*: a history of the New-England colonies,[374] "The Bostonian Ebenezer,"[375] the history of the ministry of New-England in the introduction to Book III, and the "History of Harvard Colledge."[376] These, however, are not the chief interest of the *Magnalia.*

Like the other writers of sermons, Cotton Mather wrote "character." In his "Military Duties,"[377] he portrays the good soldier, whose chief qualities should be that he is a "praying" man, a "well-Aiming" man, a "sin-hating" man. "A good soldier is a good Christian."

In a Boston lecture, he delivers his "Pourtraiture of a Good Man." It is, like the other "characters" of sermons that we have seen, an expanded "character." In almost

[372] I, 31.
[373] *Infra,* p. 187.
[374] Vol. I, Bk. I.
[375] *Ibid.,* Appendix.
[376] Vol. II, Bk. IV.
[377] (Boston, 1687).

every instance, the topic sentences of the paragraphs, if isolated and put together, would form the true character essay:

> . . . Good man, . . . is first a Just man . . . A Good Man is one that has this *good mark* to distinguish him; he is loth to do any *Hurt* unto another man . . . A *Good man* . . . is one who loves to do Good. *et cetera.*[378]

This is an example of the "type character." When he preaches after the death of Michael Wigglesworth, he reviews the Christian life of the subject, and then makes it the example of the faithful Christian.[379]

The most curious instance of his use of special lives as illustrative of model character are his examples collected as "A Token, for the Children of New England."[380] The similarity to the regular "character" is not so obvious as in the other instances noted, but he is really defining the good and pious child by examples of the lives of good and pious children.

The most famous compilation of *exempla* that Cotton Mather made was, by and large, the *Magnalia* itself. What he puts there is comparable to the undertaking that he proposes: "I WRITE the WONDERS of the CHRISTIAN RELIGION . . .

"I first introduce the *Actors*, that have in a more exemplary manner served those Colonies; and give Remarkable Occurrences, in the exemplary LIVES of many Magistrates, and of more Ministers, who so lived as to leave unto Posterity *examples* worthy of everlasting remembrance."[381] *"Plus Vivitur Exemplis quam praeceptis!"*

[378] *The Pourtraiture of a Good Man* (Boston, 1702), p. 10 f. In "a brief essay" of 1707 in which Cotton Mather warns the people against covetousness he writes a character of the covetous man, beginning, "A Coveteous Man, is he, who knows no *Greater Good* than to grow *Rich* and *Great* in this world." *A Very Needful Caution* (Boston, 1707).

[379] *A Faithful Man.* Described and Rewarded (Boston, 1705).

[380] (Boston, 1700). Or, Some Examples of *Children*, In Whom the Fear of God was Remarkably Budding, before they Dyed.

[381] "General Introduction," p. 25.

Cotton Mather was, as we have suggested, a man well aware of his own style. He begins the lives of those worthy of his history in characteristic fashion. As if warming up to his task, as if picking up his pen with a little flourish, he writes a few paragraphs by way of introduction. These are in the manner of the seventeenth century style: in epigrammatic sentences, parallel structure, abundant illustration and quotation (from church history rather than popular history), metaphor and simile, the conceit, and the pun.

He begins "The Life of Mr. John Norton":

> THERE was a famous *John* whose achievements are by our Lord emblazoned in those terms: "He was a burning and a shining light." In the tabernacle of old, erected by the order and for the worship of God, there were those two things, a candlestick and an altar; in the one a *light* that might never go out, in the other a *fire* that might never be extinguished; and yet such an affinity between these, that there was a *fire* in the *light* of the one, and a *light* in the *fire* of the other. Such a mixture of both *faith* and *love* should be in those that are employed about the service of the tabernacle: and though the tabernacle erected for our Lord in this wilderness, had many such "burning and shining lights," yet among the *chief* of them is to be reckoned, that *John* which we had in our blessed *Norton*.[382]

And he begins "The Life of Mr. John Cotton":

> WERE I master of the pen wherewith Palladius embalmed his Chrysostom, the Greek patriark, or Posidonius eternized his Austin, the Latin oracle, among the ancients; or, were I owner of the quill wherewith, among the moderns, Beza celebrated his immortal Calvin, or Fabius immortalized his venerable Beza; the merits of John Cotton would oblige me to employ it, in the preserving his famous memory. If Boston be the chief seat of New-England, it was Cotton that was the father and glory of Boston: upon which account it becomes a piece of pure *justice*, that the *life* of him, who above all men gave *life* to his country, should bear no little figure in *its* intended history; and, indeed, if any person in this town or land had the *blessedness* which the Roman his-

[382] *Ibid.*, I, 286.

torian long since pronounced *such* even, "to do things worthy to be writ, and to write things worthy to be read," it was *he* who now claims a room in our pages. If it were a comparison sometimes made of the reformers, Pomeranus was a grammarian, Justus Jonas was an orator, Melancthon was a logician, but Luther was *all*: even that proportion, it may without *envy* be acknowledged, that Cotton bore to the rest of our New-English divines; he that, whilst he was living, had this vertue extraordinarily conspicuous in him, "that it was his delight always to acknowledge the gifts of God in other men," must, now he is dead, have other men to acknowledge of him what Erasmus does of Jerom, *In hoc uno conjunctum fuit et Eximium, quicquid in aliis partim admiramur.*[383]

Such artifices as the conceit and the pun were beloved by this stylist. These are apparent in two short complete biographies which we shall partially quote here. The character of Mr. Ralph Partridge as the good minister is completely lost in a maze of conceits and puns:

When David was driven from his friends into the wilderness, he made this pathetical representation of his condition. "'Twas as when one doth hunt a partridge in the mountains." Among the many worthy persons who were persecuted into an American wilderness, for their fidelity to the ecclesiastical kingdom of our true David, there was one that bore the *name* as well as the *state* of an hunted partridge. What befel him, was, as Bede saith of what was done by Faelix, *Juxta nominis sui Sacramentum.*

This was Mr. Ralph Partridge, who for no fault but the *delicacy* of his good *spirit*, being distressed by the ecclesiastical *setters*, had no defence, neither of *beak* nor *claw*, but a *flight* over the ocean.

The place where he took covert was the colony of Plymouth, and the town of Duxbury in that colony.[384]

Even more far-fetched than this ornamentation of prose is the conceit made around Mr. Richard Denton:

Among these *clouds* was our pious and learned Mr. Richard Denton, a Yorkshire man, who, having watered

[383] *Ibid.*, I, 252 f.
[384] *Ibid.*, I, 404.

> Halifax in England with his fruitful ministry, was by a tempest then hurried into New-England, where, first at Weathersfield and then at Stamford, "his doctrine dropt as the rain, his speech distilled as the dew, as the small rain upon the tender herb, and as the showers upon the grass."
>
> Though he were a *little man*, yet he had a great *soul*; his well-accompanied mind, in his lesser *body*, was *an Iliad in a nut-shell.*
>
> I think he was blind of one eye; nevertheless, he was not the least among the *seers* of our Israel; he saw a very considerable proportion of those things which "eye hath not seen."[385]

If we are not blinded or intoxicated by these devices, we may find in these two short biographies the "character" of a good minister.

The longer treatment that Mather gives to the lives of some other exemplary men becomes biography rather than straight "character," though the idea of the "good minister" or the "good man" is still motivating the whole. The difference in these two types in the *Magnalia* is largely a matter of length, elaboration, and biographical detail, and, frequently, the addition of historical background. The lives of Bradford and Winthrop are among the best known of these. He begins them, as usual, with a flourish in the introductory paragraphs. There is to be said in favor of these beginnings, however, that here is some artistic sense of the dramatic. In Bradford's life, for instance, he builds up a suitable historical background to his character so that when Bradford is at last introduced we have greater admiration for his character and greater sympathy and praise for his governorship. In Winthrop's case, it is a matter of telling of some of the heroes of classical history first, with the idea, Let Greece boast of her heroes; New England has its Winthrops.

On rare occasions, he introduces his character less elaborately and goes at once into his example, as in his "Natus Ad Exemplar, the Life of Mr. Jonathan Burr."[386]

His most ambitious biographies in the *Magnalia* are "Pas-

[385] *Ibid.*, I, 398 f.
[386] *Ibid.*, I, 368 ff.

tor Evangelicus; the Life of Mr. Thomas Shepard"[387] and "Early Piety, Exemplified in the Life and Death of Mr. Nathaniel Mather";[388] and "Pietas in Patriam, the Life of His Excellency Sir William Phips."[389]

One need not quote further, however. The *Magnalia* is full of examples, but these were sufficient to show that, like the other ministers whom we have mentioned in the chapter on the sermon, Cotton Mather wrote the "character" and the biographical essay; and that in both, he carried to extremes those eccentricities of style to be found in the seventeenth century.

Like other ministers, too, though as usual more prolifically and elaborately, he writes the meditation—a form of prose which we have already shown to resemble the essay.

The content, manner, and purpose of his *Winter Meditations* is evident in the sub-title:

> Directions How to employ the *Leisure* of the WINTER For the Glory of God. Accompanied with Reflections, as well *Historical,* as Theological, not only upon the Circumstances of the WINTER, But also, upon the Notable Works of God, Both in, Creation, and Providence: Especially those, which more immediately Concern every Particular Man, in the whole course of his Life: And upon the Religious Works, wherewith every Man should acknowledge GOD, in and from the Accidents of the WINTER.[390]

Here, indeed, is food for contemplation, for reflection in many an essay. As one might guess, these winter meditations are not only reflective but didactic. The "Introduction" itself is an essay on winter, and might justly have that title. In this he makes comparisons between the winters of his own time and country with that described by authors in antiquity, and he makes it interesting by anecdote:

> 'Tis, as I remember, *Polydore Virgil* who relates, that when *Mathildis* was, during the Depth of Winter,

[387] *Ibid.*, I, 380 ff.
[388] *Ibid.*, II, 153.
[389] *Ibid.*, I, 164 ff.
[390] Boston, 1693.

> straitly Besieged, in *Oxford*, She arrayed her self and her followers all in white, the colour of the *Snow* upon the Ground, and by the Advantage of that Colour escaped thro' the Besiegers unto a place of Safety.

In the meditations he records some of the history of winter festivals: "it was the Month of DECEMBER, wherein the Heathen had their *Saturnalian* Jollities."[391] He is didactic:

> We should not spend them [winter nights] in such Idle Things, as the *Telling of Tales*; nor should we give cause for a poor *Tale* to be told, about our way of spending them . . . To *Sleep* all *Winter*, more befits a *Bear* than a *Man*, and much more than a *Saint*.[392]

One reflection or meditation on winter is that at such a time one should think on God's mercy. Out of this, is the reflection,

> But as the *Winter* brings much of MERCY to us, it brings much of *Hardships* too? [*sic*] *Pliny* calls the *Snow*, and the *Ice*, the *Punishments of the Mountains*. We who dwell in a *plain* Region, as well as they who dwell upon the Rigid and Ragged Edges of such *Mountains*, would be sorely *Punished*, by the Hardship of the Winter, if the Mercy of our God should not Relieve us . . . [393]

One of the best places and times for the kind of reflection that is productive of the essay on an abstract subject is the fireside on a winter day. This seemed to be true of Cotton Mather, judging not only from the preceding example, but also from

> Christianus per Ignem. Or, A Disciple WARMING of himself AND OWNING of his Lord: With Devout *and* Useful MEDITATIONS, Fetch'd out of the FIRE, by a *Christian* in a *Cold Season*, Sitting before it. A Work though *never out of Season*, yet more Par-

[391] *Ibid.*, p. 8.
[392] *Ibid.*, p. 7.
[393] Section IV, p. 40.

> ticularly, designed for the Seasonable and Profitable Entertainment, of them that would well Employ their Leisure by the Fire-Side. *Igneus esse debes, hoc est, Fervidus, in Colendo Deo tuo, ut ne ille immittat in te ignem e Caelo, et tandem te adjudicet igni infernali!*— Alsted. Theol. Natur.[394]

The difference between the meditation on a text and a meditation on an abstract theme is suggested by Mather in his introduction to this: "In the First Part, of our *Meditation,* we may either Handle a Text, or we may Answer a Case . . . or else we may Discourse on a Thing."[395]

The meditations in *Christianus per Ignem* are quite suggestive of the familiar essay: Meditation VII is "*On the And-Irons,*" Meditation VIII "*On the Lighting of a* Candle *at the Fire,*" Meditation XXXIX "*On the* Fire's *going out,*" the Appendix "*Upon a* Stove." There are forty titles to these meditations, any one of which is suggestive of the familiar essay. Reflect, for instance, "*On the* Nimbleness *of the Flame,*" (XXII) or "*On Throwing my* Pen *into the Fire*" (XL).

The purpose and application of the meditation of any of these early writers is, of course, religious; but the similarity of treatment to the essay is to be noted particularly in these of Mather. I quote one for illustration:

> On the And-Irons.
>
> There was once a Prince in the *English* Nation, concerning whom it was thought by some, that some *words* which he *spoke* hastened upon him the Fate that made him *Speechless.* Among the memorable words of that Prince, I have read, that being invited unto a Merchants House, where he saw a great pair of *Brass And Irons,* he had this Reflection thereupon. *These gaudy Appearances of shining Brass are not the Pillars that hold up the Fire;* (*as your Bishops and your Doctors are not*:) *but they are the little Creepers of Iron which bear up the Fire. So, it is not your Prelates which uphold the*

[394] Boston, 1702.
[395] *Ibid.*, p. 9.

> *Church, but it is your inferior Ministers, which take pains in their places, that uphold it; and not General Councils nor the Dignified Clergy.* If any be offended at this Reflection of Prince *Henry* about the *Fire*, their Offence will signify little to his *Ashes*.
>
> All the Remark that I shall make upon it, is This. Those *And-Irons* that are most *Serviceable*, are most *Honourable*; not those that are most Gaudy, and finished with various Ornaments, for nothing, but an useless Ostentation. It is not unlikely, That the most *Useful men* in the Church of our Lord, may not be those that are brighten'd and burnish'd with fine *Titles*, and have most of *Pomp* to set them off. It may be, they have rather been such as have said, *Odi istos Titulos.* Let my *Temper*, and my *Station* be such as may do most of *Service*, tho' I should have less *Notice* taken of me; Let me chuse the circumstances wherein I may do the best *Service*, tho' they should be those which may have most of *Meanness* otherwise attending of them: yea, though I must also therein have an *heavy Burden* lying on me; as on the *Brand Irons.* It is possible, the Work which I have to do for the Church of God, may oblige me to a very *Hot place*: *Lord* strengthen me to bear the *Heat* of all my Temptations, till the *Times of Cooling do come*! It is possible also, That the Name of Dogs may be thought good enough to be bestow'd upon those, who are to do this Work. It's no matter, if we *do so much Good*, that men can't easily *do well* without us.[396]

This has some of the elastic quality of the familiar essay in spite of its moral preachments. The author is distinctly present, making his comments on his own observations and handling his thought in his own discursive way. The title, of course, is most suggestive of this kind of essay.

Preceding these "meditations" are paragraphs that the author labels "Reflections." Here the personal equation is less evident. While both the "meditations" and the "reflections" in *Christianus per Ignem* are written to teach a lesson, the former is in its manner more closely akin to the familiar essay, and the latter in its manner markedly like the less informal didactic essay as we know it from such examples

[396] *Ibid.*, Meditation VII, p. 80.

as Bacon's. The latter is briefer than the other, more axiomatic, more direct in attack, more obvious in didactic statement, illustrated better by proverbs than by anecdotes from history. Compare, for instance, this "Reflection" with the meditation "On the And-Irons" quoted above:

Reflection II.

> To chuse *Evil Company,* is a Folly, that will be *Accompanied* with a world of Evil. What was it that betray'd *Peter*? It was his falling into *Evil Company.* He who does *That,* knows not into what he shall *Fall.* We read, Luk. 22. 55. *When they had kindled a Fire, and were sat down together,* Peter *sat down among them.* And by *Sitting down among* those, who Blasphemed and Reviled the Lord Jesus Christ, where he durst not Reprove them, he came at length to do like the rest of the *Company.* It was a Note long ago made upon this matter; *Vide quam noxia sint pravorum Colloquia, quae cogunt Petrum, ut neget Christum, quem inter Discipulos Confessus erat Dei Filium.* Alas, The Devil has not a stronger *Enchantment* for the Children of men, than *Evil Company.* Syrs, if you would be preserved from Denying of the Lord JESUS CHRIST, and from Destroying your own SOULS, be very cautious of your *Company*; under the awe of that awful word, Prov. 13. 20. *A Companion of Fools shall be Destroyed.*[397]

The real beginnings of the essay in America during our period is reached in 1710 with the publications of Cotton Mather's "Essays to Do Good." That the author had had them in mind for a long time, or that they were the result of persistent reflection on doing good, is evident from his frequent references (in his diary and other works) to the phrase that makes the title. As early as March, 1680-1681, he writes, "I shall see a *Token for good.*"[398] In February, 1683-1684, he describes "one of my Methods to do good."[399] In 1699, in the epistle to "Decennium Luctuosum," he says,

[397] *Ibid.*, Reflection II, p. 31 f.
[398] *MHSC*, series 7, VII, 3. The italics are his.
[399] *Ibid.*, p. 81.

"He Expects no Thanks for his Essayes to do Good. . ." In his diary for March 1708-1709, after one of his spiritual struggles he says, "The Flame revived; and I went on with Joy in my usual Methods of a flaming Zeal, to do good abundantly";[400] and again, in the same month, "The Work of Repentance in me, and a Resolution to be Rich in good Works, was quickened on this Occasion."[401] In May of the same year, during the serious illness of his child, he resolves to show his gratitude to the Lord if He spares him, and he "sent unto the Press, an Essay to advance Knowledge and Goodness among *Children*, . . . thus . . . from the Evil that befalls, and afflicts my Child, there will arise much good, unto many other Children."[402] One can even suspect a persistent association of ideas in such wording of sentences that follow each other as these:

"I would promote the Publication of a good *Book*, whereby the Souls of many in the Countrey may bee edified.

"I would essay to visit the *Families* of the Flock, belonging unto mee. . ."[403]

It is apparent from these quotations as well as from his use of the term in the preface, that he means by *essay*, an *attempt*—attempts to do good. The nature of these "attempts," however, is short prose pieces that have most of the characteristics of the didactic essay. It is altogether probable, when we consider Cotton Mather's love and serious use of puns, that he had his eye on both meanings of the term. That he was well aware of what the essay of the seventeenth century was is apparent by even a casual study of such didactic and informal examples as those already quoted from the meditations, or of the "character" as quoted from the *Magnalia*. If we need further proof before we analyze the actual "essays to do good," we may turn to the preface of the book itself. A book on doing good, the author comments, must be

[400] *MHSC*, series 7, VIII, 3.
[401] *Ibid.*, p. 5.
[402] *Ibid.*, p. 7.
[403] *Ibid.*, VII, 97.

dedicated to a man who is good—a true representative of a *Public Spirit*. Of such a man, he writes a "character":

> Thy patron, O book of benefits to the world, should be a general and most generous benefactor to mankind; one, who never counts himself so well advanced, as in stooping to do good unto all that may be the better for him; one whose highest ambition is to abound in serviceable condescensions; a stranger to the gain of oppression; the common refuge of the oppressed and the distressed; one who will know nothing that is base; a lover of all good men, in all persuasions; able to distinguish them, and loving them without any distinction . . . [404]

Such a man he believes exemplified in Sir William Ashhurst and in his brother-in-law, Joseph Thompson. The rest of the preface, in his telling the purpose of the book, is really a discourse "on doing good." It is distinctly didactic; it belongs to "wisdom literature"; it is axiomatic; it quotes from authority; and it illustrates by examples out of the classics and antiquity:

> For this way of living, if we are fallen into a generation, wherein men will cry, Sotah! "He is a fool," of him that practices it, as the Rabbi's foretell it will be in in the generation wherein the Messiah comes; yet there will be a wiser generation, and "wisdom will be justified of her children." Among the Jews there has been an Ezra, whose head they called "the throne of wisdom." Among the Greeks there has been a Democritus, who was called *Sophia* in the abstract. The later ages knew a Gildas, who wore the surname of *Sapiens*. But it is the man whose temper and intent it is, TO DO GOOD, that is the truly wise man after all. And indeed, had a man the hands of a Briareus, they would all be too few to do good; he might find occasions to call for more than all of them . . . [405]

He warns those who would do good that they must meet bravely misunderstanding, malice, ingratitude, and envy. In

[404] Cotton Mather, *Essays to Do Good* (Boston, 1845), p. viii.
[405] *Ibid.*, p. xiii f.

regard to these enemies of good, he makes his philosophic comments out of his wisdom and experience, and urges those who would do good to be "up and doing":

> Some have observed, that the most concealed, and yet the most violent of all our passions, usually is that of IDLENESS. It lays adamantine chains of death and of darkness upon us. It holds in chains that cannot be shaken off, all our other though never so impetuous inclinations. That no more hurt is done in the world, is very much owing to a sort of scorbutic and spontaneous lassitude on the minds of men, as well as that no more good is done. A Pharoah will do us no wrong if he tell us, "Ye are idle, ye are idle!" We have usually more strength to do good than we have will to lay it out. Sirs, be up and be doing! It is too soon yet, sure, for an "Hic situs est."[406]

The book itself is divided into sections which we may call "essays." They are like the seventeenth century essays in those qualities of manner and style that we have emphasized again and again: they are philosophical reflections on abstract subjects, commentaries that come out of the wisdom and experience of the author; they are axiomatic; they are didactic in purpose. To be sure, all of these in Cotton Mather's book are consistently on the theme of doing good, but his approach to each section is different. For "Section V" we might put the title "Of Man's Selfishness," with the ultimate preachment, "Do good to these men—convert them from their selfish ways:"

> How full, how full of devices are we, for our own secular advantage! And how expert in devising many little things to be done for ourselves! We apply our thoughts with a mighty assiduity unto the old question, "What shall I eat and drink, and wherewithal shall I be clothed?" It is with a very strong application of our thoughts, that we study what we shall do for ourselves, in our marriages, in our voyages, in our bargains, and in many, many other concerns, wherein we are solicitous to have our condition easy. We solicitously contrive, that we may accomplish good bargains, and that we may

[406] *Ibid.*, p. xvi.

steer clear of ten thousand inconveniences, to which, without some contrivance, we may lie obnoxious. The business of our personal callings we carry on with numberless thoughts how we may do well in what is to be done. To accomplish our temporal business in affairs that cannot be numbered, we find out witty inventions. But, O rational, immortal, heaven-born soul, are thy wondrous faculties capable of no greater improvements, no better employments? Why should a soul of such high capacities, a soul that may arrive to be clothed in the bright scarlet of angels, yet embrace a dunghill! O let a blush coloring beyond scarlet, be thy clothing, for thy being found so meanly occupied! Alas, in the multitude of thy thoughts within thee, hast thou no dispositions to raise thy soul unto some thoughts, "What may be done for God, and Christ, and for my own soul, and for the most considerable interests?" How many hundreds of thoughts have we, how to obtain or secure some trifle for ourselves; to one, how we may serve the interests of the glorious Lord, and of his people in the world? How can we now pretend that we love him, or that a carnal and a criminal self-love has not the dominion over us? I again come in upon a soul of an heavenly extract, and smite it, as the angel did the sleeping prisoner; Awake! shake off thy shackles, lie no longer fettered in a base confinement unto nothing but a meaner sort of business. Assume and assert the liberty of now and then thinking on the noblest question in the world; "What good may I do in the world?" There was a time, when it was complained by no less a man than Gregory the Great, the bishop of Rome, "I am sunk in to the world!" It may be the complaint of a soul that minds all other things and rarely calls to mind that noblest question. Ah! star fallen from heaven, and choked in dust, rise and soar up to something answerable to thy original. Begin a course of thoughts, which when begun, will be like a resurrection from the dead. "They which dwell in the dust, wake and sing," and a little anticipate the life which we are to live at the resurrection of the dead, when they lively set themselves to think, "How may I be a blessing in the world?" And, "What may I do, that righteousness may more dwell in the world?"[407]

[407] *Ibid.*, p. 41 ff.

For Section VIII, the title might be, "On Wasting one's Talents," and the ultimate admonition is, use your talents to do good.

Even these deliberate "lessons" of each section are not out of keeping with the ends of didacticism nor of the seventeenth century essay. The efforts to do good, moreover, were carried out, as the author predicts in his preface, in later essays to do good. Such was the purpose of Benjamin Franklin's "Do Good Papers." Such, too, became the real purpose of those familiar essays in criticism on social foibles of the day: the *Spectator* papers, the *Tatler*, the *Rambler*, the *Idler*, and the *Citizen of the World*.

After a cursory glance at Dr. Mather's voluminous output and his sometimes sententious prose, we may be led to cry, "There is a deal of a-do about style!" But careful scrutiny must inevitably lead us to admiration for much that he has written: for his biographies of Winthrop and Bradford, his political fables, his "Essays to Do Good." At his worst he merely embraced the literary vices of his age; at his best, he also embraced its virtues. The same thing may be said of his contemporaries in England. He was the literary epitome of his age in America. He was above all a scholar of the seventeenth century. And we can give him no greater praise than to say, "he could not have writ as he does if he had not read very much in his time."[408]

[408] Cf. Cotton Mather on style, Appendix C.

Part II

BACKGROUND AND INFLUENCES

LITERARY FORMS

1. Travel Books

Among the most popular books of the Elizabethan period and the seventeenth century, quite naturally, were travel books. The colonies themselves added a goodly number to these. And we find their writers imitating the type of literature of travel already in vogue.

Purchas His Pilgrimes was among the most read books of this kind. We find it in the libraries of the Mathers and others.[409] If we turn to Purchas, we shall find there some standard works of travel. Many of these are in the nature of adventure stories. No better examples of these can be found than in the related adventures of Captain John Smith, all of which were thought worthy of inclusion in this collection. Others of these accounts of travel were less colorful and more in the nature of expository accounts of the things that the writers saw.

We have found that the literature of exploitation in America followed an orderly plan such as this: a geographical survey, an account of the commodities of the new world (earth, air, water, fire), its natural resources (trees, fruits, birds, beasts), its natural inhabitants. One can turn almost at random in Purchas and find a similar order of development. For instance, the "Observations . . . of Josephus Acosta" treats "Of the fashion and forme of Heaven, at the new-found World,[410] and of the Ayre and Winds . . . Of the Ocean . . . Fishes . . . Lakes . . . Of Metals . . . Of . . . Trees, Fruits, Flowers naturall . . . Of Beasts and Fowles. . . ."[411] Similarly constructed are the accounts of "Jonas

[409] Nathaniel Morton quotes it in *New England's Memorial*. Cf. Wright p. 60.

[410] West Indies.

[411] *Hakluytus Posthumus or Purchas His Pilgrimes* (Glasgow, 1906), Vol. XV.

Pooles Voyage for Northerne discovery,"[412] and of "A Treatise of Brasill."[413]

It is obvious that the narratives of America, such as Wood's *New England's Prospect* or Francis Higginson's account of America, were following already established patterns. That the pattern was a conscious one in the seventeenth century is proved by what we find in Edward Leigh's "Hints for Travellers" in his *Three Diatribes*. Certain of his instructions do not apply here, since he had in mind the traveller's visit to civilized countries rather than to an uncultivated wilderness. His advice on the knowledge of languages and of architecture hardly applies, but other suggestions do:

> In the survey of a country, these things are observable. First. The Name and its derivation; the Latitude and Longitude of the place. The temperature of the climate. The goodness or barrenness of the ground. The populousness or scarcity of the people. The limits of the country; how it is bounded by sea or land, or both. The commodities, natural and artificial. The discommodities; either inperfections or wants. The manners, shape, language, and attire of the people. Their building; their havens and harbours. The religion and government. The history of the country and families . . .
>
> . . . The choice herbs and plants, beasts, birds, fishes and insects proper to that country . . . together with minerals, metals, stones, and earths . . . [414]

The narratives concerning America written by the colonists followed established models of books of travel.

2. Science

The scientific spirit in America has already been noted. In the chapter on "The Scientific Essay," we pointed to the colonists' active interest in the science of their day, their correspondence with such noted English scientists as Robert

[412] *Ibid.*, XIV.

[413] *Ibid.*, XVI.

[414] Reprinted in *Social England Illustrated*, An English Garner, ed. by Andrew Lang (New York, n. d.), p. 417.

Boyle, and their actual membership in the Royal Society. And we pointed to the fact that, however in error they were, they were imbued with the scientific spirit.

If we find a fondness for writing short historical essays on astronomy for the almanacs and in that, perhaps, a lingering veneration for the ancients, we find also the real citing of authority from the "moderns" such as that by "J. S." in his Almanac of 1674: "From Kepler that vigilant and ingenious Mathematician, latter [*sic*] Astronomers have received, and are of the opinion, that the Planets move in an Ellipsis . . . " We find John Foster rejecting the literal Scriptural and the Ptolemaic interpretations of the universe for the Copernican.[415]

In scientific matters concerning the universe, the colonists were as intelligently interested as their English cousins. In matters of immediate and local concern, we find them going on their independent way.

There are, however, two influences that we must note here. One is the English "anatomie"; the other is the "natural history."

The pseudo-science of "The Anatomie of Melancholy" appealed to the minds of seventeenth century writers. A seeming preparation for the age of reason in the century to follow was the seventeenth century's love of analysis of something, whether a Biblical text or an Englishman's "humour." Burton, therefore, was quoted, with and without acknowledgement. Increase Mather quoted him in his *Remarkable Providences*.[416] And in his analysis of "The Spirit of Man," Charles Morton certainly suggests the "Anatomie" and also, the medieval conception of man's "humours." For instance, his relationship of the body, soul, and spirit is reminiscent of Burton's:

> The *Soul*, which is a *True Spirit* (in a Nobler Sense, than that whereof we are now treating) being, by its *Information* of the *Body*, most Intimately conjoyned

[415] Almanac for 1675, Cambridge.

[416] For illustration of a parallel passage, see Wright, pp. 140 f.

> thereunto; while it is in the State of Conjunction, and Union in Man, *Uses* the Parts, Humours, and Members, as its *Instruments* or *Organs*, in all its Operations. Now as a Workman Receiveth nothing of his strength or skill, from his Tools wherewith he works; yet in the Exercise of his Abilities he will find himself much furthered or hindered in his business, according as his Tool is either Apt, or Unapt, for his Work. So is it in this Case: The *Soul* Receives no power from the *Body*; But in Exerting its own proper powers, is helped or hindred by the *Bodys* good or ill *Temperament*. Thus an *Ill-Tempered Brain* makes that Soul Act like a Fool, or Ideot, which had it a Brain Well-Tempered, would be both prudent and sagacious. And so also the Temperament of the *Heart*, *Blood*, and *Natural Spirits*, gives Help, or Impediment to the *Will* and *Affections*; even as, The *Organs of Sense* do, to their proper Senses. Hence that saying (*Anima Galbae male habitat*) The Brave Soul of *Galba* had but an Ill Lodging; He being a brave Spirited Man, but very sickly.[417]

He explains the influence of hot and dry, cold and moist qualities of man upon his spirit in an elaborate analysis beginning:

> And, because the *Soules* Primitive facultyes are supposed to be all Equal in every man; tis the *Bodyes Temperament*, that especially gives the great Diversity in Mens *Spirits*; we shall therefore speak of these more Distinctly; And that not Exactly according to the common four *First Qualityes* (Hot and Dry, Cold and Moyst) which are said, by their Mixture, to give the four *Complexions* (Sanguine, Cholerick, Melancholy, and Phlegmatick) of which Physicians do so often speak. But I shall Treat of them, according to the *Actives* (*Hot*, and *Cold*,) with a *Mean* Temper between them; Taking notice of the other By the way, only as occasion is offered. For it is not *Physical* composition, or *Medical* Disposition of spirits, which we have now to do with; But *Spirits* as they Relate to Humane and Moral Actions; into which these three (*Hot*, *Cold*, and *Mean*) have the greatest Influence. Besides, all men will admit of a Hotter, and a Cooler Temperament; even those who Reject Elementary Mixtures; and have

[417] See Part I, Sect. I, Memb. II, p. 20 f.

> no great Regard to the four Complexions. If any like better to have it expressed by *Matter*, more or less, moveable or moved; They may please themselves. There is no Difference in the *Thing*, however Expressions vary.[418]

The "Pseudodoxia Epidemica" of Sir Thomas Browne, of similar tendency to analysis, Increase Mather "quoted three times . . . citing the page once" in his *Remarkable Providences*.[419] In this, Browne was found suitable for use in discussing the curious ways of Divine Providence. He seems equally well suited for citation from the same book in the discussion of rainbows by William Williams:

> And if it should be asked why the Almighty chose the Rainbow and not any other Celestial appearance (if a reason might be attempted) we should say (as Dr. Brown in his *Pseud. Epid.* p. 246) because most proper for the signification intended thereby: Thunder and Lightning had too much terror, to have been tokens of mercy.[420]

In their love of learning and in their "scientific" spirit of analysis, then, Burton and Browne found sympathy in the New World.

"Natural histories," to some degree, had their influence upon those interested in recording the *natura rerum* of the New World. They were, indeed, among the popular books of the day, whether written by the ancients or the "moderns." In the field of plant and animal life, Apuleius had written his *Herbarium*; Pliny, his *Natural History*; Isadore of Seville (though interested mostly in astrology) his *De natura rerum*; Monardes, his *The New Founde World* ("Englished" in 1577 by John Frampton); and, finally, Bacon his *Natural History*. Of these, the colonist had his favorites. Bacon's work was in several libraries.[421] But,

[418] *Ibid.*, p. 26 f.

[419] See Wright, p. 142, for this statement and an example of a parallel passage. See also *Remarkable Providences*, pp. 72, 73, and 74.

[420] Almanac for 1685.

[421] E.g., Increase Mather, Samuel Lee. Cf. Wright, pp. 52 and 129.

of all, Pliny was the standard model. He is directly quoted or cited by Nathaniel Morton, Cotton Mather, John Tulley and others.[422] Even among the favorites, however, direct debts are hardly quotable. This is very naturally due to the fact that the colonist was dealing with entirely new material. New scientific data admit no old material. Here, as in the travel books, the models were merely suggestions on how to proceed. The lack of immediate debt may be due also to the fact that most of the colonists were not scientifically trained in medicine, for in this lies the great difference between them and their models. It was characteristic of these authors of the "natural histories" mentioned above that they related plant and animal life to their medicinal value. This the average writer in the colonies did not do. He chose to follow more directly the simple recording of encyclopedic information such as one finds in the travel books. Parts of these travel books were, in fact, the history of natural phenomena.

John Josselyn is the exception to this general rule. While Captain John Smith, William Wood, and others are not particularly interested in the medicinal value of plants and animals, Josselyn is. Aside from the fact, however, that he has his models in mind, there is little similarity between his works and others. It is as if, with the courage of one who knew how others had done, he began a similar work in an unexplored field. That Pliny and Josselyn's books are not more directly parallel than they are is probably due to the fact that the former was a more learned man. His encyclopedic information, like Bacon's, was venerated by the scholars of the seventeenth century. And we find Josselyn undoubtedly turning to him for his model. Where Pliny describes a plant and then lists sixteen remedies for illnesses, Josselyn mentions only one or two cures, and those he subordinates to the information on plant and animal life. In spite of this

[422] Cotton Mather cites Pliny in the *Magnalia* I, 34, and many times in his *Essays to Do Good*; John Tulley quotes him three times in his almanac for 1693 on the rainbow, snow, and "sudden blasts"; Nathaniel Morton quotes him in his *New-England's Memorial*, e.g. p. 86.

difference, however, and without further proof we would be justified in saying Josselyn was familiar with his models. However, he does definitely betray his acquaintance with "natural histories" when he opens his chapter on fishes by, "*Pliny* and *Isadore* write there are not above 144 Kinds of Fishes, but to my knowledge there are nearer 300: I suppose *America* was not known to *Pliny* and *Isadore*."[423]

The tendency to analysis among the "anatomies" and the compilation of scientific data in the "natural histories" stimulated the "scientific" writings among our colonists. Added to this, is the definite force for the development of astronomy in the almanac, inherited from England. And finally, is the indisputable evidence of learning in the reference to great scientific names such as Copernicus and Kepler.[424]

3. The Almanac

The almanac, of course, was a direct carrying over to America of a form already popular in England. It contained primarily the astronomical calendar. The character of the rest of the material differed in the two countries.

Before 1540, the almanac in England had been written and used by students and physicians—in other words, by educated men. After that date, it became a popular publication and it was gradually taken over by astrologers and quacks. Although astrology was then a respected science, it adapted itself easily to the superstition of its readers and therefore to its misuse by practitioners. In the sixteenth and seventeenth centuries, the "prognostications" of the almanac became an organ of abuse. Not only were the end of the world, sickness, and other dire calamities foretold; but political prophecies were deliberately and falsely promoted in them.[425]

[423] *New-England's Rarities*, p. 59.

[424] The almanacs are full of these and many other names.

[425] For this brief discussion, compare the history of the Almanac in England in: Eustace F. Bosanquet, *English Printed Almanacks and Prognostications* (London, 1917), "Introduction"; and Sam. Briggs, *The Origin and Development of the Almanack* (Cleveland, 1887).

In New England, on the other hand, the almanac was once again in the hands of the learned—the student and the divine. Here astronomy presently was ascendant over astrology, and prognostications were confined to the weather. With a few exceptions not even the appearance of a comet caused much superstitious excitement[426]—not even in a world that was capable of believing in witchcraft. And, as we have seen, the almanac became also an organ for short religious discourses. In Pennsylvania and New York, and to some extent in Massachusetts, the almanac was a medium for satire and invective. The editors of these were few in number, though, as in the case of Leeds, their output was comparable to others. The outstanding names among these were Clough, "N. W.," Taylor, Tulley, and Leeds. But even they cannot be called charlatans or quacks.

On the whole, the standard of the almanac in America of the seventeenth century was higher than that of its model in England and may be taken, therefore, to be of greater literary significance.

4. Histories

The historian or chronicler of New England, as revealed by his "critical" prefaces,[427] had certain definite guides for the writing of history: faithfulness to fact and simple telling. His ultimate purpose was the honest praise first to the glory of God and His earthly kingdom, and second to the glory of England. Realizing the solemn task before him, he was humble before it and, we may feel, sincerely apologetic even when he wrote his apologetic preface in the accepted manner.

These resolutions of truth to fact and simplicity of recording, along with the attitude of personal humility, are not original with our colonial historians. The fact that they were well acquainted with their English contemporaries and pre-

[426] The belief expressed in *New-England's Memorial* (p. 198) that the comet of 1664 was "no fiery meteor caused by exhalation" but was "sent immediately by God to awake the world" was becoming less usual.

[427] *Supra*, p. 111 *seq.*

decessors, however, does not make their attitude nor their principles less sincere. Rather we find our early chroniclers carrying on the spirit of the English historian of the age.

Among these, we may turn, for example, to Raleigh[428] and Camden,[429] both of whose works are found in the New England library of this period. Raleigh, for instance, begins his great task of writing the history of the world with a sense of the importance of the work to be done and his own unworthiness. He begins with the creation because he has conceived his history as a monumental work, not just to England, but to the Creator of England and of the rest of the world. He begins his famous preface with:

> How unfit, and how unworthy a choice I have made of my self, to undertake a worke of this mixture; mine owne reason, though exceeding weake, hath sufficiently resolved me . . . The examples of divine Providence everywhere found . . . have persuaded me to fetch my beginning from the beginnings of things.[430]

Camden's preface to his *Britannia* states his purpose in writing for the glory of England:

> Yet possibly I may seem guilty of imprudence and immodesty, who tho' but a smatterer in the business of Antiquities, have appear'd a scribler upon the stage of this learned age, expos'd to the various censures of wise and judicious men. But to speak the truth sincerely, the natural affection I have for my Country, which includes the good will of all, the glory of the British original, and perswasion of Friends, have conquer'd that shyness of mine . . . [431]

[428] E.g., Raleigh, in the libraries of Brewster, Eaton, Lee. See Wright, pp. 25, 36, 128. Many passages in Mrs. Bradstreet's poetical history of the world are direct transcriptions from Raleigh's history. See edition of her works by Ellis.

[429] Camden, in Brewster, Harvard, Dudley, I. Mather, etc. See Wright, pp. 26, 31, 39, 52, etc. He also is quoted by Mrs. Bradstreet, see Wright, p. 60.

[430] Walter Raleigh, *The History of the World* (London, 1614).

[431] *Camden's Britannia*, newly translated into English. Published [translated] by Edmund Gibson (London, 1695).

The moral purpose in the writing of history is also indicated in this preface:

> In the meanwhile, let them remember, that to praise the Good, is but to hang out a light to those that come after us; for 'tis a true saying of Symmachus, *Imitation receives encouragement from the promotion of the Good; and an aemulation [sic] to virtuous Actions, is rais'd by the example of another's Honour.*

Finally he welcomes those who will point out his errors.

In his *History . . . of Elizabeth* he thanks those who have helped and encouraged him, and emphasizes Truth as his object: "All such things therefore as use to obscure and prejudice the Light of Truth I resolved to remove."[432]

Among other historians with whom the New England writer was familiar was Bacon. His histories of Henry VII, of Henry VIII, and of Scotland were doubtless read by them. If they had been asked, they would have said in all sincerity that they agreed with Bacon's principle of truth. But there is, after all, a difference. Bacon was a scientist and a man of the world with little consideration in his writings for the personal equation or the emotional content. He would write a history of Henry VII, for instance, and draw him as he really was, "I have not flattered him, but took him to life as well as I could, sitting so far off, and having no better light." These words he addresses in dedication to no less than royalty itself, Prince Charles.

The New England writers, however, though quite sincere in their standard of truth, had a tendency to exaggerate the good of historic incident or person for example, or, conversely, to exaggerate the evil, also, for its moral value.

The moral purpose and the wish to write the truth in history were not necessarily Christian traits. The Greek and Latin historians had established those principles. Livy and Plutarch regard the moral good as the chief object of history. Plutarch's habit is to write the lives of two characters, a Greek and a Roman, in separate chapters and then

[432] (London, 1688). "The Author to the Reader."

add a third chapter in which he compares the two with special reference to their nobility of character and the good that they have done.

Livy is most specific on the good to be done in the writing of history:

> Here are the questions to which I would have every reader give his close attention—what life and morals were like; through what men and by what policies, in peace and in war, empire was established and enlarged; then let him note how, with the gradual relaxation of discipline, morals first gave way . . .
>
> What chiefly makes the study of history wholesome and profitable is this, that you behold the lessons of every kind of experience set forth as on a conspicuous monument; from these you may choose for yourself and for your own state what to imitate, from these mark for avoidance what is shameful in the conception and shameful in the result . . . [433]

Polybius finds history, the history of conduct:

> . . . there is no more ready corrective of conduct than knowledge of the past . . . the soundest education and training for a life of active politics is the study of History . . . the surest and indeed the only method of learning how to bear bravely the vicissitudes of fortune, is to recall the calamities of others.[434]

And Lucian emphasizes truth in the writing of history:

> The historian's one task is to tell the thing as it happened . . . For history, I say again, has this and this only for its own; if a man will start upon it, he must sacrifice to no God but Truth; he must neglect all else; his sole rule and unerring guide is this—to think not of those who are listening to him now, but of the yet unborn who shall seek his converse.[435]

[433] *Livy* (London and New York, 1909), p. 3.

[434] Polybius, *The Histories* (London & New York, 1922), I, 3 f.

[435] *The Works of Lucian of Samosaba.* Trans. by H. W. and F. G. Fowler (Oxford, At the Clarendon Press, 1905), pp. 128 f., "The Way to Write History."

On style, he says,

> As for diction and style, he is not to set about his work armed to the teeth from the rhetorician's arsenal of impetuosity and incisiveness, rolling periods, close-packed arguments, and the rest; for him a serener mood.[436]

On the accumulation of facts he cautions:

> Facts are not to be collected at haphazard, but with careful, laborious, repeated investigation; where possible, a man should have been present and seen for himself; failing that, he should prefer the disinterested account, selecting the informants least likely to diminish or magnify from partiality.[437]

Of all our historians, Bradford, perhaps, reaches this ideal which Lucian expressed.

Since the New England writers were familiar with classical literature, it is safe to assume they were familiar with these famous historians. And, indeed, Cotton Mather, the epitome of his age, mentions all the classical historians in his introduction to the *Magnalia*.[438]

> . . . Let any person of good sense peruse the History of Herodotus, which, like a river taking rise where the Sacred Records of the Old Testament leave off, . . . Let him then peruse Thucydides . . . Let him next revolve Xenophon . . . Let him from hence proceed unto Diodorus Siculus, . . . and where he is defective, let it be supplied from Arrianus, from Justin, and from Curtius, who, in the relish of Colerus, is *Quovis melle dulcior*. Let him hereupon consult Polybius . . . Let him now run over the table of the Roman affairs, compendiously given by Lucius Florus, and then let him consider the transactions of above three hundred years reported by Dionysius Halicarnassaeus . . . Let him from hence pass to Livy, . . . Let him then proceed unto the writers of the Cesarean times, and first revolve Suetonius, then Tacitus, then Herodian, then a whole army more of his-

436 *Ibid.*, p. 130.
437 *Ibid.*, p. 131.
438 See particularly pp. 28 and 29.

torians which now crowd into our Library; and unto all the rest, let him not fail of adding the incomparable Plutarch, whose books, they say, Theodore Gaza preferred before any in the world, next unto the inspired oracles of the Bible: but if the number be still too little to satisfie an historical appetite, let him add Polyhistor unto the number, and all the Chronicles of the following ages.[439]

5. *Exempla* and Courtesy Books

Character-writing we have already found in such a medium as the sermon in America. We have shown how in terminology and form its direct parallel with English models is evident. Two other influences of more remote ancestry blended well with the "character" in the early writings of America: the *exempla* and the courtesy books.

The most notable illustrations of *exempla* are to be found in the collections of lives of saintly people such as we find in those of the Church Fathers. Their purpose, as the term implies, is to hold these people up as examples to all Christians. Less abundantly and less collectively, are the lives of good men in New England held up for examples of Christians in the New World. This is to be found particularly in the funeral sermons, in which such men as Michael Wigglesworth and Samuel Willard were models of Christian behavior.[440] The qualities of the good man are pointed to purposefully as when Pemberton says of Samuel Willard, "*These things,* and many more, which we have Learned, Received, and seen in him, Let us do; . . . In this way we shall Erect for him the most Honourable Monuments in our hearts; and his Memory will be always fresh, and his Name pleasant to us thro' the Dayes of Eternity."[441]

The stimulus for such a book as the *Magnalia* may be found in the *exempla* of the Church Fathers or of Foxe's

[439] *Magnalia,* I, 28 f.

[440] *Supra,* p. 167 f.

[441] Ebenezer Pemberton, "Epistle Dedicatory," *Funeral Sermon on the Death of that Learned and Excellent Divine The Reverend Mr. Samuel Willard* (Boston, 1707).

Book of Martyrs. Every divine or theologian was familiar with both of these and everybody else—including "little Betty" of the Sewall letters—with Foxe's volume. No other New England writer was quite so ambitious as Cotton Mather in really compiling a history of American Christian heroes. Most were content with the occasional pointing out of one example in the funeral sermons, as we have noted, or in brief portraits in the chronicles.

Although Cotton Mather shows his familiarity with Foxe in the "General Introduction" to the *Magnalia,*[442] he does not mention him in that part of the book devoted to the lives of New England divines, where one might most expect it. Rather he cites the Church Fathers. He begins the introduction to "The Third Book . . . of Many Reverend, Learned, and Holy Divines" by citing Jerome, "What was it that obliged Jerom [*sic*] to write his book, *De Viris Illustribus*?"[443] In a page and a half, he crowds in other Christian fathers, using their names for illustration or authority: "Arnobius was put upon an apology . . . As Ignatius, in his famous epistles to the Trallians, . . . reports him." And he reiterates the purpose of the *exempla* in the words of Gregory: "*Ut qui Praeceptis non accendimur, saltem Exemplis incitemur; atque ac Appetitu Rectitudinis nil sibi mens nostra difficile aestimet, quod perfecte peragi ab aliis videt.*"[444]

This is the most outstanding illustration of the influence of *exempla* upon early American writing.

As we find the suggestion of *exempla* in funeral sermons, we find correspondingly the suggestion of the "courtesy book" in the election sermon. This is not a set division or standard,[445] but the differentiation is the usual and natural one, since the funeral sermon can look at a complete life and point to it for an example, but the election sermon must look

[442] Vol. I, pp. 26, 32.

[443] P. 233.

[444] *Ibid.*

[445] The use of the qualities of a prince are found, for instance, in the funeral sermon on King William by Benjamin Wadsworth.

forward and suggest the qualities to look for in the selection of a leader—the leader or civil ruler as he ought to be.[446]

Although copies of Machiavelli were in the possession at least of Brewster and of Cotton Mather, it is to be doubted whether it found much sympathy among the Puritans. Rather we are safe in assuming that Cotton Mather expressed the opinion of his contemporaries when he said, "'Twere to be wished that there might never be any English translation of that wicked position in Machiavel, *Non requiri in Principe veram pietatem, sed sufficere illius quandam umbram, et simultationem Externam*."[447] The high ethical principles of such masters of courtesy as Castiglione or of Elyot would have found greater sympathy.

And, indeed, when, by means of tables, we have compared the qualities of civil rulers as set down in the election sermons with the qualities of the prince or the governor as discussed respectively in *The Book of the Courtier* and *The Governour*, we find the same high ideals in both. In both, it is acknowledged that all men are not equal, that some possess greater talent or grace than others, that it is necessary for the superior to govern the inferior, that the superior derive their powers from God[448] and must govern in His likeness, and that the one most superior must invest others with subordinate powers. And both agree in the qualities of a good ruler: He must have knowledge and wisdom, fortitude and moral honesty. He must be righteous and just, and in this he is closest to Divinity. He must think always of public rather than private interests. Above all he must be an example to his people in virtue and in obedience to the law.[449]

[446] In these two differences lie also the two kinds of *character*: in the latter the abstract qualities of a good man; in the former, the good man exemplified by a familiar character.

[447] *Magnalia,* I, 107.

[448] In this matter of the governors and those who are governed, there is a curious transference of the divine right of Kings to the divine right of preachers to govern.

[449] See the accompanying tables for more exact comparison.

In the "character," the *exempla,* and the "courtesy book" there is one principle that unites them all and that explains the easy blending of the three: it is their underlying didactic purpose. It is this principle, too, that made them so very acceptable to the New England writer.

Just how far the New England writer derived his ideals of the Christian prince directly from the original courtesy books is open to question. Certainly, his reading was broad enough to have included these; but we cannot be so positive that he studied these as we can that he knew intimately the Church Fathers and the *exempla.* The principles of the ideal ruler had been carried into the periods of the English Renaissance and the Reformation by such men as Elyot, whom we have mentioned, and Peacham in his "Compleat Gentleman." With these, the New Englander was doubtless familiar. But should he not have read these, we may be sure that he knew the ideals of the Christian prince as portrayed in Erasmus and Quarles. It is, after all, a short step from the divine right and character of royal princes to the divine right and character of Christian princes, particularly in the Calvinistic doctrine that rationalized the theocracy of the New World. Their ideals of their administrators, if not taken from the original courtesy books, must have been derived from such books as that of Erasmus and strengthened by that of Quarles. Though the latter's *Enchiridion,* published in 1641, was dedicated to Prince Charles, a temporal prince, its Christian and moral precepts are unmistakably in accord with the highest ideals of the churchly prince, while at the same time they maintain the admirable wisdom of the courtesy books:

> Let Princes be very circumspect in the choyce of their Councellours, chusing neither by the greatnesse of the beard, nor by the smoothnesse of the face: let him be wise, but not crafty: active, without private ends: couragious, without malice: religious, without faction: secret without fraud; one better read in his Prince's business, than his Nature: and a riddle only to be read above.[450]

[450] (London, 1856), Cent. I, LX, 29.

Likewise Erasmus' *Manual of a Christian Knight*, written "unto a certain courtier, a friend of his," presents the "craft of virtuous living," which is at once the echo of the courtesy book and a guide to the Christian prince, as well as to his legion of Christian Knights:

> If thou be a prince, beware lest these perilous witches, the voices of flatterers, do enchant or bewitch thee. Thou art a lord, over the laws thou art free, whatsoever thou doest is honest, to thee is lawful whatsoever thou list . . . there is one master over all men, and he is Christ Jesus, to whom thou oughtest to be as like as possible, to whom thou oughtest to conform thyself in all things, as unto him certainly whose authority or room thou bearest. No man ought to follow his doctrine more straitly than thou, of whom he will ask accounts more straitly than of other . . . That which in other men is but a small trespass, think in thyself to be a great outrage or excess . . . First of all let them ["the common people"] learn in thee to despise such things [display of wealth], let them learn to honour virtue, to have measure in price, to rejoice in temperance, to give honour to sober lowliness or meekness. Let none of those things be seen in thy manners and conversation, which thine authority punisheth in the manners and conversation of the people. Thou shalt banish evil deeds in the best wise . . . Let not the noise of ambition . . . defend thee from contempt . . . Turn not to thine own profit things which are common, but bestow those things which be thine own, and thine own self, altogether upon the commonwealth . . . consider with thyself not how great a man thou art, but how great a charge thou bearest on thy back . . . Nothing is so comely, so excellent, so glorious unto Kings as to draw as nigh as is possible unto the similitude of the highest king Jesu.[451]

Whether the New England preacher of the election sermons was familiar only with such writings as these by Erasmus and Quarles, who as Christian writers, were sympathetic with his ideals, or whether he knew, also, as he probably did, the English books of instructions to princes and the nobility such as those by Elyot and Peacham, or whether he knew

[451] *A Book Called in Latin Enchiridion Militis Christiani* . . . , (London, 1905), pp. 217 ff.

even the courtesy books of the Italian Renaissance such as that by Castiglione, it is certain that his ideals and principles of the ruling Christian princes of New England theocracy were derived from these precepts established in such books during the Renaissance.

Table I

The Qualities of Civil Rulers
(New England Election Sermons)

A. The origin of the rulers' power.

1. Inequality of man.
   All-Wise God [did] Ordain Orders of Superiority and Inferiority among men, and required an *Honour* to be paid accordingly.[452]
   I have appointed that there shall be some of a Superiour Character, advanced to Place, Power, and Dignity above others.[453]
2. Civil Rulers . . . do not all of them stand in one equal Rank . . . There are Supream and Subordinate Powers.[454]
3. They [civil rulers] are gods Not by Nature or Essence, but by Office . . . [they] bear the *Images* and *Character* of the great God.[455]

B. Their qualities.

1. Knowledge.
   Right Reflections on their *Mortality* will suggest to such as Sit at the upper End of the World, wiser thoughts of their present State of Exaltation; and will teach them that there can be no *true Greatness* but what is found in Conjunction with *Immortalizing Goodness.*[456]

[452] Samuel Willard, *The Character of a Good Ruler* (Boston, 1694), p. 2.

[453] From Psalm LXXXII, quoted by Ebenezer Pemberton, *The Divine Original and Dignity of Government Asserted* (Boston, 1710), p. 7.

[454] Willard, *op. cit.*, p. 9.

[455] Pemberton, *op. cit.*, p. 7 f.

[456] *Ibid.*, p. 63.

2. Wisdom.

   [They must be] wise men, men of Sagacity . . . in a degree answering the Character of *Solomon*.[457]
   As Gods they must be Wise and Skillfull.[458]

3. Justice.

   [Civil Rulers] must be *Righteous* and *Just* in all their Administrations.[459]
   Knowledge without Justice will degenerate into Craft and Subtility [*sic*].[460]
   They must temper Justice with Levity.[461]
   Civil Rulers should be Just Men, and such as Rule in the Fear of God.[462]
   . . . [must be men] Fearing God.[463]

4. Men well known . . . not obscure.[464]

5. Fortitude and moral honesty.

   Able men, strong men, men of Fortitude, Courage and Resolution, that will not be diverted from their duty by frowns, nor smiles; men that have an antipathy against Flatterers, and Flattery; men that will dare to do Justice, though there are difficulties and dangers in the way.[465]
   . . . it is firstly required, that they have a Principle of *Moral Honesty* in them, . . . that they *Love Righteousness, and Hate Iniquity*: that they be *men of Truth*; . . .[466] he must be one that respects the Cause, and not the persons in all his Administrations . . . [without] Bias . . . whom neither Flattery nor Bribery may be able to remove out of his way.[467]

6. Public rather than self-interest.

   . . . he must be one who prefers the publick Benefit

[457] Thomas Bridge, *Jethro's Advice* (Boston, 1710), p. 7.
[458] Pemberton, *op. cit.*, p. 30.
[459] *Ibid.*, p. 36.
[460] *Ibid.*, p. 37.
[461] *Ibid.*, p. 43.
[462] Willard, *op. cit.*, p. 8.
[463] Bridge, *op. cit.*, p. 8.
[464] *Ibid.*, cf. p. 7 f.
[465] *Ibid.*, p. 8.
[466] Willard, *op. cit.*, p. 9.
[467] *Ibid.*, p. 10.

above all private and separate Interests whatsoever.[468]
Every man ought to, and one of a Publick Spirit will deny himself out of respect to the good of others.[469]

7. His life, exemplary.

[He] must use utmost endeavours that his own life may be an exemplification of Obedience, and others may learn by Him, what a Veneration he hath for the Laws.[470] . . . *a Terror to Evil Doers and an Encouragement to them that do well.*[471]

Table II

The Qualities of a Prince or a Governour
(Courtesy Books)

A. The origin of the rulers' power.

1. (a) . . . god gyueth nat to every man like gyftes of grace, or of nature, but to some more, some lesse . . .[472]

   (b) . . . suche ought to be set in a more highe place than the residue . . . that . . . other of inferiour understandynge may be directed to the way of vertue and commodious liuynge.[473]

   (c) Men have been placed by God under the word of princes.[474]

2. . . . it is expedient and also nedefull that under the capitall gouernour be sondry meane authorities . . .[475]

3. (a) . . . he doth approche most nyghe unto the similitude of god; . . . as one excelleth an other in that influence, as therby beinge next to the similitude of his maker, so shulde the astate of

[468] *Ibid.*, p. 11.

[469] I. Mather, *The Excellency of a Publick Spirit* (Boston, 1702), p. 7.

[470] Willard, *op. cit.*, p. 12.

[471] *Ibid.*, p. 14.

[472] Thomas Elyot, *The Governour.* Everyman ed., p. 4.

[473] *Ibid.*, p. 5.

[474] Castiglione, *The Book of the Courtier* (New York, 1903), p. 262.

[475] Elyot, *op. cit.*, p. 16.

his persone be auanced in degree or place where understandynge may profite.[476]

(b) . . . from god only procedeth all honour.[477]

(c) . . . divine princes . . . have been sent by God on earth, and by Him made to resemble one another in youth, in martial power, in state, in beauty and bodily shape, to the end that they may be of one accord for this good purpose also.[478]

B. Their qualities.

1. Knowledge.

(a) Knowledge and reflection implied in the education of the "governour."[479]

(b) Hence . . . it is needful to know and to govern one's self with that foresight which is the necessary companion of all the virtues.[480]

(c) Thre noble counsayles of reason, societie, and knowlege.[481]

(d) . . . ignorance, whence spring all sins.[482]

2. Wisdom.

(a) Thre noble counsayles of reason, societie, and knowlege.[483]

(b) The noble philosopher . . . *Tullius Cicero* . . . saith in this wise, Sapience is the science of things diuine and humaine . . . This definition agreeth wel with the gifte of sapience that god gaue to Salomon, king of Israell, who asked onely wisedome to gouerne therwith his realme.[484]

[476] *Ibid.*, p. 5.
[477] *Ibid.*, p. 112.
[478] Castiglione, *op. cit.*, p. 276.
[479] Elyot, *op. cit.*
[480] Castiglione, *op. cit.*, p. 277.
[481] Cf. The education of the governour. Elyot, *op. cit.*, Bk. III, chap. III.
[482] Castiglione, *op. cit.*, p. 264.
[483] Elyot, *op. cit.*, Bk. III, chap. III.
[484] Elyot, p. 268 f.

3. Justice.
   (a) The moste excellent and incomparable vertue called iustice is so necessary and expedient for the gouernour of a publike weale, that without it none other vertue may be commendable.[485]
   (b) . . . of the cares which belong to the prince, the most important is that of justice . . . justice also fosters that piety towards God which is the duty of all men . . .[486]
4. The prince or the governour is well known.
5. Fortitude and moral honesty.
   (a) Elyot recommends that the governours have their own source of revenue so that they may "lyve without takyng rewardes: it is lykely that they wyll nat be so desirous of lucre . . ."[487]
   (b) A noble man aboue al thinges aught to be very, circumspecte in the election of suche men as shulde continually attende upon his persone [that is, he should be swayed neither by friends nor flatterers].[488]
   (c) Cf. Elyot's chapters on "Fortitude."[489]
6. Public rather than self interest.
   (a) They shall nat thynke howe moche honour they receiue, but howe moche care and burdene. Ne they shall nat moche esteme their reuenues and treasure, . . .[490]
   (b) Let them thynke the greatter dominion they haue, that thereby they sustayne the more care and studie.[491]
7. Their lives exemplary.
   (a) The most sure fundation of noble renome is a man to be of suche vertues and qualities as he desireth to be openly publisshed.[492]

[485] *Ibid.*, p. 195.
[486] Castiglione, *op. cit.*, p. 270.
[487] Elyot, *op. cit.*, p. 17.
[488] *Ibid.*, p. 189.
[489] *Ibid.*, Bk. III, chaps. VIII-X.
[490] *Ibid.*, p. 118.
[491] *Ibid.*, p. 118.
[492] *Ibid.*, p. 119.

(b) They shal also consider that by their pre-eminence they sitte, as it were on a piller on the toppe of a mountaine, where all the people do beholde them.[493]

(c) . . . all men would gladly obey the laws, when they found that he himself obeyed and was as it were the guardian and incorruptible minister of the same.[494]

[493] *Ibid.*

[494] Castiglione, *op. cit.*, p. 271.

SEVENTEENTH CENTURY PROSE STYLE

"Seventeenth century prose" is more than an ordinary caption for a period in literary history; it is more than a mere divisional study. It is as vividly meaningful as "the drama of the Restoration and the eighteenth century," or "Elizabethan drama," or "the poetry of Romanticism," or "the nineteenth century essay." The phrase connotes an age in which some of the best and some of the worst prose of our English literary history was written. It means the prose that is as involved as Milton's at his worst or as sonorous and moving as it is at his best, as learned and as engaging as Sir Thomas Browne's or Robert Burton's, or as packed full of wisdom and unforgettable phraseology as Bacon's. These are the qualities of seventeenth century prose: the abstruse, the learned, the sonorous, the simple, the rhythmical, the epigrammatical.

Having mentioned the great names of this period, we turn, with perhaps some unfairness, to the writers of the same time in America. Here we were neither so productive nor so great. But at our worst, we were no worse than they; at our best, we were not to be ashamed. And the characteristics, good and bad, of English prose of the seventeenth century were also evident in America.

Like our English contemporaries, we were at our worst starting no new school of rhetoric. Like them we were affecting the rhetoric inherited from the classics and carried on and re-emphasized by the medieval tradition. Scholasticism was still manifest in the extremely logical methods of analysis and the artificial question and answer in the sermon, in the embellishments of quotation and turn of phrase and figure, and in the abundant use of cited authority.

The artificial style is well illustrated in its extreme protagonists, John Cotton and Cotton Mather. The conscious analysis of John Cotton's sermons must have needed his purported "golden voice" to carry his congregation to enthusiasm. His famous farewell sermon to the people of the future Massachusetts Colony is characteristic of all his dull sermons: a text, a minute analysis step by step of its phraseology with its "firstly's", "secondly's," "thirdly's"; its "question" and "answer"; its artificial application. It is little more than an outline, of which the following passage is characteristic. The text is, *Moreover I will appoint a place for my people Israel, and I will plant them, that they may dwell in a place of their owne, and move no more* (2 Sam. 7.10). After an introductory paragraph Cotton says:

> . . . the Lord bids *Nathan* to shut up his speech with words of encouragement, and so he removes his discouragement two wayes
>
> First, by recounting his former favours . . . Secondly, by promising the continuance of the like or greater . . . And five blessings God promiseth unto *David* . . .[495]

Then in five sentences he defines them, beginning each with consecutive numbering, "The first is . . . Secondly . . . Thirdly . . ." *et cetera.* Immediately following this is "In this 10 verse is a double blessing promised:

> "First, the designment of a place for his people.
>
> "Secondly, a plantation of them in that place, from whence is promised a threefold blessing.
>
> "First, they shall dwell there like Free-holders in a place their owne.
>
> "Secondly, . . ."[496]

This involved piling up of analysis upon analysis is hardly relieved by an occasional "Question" and "Answer":

"*Quest.* Wherein doth this worke of God stand in appointing a place for a people?

"*Answ.* First . . ."[497] and then the numerical division begins all over again.

Though not very frequently carried to such extreme, this, in general, was the method used by New England divines in

[495] *God's Promise to His Plantation* (London, 1634), p. 2.
[496] *Ibid.*, p. 2.
[497] *Ibid.*, p. 3.

the composition of their sermons, and may be said to be an outgrowth of the sophistic love of abstruse analyses.

We have already noted the use of the epigram, parallelism, and illustration in the sermon in America. We have noted, also, in the works of Cotton Mather the extreme use of the figure in the conceit[498] and the pun and the conscious display of learning in his accumulation of illustration, anecdote, and quotation from the classics.

The extent to which Cotton Mather could go is illustrated in his *Magnalia,* which he wrote with a conscious eye to posterity. If it is the extreme example of the display of learning in America, it is also the extreme example in the writing of Cotton Mather himself. Let us open the book at his "General Introduction":

> I cannot say whether the style wherein this Church-History is written, will please the modern criticks: but if I seem to have used *αωλ στατη συνταζει γραφης*, a simple, submiss, humble style, 'tis the same that Eusebius affirms to have been used by Hegesippus, who, as far as we understand, was the first author (after Luke) that ever composed an entire body of Ecclesiastical History, which he divided into five books, and entituled, *ὑπομνηματα των εκκλησιαστικῶν πραζεων*. Whereas others, it may be, will reckon the *style* embellished with too much of *ornament*, by the multiplied references to other and former concerns, closely couched, for the observation of the attentive, in almost every paragraph; but I must confess, that I am of his mind who said, *Sicuti sal modice cibis aspersus Condit, et gratiam saporis addit, ita si paulum antiquitatis admiscueris, Oratio fit venustior.* And I have seldom seen that way of writing faulted, but by those who, for a certain odd reason, sometimes find fault that "the grapes are not ripe." These embellishments (of which yet I only—*Veniam pro laude peto*)

[498] The use of the conceit and the artificial turn of phrase was admired by John Norton. Introducing his sermon *Abel being Dead yet speaketh,* he says, "It is the priviledg [*sic*] of the blessed who lived in Heaven, whilst they lived on Earth; That they may live on Earth, whilst they live in Heaven. And 'tis a part of the Portion of the Saints, that (together with the benefit of the living) they may enjoy both the life and death of those, who lived and dyed in the Faith. *Life and Death are yours.* (Boston, 1658).

are not the peurile spoils of Polyanthea's; but I should have asserted them to be as choice *flowers* as most that occur in ancient or modern writings, almost unavoidably putting themselves into the author's hand, while about his work, if those words of Ambrose had not a little frightened me, as well as they did Baronius, *Unumquemque Fallunt sua scripta.* I observe that learned men have been so terrified by the reproaches of pedantry, which little smatterers at reading and learning have, by their quoting humours, brought upon themselves, that, for to avoid all approaches towards that which those feeble creatures have gone to imitate, the best way of writing has been most injuriously deserted. But what shall we say? The best way of writing under heaven shall be the worst, when Erasmus, his monosyllable tyrant, will have it so! and if I should have resigned my self wholly to the judgment of *others,* what way of writing to have taken, the story of the two statues made by Policletus, tells me what may have been the issue: he contrived one of them according to the rules that best pleased himself, and the other according to the fancy of every one that looked upon his work: the former was afterwards applauded by all, and the latter derided by those very persons who had given their directions for it. As for such unaccuracies as the critical may discover, *Opere in longo,* I appeal to the courteous for a favourable construction . . .[499]

This part of a page is only one of thirteen similar pages of his General Introduction and of many more similar pages of introductions to each of the seven books of the *Magnalia.* Only in a little less degree is it typical of the biographies throughout the book. I quote this passage at length because it illustrates many things. In the first place, it is a discussion of his own style. It is written by a man with the love of learning, but without any saving sense of humour. How else can one explain not only his grave piling up of conscious samples of his learning, but also his audacity in suggesting that anyone might mistake his style of writing for the simplest? In the second place, with the possible exception of the conceit and the pun and the use of parallelism, balanced

[499] *Op. cit.,* I, 31 f.

construction, and epigram, this passage illustrates all the tricks of seventeenth century prose: the quotation of authority, particularly from church history, the flourish of Greek and Latin quotation and phraseology, a rarer indulgence in English proverb, the curious use of pagan and Christian names in juxtaposition (Polyanthea and Ambrose appearing in the same sentence), the metaphor (as in "choice flowers"), and the illustration from classical story. And finally, this passage illustrates the scholar's contempt for his critics upon whom he looks from his high pedestal of learning. To him they are merely "smatterers at reading and learning."[500]

[500] It is of interest to note, in connection with this quotation, the conclusions of Kenneth B. Murdock on the reading and writing of Cotton Mather. He shows that Mather, like his contemporaries, had frequent recourse to such compendia of information as Samuel Clark's *Mirrour or Looking Glass both for Saints and Sinners,* to which he referred by quotation or allusion about seventy times. Among many other writers whom he quotes or cites, Thomas Fuller is next in frequency to Clark. Mr. Murdock thinks, in fact, that the whole plan of the *Magnalia* is derived from Fuller. "Without Fuller the book might still have been written, but it is hardly likely it could have taken its present form or have been as artistically successful as it is. Combine the *Worthies,* the *Church History,* the *Holy and Profane States,* and you have the basic outline of the *Magnalia.*"

And Mr. Murdock shows, too, that Mather's interest in writing the *Magnalia* was that of man-of-letters rather than theologian:

"The Cotton Mather of the *Magnalia,* then, is not the pedantic scholar, the eager delver into theological and philosophical mysteries, or the seeker after truth, preoccupied with ideas, doctrines, and theories. Nor is he conspicuously concerned with science. In the *Magnalia* there is far more of Mather the lover of books, the would-be artist, and the practical moralist. He was either incapable of going deeply into purely technical problems, or, more probably, uninterested in doing so. . . He had some taste for style in others; he set out to develop a style himself. However he may have failed, however outmoded his conception of prose may have been, there are inescapable signs that he aspired at least towards an artistic standard."—From the manuscript copy of Kenneth B. Murdock, "Cotton Mather's Reading for the *Magnalia Christi Americana,*" read before the Modern Language Association in 1936 and quoted here by Mr. Murdock's kind permission.

So reads the extreme example in America of seventeenth century learning. If we seem to quote Cotton Mather and John Cotton rather lengthily it is with the knowledge that they represent the summation of the learning among New England writers. In only less degree, the other educated men were like them: that is, they were learned men and well influenced by seventeenth century mannerisms of style.

The family of the Mathers was undoubtedly the most style-conscious and "scholasticall" of all the New England divines. Samuel Mather introduces Samuel Stone's "Congregational Church Is a Catholike Visible Church" with one of the most painful examples of "logicall and scholasticall" prefaces. Stone has been involved in a theological dispute with Hudson and Cawdrey *an Ecclesia instituta sit genus an integrum.* There is only one way to settle such a question, thinks Mather, and this is by logic:

> *Now Logick is of most general use. Divinity,* ratione finis; *for it is the universal end of all*: physica ratione χτήυεως; *for every art riseth here*: *but Logick* ratione χσήνεως; *is most general*; *there is no art but useth the help of Logick*; *nothing can shew it self to the eye of the mind of man, but in this light. Hence mistakes in Logick are not unusual in Writers upon this subject. A man cannot apprehend* M. Hooker's *double consideration of the Church, as* totum essentiale & organicum; *nor why as* totum essentiale *it is* Ecclesia prima, *if he do not know* genus *and* integrum *and* argumentum primum *and* ortum *in Logick*; *nor judge his method to be other then leaping, if he do not know the method of the first part of Logick. Nor will his proving that Christ gave the Keys to a Visible Church, entitle the Church of* Boston, *or any other Church to them, unless it be also proved, that the visible Church is a* genus, *and that every individual Church, as that of* Boston, *is a* species *or part of this* genus: *Nor will it ever appear whether the visible Church be* genus *or* integrum, *till it appear what* genus *and* integrum *be.*[501]

[501] Samuel Stone, *Congregational Church Is a Catholike Visible Church* (London, 1652). Preface by Samuel Mather.

Paradoxically he recommends this discourse to any who may reply to Stone's work because it is an example of clear and succinct style:

> If any shall attempt to reply, let me desire him to imitate this, which may be a patterne for all discourses of this nature in clearness, and succinctness, and close pursuing the point in hand, without distastful reflections and diversions from things to men. Many polemical writers are so filled with odd pangs of their spirits, as causeth a secret kind of disrelishment and offence to the Readers.[502]

The quoting of authority in such a case as that in the introduction of Mather's *Magnalia* is done with an eye to literary effect. The quoting of authority in polemics was done of necessity. Here it was used not only for oratorical effect, but for the actual strengthening of argument. The written literary effect and the oratorical effect may be considered as the same end. But the strengthening of an argument is not so much concerned with display, as it is with the reasoning process. In this there is a definite sympathy between the Calvinists and the medieval clergy, to whom the former were largely indebted for their knowledge of scholastic methods. Both were concerned with the *summum bonum* of salvation. Both were striving to establish the dogma of their faiths, which not only embraced certain ideals about the hereafter but also dictated the manner of living in the present. The skeptic, therefore, must be overwhelmed by the evidence in favor of established doctrines. It was natural, then, that the followers of Calvin, in a state in which the authority of dogma embraced also the authority of a political hierarchy, should find the methods of scholasticism especially to their taste. The characteristics of medieval scholasticism are also

[502] The frequent quoting of authority, in spite of the opportunity it gave an author to show his learning, was—and is—a fundamental need in any non-fictional writing, particularly of the essay in criticism. One may challenge the truth of a statement by an author if only he utters it. One cannot question so easily a statement that is supported by the authority of several others.

the characteristics of the New England colonist: faith in an ideal, deference to authority, the rationalization of dogma, and the interest in learning, out of which dogma may be derived.[503] The preparation for the dissemination of such ideals was the study and practice of grammar, logic, philosophy, and the sciences. It is not surprising then to find the laws of Harvard, a university founded by Puritans, requiring the following:

> Every student who, on trial, shall be able to translate from the original Latin text, and logically to explain the Holy Scriptures, . . . and shall also be thoroughly acquainted with the principles of natural and moral philosophy . . . may receive the first degree . . . ;

and

> Every scholar who has maintained a good standing, and exhibited a written synopsis of logic, natural and moral philosophy, arithmetic and astronomy, and shall be prepared to defend a proposition or thesis; shall also be versed in the original languages, as aforesaid: . . . shall be admitted to the second, or Master's degree.[504]

Thomas Shepard and his contemporaries respected the weight of authority from antiquity and, also, from more "modern" thought. The former, in the preface to his *Theses Sabbaticae, or, the Doctrine of the Sabbath,*[505] says, "It is easie to demonstrate by Scripture and argument, as well as by experience, that Religion is just as the Sabbath is, and decays and growes as the Sabbath is esteemed . . ." And he does demonstrate, in impressive manner, by authority from church history: he explains Clemens and Origin on the doctrine of the Sabbath; he points to Constantine as a beginner in upholding the true belief, and to Charles the Great who firmly established the Sabbath day; and he reminds his reader of "the darknesse of Popery" which nearly obscured the true doctrine, and of the Reformation which re-established it.

[503] Cf. Henry Osborn Taylor, *Thought and Expression in the Sixteenth Century* (New York, 1920), Vol. I, chap. XVII. "John Calvin."

[504] *Magnalia,* II, 25.

[505] (London, 1655).

In the dispute between Roger Williams and John Cotton over religious toleration, each quotes many authorities. John Cotton depends almost wholly for his effect upon an impressive array of citations. Williams is less pedantic. Let us look for a moment, at their dispute of the *Bloudy Tenent*.

Williams introduces his *Bloudy Tenent* with a letter entitled "Scriptures and Reasons written long since by a *Witnesse* of Iesus Christ, close *Prisoner* in *Newgate*, against *Persecution* in cause of *Conscience*; and sent some while since to Mr. Cotton." He adds also Mr. Cotton's reply to this letter.[506] The two letters make perfect introductory illustration of tolerance and persecution. The "Scriptures and Reasons," on the side of toleration, is in itself a magnificent example of the seventeenth century practice of quoting authority in polemical disputes. But with this letter we are not here concerned since it was written by a man who was not an American. It is of interest to us only because it was published several years after it was written with a reply from Cotton and because it was the immediate occasion of the *Bloudy Tenent* series. Through his reply, Cotton attacks the liberal religious principles of Roger Williams.

The curious fact about writings in religious controversy among these learned men was that the opponent of an argument could use the same tools as his enemy. *The Answer of Mr. John Cotton* to the arguments of the "prisoner," although perhaps more full of the expression of personal opinion, refutes the first point by point by quoting authority from the Bible, a few kings, and some Church Fathers: "First it is not unlawfull to persecute any for *Conscience* sake *Rightly informed*; for in *persecuting* such, Christ himselfe is persecuted in them, *Acts* 9.4." Then follow citations from Tit. 3.10; Phil. 3.17; Rom. 14.1, 2, 3, 4; and a number from Matthew, and many others. He explains away the Prince and the King of Bohemia whom the "prisoner" had cited and turns to Constantine the Great who banished

[506] For the history of this case, see the Editor's Preface to the *Bloudy Tenent* in *Narr. Pub.* III, i-xiv.

"Arrius with some of his fellowes. Sozom. lib. I. *Eccles. Hist.* cap. 19.20." And he calls upon Williams to remember Queen Elizabeth and King James and how they proceeded against the Papists. He has an answer for each item quoted by the "prisoner" from the Church Fathers. In spite of his own words, "To shut up this Argument from Testimonie of *Writers,*" he does not end abruptly but proceeds with Augustine, Bernard, Calvin, and Beza before he writes several paragraphs of conclusion.

Since Williams refutes the whole of Cotton's reply in a long treatise, the *Bloudy Tenent,*[507] he, too, makes the best of authority and illustration, but with some sense of moderation. He may quote from the history of his recent England, "Well spake that famous *Elizabeth* to her famous *Attorney* Sir *Edward Coke*:[508] Mr. *Attourney,* goe on as thou hast begun, and still plead, not *pro Domina Regina,* but *pro Domina Veritate.*"[509] He may combine a number of historical examples in one paragraph:

> And yet *Caesar* (as a *civill* supreme *Magistrate*) ought to defend *Paul* from Civill *violence,* and *slanderous accusations* about *sedition, mutiny, civill disobedience, etc.* And in that sense who doubts but *Gods people* may appeale to the Romane *Caesar,* an Egyptian *Pharaoh,* a Philistian *Abimelecke,* an Assyrian *Nabuchadnezzar,* the great *Mogol, Prester Iohn,* the great *Turke,* or an Indian *Sachim?*[510]

Or he may depend simply, as he most frequently does, upon the supreme authority of the Bible:

> This was and is the summe of all true preaching of the Gospell or glad newes, *viz.* That God anointed Jesus to be the sole King and Governour of all the Israel of God in spirituall and soule causes, *Psal.* 2.6. *Acts* 2.36

[507] *The Bloudy Tenent* of Persecution, for cause of Conscience, discussed, in a Conference betweene Truth and Peace (London, 1644), *Narr. Pub.*, Vol. III.

[508] Coke was a patron of Williams. See editor's note, p. 57.

[509] *The Bloudy Tenent. . . Narr. Pub.*, III, 46 f.

[510] *Ibid.*, p. 159.

> Yet this Kingly power of His he resolved not to manage [28] in His owne Person, but Ministerially in the hands of such Messengers which he sent forth to preach and baptise, and to such as beleeved that word they preached, *Iohn* 17. And yet here no *Arrogance* nor *Impetuousnesse.*[511]

The three men whom we have just discussed, Cotton Mather, John Cotton, and Roger Williams, are representative of the learned men of their time in America. There were others of course. Wright states that at least thirty books are cited or quoted and over thirty referred to "familiarly" by Increase Mather; and nearly forty quoted or cited by Bradford in his polemical writings.[512]

Although the writings of Colonial America were mostly sermons or, if not, works written by those venerating the religious life, and though their authors, therefore, were most fond of quoting from the Bible or church history, reference to pagan authors was not out of order. John Norton, in his funeral sermon on John Cotton, *Abel Being Dead Yet Speaketh,*[513] quotes Xenophon and Plutarch: "An honest-minded man (saith Xenophon) gets by enmity: And Plutarch writes a Treatise concerning benefitting by our Enemies."

In his letters to his friends, Samuel Sewall seemed particularly fond of Ovid. In a letter to Cotton Mather, he "cannot well brook [his] charging Ovid with Stumbling, and blundering" and defends the poet by quoting "a most Noble and excellent Exordium becoming the Ingenius Author."[514] And in a letter to Nicholas Noyes, quoting Ovid, he indulges in a bit of literary fun:

> My Brother in a Letter had raised my Expectation of receiving a distich or 2 from you; and the disapointment

[511] *Ibid.*, p. 77.

[512] See Wright, pp. 142 and 158 respectively. He lists also nearly three hundred cited or quoted, and nearly two hundred not cited or quoted by Cotton Mather.

[513] (London, 1658).

[514] *MHSC*, series 6, I, 372-3.

[*sic*] puts me out of Tune. But I recover, and am very Thankful to you for your Elaborat Answer to my Propositions. You may be sure, I am in no condition in the world to make any Reply at this time; Finding myself under the Circumstances of the poor fellow mentioned by Ovid in the latter end of his 12th Book Met.

Tela retusa cadunt, manet imperfossus ab omni ictu.
Saxa trabesq[u]*e super, totosq*[u]*e involvite montes;*
Vivacemq[u]*e animam missis elidite sylvis.*
Sylva premat fauces et erit pro vulnere pondus.
---- ---- ---- ---- ----
Orbrutus inmani cumulo sub pondere Coeneus
Aestuat arboreo . . .

. . . O the Cruelty and Injustice of Antichristian Tyranny! Justly provoked Juno, after awhile relented, pitied the misery of metamorphosd [*sic*] Io, and restord her to her native features:

Ut lenita dea est, vultus capit illa priores:
Cornua decrescunt, fit luminis arctior orbis,
Contrahitur rictus. . .

Whereas poor innocent Helvidius, after more than a thousand years Unreasonable Torture, is still compell d to continue his old fashion of bellowing and Barking in stead of speaking with humane voice. Piscator's Censure is more tolerable; *Peccavit olim Helvidius,—peccant hodie Papistae.*[515]

The familiarity of the New England writers with Latin is illustrated by their easy use of Latin epigram. If these phrases and quotations were not sufficiently simple to be easily interpreted, they were accompanied by an English translation, sometimes literal, sometimes free. William Wood likes the occasional use of the Latin proverb, which he accompanies frequently though not always with the English: "But as it is an Axiome in Nature, Nullum violentum est perpetuum, No extreames last long, so this cold winde blowes seldome above three dayes together. . ."[516] As a rule, however, he finds no necessity of translating his

[515] *MHSC*, series 6, I, 315-18.
[516] *New England's Prospect*, p. 4.

Latin phrases, a fact which further goes to prove that to the average reader, not necessarily to a scholar, Latin was not unfamiliar ". . . in them [the Indians,] the old proverbe may well be verified: (Natura paucis contenta) for though this be their daily portion, they still are healthfull and lusty."[517]

This familiarity of the average reader with Latin is further attested by the fact that the quotations were not limited to a few set phrases such as have been taken over from Latin and French into our language and now find their place in our twentieth century dictionaries. There was a stimulating variety and not very frequent repetition. Moreover, the almanac, the kind of printed matter that came the nearest to being popular literature, is full of Latin phrases. Josiah Flint uses Latin and a little Greek in his essay on "The Worlds Eternity is an Impossibility":[518] "Among other their malepert and audacious attempts, they endeavour to. . . coequalize a point with him *cujus centrum est ubique et circumferentia nullibi*? . . . Which beside the many Scriptural demonstrations founded upon the αυτός ἔφη of Truth itself. . ." Nathaniel Chauncey,[519] Israel Chauncey,[520] Alexander Nowell,[521] William Brattle[522] are a few of those who used the Latin phrase or the Latin proverb in their almanacs.[523]

The frequent use of Latin is, after all, not to be wondered at since it was the language of the school, and, until comparatively recent times in relation to this period, the language of books. It is a familiar fact that Francis Bacon wrote in the Latin because he believed it would always be read, and that the writing in the vernacular came into its own really

[517] *Ibid.*, p. 66.
[518] Cf. p. 408. *Almanac* for 1666. Cambridge.
[519] e.g. *Almanack* for 1662. Cambridge.
[520] *Almanack* for 1663. Cambridge.
[521] *Almanack* for 1665. Cambridge.
[522] *Almanack* for 1682. Cambridge.
[523] There were collections of Latin proverbs for general use. An example is Erasmus' *Adagia*.

with the great prose period of the seventeenth century. And granted that the "reading public" was fairly familiar with this language, we can conceive that the use of Latin phraseology, when not too frequent, might not appear so much an affectation to them as it does to us. Even when used at length, it gave weight to one's writing as an expression of the knowledge and scholarship that was held in profound respect in this period.

If, on the one hand, Cotton Mather and John Cotton at their worst represent the sophistry of the age; on the other hand, not all the writing of this period was so overburdened with mannerisms. It is quite possible that the average New England citizen did not find the sermons and theological discussions, "logicall and scholasticall" as they were and weighted down with authority, altogether easy to peruse in cold print. Spoken in the voice of the minister they had sounded, no doubt, much more impressive. Samuel Willard, at least, had begun to suspect as much. When he "was desired to let" his sermon, "A Brief Discourse of Justification," come abroad, he considered that "the smalnesse of the Book might invite some to read it, that would not allow themselves time to peruse larger tracts on the Subject; or to be at the expense to purchase them . . . in it I made it my endeavour to avoid all controversy or dispute, and laboured with all plainness to suite expressions to common capacities. I hoped it might on that account yield some advantage to more unlearned Christians, to whose perusal I do more especially recommend it."[524]

There were influences other than these sophistic tendencies. Paradoxically, the proverb, so frequently introduced affectedly, must, along with the essays of Bacon, ultimately influence prose for terseness of expression.

Francis Bacon was read, imitated, and quoted in America. Roger Williams in his dedicatory letter "To the High Court of Parliament," introducing *The Bloudy Tenent* quotes: "And yet, saith that learned Sir *Francis Bacon* (however

[524] Samuel Willard, *A Brief Discourse of Justification* (Boston, 1694).

otherwise persuaded, yet this he confesseth:) 'such as hold *pressure* of *Conscience* are guided therein by some private interests of their owne.' "[525]

In America's first anthology, *The Temple of Wisdom for the Little World*, Daniel Leeds includes forty "Essaies And Religious Meditations of Sir Francis Bacon, Knight, Attorney General to King James the First."

We have already discovered sundry echoes of Bacon. In summary, we may review: Thomas Shepard, advising his son who is about to enter college, says:

> Lett your studies be so ordered as to have variety of Studies before you, that when you are weary of one book, you may take pleasure (through this variety) in another: and for this End read some Histories often, which (they say) make men wise, as Poets make witty; both which are pleasant things in the midst of more difficult studies.[526]

The influence of the Baconian essay is suggested by discussions of books and studies in sundry New England writings. William Brattle's epigrammatic essay on reading already referred to[527] is suggestive of Bacon in thought and manner. William Morton's preface to Cotton's *The Way of Life* begins, "Hee resolved well that said, Books and friends would I have few and choice; He advised well that wisht, Be courteous to all, familiar with few . . . "[528]

The great influence of the Bible on this period is obvious because of its overwhelming evidence on every page of Puritan writing. Perhaps we may suggest here, merely, that the wise sayings of Solomon[529] fitted in with the century's love of epigram and proverb and that the sufferings of Job appealed most to the sufferings of the colonists. This is merely a guess, but the frequent appearance of quotation from "Proverbs" and "The Book of Job" suggested the idea

[525] Cf. Bacon's essay, "Unity in Religion."

[526] Cf. Bacon's *Of Studies*, and Wright's reference to, p. 138. Cf. *Supra*, p. 88.

[527] *Supra*, p. 34.

[528] Cf. *Supra*, p. 97.

[529] For quotations from these see the section above on "Science."

that quotations from these might be more frequent than others. And yet, once having stated this, one thinks also of the consolations of the Psalms and the inspiration of I Corinthians and the guiding light of the Gospel of Matthew to which they turned. Whatever their inspiration, the influence of the King James Bible upon their prose was as inevitable as it was upon the prose of seventeenth century Englishmen. On the one hand, was the succinctness of the proverb; on the other hand, the rhythm of Biblical prose.

The rhythm of Biblical prose is attained largely by the use of parallel structure and the long sentence that grows out of it. Fortunately the King James version of the Bible, the one most familiar to the seventeenth century preachers, made no distinction between the verse and prose of the original. If it had, the influence of rhythmical parallelism on English prose might not have been so great.

Thomas Hooker, who, as we have already noted, was at times a bit "scholasticall" in spite of himself, was also influenced for good by the Bible in the writing of his prose. We may discover in him, however unconscious the trait may have been, some of its methods of parallelism. Other writers were similarly influenced, but he will stand for a marked illustration.

First, there is the parallelism in the Bible that is the repetition of an idea already stated:

> "The Lord of Hosts is with us;
> The God of Jacob is our refuge."

Compare this of Hooker: "he loveth his sin as he loveth his soule; Nay, he maketh his sin his God."[530]

Another kind of parallelism is that of antithesis:

> No servant can serve two masters
> For either he will hate the one,
> And love the other;
> Or else he will hold to one,
> And despise the other.
> Ye cannot serve God and Mammon.

[530] Thomas Hooker, *The Saints Dignity and Dutie* (London, 1651) Sermon VII, p. 228. "Wilful Hardnesse."

Although one does not find a completed verse structure like this in Hooker's work, one finds the adaptation of antithesis as in the following:

> All mens estates in this world are either *holy*, or *unholy*; either they are *in a state of grace and salvation*, or *in a state of sin and condemnation*. Hence therefore you may take a scantling of your conditions, and plainly and clearly see how it is with you: *Whether you be of the number of those that have infallible Evidences of the work of Gods Spirit in the Ministerie of the word*, tending to holiness and sanctification, or *whether you be yet in the gall of bitterness, and in the bond of iniquitie. Whether you be as you came into the world*, the children of wrath still, or *whether you be begotten again by the immortall seed of the Word, to a lively hope*, and to an inheritance with the Saints in light.[531]

The fact that the use of antithesis in Hooker's work is not absolutely parallel in construction is a virtue. The variety of adaption in this example shows the skill of an experienced writer. For instance, the last sentence does not end at the word "hope," but is brought to a rhythmical and satisfying period by the addition: "and to an inheritance with the Saints in light." The best prose of the seventeenth century uses parallel structure no more skillfully. It is, at its best, such an adaptation. Hooker's prose, indeed, anticipates the variety of parallelism that reached its highest art in the prose of Newman in the nineteenth century.

Hooker, too, was skillful in the use of analogy or parable for illustration. For instance

> If a curious workman after he hath made a clock or a watch, shew the frame thereof to a man ignorant of that Art, and declare to him the manner of making it, happily he will conceive his words, and his reasons, and perceive that he saith truth, but he cannot make such another, because he hath not the art it self of clock-making: My brethren, so it is here, There is a curious frame in the soule of a Christian, of grace, of faith, of repentance, of holinesse, of love, patience and the like;

[531] *Ibid.*, p. 234. Italics mine.

> a blessed disposition of heart, whereby the soul runneth right toward God and every holy dutie, and strikes right (as I may say) in all holy obedience to God; this is a frame reared up by the hand of the Spirit of God alone, in the heart of a Christian.[532]

The writings of Thomas Hooker, Benjamin Colman, and Roger Williams at their best are representative of early American prose that is most comparable to the English prose of the seventeenth century. Colman's excellence is manifest in his portrait of the hypocrite,[533] which, on analysis, will be seen to be dependent for its effectiveness upon parallel thought and structure.

The use of climax and cresendo combined with parallel structure is one of the most effective of devices in Old Testament poetry.[534] Roger Williams' impassioned prose uses parallelism; but its best effect is the result of a combination of the simple and the long sentence and the use of climax. In the following example the first sentences are simple and strikingly figurative. The sentences that follow grow in length and in a sense of climax, which is emphasized by the skillful use of parallelism: "I have been charged. . . I have been blamed. . . [and then for variety] It hath been told me that I labored. . ." *et cetera,* and finally, "this, and ten times more, I have been censured for . . . and at this present am called a traitor. . ."

> WELL BELOVED FRIENDS AND NEIGHBORS,—I am like a man in a great fog. I know not well how to steer. I fear to run upon the rocks at home, having had trials abroad. I fear to run quite backward, as men in a mist do, and undo all that I have been a long time undoing myself to do, viz.: to keep up the name of a people, a free people, not enslaved to the bondages and iron yokes of the great (both soul and body) oppressions of the English and barbarians about us, nor to the divisions and disorders within ourselves. . . I have been

[532] *Idem,* Sermon VI, p. 210. "Culpable Ignorance . . ."

[533] *Supra,* p. 160.

[534] For this discussion of Biblical verse, cf. R. G. Moulton's *The Literary Study of the Bible* (Boston, 1895), Bk. I, chaps. I, II.

> charged with folly for that freedom and liberty which I have always stood for; I say liberty and equality, both in land and government. I have been blamed for parting with Moshassuck, and afterward Pawtuxet, (which were mine own as truly as any man's coat upon his back,) without reserving to myself a foot of land, or an inch of voice in any matter, more than to my servants and strangers. It hath been told me that I labored for a licentious and contentious people; that I have foolishly parted with town and colony advantages, by which I might have preserved both town and colony in as good order as any in the country about us. This, and ten times more, I have been censured for, and at this present am called a traitor by one party, against the state of England, for not maintaining the charter and the colony; and it is said I am as good as banished by yourselves, and that both sides wished that I might never have landed, that the fire of contention might have had no stop in burning.[535]

Professor Ernst, who analyses other examples of Williams' prose,[536] summarizes his work in the *Bloody Tenent* thus:

> He had given full expression to the spirit of rebellion back of the Civil War then raging in England. The book is chuckful of quotable sentences and paragraphs which shock and startle the reader into attention by their apt phrasing and skillful repetitions. . . His style has the dash, vigor, and earnestness of a mind made up and passionately sincere. *The Bloody Tenent* still lives and pulsates because it grew out of the heart and soul and sinews of its age.[537]

The best prose of early America is to be found in such passages as these from Roger Williams. Worthy of praise, too, is the prose of Benjamin Colman, Thomas Hooker, and Cotton Mather.

The display of sophistic, the terseness of epigram, and the rhythm of Biblical prose influence for good and ill the prose of seventeenth century America.

[535] *Pub. of Narr. Club*, VI, 262 f.

[536] James Ernst, *Roger Williams, New England Firebrand* (New York, 1932), chap. VIII. "A Writer of Books."

[537] *Ibid.*, p. 246.

THE CLASSICAL INHERITANCE

It might have been possible for America of the seventeenth century to have inherited the qualities of ancient rhetoric only through the medieval church or English literature of the seventeenth century. It might have been possible for its writers to have acquired their ideas of composition through such contemporaneous textbooks as Ralph Johnson's *The Scholar's Guide*[538] or through the earlier *Arte of Rhetorique* of Thomas Wilson. However, though thoroughly familiar with the literature of the church and with English writing, they were also acquainted with original sources—especially the Latin, and if not the Greek directly, at least the Greek through the Latin. It was the natural thing, then, that every student entering college had to be able to read Cicero and to speak and write Latin and that, after his matriculation, he found an important part of his education devoted to a training in oratory. A freshman

> must speak in public on the stage eight times a year . . . Sophisters must be present at a public debate twice a week . . . bachelors will discuss in public philosophical questions once a fortnight . . . every scholar shall be prepared to defend a proposition or thesis . . . [a candidate for Doctor of Divinity] shall pronounce one oration in Latin and one in English in a church, or the college-hall.[539]

In these stated rules there is apparent the connection between the classical past and the seventeenth century, between Latin oratory and the training for an American minister of the Gospel.

Charles Morton was a minister of the Gospel in Cambridge, Massachusetts. He was respected by his colleagues and listened to by the generation of young ministers and

[538] London, 1665.

[539] See Laws of Harvard, *Magnalia*, II, 24-25.

students of the ministry whom he taught. It is therefore of interest to note the address of advice and instruction that he gave those "who are entring into the Sacred Work."

After emphasizing the grave religious significance of their calling and urging them to constant prayer, he makes this curious observation:

> Thus you shall avoid the unsavoury Way of Moral Philosophy Lectures, instead of Gospel Preaching, more fit for the *Rostra* or Theatre of Heathens, than the pulpit or Assembly of Christians; and better comply with the exemplary Resolution of the Apostle, who determined *to know nothing but Jesus Christ, and him crucified.*[540]

One might suppose from such a resolution and its contemptuous reference to the "heathen," that he would not recommend a study of the ancients; but the instructions which he subsequently gives are certainly those of the classical models. To the authors of these he makes no reference. The paradox may be explained by the fact that he does cite as authority the theological books of instruction through whom the classical theories could, with impunity, be handed down to the young students. The attitude of Charles Morton toward the "heathen" and toward moral philosophy was, however, unusual. The course of instruction in our first university bears testimony to the respect in which the classics and moral philosophy were held.

There was, indeed, between the ancients and these divines a sympathy and understanding that had a moral and ethical basis. This is no more evident than when the latter speak apologetically in behalf of "the heathen." A translation of Plutarch's *Morals* "by several hands" shows this attitude in its dedication:

> . . . the Author . . . was the wisest man of his Age, and if he had been a *Christian, One of the Best* too; but it was his severe *Fate* to flourish in those Days of *Ignorance,* which 'tis a *favourable Opinion* to hope the *Al-*

[540] Report of an address of Charles Morton to young divines in Edmund Calamy, *A Continuation of the Account of the Ministers* (London, 1727), I, 199.

> *mighty* will one time wink at, that our Souls may be with these Philosophers together in the same State of Bliss; . . .[541]

Although this is from an English publication, it mirrors the exact attitude of our divines toward the ancients.

The models of oratory or the books of rhetoric were usually those of Cicero and through Cicero those like Isocrates and Aristotle, who had established certain criteria of composition. In the use of these theories of the ancients, the New England teachers were continuing an unbroken chain from the past, which had been handed down first by the Church Fathers, then stimulated by Renaissance learning, and emphasized again by the preaching and oratory of the Reformation and of the seventeenth century. Such textbooks as Wilson's *Arte of Rhetorique* are the mere echo of Ciceronian principles.

Cicero and Quintilian, who in turn echoed Cicero, Demosthenes and other models, explain the classical principles of rhetoric as completely as we can find them anywhere.[542]

The most important requisite for the successful orator shows at once the innate sympathy between the ancients and the seventeenth century preachers. It is the indisputable premise of both that "above all . . . he must be a good man."[543] And inextricably bound with this is the underlying reason why he must be a good man. The orator wishes to be the "regulator of times and persons."[544] He has a moral responsibility to those who hear him and who may be influenced by

[541] *Plutarch's Morals.* Translated from the Greek By Several Hands (London, 1699), Vol. I, third edition.

[542] Although the New England fathers very likely had fewer texts of Quintilian in comparison with those of Cicero (Cotton Mather quotes Quintilian in *Essays to Do Good,* e.g. Sec. XV), we shall turn to the *Institutio Oratoria* to supplement or verify the discussion. Quintilian's long and careful treatise, with its impartial and sane criticism, gives not only the foundations upon which ancient rhetoric was laid, but reveals, in his clear judgment of the times, the affectations of rhetoric.

[543] *Quint.,* XII, i.

[544] *The Orations of Cicero,* ed. C. D. Yonge (London, 1852), IV, 417. "The Orator," XXV.

what he says. There is also the implied principle that an oration can not be effective if its author is not sincere and honest.

First, the orator must be a good man. Second, he must be a man of knowledge. Bacon, "who took all knowledge to be his province" expresses the seventeenth century ideal of a Ciceronian doctrine, "scientia comprehendenda rerum plurimarum."[545] That our first Americans also set this ideal for education is evident again in the requirements of their schools, particularly for those entering the ministry.

The three traditional purposes of classical oratory were *docere, conciliare,* and *movere.* Since the end of pulpit oratory was to teach, the appropriate Latin parallel of the term was *docere.* Although the New England minister might use the means of persuading or moving, his ultimate purpose was to teach. He must sublimate the means to the end. And so Charles Morton tells his young students in his second cardinal point of his counsel:

> often call to mind the End of Preaching, which is, to teach what Men *should,* not to shew what you *can* do: Not *dicere,* but *docere*: Not *eloqui,* but *alloqui* . . . Direct your Speech . . . as designing to teach and touch the tenderest Part of their Hearts.[546]

He insists that they must confine themselves to the oratory that is appropriate to them as young men:

> I would not have young Men so personate Fathers, as to put on affected Gravity, nor conceit to themselves greater Authority, than indeed they have. This would render them and their Discourse more ridiculous than reverend. (See Keckerman *De Oratoria Concionatorum,* at the End of his *Logick.*)[547]

In spite of the reference to Keckerman, his instructions of this head amount to nothing more than the rhetoricians' sense of *decorum.*

[545] M. Tulli Ciceronis, *De Oratore,* I, v, 17.
[546] Calamy, *op. cit.,* p. 199.
[547] *Ibid.,* p. 200.

Decorum, however, was usually employed among ancient rhetoricians to mean the appropriate adaptation of style to subject matter and the occasion upon which a speech was delivered. Although Morton's instructions do not emphasize this matter, the divines were aware of its governing principles. There was, perhaps, nothing in their writings so specifically separate and obvious as the three styles in ancient rhetoric—*genus tenue, genus medium,* and *genus grande.* Neither was there, for that matter, a strict holding to these demarcations in the actual practice of the ancients. But our ministers were aware of proper adaptation of style to the subject matter and the occasion. The artificial style of Cotton Mather clamors so insistently for our attention that we think of it as representative of all his writings. And yet even he recognized the fundamental principle of *decorum* when he preached the funeral sermon of Michael Wigglesworth, a sermon which could hardly be more direct or more simple. And Roger Williams recognized it when, on the one hand, he disputed with John Cotton in the style laden with quotation from authority, and, on the other hand, when he pleaded his case with the people of Providence. Before Mather or Williams delivered these speeches, they must, if we may judge from results, have determined where they were to speak, what they were to say, and in what style they were to express themselves. They must have followed, in other words, the principles stipulated by Cicero and reiterated by Quintilian: *non omni causae neque auditori neque personae neque tempori congruere orationis unum genus.*[548]

In order to learn appropriate speech, the beginner was directed to the study of models. Quintilian had said,

> Id autem consequemur optima legendo atque audiendo; non enim solum nomina ipsa rerum cognoscemus hac cura, sed quod quoque loco sit aptissimum.[549]

Reading the best writers and listening to the best orators shows reverence not only for the past but also for the best

[548] *Quint.*, XI, i, 4. Cf. *De Oratore,* III, lv, 210.
[549] *Quint.*, X, i, 8.

of the present. Although reading and meditation were essential in the training of the New England preacher, the importance of listening to and disputing with his contemporaries was quite as important. The dispute and the discussion was in the nature of the old Socratic method, which finds its echo again in the advice of Thomas Shepard to his son:

> Single out two or three scholars most Godly, Learned and studious, and whom you can most love, and who love you best, to be helps to you in your Studies; Gett therefore into the acquaintance of some of your Equalls, to spend some time with them often in discoursing and disputing about the things you hear and read and learn; as also grow acquainted with some that are your Superiours, of whom you may often ask questions and from whom you may learn more than by your Equals only.[550]

Charles Morton advised the young candidates for the ministry that the only way to transmit good to others was first to receive it themselves and then transmit it to others. Although private study would enrich them with ideas, "practical Holiness" was more important: "Be diligent in hearing the most pious and practical Preachers, and such as you see do most prevail with the Hearts of Men."[551]

If the prospective orator met the requirements of being a good man, if he endeavored to make all knowledge his province, and if he studied the great models, living and dead, he was then ready to think of composing his speeches. Here, again, in the composition of the sermon, are the echoes of classical models.

The traditional five parts in the preparation, composition, and delivery of a speech, which were analyzed by Aristotle and echoed by Cicero, were *inventio, dispositio, elocutio, memoria, actio*.[552] *Inventio*, or the compilation and analysis of

[550] *Pub. Col. Soc. Mass.*, XIV, 194.

[551] *Op. cit.*, p. 205.

[552] In this discussion, I have made use of the analyses given by Charles Sears Baldwin in his *Ancient Rhetoric and Poetic* and *Medieval Rhetoric and Poetic* (Macmillan, 1924 and 1928, respectively) and the texts of Cicero's essay on the orator.

material, although not apparent, of course, in the finished form of the sermon, is still apparent in such preparations for the sermon as we find in the "commonplace books." These were personal notebooks filled with quotations and references, which were carefully classified in marginal notes for future use. When the minister wished to compose a sermon, he could find material on his subject at hand for appropriate use. Such a book or books Thomas Shepard advises his son to prepare even while he is in college.[553]

Charles Morton also advises his students:

> This [the selection of appropriate texts, *et cetera* to his subject] may be done ordinarily by first collecting most of the Scriptures relating to your Subject, and afterwards refering [*sic*] each to its proper Branch or Kind . . . first be furnish'd with Scriptures, and out of them draw your Heads, which will of Course be well confirm'd by them.[554]

This was the preparation before actual composition and corresponds to *inventio*.

When the subject was chosen and the material appropriate to it was collected, then followed the arrangement of material, known among the rhetoricians as *dispositio*. This, particularly in forensic or deliberative oratory, was in turn composed of *exordium, propositio, narratio, confirmatio, refutatio, peroratio*. Although the sermon was not forensic, it inherited in its love of analysis and its anticipation of doubt or argument many of the traits of judicial procedure. The pulpit had taken the place of the Forum. The presentation and refutation of argument had already been practiced in college when the sophist was required to defend a thesis. The method was carried on after he became a minister of the Gospel. He had the advantage over the lawyer in that he need not be disputed, but his arguments assumed the unspoken doubt and the questioning of an opponent. Hence we may well find the parts of *dispositio* in the sermon, though

[553] *Op. cit.*, p. 194, Par. 7.
[554] *Op. cit.*, p. 205.

not necessarily in the same order. There is usually the presentation of the text, a moral saying to be proved true; then may follow a statement of what the orator intends to do; after that comes the analysis of the meaning of the text and a confirmation of its truth by illustration; finally there is the return to the text and its application. Sometimes there appears also a refutation, in question and answer, of arguments not really stated by an opponent, but proposed by the orator himself, who recognized the probability of such a question in his hearer's mind. In polemics, the refutation and all the other parts of ancient orations are even more evident. Here one has an actual opponent. It is easy to see how the study of the methods of ancient oratory combined with the study of formal logic would lead to the extreme analysis that one sometimes finds in the early sermons of America.

Elocutio was the third step in the preparation of a speech, and, of course, is the consideration of style since it deals with the choice of words and sentences. "One thing there will certainly be," said Cicero through the mouth of Crassus,

> which those who speak well will exhibit as their own; a graceful and elegant style, distinguished by a peculiar artifice and polish. But this kind of diction, if there be not matter beneath it clear and intelligible to the speaker, must either amount to nothing, or be received with ridicule by all who hear it . . . the proper concern of an orator . . . is language of power and elegance accommodated to the feelings and understandings of mankind.[555]

As a means to this end he recommended appropriate choice of words and the frequent use of periodic and rhythmic sentences. He would recommend Demosthenes rather than the Sophists, the clear and rhythmical prose rather than the highflown or strained. That our own divines were more or less under the sophistic influence that reached its height in the medieval period cannot be denied; and yet their theory of rhetoric echoed the more conservative tendencies of Demosthenes and Cicero. Quoting Thomas Shepard again,

[555] *De Oratore,* I, XII. Bohn Edition.

" . . . as in your orations, so in all you do, labour for exactness, and accurateness, let not crude, lame, bungling Stuff come out of your Study." And Charles Morton said,

> I would advise you . . . not to run into the newfangled Method of roping Discourses, without observable Method: Wherein a Torrent of Words was like Water over a Mill-Wheel, and the continu'd oratorical Flash leaves not Space for distinct Observation.[556]

The best seventeenth century prose, whether it be that of Jeremy Taylor's in England or Roger Williams' in America, had the qualities not only of appropriate diction but of moving rhythmical sentences. Here, I should say, that, although the theory of such prose and its beginnings had its roots in ancient rhetoric, the immediate stimulus or pattern was the prose of the Bible.

Memoria, the fourth step in the delivery of a speech, was, as Quintilian suggests, the necessary link between *inventione* and *elocutione*.[557] Without memory, the orator could not achieve anything, however perfectly he had gathered or arranged or composed his material. Its importance is implied in ancient and seventeenth century rhetoric in the study of models. Thomas Shepard sees a practical aid to memory in listening to good speakers:

> Mark every mans Disputations and Conferences, and study to gett some good by every thing: and if your memory be not very strong, committ every notion this way gained unto Paper as soon as you gett into your Study.[558]

Charles Morton declares that a minister is a more effective speaker if he does without notes but that, if his memory is faulty, he may use them "not proudly and foolishly, but humbly and wisely . . . if they [Preachers] be excellent good with them [notes], they would be excellently better without them."

[556] *Op. cit.,* p. 207.
[557] Cf. Baldwin, p. 83, and *Quint.,* XI, ii, 1-3.
[558] *Op. cit.,* p. 194.

If the beginner is timid, he must analyze himself for the kind of memory he wants and how he must achieve it:

> Ask that therefore, whether you want a rational or useful Memory, or a serious and suitable Intention to your Business: And see whether it be a natural or moral Defect. (See *Reynold's Passions*, chap. iii. *Of Memory.*) Whether 'tis modest Bashfulness, or proud Fear of Disparagement, that makes you so distrust yourself. Whether the Accuracy of Speech be not more minded than the Efficacy.[559]

With the speech composed and the memory trained, the minister is ready for *actio,* or delivery of his sermon.

> Direct your Speech [said Charles Morton] not as if you intended to beat the Air over Mens Heads, but as designing to teach and touch *docere* and *movere* the tenderest Part of their Hearts . . . a Father or Tutor does not make Orations, or Speeches to his Children or Scholars, but in a familiar Way, (*humano more*) he inculcates his Instructions, so as he judges will make the best Impression.[560]

Specifically on *actio* he advises,

> Now because through the intimate Conjunction of Soul and Body, there is great Communication and Influence to and from the Affections, by the Deportment of the Outer Man, let me here caution you against the Errors in Elocution. Avoid all odd and extravagant Tones: *Homoitonia's* (the same Cadencies and Elevations, however the Matter varies.) *Homotonia's* (the same even Sound throughout:) Beginning Sentences with a strong Voice, and slackening the Strength towards the Period; whenas the contrary is most vivacious, and holds up Mens Attention. Also beginning leisurely, then huddling and precipitating in the Close of Sentences; which is a Kind of *string halt* in Speech. Especially beware of over fast speaking throughout, without due and convenient Pauses. For Men will need a little Time to think, as well as you to breath. Beware also of impertinent Repetition of Words and Sentences, which dead and flatten much the Intention of the Audi-

[559] *Op. cit.*, p. 201 f.
[560] *Op. cit.*, p. 199 f.

> tors. Add to this the Errors of Gesture and Countenance, and the Defects of and Super-abundance in Action, or what else is unbecoming or unpleasing. For you must please to Edification. As I would not have you nice, so I would not have you slovenly in so great a Performance. Do all *humano more*, as was said. What is most natural will prove most artificial. Only for this I advise you to desire some Faithful and Prudent Friend, to observe and warn you of your Defects in the Beginning, least you get some scurvy Habits that you can never leave while you live.[561]

The attributes of posture, gesture, and the quality of voice were those discussed in detail by the rhetoricians.[562]

In summary, the five parts of classical rhetoric survived in the oratory of seventeenth century America. It was evident in the college training of the minister and in the actual practice of composition.

We have neglected thus far to speak of the three branches of rhetoric that Aristotle classified and that later rhetoricians accepted: the "deliberative," which considers the expediency of a proposal or measure; the "judicial" or "forensic," which considers a question, like a case in the courts; and the "demonstrative" or *epideictic*. With the "deliberative," we have here little to do. And we have already suggested the survival of forensic oratory in the sermon in its exhaustive analysis and its presentation of question and answer. We have left the epideictic.

Epideictic, as its original meaning and its synonym "demonstrative" indicate, connoted display of delivery and its consequent pleasure derived by the audience.[563] Quintilian objected that this definition was too narrow because all three kinds of oratory are devoted partly to subject-matter and partly to display.[564] His definition emphasizes aim rather than manner and makes epideictic embrace that oratory which

[561] *Ibid.*, p. 204.

[562] Cf. *Quint.*, XI, iii.

[563] For a discussion of *epideictic* literature, see Theodore Chalon Burgess: *Epideictic Literature.* Chicago University Press, 1902.

[564] *Quint.*, III, iv, 14.

is persuasive and advisory and also that which holds up its subject to praise and blame. Under this definition would come all panegyrics and encomiums.

Now the early literary types in America have essentially these persuasive and advisory qualities. The short didactic compositions, especially, and the sermon, in order to persuade the readers or hearers to virtuous action, hold up the good for praise and the bad for blame. And other writings not didactic—such as the "pamphlet of newes"—are also encomiastic and laudatory. In these qualities the early essay in America inherits from the classics the characteristics of *epideictic* literature. The traditional pattern is evident when we examine the instructions of Menander, Rhetor on the writing of encomiums. Praise might include, we find, that of a country, a city, a person, or anything worthy of praise.

Praise of a country included its geographical position, its physical aspects, its advantages and disadvantages, its natural resources:

> The nature of every country we judge from these six points: whether it is mountainous or level; whether dry and waterless or damp and well watered; and whether fertile and productive or barren and unproductive. For from these features we recognize the goodness and badness of a country.[565]

The country is further to be praised from the pleasure or use it will give—the former by its beauty and variety of scenery, the latter for its natural resources. In these instructions for the encomium of a country, need one be reminded of the methods by which such men as Captain John Smith, William Wood, and Francis Higginson composed their encomiums of America?

The funeral and election sermons, which formed such an

[565] This and the following excerpts from Menander are translated by Professor Schumann of Indiana University. The text of Menander used for this thesis is that in the edition edited by C. Walz, *Rhetores Graeci* (London, 1836), pp. 127-330.

important part of the New England sermons, may be seen to have inherited much of their framework from the classical manner of composing the lament, the consolatory speech, the funeral oration, and the public address (panegyric). This is evident in the instructions of Menander, Rhetor and of Quintilian.

The panegyric, according to the latter, might be praise of gods or praise of men. If one substitutes "God" for "gods" and "Christian men" for "men," one finds the sermon a frequent panegyric in praise of God or in praise of a good man.

In the development of an oration praising men, Quintilian specifies the following items to be included:

1. The period preceding birth: country, parents, ancestors.
2. Individual character: physical endowments, external circumstances.
3. Glory of deeds may be enhanced by emphasis on the smallness of his resources.
4. Glory of deeds may be enhanced by the fact that he was unspoiled by wealth.
5. The chronological order of his life may be given, or his virtues may be considered separately.[566]

Menander, Rhetor elaborates more specifically upon those points in his instructions of Public Address, Consolation, and the Funeral Oration.

Public address, of course, had to do with the praise of a living ruler. In it excellent qualities of character were glorified, in the matters of his public benefits, his courage in war, and in his prudence, justice, *et cetera*.[567] The speeches of

[566] See *Quint.*, III, vii. Cf. *De Oratore*, II, xi.

[567] The specifications of these classical texts were not incompatible with the later characteristics of ***exempla*** and character, or the qualities of the ideal prince. They are, simply, more inclusive and pertain particularly to the whole composition.

consolation and of the funeral did the same thing for the dead, but added, of course, a more detailed biography, and, particularly, the expression of grief for the "fallen one"[568] and the consolation to those left behind.[569] The speech of consolation added, for its ultimate purpose of lessening grief, the comment that the departed one was now in the Elysian fields. The similarity to such speeches among the Christians during nineteen hundred years is so obvious as to need little comment. The grief for a young person "cut off in the flower of his youth,"[570] the glorification of the deeds of a good man accomplished in spite of ease or adverse circumstances, the assurance of a happier life beyond are all familiar subject matter to Christian people.[571]

Classical methods required that the subject's ancestry must be praised. Wadsworth's sermon on King William says, "He descended from an Ancient and Illustrious Family . . ."[572] and praises the deeds of his family.

The subject's character must be extolled, his deeds glorified, and his virtues praised. Menander specifies that he must be shown to have the qualities of "prudence, justice, moderation, courage." Wadsworth says of King William:

> A Prince the best qualify'd for a Throne, being great without Pride, true to his word, wise in his deliberations, secret in his Counsils, generous in his Attempts,

[568] "The one who makes a consolatory speech grieves himself for the fallen one."—Menander, "On Consolation."

[569] "Meanwhile you have opportunity to put in remarks:—that cities also perish, and there are races which have entirely perished, and that the departure from the present life is a blessing, removing one from injustice, greed, and cruel Fortune."—*Ibid.*

[570] "He was a young man . . . and fell in the flower of manhood."—*Ibid.*

[571] "I believe that the departed will inhabit the Elysian field, where are Rhadamanthus, Menelaos, the child of Peleus and Thetis, and Memnon. And more likely he is dwelling now somewhere with the gods and inhabits the upper air and overlooks things here. And very likely he is blaming the lamentations. For the Soul, being akin to the divine, descending from there hastens back up to its kin."—*Ibid.*

[572] *Op. cit.*, p. 5.

> undaunted in Danger, Valiant without Cruelty. Who loves Justice with moderation, Government without Tyranny, . . .[573]

The virtuous action of the person praised may be, according to classical authority, enhanced by pointing out that he was unspoiled by wealth or power. In a parallel way, Wadsworth says,

> Some Persons when advanced to highest Power and Authority, have given up themselves to the most sluggish ease, the most shameful Licentiousness, and the most bruitish pleasures: . . . Such were several of the *Roman Emperors* . . . But our Deceased, Bewailed Sovereign, was quite contrary. He was ever ready to deny Himself . . .[574]

Even the reference to the Roman emperors (a reference more expanded in the original than we quote here) is reminiscent of classical instructions to incorporate, by way of illustration or authority, what was said or done by some notable person in history or literature. The abundant use of authority in later sophistic is an accumulative process of the same idea.

Virtuous action, according to these rhetoricians, may be emphasized not only by showing the man to be above the petty use of wealth and power, but also, at the other extreme, by showing his commendable actions in spite of poverty or other adverse circumstances. Cotton Mather's funeral sermon on Michael Wigglesworth, although it gives the family background and the chronological sequence of events, does, for the most part, praise the victory of the man over adverse circumstances.

On the whole, these are very striking resemblances of our early sermons having to do with the praise of one living or dead to the general process of composition for the classical

[573] *Ibid.*, p. 7.
[574] *Ibid.*, p. 8.

orations of consolatory speeches, funeral sermons, and public address.[575]

There are two other forms of specified literary composition in later classical writing that bear directly on our subject and that serve once more to bind together the aphoristic essay and the sermon. For the undoubted ancestors of these are the *chria*, or moral essay, and the *epigram* of ancient rhetoric.

Quintilian instructs: the pupil "should be set to write *sententia*, *chriae*, and *ethologiae*, of which the teacher will first give the general scheme, since such themes will be drawn from their reading."[576] In these three types that he mentions are surely the literary ancestors of the popular aphorism, the moral essay, and the "character"—all integral parts of the seventeenth century prose of England and America. "In all of these exercises," he continues, "the general idea is the same, but the form differs: *aphorisms* are general propositions, while *ethologiae* are concerned with persons. Of *moral essays* there are various forms: some are akin to *aphorisms* and commence with a simple statement." Here he gives several examples, one of which is " 'Milo, having accustomed himself to carrying a calf every day, ended by carrying it when grown to a bull.' All these instances," he points out, "are couched in the same grammatical form . . ." We can remember such beginnings are characteristic of the essay and sermon.[577]

But we can go further. Hermogenes, in the second century, sets down some "elementary exercises" for sophistic, among which instructions for developing the *chria* are carefully given:

> A chria is a concise exposition of some memorable saying or deed, generally for good counsel.
>
> Some chriae are of words, others of deeds, still others

[575] Menander further states that "death lies beyond life and that heroes and children of gods do not escape it." "On Consolation." This is distinctly the repeated note of the seventeenth century funeral sermon.

[576] *Quint.*, I, ix, 3.

[577] *Supra*, p. 156.

> of both: of words, i.e., essentially sayings, as "Plato said that the Muses dwell in the souls of the fit"; of deeds, i.e., essentially doings, as "Diogenes, seeing an ill-bred youth, smote his tutor, saying, 'Why did you teach him thus?' " . . .
>
> Let this working out [of the chria] be as follows: first, brief encomium of the sayer or doer; then paraphrase of the chria itself; then proof or explanation. For example, Isocrates said that the root of education is bitter, but its fruit sweet: (1) encomium, "Isocrates was wise," and you will slightly develop this topic; (2) chria, "said, etc.," and you will not leave this bare, but develop the significance; (3) proof, (a) direct, "the greatest affairs are usually established through toil, and, once established, bring happiness"; (b) by contrast, "those affairs which succeed by chance require no toil and their conclusion brings no happiness; quite the contrary with things that demand our zeal"; . . . (c) by illustration, "as the farmers toil ought to reap fruit, so with speeches"; (d) by example, "Demosthenes, who shut himself up in his room and labored much, finally reaped his fruit, crowns and public proclamations." (e) You may cite authority, as "Hesiod says, 'Before virtue the gods have put sweat'; and another poet says, 'The gods sell all good things for labor.' " (4) Last you will put an exhortation to follow what was said or done.[578]

His instructions for the proverb are similar:

> A proverb is a summary saying, in a statement of general application, dissuading from something or persuading toward something, or showing what is the nature of each: . . .
>
> The working out is similar to that of the chria; for it proceeds by (1) brief encomium of him who made the saying, as in the chria; (2) direct exposition; (3) proof; (4) contrast; (5) enthymeme; (6) illustration; (7) example; (8) authority.[579]

These instructions for the *chria* and the proverb sound familiar and they display, indeed, the processes of development, as we found them, in the analysis of the didactic essay and the sermon: a notable beginning sentence that is usually

[578] Baldwin, *Medieval Rhetoric*, pp. 26, 27.
[579] *Ibid.*

a saying of a distinguished person; perhaps, though not necessarily, a tribute to the wisdom of the one quoted; and a development of the saying, showing its truth, by the processes of exposition, of proof by expansion or contrast, of illustration, of example, of authority; and finally the exhortation or moral derived from the whole.

The *chria* and the *epigram,* the sermon and the essay, whether written or spoken, are, like the epideictic oratory of Quintilian's definition, persuasive or advisory, holding up their subjects to blame or praise.

THE TIMES OPINIONISTS ANSWERED

From the time that Captain John Smith originated American literature with his account of Virginia to the time that Cotton Mather published a collection of short prose pieces which he called *Essays to Do Good*, our first settlers maintained a versatile and "lively" interest in writing and planted a rich field for our later non-fictional prose.

The surprising fact about these authors in a wilderness is that their writings were neither crude in expression nor limited in subject. Their work is not a collection of haphazard jottings; nor is it confined to moral preachments. Though the religious note, like the *motif* of a symphony, threads its way through most of their writings, it does not dominate their literary expression. On the other hand, in regard to literary forms, there is sufficient repetition of kind to indicate an awareness of literary composition. There are to be found, therefore, certain literary types predominating: besides the more casual writings of the letter, the diary, and the autobiography—and even they have certain similarities—there are the "pamphlet of newes," the short didactic and informative "essays" of the almanac, the scientific "essays," the critical prefaces, the meditation, and the sermon. And incorporating all the styles and forms of the age, like a kind of literary epitome, looms the work of Cotton Mather, a man as conscious of literary style as any other prose writer in England or America of the seventeenth century.

That our forefathers were alert to timely matters is evident in their papers of immediate interest and concern, in their almanacs, and in their scientific papers. The "pamphlet of newes" described the new country in glowing, yet frequently accurate terms, and in so doing imitated in form the travel books established during the period of Elizabethan adventure. More frequently than otherwise the enthusiasm manifest in these pamphlets raised the quality of prose from a mere recording to that of real literary flavor. Captain

John Smith, William Wood, and Daniel Denton, for instance, at their best and most accurate moments, anticipate the later American writers of nature. On the other hand, there were also the simple and unadorned records in the work of men like William Penn.

Quite a different group of writings, the "witchcraft papers," also showed the colonists' interests in concerns of the day. Here one is impressed not so much by the fanaticism of 1692 as by the logical arguments presented for and against the case of witchcraft. Granted a belief in the existence of Satan and his cohorts, their thought becomes surprisingly analytical and critical. Although there were many zealous papers "proving" the existence of witches, there were also papers that showed a spirit of skepticism and an anticipation of the age of reason. Indeed, this critical spirit probably accounts for the fact that the period of hysteria was short-lived compared with its history in other countries.

There were many other papers on miscellaneous questions of the day, but perhaps the most interesting of these are George Keith's and Samuel Sewall's protests against slavery, William Hooke's effusion on the horrors of war, and Ward's caustic remarks on people and customs that irritated him.

One of the most interesting sources of literary beginnings in early America is the almanac, of greater importance in America than in contemporary England because its composition was in the hands of educated men. Here are paragraphs of miscellaneous information, of moral uplift, and of scientific observations. Such people as the Mathers found it not a bad practice to fill up a space "that would otherwise be vacant" with a short moral discourse. And they and others, too, found it appropriate to put into their almanacs discussions of astronomical matters.

America's first scientific articles began in these and in the letters and travel books of the time. Here, again, one is impressed not so much by superstition as by the actual scientific spirit of investigation; not so much by assumptions as by the consistent attempts at accurate observation. Astronomy was taking the place of astrology; and geology, botany, meteorology, zoölogy, medicine, and anthroponomics were taking their place as the beginnings of our scientific literature. Some observations, like Winthrop's accurate description of the "basket-fish," found their way to the Royal Society of London, of which Winthrop and Cotton Mather were members. And such studies of Indian life as are to be found in the work of Smith, Wood, and Williams are sufficiently accurate and interesting to be a permanent source of information and enjoyment.

The interest in timely matters such as we find in the "pamphlet of newes" and scientific papers showed very naturally in the letters, diaries, and journals. Obviously the most important news to friends in England would be a description of the new country or an account of the colonists' activities. These matters, along with gossipy items about the neighbors, were the content of the personal records. In the letters, also, was advice, frequently couched in the epigrammatic sentiments of "wisdom literature," to members of the family. And into the diary and the autobiography crept the more subjective note of religious fervor, of intimate struggles with God and of adult confessions of childhood sins, in the manner of *Grace Abounding*.

The prefaces and introductions to publications in America before 1710 betray our forefathers' insatiable desire to express themselves. Here they seem at liberty to do as they please. In the South, Captain John Smith and George Alsop talk in bantering familiarity with their patrons and readers. In the New England colonies, in more serious vein, the eminent divines take occasion to analyze the subject of the book or occasionally to give their critical estimates of literature. The latter provide for us our beginnings in literary criticism, notably in the *Bay Psalm Book* and in the prefaces to histories. In the former, are definite theories on literal translation and the writing of verse; in the latter, theories of correct historical writing: truth to fact and simple telling. The most notable contributor to the preface in literary criticism is Cotton Mather, especially in his introductions to the different books of the *Magnalia.* Here he expounds his ideas on style and on historical writing. In him, above all the rest, is the conscious formulation of theories of writing, apparent in such examples as his defensive preface of elaborate writing and his definitions of poetry and style.

The prefaces, the almanacs, and the timely papers were the media for the satire and invective of our seventeenth century. Here the almanac-makers betrayed their jealousy of rivals in their caustic accusations of inaccuracy and ignorance. Here John Cotton and Roger Williams indulged in polemical invective. Here Nathaniel Ward expressed in sharp and clever thrusts his intolerance of toleration. And here Cotton Mather created his simple and well-written "Political Fables."

Perhaps the most literary of the early types of American prose were the meditation, the religious discourse, and the beginnings of biography. Contrary to the supposition that these, like poetry, would be limited by religious dogma, they were, perhaps, the most creative of all the types of our early literature, excepting, of course, the individual work of Cotton Mather. They are the most akin to one of our creative forms, the essay. Whether the meditation exists individually or collectively, it is like the essay in substance. It has the brooding, meditative quality, the subjective outlook upon life. The sermon itself, in expanded form, is like the aphoristic and didactic essay of the seventeenth century: the striking thesis, its development by explication, illustration, anecdote, and its moral conclusion. It is like it in its use of epigrammatic statement. And it is like it, finally, in its predilection for the abstract theme. In the sermon, also, are to be found the use and influence of other established literary forms: of character and *exempla,* particularly in the funeral sermons of eminent men; of courtesy books, especially in the election sermons. Here, too, is the inheritance of the classical and medieval rhetoric: in the preparation, composition, and delivery of the sermon are the methods of rhetoric established by Aristotle and Cicero; in the tendency to display and the motivation of praise and blame is the legacy of epideictic oratory; in the logical development and the love of authority, are the influences of forensic oratory and of medieval sophistic; and, finally, in the development of the sermon, as well as the seventeenth century essay, is traceable the form of the *chria*. Here then, in the sermon, are manifest many forces of literary models at work. Surely the sermon is, indeed, the most potential literary creation of seventeenth century America.

And out of the sermon, especially of the funeral sermon, like a kind of literary by-product, was developing the literary biography—truly biographical in proportion as the authors added data from the lives of the eminent and good men whom they portrayed.

Altogether what have we inherited from this literary beginning? We can make only tentative conclusions, but the strong sympathy between our literary feeling, then and now, would seem to justify our theories in this direction. In our critical essay may be traced the inherited love of analysis so very characteristic of the chief forms in the "creative literature" of Colonial times. To this branch, with its conscious sense of form, we must inevitably owe our later sense of logical development in the formal essay.

Our chief inheritance from the past would seem to be the didactic impulse which we found was the motivating force of these forms of literature from the short essays of the almanac to the sermon; and revolving around this, the rhetorical inheritance of the classics. For it was the early didactic essay or sermon that inspired other noteworthy writers who succeeded our preachers. A memorable lesson or moral was most effective in epigrammatic form. The truth of this was recognized by Franklin in the eighteenth century and Emerson in the nineteenth. We speak of Franklin as a Yankee. He was really the Puritan grown more shrewd and sophisticated. He was still extremely moral in his writings and given to delivering preachments. Poor Richard, worldly wise, speaks in moral epigrams. Silence Dogood, who shrewdly comments upon her contemporaries, owes her existence to Cotton Mather's *Essays to Do Good*.

We do not now think of this moral quality as a part of our national character. And yet, our critical articles to-day are extremely didactic, though we hide our purpose of teaching very subtly. A great part of our apparently impersonal criticism has its impetus in the desire of the writer to teach the public to see things as he thinks they are. Such a writer, of course, does not state a moral. The sermon now remains in the pulpit. But the moral purpose, the desire to teach, the love of analysis, are permanent attributes of our character. We are essentially a nation of reformers with its center still in New England.

Our literature is fundamentally *epideictic*. Our essays, our editorials, our political orations are persuasive and advisory; and they hold up people and things to praise and blame. And in the recent past, at least, the display implied in the term *epideictic* and the methods of rhetoric in classical oratory were still characteristic of our oratorical literature. Edward Everett reached the heights in this kind of oratory. Mr. Burgess says,

> This most Hellenic of modern speakers, throughout his long and noteworthy career as an orator, devoted himself almost wholly to themes which must be classed as epideictic. His oration on Washington presents one of the most perfect compositions in the history of this most conspicuous form—the eulogy. Many others, whose chief activities were in court speeches or in the discussion of state questions, have won even greater distinction in orations clearly belonging to the epideictic branch. Robert Winthrop, Rufus Choate, Daniel Webster, Wendell Phillips, George William Curtis are notable names.[580]

It was in vain, for a time at least, that Lincoln demonstrated at Gettysburg that an effective speech need not be elaborate or lengthy. Orators to-day realize the effectiveness of short speeches. Nevertheless the appeal of epideictic

[580] Theodore Chalon Burgess, "Epideictic Literature," *Studies in Classical Philology*. Vol. III, Reprint (University of Chicago Press, 1902).

oratory is still with us, stripped a little of its sophistic elaboration because the times call for brevity.

Aside from the short-story, which we have made our own peculiar creative art, the essay has been a constant medium for our American literature. Our magazines are dependent upon them. Our nation is, first of all, a nation of prose, particularly short prose. It suits our practical sense and our need of a short medium in which we can express our inherited zeal for reform and analysis. The creative arts of fiction and drama did not take their important place in America until the nineteenth century, and until then poetry was occasional and episodic. The seventeenth century on the other hand, prepared the way, at least, for the essay of analysis and instruction.

Two accusations have been hurled by the "Time's opinionists" against this early period of American literature: one, that the writings were chiefly theological and two, that they were not original but imitative. These accusations are true, but not with the implications with which they were uttered. All writing during this period was imitative and most of it was theological. But these facts are virtues rather than failings.

The stern moral codes of Calvinism had, indeed, suppressed the youthful creative spirit that characterized the Elizabethan period in England so that America was poor in beginnings of verse and drama. On the other hand, the classical training of the minister and his constant activity in speaking and writing continually promoted a literary interest and a taste for the best in thought and form. It is to be noted that the South, unhampered by such disciplinary training, was interested chiefly in the transitory tales of adventure and contributed much less of lasting value. The very qualities of these religious colonies were, after all, the *raison d'etre* for the literature that was established in America and that formed the background for that "New England culture" that has since been its proud boast.

The New England preacher composed his sermons not only to be spoken, but to be read. The immediate impulse of these compositions had been to teach (*docere*) the congregation the ways of the righteous. But, because of the ethical and moral sympathy between the theologians and classical rhetoricians; because of the tradition of oratory handed down from the classics through the Church Fathers and through the study of Cicero; because the Renaissance had revived classical learning, and the Reformation, carrying on the classical tradition, had stimulated it through preaching and oratory, New England inherited the wealth of the past. Having contemplated the stars and the earth and found them of mysterious and divine force, the New Englander made our first reasonable efforts at scientific truths. Having an innate love of analysis, he investigated and criticized the problems of the day. Having meditated upon the moral forces that govern all peoples of all time, he treated with respect the classical tradition and created for his own community his sermons modelled upon the principles of rhetoric. The immediate impulse for expression was Calvinism; but its method was classical rhetoric.

Our answer to the "Time's opinionists" is that, though the period of American literature from 1607-1710 may have failed to produce literature that may be called "great"; though it may be said, in fact, to be practically devoid of the happy spirit that is the inspiration of *belles-lettres,* it did establish a worthy background for later, more sophisticated literature. Our early literature, produced in a difficult period of settlement, might justifiably have been an unadorned and dutiful record of facts, a "literature of knowledge." But, instead, it was touched by the personal interpretations which lifted it, however naïvely, into the "literature of power." It had a literary consciousness manifest in its active interest in the world of men and of God, and in its recognition of certain established literary forms. It was perhaps fortunate that the beginnings of our prose occurred simultaneously with the greatest prose period of England, and that, although we had no John Milton or Jeremy Taylor, we were influenced like them by stern moral codes, strict mental discipline, and respect for the past.

POETRY

Cotton Mather, addressing young men about to enter the ministry, recommended to them "some acquaintance" with poetry. "I cannot wish you," he said, "a Soul that shall be wholly *unpoetical*."[581]

The Puritans had closed the theatres not because they distrusted the art of drama as such but because it had become corrupt. They did not wholly reject the other arts, and when "souls poetical" were inspired, they composed verse.

To discuss each poet of all the English colonies would require another volume. It seems sufficient here to examine certain characteristics of their poetry and to discuss more completely only a few outstanding poets.

One of the noteworthy facts evident in previous chapters of this study, is that most of the prose types had their counterparts in poetry; and, indeed, they were often intertwined. William Wood sang his praises of New England in poetry that ended every chapter of his "true, lively, and experimental description" of the colony.[582] John Josselyn, botanist, ended his text with a delightful portrait of an "Indian Squa," done up in rhyming couplet.[583] Sarah K. Knight, after a hard day's journey by horseback, during her trip from Boston to New York and back, adorned her journal in amused, bemused, or romantic sentiments in lively, rhyming couplets, about the country and people she saw. Kept awake in an inn by rowdy guests next door, she prayed for the aid of "potent rum" to silence them.

> I ask thy aid, O potent rum!
> To charm these wrangling topers dumb.

[581]*Supra*, p. 336.
[582]*Supra*, p. 12 f.
[583]*Supra*, p. 72.

Thou hast their giddy brains possessed—
The man confounded with the beast;
And I, poor I, can get no rest.
Intoxicate them with thy fumes!
O still their tongues till morning comes!

Thomas Morton, a seventeenth century hippie, annoyed by the frowns of the Puritans, composed a merrie drinking song celebrating May Day and beginning:

Drink and be merry, merry, merry boys;
Let all your delight be in Hymen's joys
Make green garlands, bring bottles out,
And fill sweet nectar freely about; . . .[584]

Another Morton, Charles, a respected minister and teacher at Charlestown, interspersed his text on physics with philosophic couplets.[585] Roger Williams ended every chapter of his book on the Indian language with skillfully wrought stanzas on the subject just discussed.[586] The almanac makers and Nathaniel Ward were experts in the art of satiric verse—Ward's, again, scattered among his prose.[587] Cotton Mather and many others, with varying degrees of success, wrote elegies on the deaths of prominent colonists. And Richard Mather, with two other ministers, plodded their conscientious way through the translation of the Psalms to make them fit established meters and tunes for hymn singing.[588] The result was the *Bay Psalm Book*, which, however it butchered the original, was completely accepted by the Puritans for church services.

In the southern colonies there were, also, active writers of verse. George Alsop adorned his chapters on *A Character of Maryland* with poetry.[589] Richard Rich wrote a long and often vivid account in ballad stanzas of the wreck of Sir Thomas Gates' company on the shores of the Bermudas and

[584] (This may be an adaptation of some English song for May Day).
[585] *Supra*, p. 38 f.
[586] *Supra*, p. 75.
[587] *Supra*, p. 135 and 47–55 *passim*.
[588] *Supra*, p. 107 f.
[589] *Supra*, p. 14.

their eventual success in reaching America. It has been suggested that it inspired Shakespeare's writing of *The Tempest.*

The seas did rage, the winds did blow,
  distressèd were they then;
Their ship did leak, her tacklings break, in
  danger were her men.
But Heaven was pilot in this storm, and to
  an island near,
Bermoothawes called, conducted them,
  which did abate their fear.

But yet these worthies forcèd were,
  oppressed with weather again,
To run their ship between two rocks, where
  she doth still remain;
And then on shore the island came,
  inhabited by hogs,
Some fowl and tortoises there were. . . .

The full title of the poem describes the island where the ship was wrecked as an "Island of Devils." The future hope of these suffering people lies in the birth of "a son and a daughter," and, after "two and forty weeks," the group sets sail again and finally reaches Virginia. The details of the storm, the island of devils, the romantic suggestion of the hope in the two young people, the departure for civilization lend credence to the possibility that Shakespeare's imagination was stimulated by Rich's poem.

Perhaps the strangest phenomenon, in some respects, was the translation of Ovid's *Metamorphoses* by George Sandys, while he attended to official business in the government of Virginia,—one of the finest pieces of literary work to come out of the English colonies. He began it in England and stayed with it in Virginia, despite what might seem a discouraging background with a colony just emerging from a wilderness. To quote only a few lines from here would do it an injustice.

Philip Pain, a young man who lost his life by drowning, wrote some melancholy but effective poems on the inevitability of death.

This World a Sea of trouble is, and Man
Is swimming through this vast wide Ocean.
The billows beat, the waves are angry, and
'Tis seldome that he spies a helping hand
  To buoy his head up. O great God, let me
  Be kept from sinking into misery.

These poets of the northern and southern colonies mentioned above are only a few representative ones. Among the rest, there are three outstanding: one whose volume of verse was the first published by a British American—and the first to be published by a woman, British or American; another, whose most famous poem was read almost as much as the Bible; and a third, whose poetry was not discovered until the twentieth century.

The first of these is Anne Bradstreet, whose *The Tenth Muse* was published in London in 1650 without her previous knowledge. It is doubtful that so modest a woman as she was would have consented to so immodest a title. Reared in affluent surroundings on the estate of the Earl of Lincoln, whose most trusted friend and steward was her father, she had access to a fine library. Her father, also a poet of sorts, encouraged her in education, and she devoured such books as Du Bartas' *Divine Weeks and Works* and Sir Walter Raleigh's *History of the World*, the two books of greatest influence on her early poetry. At the age of eighteen, just two years married to Simon Bradstreet, she emigrated with her family with the Massachusetts Bay Colony in 1630. Used to comfort and ease, her "heart rose" against the prospect before her when they arrived at their new home of Salem. Yet in spite of these new trials, or perhaps because of them, she turned to the writing of poetry that was to compose her first volume. She continued in spite of bad health and presently a growing family that was to number eight children.

That first volume was highly imitative in verse structure and subject matter of Du Bartas and in subject matter, too, of Sir Walter Raleigh. Seeing her verse in print, she was embarrassed at its weakness. Over the years that followed she composed lyric poetry of a personal nature, freer in form and subject matter, that was to enlarge the first edition into a second, not published, however, until two years after her death. Her later work showed maturity and charm. Among these is the familiar "To my dear and loving Husband," which has appeared in nearly every anthology of early American literature since Conrad Aiken discovered her worth for that purpose in 1929.* Her love poems and her elegiac verse can stand proudly beside seventeenth century English verse. Her "The Flesh and the Spirit" received high praise from the distinguished critic Samuel Eliot Morison, who has also called her "the greatest American poetess before Emily Dickinson." Her "Contemplations" will always be a fine representation of her work not only for their skillful poetic form but for their lofty poetic ideas, not the least of which was the recognition of beauty and God in nature.[590]

> Silent alone, where none or saw, or heard,
> In pathless paths I lead my wandring feet,
> My humble Eyes to lofty Skyes I rear'd
> To sing some Song, my mazed Muse thought meet.
> My great Creator I would magnifie,
> That nature had, thus decked liberally:
> But Ah, and Ah, again, my imbecility!

Michael Wigglesworth, the second poet of special mention, was the author of *The Day of Doom* (1662) which is to us now a literary oddity of only historical importance but was in its day almost as familiar and as widely read as the Bible. It was, in fact, considering the small population, a best seller. Its first edition of 1800 copies was almost exhausted within a year after publication. There were other related poems in the volume and there was to be another with the title *Meat Out of the Eater.* If one can forget its jogging ballad stanzas, repetitious in meter and rhyme, one can find in it some powerfully descriptive passages concerning human beings faced

*The Trent and Wells anthologies of colonial American literature (1901), had admirable selections from her poetry, but later anthologists failed to do her justices.

[590]For a critical study of her work, see this author's Anne Bradstreet (New York, 1965.)

with the terrifying day of the last judgment. The purpose of the poem was to jolt the poet's contemporaries out of their growing complacency and to refresh their memories on Calvinistic dogma, reminding them of the doctrine of election and of the inevitable day of doom. It taught adults and it taught children, who memorized all or parts of its two hundred twenty-four stanzas. Our amusement at the frequently quoted lines as to God's modified punishment for the children who "from the womb unto the tomb were straightway carried" —to send them to "the easiest room in hell"—has blinded us to its more meritorious stanzas. For example there is sheer terror, ably described, in stanzas 11 and 12:

> Mean men lament, great men do rent
> their Robes, and tear their hair:
> They do not spare their flesh to tear
> through horrible despair.
> All Kindreds wail: all hearts do fail:
> horror the world doth fill
> With weeping eyes, and loud out-cries,
> yet knows not how to kill.
> Some hide themselves in Caves and Delves,
> in places under ground:
> Some rashly leap into the Deap,
> to scape by being drown'd:
> Some to the Rocks (O senseless blocks!)
> and woody Mountains run,
> That there they might this fearful sight,
> and dreaded Presence shun.

Other stanzas are equally vivid. The lack of interest on our part is due partly to the fact that Calvinist doctrine seems remote to most of us, but largely because we grow tired of the verse form. Michael Wigglesworth had one thing to talk about—the approaching Day of Doom—and practically only one way to say it,—in the ballad stanzas. Only a few of his shorter poems like "Vanity of Vanities" and one longer, "New England's Prospect," sublimate their form to their content sufficiently to make us forget the former in our interest in the subject. "New England's Prospect,"[591] furthermore, varies its

[591]The complete poem can be found in *Proc. Mass. Hist. Soc.*, 1st Ser., XII (1873), 83–93.

verse form. Unfortunately the oddities of *The Day of Doom* have overpowered the virtues of "New England's Prospect"; but, even so, in the former the poet is able to take a Biblical verse or a theological argument and turn it into a thing of terror. In America of the seventeenth century, the poem was not taken lightly.

America's scholarly discovery of the twentieth century was the manuscript poems of Edward Taylor, New England preacher of Westfield, Connecticut, who emigrated from England to America when he was twenty-six. Though he wrote poetry voluminously, only a very few of his poems were published in his lifetime, and his request that they not be published was respected for more than two centuries. Most of them lay in manuscript form in the archives of Yale University until Thomas H. Johnson gave some of them recognition in the *New England Quarterly* in 1937.[592] After that, other scholars became interested in the poet, and in 1960, after publishing articles about him, Donald E. Stanford issued a complete edition of *The Poems of Edward Taylor*,[593] a monumental task since Taylor's fine script is almost indecipherable.

Edward Taylor and Michael Wigglesworth had their eyes on the Hereafter; but, though their theology, which embraced Calvinism and the doctrine of the elect, was alike, their attitudes and their means of expressing it were poles apart. Basically they were inspired by the same subject, the act of communion in the church, but their feelings for it were like darkness and light. According to Puritan belief, one was truly converted to God and the church through *sanctification*, a kind of mystical union with Christ, most properly felt in the act of communion. Then and then only would one become a member of the Christian family with Christ as the head.

Perhaps because of his first hazardous years in Massachusetts and his ill health, Wigglesworth's mind was abnormally ridden with a sense of guilt even over the most trivial matters, over anything that gave him pleasure. He was respected as

[592]Vol. X (June, 1937), pp. 290–322.

[593]Yale University Press, 1960. For a critical study of Taylor, see also Norman S. Grabo, *Edward Taylor*, (New York, 1961).

a teacher at Harvard, from which he graduated, and as a physician; yet nothing brought him a sense of security about this world or the next. He could not, therefore, partake of communion without despairing doubt. It is no wonder, then, that he had a morbid dream that inspired his most famous poem or that his mind dwelt on the terrors of hell; no wonder that, in brooding over his own supposed failures in the face of Heaven, as his diary shows, he was moved to warn others of the day of doom ahead of them. Though Taylor was aware of his own disease of sin, his hope for cure was always dominant:

> Woe's mee, Undone! Undone! my Leprosy!
> Without a Miracle there is no Cure.

Meditation 27 in "Preparatory Meditations" (Second Series) begins on this self-accusing note but ends, as most of his poems do, on a note of hope and faith.

> Lord, Cleanse mee thus with thy Rich Bloods Sweet Shower
> My Issue stop: destroy my Leprosy.
> Thy Holy Oyle upon my Head out poure
> And cloathe my heart and life with Sanctity.
> My Head, my Hand and Foot shall strike thy praise,
> If thus besprinkled, and Encamp thy Wayes.

Despite his awareness of hell, Taylor's eyes are on his admission into heaven, an experience and a place which he describes in rich, sensuous images, as in Meditation 47 (First Series).[594]

> My stain will out: and swelling swage apace.
> And holy Lusters on my shape appeare.
> All Rosie Buds: and Lilly flowers of grace
> Will grace my turfe with sweet sweet glory here.
> Under whose shades Angells will bathing play
> Who'l guard my Pearle to glory, hous'd in clay.
> Those Gates of Pearle, porter'd with Seraphims,
> On their carbuncle joynts will open wide.
> And entrance give me where all glory swims

[594]Donald E. Stanford, *The Poems of Edward Taylor* "Preparatory Meditations." (New Haven, 1960) .

In to the Masters Joy, e're to abide.
O sweet sweet thought. Lord take this praise though thin.
And when I'm in't Ile tune an higher pin.

In Taylor's poetry, then, there is none of the real terror contained in Wigglesworth's.

The inspiration for most of Taylor's poetry is the sacrament which he approached with joyous conviction. Most of his poems are meditations in preparation for the sacrament, each of which accompanies a sermon. They are the work of a skilled and sophisticated poet, in marked contrast to that of Wigglesworth. The earlier poet wrote in simple form and language that was concrete and easy to read in order to reach a large audience; the later poet wrote, apparently, for his own satisfaction. Influenced by Herbert and other metaphysical poets, his thought is hidden in complex symbolism. He uses, however, simple images derived from the familiar and the domestic as in the often quoted poem, "Huswifery," which is built around a consistent and sustained image of the spinning wheel. Meditation Eight (First Series)[595] in the service of communion is described with domestic images familiar to every Puritan. The bread of Holy Communion is

Food too fine for Angells, yet come, take
and eat thy fill. It's Heavens Sugar Cake.[596]

Edward Taylor may never have achieved the greatness of contemporary English metaphysical poets, but then they were giants. His poetry, however, is often distinguished. It is always challenging even when the challenge is to extricate the meaning among complicated imagery—even so, he was clearer than many of his English contemporaries. He has sometimes been called our first real poet. This is highly debatable since the lyrics of Mistress Bradstreet stand on their own right as excellent poetry.

[595]Preparatory Meditations.

[596]An excellent analysis of Taylor's work may be found in Norman S. Grabo, *Edward Taylor* (New York, 1961). Also, the best study of Taylor's poetry with sermons is *Edward Taylor's* CHRISTOGRAPHIA, edited with an introduction by Mr. Grabo. (New Haven, 1962).

The Times' Opinionists must recognize eventually that Anne Bradstreet and Edward Taylor must take their place among seventeenth century poets on their own right. Their ideas, their emotions, their expert writing raise their poetry above mere historical curiosities. It must recognize, also, that one of the Puritans' favorite pastimes seemed to be the writing of poetry.

ALMANACS

A breif [*sic*] *Explication and proof of the Thiloaick Systems.*[1]

That which the studious in Astronomy have propounded to themselves, as the main end & scope, to which they have directed their endeavours, hath beē ye finding out of some rational way, for ye salving of ye Coelestial appearances; In order to which there hath been a three-fold hypothesis invented; sc: the Ptolemaick, Tychonick & Philolaick; To let pass any further mention of the two former, the frame of ye last is as follows:

In the lowest room of the World, is placed the Sun, which challengeth to it self a centrall motion, finish't in ye space of about 26 dayes; which is evidenced by the late admirable invention of the Telescope, by which, the Solar spots are discovered to move round the body of ye Sun, from the celerity of whose motion nigh the middle of ye Solar disce, & tardity when they approach either limb of ye same, may more then conjecturally be drawn that they are contiguous to the body of ye Sun, of whose motion they participate: Next in order above ye Sun, moves ye Planet Mercury, and finishes his course in about 88 dayes. To whom succeeds Venus who accomplisheth her period in 225 dayes, After Venus is placed ye Earth, which besides her diurnal revolution in 24 houres, hath an Anual periodical motion through ye Ecliptique, performed in 365 dayes: about the Earth as its center, the secondary Planet the Moon is carryed, which goes from, & returnes to, the same point in ye Zodiaque in ye space of 27 dayes, which measures the periodical month. The next primary Planet is Mars, who finisheth his course in 2 yeares.

[1] Zech. Brigden, *An Almanack ... for 1659* (Boston). Only known copy, LC.

Jupiter takes his place next after Mars and paceth round ye Sun in 12 yeares; about whom as in an epicycle move 4 other Planets, notizable to ye eye without the help of the Telescope. The last primary Planet, which is highest in place, & consequently slowest in motion; is Saturn, who runs his circuit in no less than 30 yeares: and as the Earth & Jupiter had their moōs or concomitatns [*sic*], so is ye body of this Planet environed by two secondary Planets, not visible without ye help of the forenamed Instrument. In the outmost surface of this visible world, is seated ye Spheare of the fixt Stars, which are altogether voyd of motion, but changably retayn the places assigned them at their Creation.

That this is the true & genuine Systeme of the world, is plainly evinced from its exact squaring with the Phaenomena, for, hence is drawn the reason why Venus & Mercury are never in opposition to ye Sun, & why the contrary is to be seē in the 3 superiour Planets: as also the reason of ye direction, retrogradation & station of ye two inferiour, and three superiour Planets, and why ye Earth and Moon are not subject to the like passions. Further hence may the true places of ye Planets be obtained, and their several inequalityes rectifyed to every point; as is evidently declared & proved by *Mr. Vincent Wing* in his *Astronomia Instaurata.*

Lastly, hence is taken away that gross difformity of motion, & farrago of cōcentrical, eccentrical and epicyclical, whimsyes, which pester the other Hypotheus, they being but meer figments and altogether incompossible with ye uniform motion of ye Planets.

The Objections usually brought to evert the truth of this Systeme are easily answered, by the following propositions:

1. That the *Orbis magnus* in which ye Earth runs its annual circuit, in respect of the Starry sphear, hath no sensible magnitude. *Galalous.*

2. That there is no common Center of gravity: *Kepler, Galil., Digby, Origanus.*

3. That the motion of the Earth from West to East, is communicated, as to all earthly bodyes, so to that portion of

ayre which is contained win [*sic*] y[e] Concave of y[e] Moons Orbe. *Dr. White.*

4. That a common motion of bodyes can imprint no force at all, to hinder, or further their different particular motions. *White Gossend.* Want of room forbids the application of these titles, which yet by the desirer of satisfaction are easily applicable, for the solution of y[e] ordinary objections, whether Astronomical or Physicall.

Those objections that are back't with Divine Authority, though they are most weighty, yet by the maintayners of this Systeme, are not let pass without an answer, the breif wherof is

That the Scriptures being fitted as well to the capacity of the rudest mechanick as of the blest Philosopher, do not intend so much propriety & exactness as playness & perspicuity; and in Philosophicall truths therein contayned, the proper literal sense is alwayes subservient to the casting vote of reason. *Scharpius. Gossend. Fiscerinus.*

The most seemingly contradicting Scripture is *Psal*: 104. *He hath builded* (?) *the Earth*; *upon its Basis, that it should not be removed for ever.*[2] But 1. Place is sometimes taken for the same with order, and in this sense the Earth doth not change it's place, or is not removed. Or 2. The Basis of a figure, is that wheron it rests, answerable to which in y[e] Earth is its center, on which the Earth is so founded, that it cannot suffer a total dissipation.

A breif Discourse of the Rise and Progress of Astronomy.[3]

Man at his first Creation, being endued w[t] an immortal soul, no less enflamed with an insatiable desire after, then active in the eager attainment of all knowledg, was no sooner set by out of the hands of his Maker, upon the Theatre of this Terrestrial world, against those Celestial Lights (though to enamour his soul not incrustate his body as some fabulous

[2] "Who laid the foundations of the earth,
That it should not be moved forever." (Psalm CIV, 5)

[3] S[amuel] C[heever], *An Almanack for . . . 1661* (Cambridg).

Jewish Doctours have fondly conceited,) but being of an upright countenance, an Emblem of his Soveraignty over the Creatures, he quickly fixed his eyes upon those glorious objects then presented to his view, and was as quickly acquainted with their regular harmonious motions, But man now since the lapse, is fallen at so great a distance, that his dim Intellectuall ey by reason likewise of the dark *medium* of ye body can at first give but a probable conjecture, not get a distinct perception of any object whatsoever, so that its no wonder if this as all other sciences in every age do receive but by degrees some small addition, though such indeed was the slow progress this science for a long time made, that minutes not degrees would have been the fittest model to measure her secular motion by. But for the originall thereof, when once it became a nationall study, Egypt (if we may credit her) will willingly assume the invention thereof upon her selfe, from whence this science soon passed into *Greece.* Amongst whom sundry by their curious observations, of the places of the Planets, Eclipses, & Solstices, brought no little light to Astronomy, though in what manner those motions were performed, was to them unknown, Till at length *Aristarchus Samius* conceiving it far more rational to assign an uniform motion to those Celestial bodyes, and that those strange antick gestures of the Planets, of running back, standing still, comming close to us, and then flying from us were no way consistent with the common received principles of Decency; took no little paines to find out some rational Hypothesis to salve these *Phenomena*, trying therefore every way, at length set the earth a going, and allotting it a place among ye other Planets, soon drew out the real platform of the visible world, which Hypothesis, *Pythagoras* & others in that age readily embraced, But their followers fearfull to goe on in his way, thought it farr more secure to come down and rest in the Center, and they chose therefore to sit vailed in obscurity, apprehending it better reason that the light should turne about to them, then they to it. And now *Eudexus* a man probably better skilled in Architecture then Astronomy, frames in his Dedalaean fancy a strange Fabrick of solid

Orbes enclosed one within another, which by the help of his confederates he at last erected in the heavens, but not living to finish the work his successours, some adding concentrick, some excentrick Orbes to salve the appearances, endeavoured to finish it. Though nothing was done to any purpose, till *Ptolomaus*, 140 yeares post *Christum*, by thrusting in a parcell of Epicycles, was enabled in some measure, as he thought to salve the *Phenomena* which forme of his remained 800 yeares without any great alteration, But this being not yet able to serve the turne, and Posterity finding it indeed too chargeable to keep this costly aedifice in repair, being forced ever and anon to clap in new Epicycles and other Circles to uphold it; to avoide therefore the trouble and charge of new wheeling and joynting this crazy engine, resolved rather to take it quite down, and find out some more easy and rationall way. And now upon diligent perusall of the Records, the ancient opinion of the Earths motion so long slighted, is againe received into favour, the senses continually wafted to and fro therein are voted down as unable to give in true intelligence, their verdict is quite rejected, & Reason is at last landed ashore upon the *Terra Novicognita* of the other Planets, that descrying the motion of this tottering barge, she may accordingly give in true information. *Copernicus* now appeares, and allowing the Earth her diurnall and annuall motion, cleares up by infallible Geometricall demonstrations that all the motions are performed about the Sun the undoubted Center of ye Planetary Orbs, But yet this opinion was not so generally received, but it found opponents, *Tycko* will allow ye Sun ye Center of five of the Planets, and that they can keep their time & distance in the Air without any solid Orbes, but will by no meanes yeild to that Paradox of the Earths motion, and therefore to salve the *Phenomena* rakes up the old rubbish, and introduces imaginary Centers filling the Heavens with fained circles and contrary motions, nor did this his fondling dy together with him, but after his death it was fostered and dandled by his successours, especially *Langomontanus*, who upon this Hypothesis framed tables of the Planetary motions, though how distentaneous they are from the Heavens, the *Ephemerides* of *Erchstadius* as well as of *Argelus* composed from thence do evidently demonstrate. Whereupon in this fast age, *Galilaeus, Bulliadus, Kepterus, Gassendus* and sundry other mathematicians, have learnedly confuted the Ptolemaich & Tychonick Systeme, and demonstrated the Copernican Hypothesis to be most consentaneous to truth and ocular observations as the Ephemerides composed from thence clearly evince, although there are not, and questionlesse never will be wanting those who will be still pleased to censure and cavill at the Hypothesis, as no way suting their own fancy. Thus after many sore and tedious throwes, time obstetricating, at length

Experientia scientiam, Scientia veritatem,
sed veritas odium peperit.

FINIS

The primum mobile[4]

It is received maxim in Philosophy; *Frustra fit per plura, quod potest fiers per pauciora*: which makes Neotericks Lodg [*sic*] the Sun in the Center, to disanull [*sic*] those enterfarings, doublings and redoublings of Circles, which surcharge the Planets with Quicksilver motions, which sometimes inverts, now and then transcends, anon infringes the axioms of Nature. Therefore Method as well in the Heavens, as in Logick, dictates, to them to seek out a new Cause of their motions, besides their Locomotive Soul, which is *Aphilosophen,* and is found as much in Smoak, as in the Heavens.

But as it is said, *Nihil simul inventum et perfectum*: By time and experience Philolaick Astronomers, have found a Clearer Hypothesis to build their Conclusions upon.

The Sun is affixed to his Center form not to move out of it, and yet moves from West to East in the space of 26 dayes, which is proved by Optick Glasses, which discerne lesse bright parts in the Body of the Sun, like fulginous vapours, which move throug [*sic*] the disk of his Body in 13 or 14 dayes.

[4] Nathaniel Chauncy, *An Almanack for . . . 1662* (Cambridg).

As the Sun circumvolues [*sic*] his axis, he sends forth estluxes of light, laden with Electricall Virtue which is the primary cause, amongst Secondary causes of the diverse motions of the greater and lesser planets, according to their intervall distance, or disposition in them to motion, with which magnettical Virtue (whilst the wheels about) he Blases them the same way.

Which is proved both Negatively and affirmatively.

1. Negat: Either they are moved by the magnetical Virtue of the Sun or a *formain formante,* or by intelligences: not by the Second way for, from whence come their irregular Phoenomena's & Anomelous motions: not from this internal principle or Locomotive Soul, for why? It implyes a contradiction, *Nam omnis formis naturalis movet Uniformiter.* Not by one of the Aristotelean Intelligences, for he must be either in the Center of Circumference: not in the Center, for he would then be many Diameters of the Earth distant from some of the Stars, and therefore not move them for *modus operandi Sequitur modum ejsendit.* Not in the Circumference, for then the principle of individuation will be where the body is not.

2. Affir: The Sun (with his influence) in such sort moves those Planets quickest which are neerest itselfe, and those more slow which are farther off: and the same Planet moveth Swiftest when neerer to the Sun, slower when further off: which is plaine in the Magnet, who in a great interval drawes [*sic*] iron more remisely, in a less more [*sic*] Swiftly.

Now the Planets are either primary or Secondary; primary are those who respect the Sun as ye propper [*sic*] Center of motion & Virtue. The Secondary are those, who respect some one of the Primary Planets, as the Center of their motion, as 4 about *Jove*, 2 about *Saturne,* about the earth, which move swifter or more slowly according to her distance from the primary Planets, which is plain in the Moones Apoge's and Periges. Though probable as Pemble saith *Nihil de Caelo, adhuc Certe Novimus*: The Sun by his Magneticall Charmes makes the Primary Planets Dance this Constant Course of inconstancy these illipticall Sallyes, Ebbs and flowes: So that we may say there are certain Oeconomical rules engraven upon every individuall Planet whereby it Expects warrant, and direction for each severall operation from his Superintendent.

The Worlds Eternity *is an* Impossibility.[5]

Impious, Blasphemous, and detractive from the transcendent excellency of the Divine Majesty, have been the bold assertions of men unacquainted with, and unguided by the Spirit of Truth of him who is *Amen, the God of Truth.* Among other their malepert and audacious attempts, they endeavour to enthrone the *World* with the *Antient of Dayes,* to extend a Minute to Eternity, and coequalize a point with him *cujus centrum est ubique et circumferentia nullibi*? Affirming some that the *World was,* others that the *World could be from Eternity.* Which beside the many Scriptural demonstrations founded upon the *αὔτος ἔφη* of Truth it self, Reason presuming none so unreasonable as to maintain the *former,* presents the World with these Arguments to disprove the *latter,* drawn from these four *Topicks*: 1. *A parte creantis.* 2. *A parte creaturæ.* 3. *A Natura creationis.* 4. *A Natura AEternitatis.*

1. *A parte creantis,* because God could not produce by creation, or an external act, a Being coeternal with himself; not to imply any impotency in the Omnipotent, but rather to express his infinite perfection, whose perfect Nature admits of no jarring contradictions: nor hath he made *impossibilities* the object of his power. For that an *efficient* should extrinsecally [*sic*] produce *another entity* contemporary, much more coeternal with it self implies a contradiction.

2. *A parte creaturæ,* though Reason nor Religion will not permit the least *Iota* of detraction from the Almighty, who is *Jehovah,* giving Being to all things, to assert that his infin-

[5] Josiah Flint, *An Almanack . . . for 1666.* (Cambridge). Only known copy, AAS. Josiah Flint, belonging to an old school of thought, is obviously shocked by the new order.

ite power is not eternal and unchangeable, which is *Deus potens, aeternus et immutabilis*: Yet 'tis true and certain, the *Creature*, or rather *Nothing*, which was its first Principle, could not admit a possibility of Being from Eternity; (*In esse subjectivo non objectivo*) for the *Divine Idea* (If I may speak in the dialect of some learned and pious) being God contemplating himself as imitable in the creatures fabrick, or as it was capable to receive the impression of the *Image* or *Vestigium* of those divine perfections which were in himself; it follows that whatever perfection was eminently in God, and the creature was Analogically capable of, was according to divine wisedome expressed (for otherwise the *Idea* or *Exemplar* would not have been consentaneous to the τὸ πρατ'λολэтlo But *Eternity* not being communicated to any created Being, implies that it is no communicable property, so that though we grant *Potentia, Conveniens in Deo,* to be a creator from eternity, yet the incommunicability of Eternity to the Subject, inferrs an impossibility of its eternal existence . . . creation would not be distinguisht [*sic*] from providential conservation, *a creature* might be *ens et non ens* created, and preserved, in the same moment. *Nam creatio ponit non presupponit objectum sed conservatio praesupponit non ponit subjectum.*

4. *A natura AEternitatis.* For Eternity admitts no parenthesis of time, *AEternitatis est interminabilis existentiae possessio.* So that to make the World Eternal is to assert it cosubstantial with *ens primum,* to call the creature Creator, to confound the Truth in contradictions and to give the effect one of the incommunicable properties of its Cause.

A brief Geographicall Description of the WORLD.[6]

The World is by Geographers divided into four parts, *Europe, Asia, Africa,* and *America.*

[6] D[aniel] R[ussell], *An Almanack for 1671* (Cambridge).

Europe, bounded on the North with the *Northern Ocean*, on the South with the *Mediterranean Sea*, on the East with the River *Tanais*, and on the West with the *Western Ocean*, Contains in it these Provinces; *Germany, Italy, France, Spain, Denmark, Norway, Swedeland, Moscovia, Potonia, Hungaria, Schavonia, Graecia*. The most eminent Islands of it are, *England, Scotland, Ireland, Sicilia, Candia, Corsica, Sardinia, Nigropont*. The length of this part of the World is 3000 Miles, the breadth 900.

Asia, the most famous Country in the World, is bounded on the North with the *North Ocean*, on the South with the *Red Sea*, and the Gulfs adjoyning, on the East with the *East Indian Ocean*, and on the West with the Flood *Tanais*: Whose principal Regions are, *Natolia, Syria, Palaestina, Armenia, Arabia, Media, Assyria, Mesopotamia, Chaldaea, Persia, Parthia, Tartaria, China, India*, and the Islands thereof.

Africa is bounded on the East with the *Red Sea*, on the West with the *Atlantick Ocean*, on the South with the *Southern Ocean*, on the North with the *Mediterranean Sea*. The chief Provinces are, *Aegypt, Barbary, Aethiopia, Nubia, Abassines, Alonomatapia, Lybia*. The chief Islands are, *S. Laurence, S. Thomas, Cape de Verde Island, Canary Islands, Madras*, &c.

America, the fourth part of the World, and of latest discovery, is bounded on the East by the *Atlantick Ocean*, on the West with the *West Indian Ocean*, on the North with the *Northern Ocean*, on the South with the *Megallanick Sea*. It consists of two parts, *Mexicana* and *Peruana*. The Provinces of *Mexicana* are, *Nova Hispania, California, Terra Florida*; *Virginia, New England, Nova Francia, Estotiland*. The Islands of it are, *Greenland, Iceland, Friesland*. The Provinces of *Peruana* are, *Brasil, Pis . . de Cabatina, Peru, Chila, Charos, Chien, Patagonos*. The chief Islands are, *Hispaniola, Cuba, Jamaica, Insulae Margaritta, Maiucco Islands, Java Major* and *Minor, Salamonis Insula*, &c.

The names of the chief Seas are, the *Ocean Sea, Narrow*

Sea, Mediterranean Sea, Caspian Sea, East Indian Sea, Red Sea, Persian Sea, South Sea, &c.

Prognosticks of unhealthy Seasons.[7]

The wind blowing Much from the South without rain: wormes in oak-apples: Plenty of frogs, flyes and poysonous creatures: Great and early heates in Spring: Years with little wind and thunder: Flesh or fish soon putrefiing in the open air.

Signs of Wind

Red clouds either in the morning or evening often shooting of stars is a certain sign of wind to follow from that quarter whence they fly: Thunder in a morning is a sign of wind: Spiders will be vediligent before a wind. High winds commonly accompany eclipses of the moon, and calm weather the eclipses of the Sun.

Signs of a Storm

Smaller Stars disappearing; The oft changing of the wind; Lightning from all quarters when the sky seemes to be cleer, are foretokens of a tempest. when the Rayes of the Sun appear before the sun is up, it is a sign of wind and rain the same day; Great heats in summer, end [*sic*] most commonly either with thunder-showers or else wind & rain for many dayes.

Signs of hot weather

Many Batts flying abroad sooner then ordinary, Stars seeming dim and fiery red, a white mist arising out of moors or waters before sun rise, or after sun setting, Kites flying high, Crows and Ravens gaping against the Sun, store of flyes playing in the sun-shine towards night.

Signs of cold Weather

Clouds flying low, seeming to touch the tops of hills is a sign of cold weather, Great companyes of small birds gath-

[7] J[ohn] F[oster], *An Almanack . . . for 1676* (Boston). Only known copy AAS.

ered together in the beginning of Winter, do foretell either cold storms or frosty weather, The extraordinary twinkling of the stars foretelleth an hard frost; Clouds upon heaps like Rocks, in summer hail, and in winter frost and snow.

Signs of fair weather

When the Moon appeares bright and fair soon after the change, or three dayes before the Full, Clouds with golden edges towards Sun-setting, Mists in the evening, The Crow crying betimes in the morning, any of these are usual signs of fair Weather.

A brief Essay to promote a religious improvement of this preceding Calender.[8]

Christian (who ever thou art, into whose hands the foregoing Account of this following year shall come) thou are desired to take notice, thar [that?] the Composer of this (his intended last of this kind) hath a designe, (through and beyond the glittering out-side of the beautiful Heavens, to lead thee into the Palace of the inconceivably glorious King: where, what is to be seen and Everlastingly enjoyed, is far above mine (or an Angels) ability to relate, or thine to understand. Though I never was so Astrologically opinionated, as to think that the Stars were intended for windows, through which poor mortals might peep and steal a look into the sacred Decrees, and secret Counsels of the most High: yet sure I am, they are a considerable part of the Heavenly Host, Deut. 4.19. by which as Instruments the Sovereign Lord and Ruler of the World bringeth about and Effecteth great things, Judg. 5.20. and that in a way to man, past finding out, Joh. 9.9,10. and Chap. 38.31,32. By their Light, the poor Heathen from their dark Dungeon could discern an Eternal Almighty Deity, Rom. 1.20. how much more of the Admirable glory of that first and best of Beings, who made and upholdeth all things by the word of his Power? may Christians be advan-

[8] J[ohn] S[herman], *An Almanack . . . for 1677* (Cambridge).

taged, from off a Mount of Vision, to discover and observe: May they not be looked at as the Imbellishment and Imbroydery of the beautiful Cover of the great Volume of our Heavenly Makers works? or a Divine Hymne, printed off in Letters of gold, to be made use of by all the Sons of God, Job. 38.7. in singing out the high praises of the ever-glorious Creator, Psal. 145.10, and 148.3. Their number none can count, nor measure their stupendous distance from this Earthly Globe, nor determine their Magnitudes, vastly transcending, what to Ocular Inspection do sensibly appear. The great God by his spirit hath garnished the Heavens—Lo these are part of his wayes: but how little a portion is heard of him? but the thunder of his Power, who can understand, Job. 26.13,14. To speak Truth, nothing considerable of this piece of his works is known by the wisest and best learned of men, but their motions, concerning which, from long Experience; frequent, careful and costly observations, Rules and Tables have been found out and framed, by which for any Time given, whether past or to come, their place and walk (very near exact Truth) may be discovered and declared. Hence in this preceding Calender, an Account is given of the Suns and Planets motions, with some of their principle Aspects: by which thou art Advantaged to see and Consider how this part of the Heavenly Host, doth (in all their motions and marches, as if called forth by their Names) wait upon and follow their Sovereign Lord and Leader, ready to fulfil his pleasure, in an exact observance of, and obedience to that Inviolable Law and Command he hath laid upon them. And may not this make us blush, and fill us with shame and Confusion of face, that being Creatures made capable of, and called to far more High and Heavenly Imployments and Enjoyments, we should yet indulge ourselves in sloth, idleness, and vanity, and run a Course Cross, and contrary to the holy, just, and good Law, and will of him in whom we live, move, and have our Being, who is the Sovereign Lawgiver, able to save and to destroy. Let me further intreat one thing of thee, and I will adventure to promise thee a good year: the Request is in itself Reasonable, and may to thee be Eternally profitable. Its only this: duly to prize, and diligently to improve Time, for obtaining the blessed End it was given for, and is yet graciously continued to thee by the Eternal God.

This paper perused, will shew thee, with how swift a motion dayes are running into weeks, and weeks into Moneths, the last of which being in number but the 12th, is hastening to lodge the Year in that grave, from which it can never obtain a Resurrection. Remember Time is given to be improved for Eternity. what thou sowest in the one, thou must be ever reaping in the other. *Morieris, Orieris, Eris, Is.* After a short Life followeth a certain, uncertain Death, after that a Resurrection, then an Eternity of bliss, or woe without Change. Of 365 dayes allowed to the making up this Year, which shall be thy last, thou knowest not, but that any one of them may be it: thou oughtest to know, and so Consider, that thou mayest pass the Time of thy sojourning here in fear. Art thou young, thou mayest Probably never live to be old, if old, shalt never again be young. Be we then all with our Loyns girt up, and Lights burning, waiting the coming of the Lord. *New-England Remember,*—Forget not thy last yeares *Miseries, Mortalities, Mercyes.*

FINIS

Of the Eclipse of the Sun.[9]

That which we call an Eclipse of the Sun, might more aptly be stiled an eclipse of the Earth, for indeed the Sun at such a time is not diprived of any light, but the Earth, by reason of the intervening of the Moon; yet because the Sun in respect of us is deficient, hence we call it an eclipse of the Sun.

This solar eclipse is an obscuration of the sun arising from a diametral interposition of the moon between the sun and our sight.

This eclipse of the Sun (if natural) happens only when there is a new Moon, for then only can there be an interven-

[9] William Brattle, *An Ephemeris . . . for 1682* (Cambridge).

ing thereof between the sun and our sight, (and hence the eclipse which happened at the time of Christs suffering was a preternatural or miraculous Eclipse, for it is evident, that it was at *Easter* when the moon was at the full; etc.) but yet there is not an eclipse of the sun every new moon, that is, every time the moon is in conjunction with the sun; because of the latitude of the moons orbit, which the suns is without: For you must understand, that the ecliptick line, in which the sun alwayes doth continue, is a line in the Zodiak without any latitude, whereas the Zodiack in which the moon keeps (she straying out of the Ecliptick) hath latitude, so that there may be a conjunction of them, that is, they may both be in one sign and yet not cause an eclipse: but when the moon comes to be in the same point of the ecliptick where the sun is, and hath little or no latitude, then there happens to be an Eclipse.

The same eclipse of the sun may be total in some parts, partial in others, and none at all in other parts of the world. But if any one should count it strange, that there should be a total eclipse of the sun, or (which is all one) that the moon, which is several hundreds of times less than the sun, should ever wholly hide it from us, he may hear [*sic*] read a reason for it, namely, the nearness of the moon to our sight; A mans hand put before his eye will hide a thing, (suppose a man) that is a thousand times bigger then his hand from his sight, and that though his hand be no nearer his eye in respect of the man (the object of his sight). then the moon is to our sight in respect of the sun; seeing then this seems no what strange, why should that? whenas the reason of both this, and that, is the same.

To the Reader.[10]

It was above 2,000 Years ago an *inspired praediction* of that *Zachariah,* who has not ineptly been called the *Sun among the smaller Prophets,* that when the Messiah should set up his Kingdome in the World, *there should even be upon the Bells of Horses, Holiness to the Lord,* Zech. 14.20. i.e.

[10] Cotton Mather, *The Boston Ephemeris for . . . 1683* (Boston).

the very meanest things should have *Holiness* interwoven, and be consecrated unto a *Divine Service.* Reader, a sorry *Almanack* will become Noble, if it may share in such an Honour: and what should hinder it from doing so? Such an *Anniversary Composure* comes into almost as many hands, as the *best of Books*; and why should not every eye be entertained with what is Intelligible, and may be profitable? Though we don't go with *Schiller* to put *Christian Names* upon the *Constellations,* let it not be absurd to beseech the Readers of an *Almanack* to become *Christian* Men: Hath not the *Parallel project* of *Protestant Primers*; yea, and *Protestant Almanacks* too, on this very score had the good word of all honest *Protestants*? Think it not strange! *Id ante nos fecerunt alii.* Another place once saw the harmless design of a *Scripture Kalender. New-England* too ha's enjoyed more then once the well-contrived *Almanack Addresses* of a most skilful *Mathematician,* and Reverend Divine: We say, *What if we should run after them.* And our *first Essay* of this Nature shall be to present thee with,

1. A *probable Account* in what *Order,* at what *Time,* and by what *Hands,* the Books in the *Bible* might be Written.

Reader, As one of thy main works in the World is to search like a *Miner,* in thy Bible: So one of the most considerable *Questions,* which thou art to be askt, is, *Understandest thou what thou readest*? And as *Innumerable helps* are herein improvable, so none of the least despicable are *Chronological* ones; Our *Almanack* would gladly convey thee one of that kind. And since a considerable lift to an insight into the Scripture, is to get a right *Idea* of the Order in its Books; Vouchsafe in a few curt *Laconisms* to receive the guesses of the Learned thereabout.

In the *Old Testament*: *Genesis* (an History of the Church for about 2368 years) seems written (by *Moses*) a little before *Israels Exodus* out of *Egypt,* A. M. 2450. *Job,* the *Person,* probably lived about the time that *Jacob* went into *Egypt,* and was one of *Abrahams* Kindred: the *Book* some think written by *Elihu,* some by *Solomon,* most by *Moses.* Fixing on A. M. 2450. *Exodus* (in the 12 first Chapters an History of 140 years, and in the rest of two years more) was perhaps written about A. M. 2454. *Leviticus* (a relation of one moneths transactions) might also be written A. M. 2454. *Numbers*, a Story of 38. years, reaching to A. M. 2492. possibly was then penned. *Deuteronomy* (an account of a Moneth and half) might likewise be written by *Moses*, A. M. 2492. Though some passages at least, in the *Pentateuch*, seem ascribable to another Hand, why not *Joshua's*? *Joshua* declares about 18 years Revolutions, A. M. 2517. though his conclusion is manifestly the addition of another. *Judges*, reaches from the death of *Joshua* to the Government of *Eli*, about 292 years, and might be written (tis imagin'd) by *Samuel*, A. M. 2840. *Ruth* admits most various and undeterminable conjectures. 1. *Samuel* (an History from A. M. 2809, unto A. M. 2889.) might about that time (as the notion of the *Jews* is) be written by the then *High Priest*. II. *Samuel*, (an History from A. M. 2889. unto A. M. 2929.) might then be written by a like person. *Proverbs of Solomon* seem to be penned by him, in great part for the immediate use of his Son *Rehoboam*, about A. M. 2940. though some of them were collected at sundry seasons after his death. *Ecclesiastes* and *Canticles* (the fruits and discoveries of that great Man's Repentance) challenge their date somewhat near A. M. 2968. *Jonas* seems to Prophesie about A. M. 3124. *Hosea* was his contemporary, and prophesied at least 70 years. *Joel* prophesied at the same time. And *Amos* too. *Isaiah* (that *Evangelist*! that *Apostle*! that unimitable exemplar of *lofty Language*!) Prophesied A. M. 3138. and continued at his blessed Masters work, some say 80 years, though others allow him but 47. *Micah* lived in his dayes: and was certainly very long improved as a divine Embassador. Habakkuk seems to Prophesie A. M. 3220 And the consolatory *Nahum* (to some) about the same time. *Zephaniah* comes after, about A. M. 3316. And *Obadiah* also. *Jeremiah* sounds the Trumpet, about A. M. 3328. continues a Preacher about 43 years: writes his *Lamentations* about A. M. 3340. And after this (the *Jews* say) the two Books of *Kings*, (a History from A. M. 2929 to A. M. 3360. *Ezekiel* is visited with divine Visions, A. M. 3350. And about the same time *Daniel* flourished. *Haggai* and *Zechariah* begin their work, about A. M. 3527. *Malachi* brings up the rere of the Prophets, 3537. The two Books of *Chronicles* are supposed by not a few to be of *Ezra's* compiling (if sundry hands were not therein employed) an History from the Creation to A. M. 3419. The Book *Ezra*, written by himself, continues that History, and might be written A. M. 3563. *Nehemiah* writes the Book which bears his Name, about A. M. 3570. And many deem he wrote the Book of *Esther* too, about A. M. 3572 The Epitome of the *Bible*, h. e. [*sic*] the Book of *Psalms*, though most of them were Penned by the Lovely *David*, *Israels sweet Singer*, were not all compiled till the dayes of the *Maccabeas*.

In the *New-Testament*, *Matthew* first writes his Gospel, about A. C. 42. *Paul*, of his 14 Epistles, writes four, *i.e.* to *Thessalonians*, 1.2. to *Titus*, to *Galatians*, to *Corinthians* 1, about A. C. 51. Two more *viz.* to *Corinthians* 2. to *Timothy*, 1. about A. C. 52. To *Romans*, A. C. 53. *Luke* writes his Gospel from the mouth of *Paul*, much about this time. *Paul* writes (in Bonds) to *Philippians*, to *Colossians*, to *Philemon*, to *Ephesians*, to *Hebrews*, about A. C. 56.57. *Peter* writes his first Epistle, and *Jude* his Epistle, and *Mark* his Gospel from the mouth of *Peter*, about that time. *Luke* writes the *Acts* about A. C. 60 so doth *James* his Epistle. And *Peter* his second Epistle. *Paul* writes to *Timothy* 2. A. C. 64. *John* writes his three Epistles before his Banishment, A. C. 87. and after that his *Gospel*, and his Revelation.

Thus hast thou an huddled account of the successive delivering to the Church that Heavenly Book, which contains the *Oracles of God*, in which they that have had leisure have counted not only the Chapters to be 1189. but also the Verses to be 31171. And of which thou mayest be sure to dispatch the Reading in a year, if thou wilt give thy self time to revolve three *Psalms*, fifteen *Chapters* of the *Old Testament*, and five of the *New* in a Week. Do so; And say,

> *Sancte Liber! venerande Liber! Liber optime! nobis:*
> *O animae nostrae Biblia dimidium!*

But then thou art invited to Consider,

II. A serious *Reflection* on Mans mortal and Momentary life. For

Reader, We must have *one Word* more before we part;

The *Shrub* that is now writing, had not stept out of his Road, & devoted a few of his *Horae subcesivae*, to try what he could do in the foregoing *Mathematical composure*, if he had not therein foreseen an opportunity to approve himself a Friend to thine everlasting welfare. And as the universal medicine of *Soul-distempers*, & the grand Instrument of *Soul-good*, is *consideration*! *consideration*! [*sic*] how much commanded, and commended in the *Scriptures* of *God*? & by the *Dictates* of *Reason*? So I cannot presently call to mind any matter of *Consideration* more suitable to be pressed in such a *Measurer of time* as an Almanack is, then what the *Measure of thy time* in this world is like to be. Oh! let a *Rude Pen* expostulate a little with thee! and if a *King* gave a young-man a Pension to Ring every day that Lesson to him, *Remember thou art but a Mortal Man*! If an *Emperour* had one appointed at certain times to salute him with *Live mindful of thy Death*! If *Jerom* could declare, *Whatever I do methinks I hear the sound of the Arch-Angel's Trumpet, Arise yee Dead*! Let, let not an *Ephemeris* be blamed for seeking to do thee such an office of love as to say, Having obtained *Help* from the God in whom thou livest, thou art brought to the beginning of another Year: And the lease of thy Souls dwelling in its *Clay Tabernacle* is *hitherto* prolonged [Eben-Ezer!] But what? Are thy *inward thoughts* that this is thy *Resting place*? and that thou shalt abide here for ever? Oh folly! surely thou needst not have *Scripture* quoted to demand, *What man is he that liveth and shall not see death*? or to convince, *That it is appointed for men once to die*. For dip where thou wilt in thy Bible, and this thing will accost thee. But thy *eyes*, & *ears* may enough mind thee of thy death: thy very *food* and *raiment* (the reliques of *dead creatures*) & the frequent *tolls* of the mournful Bell for thy *dead Friends*, say aloud unto thee, *Thou shalt die, and not live*! And truly as Xerxes wept over his vast *Army*, because in an Age, not a man of that multitude would be alive, such a *thought* cannot but warmly possess the *Writer* concerning all the Readers of this Address. Under such an Influence let be annex'd. Oh! know! Thy *Life* will not, and cannot be *Long*. Every one that is *born of a Woman,* every mothers child, is of *few dayes*; Yea, and that if his dayes be not only compared with the duration of *Eternal Beings*: but compared the temporal duration of his great *stage,* the *World*: ay, and of some animate creatures in it. Wouldest thou know how long at most thou art like to be an Inhabitant on this Earth? I might turn thee both to the *account* which some *instances of Longevity* give about themselves, in *Job* 7.8. & 10.20. & 16. ult. in *Gen.* 47.9. in *Psal.* 39 5. And to the *Similitudes* which Mans frail life is represented by, in *Job* 14,2. *Psal.* 103.4. *Isai.* 40.6,7. 1 *Chron.* 29.15. *Jam.* 4.14. and in *Job* 9.25, 26. where there is an allusion to what every *Element affords,* and that with a *gradation* too. But what needs it? when not only the very *Heathen* could write rationally *de brevitate vitae*? But even the most *stupid* among Mortals will of their own accord, resemble the *Condition* of Men in this World, to that of *Leaves* in *Autumn.* The *Souls* of men in their *Bodies,* to a young *Bird* in a *shell,* that will quickly break out and fly away: or to a *Candle* in a shattered *Lanthorn,* ready to be puff'd out by every wind. The *continuance* of men in the land of the living, to the vanishing of a *Vapour,* or the swiftness of a *Torrent,* gliding and whirling down apace into an *eternal Ocean.* And oh! know! thy *Death* may be sudden, and unexpected: where, ay! where is the man that do's *know his time,* or dares *boast of to morrow*? Reader, on the *Evening* wherein this is written, I call to mind near twenty *sudden Deaths,* which we have seen in the two or three last Moneths. And verily, *Except thou repent*! The famous *Waldo* from whom the *Waldenses* had their Name, became a *Convert* at such a sight: And will it not so much as make thee apprehend that even in a moment, thou mayest also go down into the Grave? Oh! let it do so! Wherefore I cannot be so unkind as to dismiss thee, before I strike home the nail I have to drive in one *Importunate Request.* For whoever thou art, I intreat thee! I beseech thee!! I conjure thee! by all that thou hast any value for; that thou wilt [Oh! why! I beg thee! why wilt thou not? at least *once* however!] set apart a few *Sands* of an *Hourglass* to be run in such thoughts as these: "I am now in this World! but as sure as I am now alive, I shall not alwayes, nay, I shall not long, and I know not how long, I shall be so: yea, tis a most vain thing for me to imagine any other, but that very certainly and speedily this very Body of mine will become a cold, a blew, an unsavoury lump of *Clay*: a few dayes more, & the dayes of my own black *Funeral*, and my Friends *Mourning* over me, Ah! *He is gone*! will overtake me! Then, then will the *Spark* of *Immortality* now within my breast be flown into the *world of Souls*, and will be fixed down like a *Rock* in a state of weal, or a state of wo, for infinitely more then as many millions of ages, as the *Heaven* hath *Stars*, or the *Shore sands*, or the huge *Ocean* drops of water in it."

Such thoughts as these on the one hand should, and would make thee moderate in the pursuit of all inferiour goods, rivet the Book of *Ecclesiastes* in thy mind, and cause thee to take the wholsome *Counsel*, in 1 *Cor*. 7.29. and they on the other hand, ought, and might make thee to Redeem they short time by a timely *Provision* for a long *Eternity*: and do as all wise men do, 2 *Cor*. 4.18. And so tis hop'd if thou art already converted, thou wilt give all diligence for an open and abundant entrance into the Kingdome: Or if thou art a *Stranger* to Religion, thou wilt cry no more with unconverted *Austin, By'nd by and anon*. But thou wilt unfeignedly turn from all thy *Idols*, to God in Christ without delay.

Concerning Lightning, and Thunder, withsome Observations and Cautions touching the same.[11]

Lightning is an Exhalation hot and dry, as also hot and moist; which being Elevated by the Sun to the middle Region of the Air, is there included or shut up within a cloud and cannot ascend; but by an Antiperis . . . grows hotter and is

[11] N. Russel, *Cambridge Ephemeris*, 1684. Only known copy, MHS.

enkindled, attenuated, and so seeks for more room, which it not finding in the cloud violently rends the same, breaks out of it, and continues burning so long that it comes to the very ground. By its rending of the cloud, there is caused a most dreadfull noise or rumbling, and this we call Thunder: So that Thunder is improperly reckoned among the kinds or *Species* of *Meteors*.

Of Lightning, [*fulmen*] there are three sorts, *viz.* piercing, [*Terebrans*] dashing in peices [*sic*] [*disentiers*] burning [*urens*] Piercing Lightning (which is also called white Lightning,) does consist of a most Subtile and thin exhalation and is very penetrating.

Observ. By reason of its subtile nature, many strange effects are produced thereby; A sword blade will be melted in its scabbard, and the scabbard not hurt at all: The pores in the scabbard are so great, that this Lightning passeth through them without any hurt, but coming to a mere solid body (as the sword blade is) it meets with opposition there, and so through its heat melts it.

The *Second* sort of Lightning, is such as consists of a more fat and thick exhalation, which meeting with things, burnes not to ashes, but blasts and scorcheth them.

Observ. With this Lightning, there happens to be (yet seldome) a Stone, that is called a Thunder-bolt, which breaketh forth with the exhalation, (as a bullet out of a gun) and breaks into pieces whatever it meets. When it strikes the earth it is reported to go not above five foot deep.

The *Third* sort of Lightning is fulmen urens [*burning Lightning*] and is more fiery then flamy; of a more grosse and earthy substance then the preceding sorts.

Observ. If Lightning kill one in his sleep, he dyes with his eyes opened, the Reason is because it just wakes him and kills him before he can shut his eyes again: If it kills one waking his eyes will be found to be shut, because it so amaseth him, that he winketh and dyes before he can open his eyes again.

Caution. It is not good to stand looking on the lightning at any time, for if it hurts no otherway, yet it may dry up or so waste the Chrystalline Humour of the eyes that it may cause the sight to perish, or it may swell the face, making it to break out with scabs, caused by a kind of poyson in the exhalation which the pores of the face and eyes do admit.

FINIS

Concerning a Rainbow.[12]

The Rainbow is described, the Image of a many coloured bow appearing in a dark, uneven, hollow, and dewie cloud, caused by the reflection of the Suns beams opposite to it.

The Reason why the Image of the Sun does not appear as it does in a Parelius is, because the cloud is uneven, and by reason of its scituation, but it appears round because the cloud is concave, and likewise because the Rays of the Sun falling on the middle of the cloud, they gather themselves to equal Angles:

Observ: If at any time there appear more Rainbows then one, it is to be noted, that only the first is caused by the Sun beams, the other is caused by the resplendency of the first.

There is a twofold final cause of Rainbows, Natural and Supernatural.

The Natural is twofold, 1. It is a sign of Rain *viz.* when it appears in a very watry cloud, that it is ready to fall into drops, or when the colours of the bow grow little and little till at last they are buryed in a black cloud; this is rarer then the contrary but when it happens is almost an infallible token of Rain ensuing. 2. It is a token of fair weather, when the colours of the bow gradually grow clearer and clearer till at length they vanish away.

The Supernatural end of the Rainbow is to be a sign or symbole of Gods mercy to the world in never destroying it again by a deluge *Genesis 9*.

Whether or no there was any existence of Rainbows before the Floud is a Question? answered by some Affirmatively by some Negatively;

[12] W. Williams, *Cambridge Ephemeris*, 1685.

But the Affirmative voice seems to be most clear and rational; For since these bows are grounded on nature as much as a Parelius, Paraselene or any such like object: we must either assert that nature was Supernaturally hindered in its operations (in that respect) till after the floud which is unreasonable, Or else must maintain that a suitable cloud never opposed the sun and gave occasion for a Rainbow till after the Floud, which cannot but be accounted very strange, no lesse then 16 hundred years intervening between those two AEraes:—As for that of *Genesis. 9.* It may imply that God never let his bow in the clouds for a token of a covenant e[r]e that time. And if it should be asked why the Almighty chose the Rainbow and not any other Celestial appearance, (if a reason might be attempted) we should say (as *Dr. Brown* in his *Pseud. Epid.* p. 246) because most proper for the signification intended thereby: Thunder and Lightning had too much terror, to have been tokens of mercy; Comits appeared too seldom to put us in mind of a Covenant to be remembered oft: and might rather signifye that the world should be once destroyed by fire then never again by water: Thus the learned *Doctor,* which (together with what precedes and follows) whether satisfactory or no we know not yet trust it cannot be offensive unto any.

According to *Syr.* look upon the Rainbow, and praise [h]im that made it.

Concerning late marvellous Astronomical Discoveries in the Planets.[13]

Before the last Age *Telescopes* were altogether unknown to the world, but since their invention, most wonderful discoveries in the Heavens have been made. It is now Evident that all the Planets are so many *Opaque dense* bodies without any light whatever, and all of them (except the Sun) change their faces like the Moon, so that *Venus* and *Mer-*

[13] Nathaniel Mather, *The Boston Ephemeris, 1686* (Boston).

cury sometimes appear like an half Moon, and sometimes quite round, according as they are more or less opposite to the Sun, and they have spots in their Superficies just as the Moon has, and of the same blackness. There is also observed that the black spots in the Convexity of the body of the Sun are variable, and do move regularly towards the West, finishing their Revolution in about 26. or 27. dayes, which proves that the body of the Sun turns upon his center with that Motion. These solar spots are judged to be Evaporations from the Body of the Sun, like as Vapours are to the earth which arise from thence, and form themseves into Clouds. There have been also notable discoveries in the Moon, which there is not here space to enlarge upon; only it is evident that the Lucid parts of her Body are rugged like the Earth, and the spots of the Moon resemble the Sea; and the surface of this Planet is set all over with certain round hollows, like pits or wells of several magnitudes. It is also very surprizing that in her Eclipse, when it is Eclipsed a fingers breadth or two to the naked eye, it is not at all Eclipsed if you look on it with a Telescope; and when it is quite freed from the Eclipse in the Telescope, it yet appears to be Eclipsed a fingers or two breadth to the naked eye (as was observed at *Boston* in the Eclipse on *November* the 30. 1685).

By the help of the Telescope we discover that *Saturn* is not an intire round Globe (as in all former Ages was believed) but that it is composed of two parts, and besides its body it doth consist of a Ring, which encompasseth him about after the manner the Horizon in our Artificial Globes doth encompass them, and is flat upon the verge as they be; sometimes he appears without his Ring. Mr. *Hugens* has observed that when it arrives at 20 deg. and half of *Pisces* and *Libra,* it appears round and without Arms. 1671. it appeared all round, So again in this last year. [*sic*] 1685. and so it will again 15 years hence. Mr. *Azout* conjectures that within a few years the shadow of the little Moon which attends *Saturn,* will be seen upon the Body of the Planet: as for the four little Moons which move round the Body of

Jupiter, rising East of him and setting West; those that are the nearest to his Body finish their Revolution with greater Expedition than those that are further off, *viz*. The first which is distant 3. minutes, finisheth his course in 18. hours, 28. min. 30 *sec*. The second is distant from 4 5. min. and ends his Revolution in 3. dayes, 13 hours, 18 min. The third is distant, 8 min. and finisheth his Revolution in 7. dayes, 3. hours, 35. sec. The fourth is distant, 13. min. performs his course in 16 dayes, 18. houres, 9. min. 15. sec. When these little Moons are found interposed between the Sun and Him, they give a shadow upon the Body of *Jupiter*. Perhaps hereafter some notable Discoveries respecting the other Planets, and something more of these also may be mentioned.

These things may seem strange and vulgar minds are unapt to believe them; but they are real truths: Should a man affirm that there may be a slowness of motion proportionable to the supposed swiftness of the Sun, or that a Body may be continually in a direct motion not one minutes time wherein it did not rid some space, and yet that the Body in 10. years together should not move near so far as an hairs breadth, who almost would credit such an assertion. Nevertheless the learned Doctor *Wilkins* and others have by Mathematical demonstration evinced it to be true.

FINIS

Short Rules in Husbandry.[14]

Remove young trees either in the end of October, in November, or else not till February, the Moon increasing. In the first month in warm Weather graft. The best way of Grafting in this Country is to cut off the Stock even with the Ground, and cover the Joynt with Earth. In the 11 Month trim off superfluous Branches from Fruit Trees. Gather all Fruits you mean to keep in a dry time, when the Moon is about the Full. Geld Cattle when the Sign is in the

[14] Daniel Leeds, *An Almanack for . . . 1687*. (Broadside, New York, 1687.)

Head, Thighs or Knees, and the Moon in her last Quarter. But being confined therefore;

Mend, modest Reader, what thou findst amiss,
But let the Author know what fault it is.
All men have err'd since *Adam* first transgrest.
If I commit no Faults I'm one o' th' best.
But here my Comfort is, though I offend,
I to my Faults can quickly put an END.

Prognostica Georgica: *Or the Country-mans Weather-Glass. Prognosticks of Tempests.*[15]

The obscuring of the smaller stars is a certain sign of Tempests approaching, the oft changing of the Winds is always a fore-runner of a *Storm.*

Of Winds.

The resounding of the Sea upon the shore, and murmuring of the Winds in the Woods without apparent Wind, shew wind to follow; shooting of stars (as they call it) is an usual sign of wind from that quarter the star came from, Redness of the *Skie* in the morning is a token of Winds, or Rain, or both: if the circles that appear about the *Sun,* be red and broken, they portend wind: if thick and dark, Winds, *Snow,* or Rain: The like may be said of the Circles about the Moon: *Luna rubicunda fiat, &c.*

Of Rain

If two Rainbows appear, they are a sign *of Rain*: If the *Sun* or Moon look pale, look for Rain, according to that verse, *Pallida Luna pluit,* &c. if a dark Cloud be at *Sunrising,* in which the *Sun* soon after is hid, it will dissolve it, and Rain will follow: *Nebula ascendens indicat imbres nebula descendens serenitatem,* if the *Sun* seem greater in the East than commonly, it is a sign of Rain, if in the West about *Sun-setting* there appear a black Cloud, you may expect Rain

[15] John Tulley, *An Almanack for . . . 1687* (Boston).

that night, or the day following, if in the winter time thick white Clouds appear in the south-east near the Horizon at Sun rising, they portend snow, a day or two after. If black Clouds appear there, it is a sign of Rain.

Sero Rubens ceolum eras indicatesse serenum,
Sed si mane rubet ventures indicat imbres.

Of Fair Weather

If the Moon look bright and fair, look for Fair Weather. Also the appearing of one Rainbow, after a Storm, is a known sign of Fair Weather. If Mists come down from the Hills, or descends from the heavens, and settle in the valleys, they promise fair hot weather: Mists in the Evening shew a fair, hot day, on the morrow. The like when mists rise from the waters in the evening. Much more might be added, but I would not tire the Reader, craving but what the Poet doth,

. . . [*sic*] *Si quid novisti rectius istis*
Cundidus imperti, sinon, his utere mecum.

Of the Ecclipses, 1687.

There will be two Eclipses of the Sun this year, The first will be the first day of *May,* The second the twenty sixth of *October,* which near the line will appear great Eclipses, but not visible to us, and therefore needless to be minded here.

A *PROGNOSTICATION.*[16]

For the Year 1688. Calculated for the Meridian of *BOSTON*; and may without any sensible Error serve for any other place in *NEW-ENGLAND.*

Thus Reader, by our Astrologick Art,
Future Events we unto thee impart;
But yet 'tis with this Reservation, tho'
If they come not to pass, we'd have them do.
For all Predictions do to this belong,
That Either they are *right, or* they are *wrong.*

[16] John Tulley, *An Almanack for . . . 1688* (Boston).

January's Observations

The best defence against the Cold
Which our Fore-fathers good did hold.
Was early a full Pot of Ale,
Neither too mild nor yet too stale,
Well drenched for the more behoof
With Toast cut round about the Loaf,
The Weather is very cold; but where *Jeal-
lousie* is hot, that house is Hell, and the
Woman the Master Devil thereof.

February's Observation

You lads and Lasses would repine,
Should we forget St. *Valentine*:
When Young men do present their Loves
With Scarfs, with Ribons, & with Gloves,
And to shew manners not forgot all
Give them a lick under the Snot-gall,
Then one a Cursie dops anon,
And smiling says, *I thank thee, John.*

On the Twenty eighth day of this month is like to be a very comfortable smell of *Pancakes* and *Fritters*. The Nights are still cold and long, which may cause great Conjunction betwixt the Male and Female Planets of our sublunary Orb, the effects whereof may be seen about nine months after, and portend great charges of Midwife, Nurse, and Naming the Bantling.

MARCH

Now if thy Body be not well
This month for Physick doth excel;
But choose a Doctor skill'd in Art,
Not *Quacks* growing rich by others smart.

If some great Person do not die this month, either in *Europe*, *Asia*, *Africa*, or *America*, let them light Tobacco, or make Bum-Fodder with our Observations.

APRIL

This being now the time of *Spring*,
Young Folks do love like any thing.
But Love is made of different mettle,
Of Joy, and pain; in *Dock out Nettle.*
A painful pleasure pleasing pain,
A gainful Loss, a loosing Gain,
And therefore Freinds take my advice,
Love none but vertuous, rich, & wise.

This is a very *Fickle* month, and therefore no more like a *constant* month than an Apple is like an Oyster. Many people shall be desirous to marry, but when they *have* a wife, they know no more what to do with her, than a Taylor knows how to make a *Horse-shoe.*

MAY

This is Love's month, else Poets lie, what then?
Why then, young maids are apt to kiss young men:
But for old *maids unmarried, 'tis a sign,*
They either do want beauty, *or else* Coyn.

Many Weddings this Month: but the people couped very unequally, a sneaking Woodcock joyned to a wanton Wagtail, a Henpeckt Buzzard to a chattering Magpie.

Mars in a Trine aspect with *Jupiter,* denotes, that a Dung Cart full of nail pareings will be better to dung Land than a Bushel of live Buggs or *Musquitoes.*

JUNE

The Sun is entred now into the Crab,
And days are hot, therefore beware a Drab;
With French diseases, they'l thy body fill,
Being such as bring Grist *to the Surgeons Mill.*

If any are bound for *England,* and would know whither to go for several sorts of Belly timber, I shall direct them to *Devon-shire* for White-pots, To *Essex* for Veal, to *Nor-*

folk for Dumplins, to *Tewxbury* for Mustard, to *Banbury* for Cakes, to *Kingsnorton* for Cheese, and to *Darby* for Ale.

JULY

Now wanton Lads and Lasses do make Hay,
Which unto lewd temptation makes great way,
With tumbling on the cocks, which acted duly,
Doth cause much mischief in this month of July.

I assure you upon the word of an Ass-trologer, we shall have no hard Frosts, nor deep Snows this month, but much blustering Weather with those women whose Husbands have been at the Ordinaries all day, and at night come home drunk.

AUGUST

Now doth the Dog-*Star rule, therefore you must*
For your health's sake astain from fleshly Lust.
Better it is your business hard to ply,
For to get in your Barley, Wheat, and Rye.

Now the *Indian Sanupps* with their *Squaws* shall dance the *Canaries,* having for their musick the Roaring of *Lions,* the Howling of *Wolves,* Lowing of *Oxen,* Bleating of *Calves,* Croaking of *Toads,* Hissing of *Serpents,* Barking of *Doggs,* Screeching of *Owls,* Wawling of *Cats,* Buzzing of *Musquittoes,* and Screaming of *Peacocks,* which (together with their own ravishing & melodious Voices) will make a most harmonious Sound.

SEPTEMBER

Now Landlords they prick up their ears,
Because St. Michael's *day appeares.*

Now the Farmers barns are full, and a full barn makes a full Purse & a joyful heart; it makes the Bakers bread heavier, and the Brewers Ale stronger: All you that love Toast & Ale, pray for full barns.

OCTOBER

Who takes a Giglet to his wife,
Must look to lead with her this life,
Each morning she will have brought up
A Candle in a silver Cup,
Then lie abed and take her ease,
And goe abroad when ere she please.

Now an apparition of Pork and Turnips will be very comfortable to an hungry Stomach.

NOVEMBER

Cold shivering Winter *now makes his addresses,*
Adorned with his silver'd colour tresses.
Then get both wood and Rum if thou art able,
For now you'l find they'l both be comfortable.

The Moon being in Conjunction with *Scorpio*, presageth, that this month we shall have plenty of *Frost-fish* and scarcity of *Butter* which shall make many to *boil* them, whereas they are better *fryed.*

DECEMBER

This month the Cooks do very early rise,
To roast their meat, & make their Christmas pies.
Poor men at rich men's tables their gutts forrage
With roast beef, mince-pies, pudding & plum porrige.

This month, Money & Rum will be in great request; and he that hath the *first* shall not need fear wanting the latter. We will end our monthly Observations thus, *That,* Those who lose their whole estates at *Cards* and *Dice,* may die *Beggars* without being pittyed.

Of this you may see more at large in a Treatise called *The game of Hazzard Explain'd.* Fol. 110. originally written in *French,* and now done into *English* by *D. C.*

We shall now give you our judgement of such things as without the help of any *Lapland* Devil we may safely prognosticate will assuredly come to pass. We find then by the position of *Mercury*, a great plenty of such people who are thus described by the Poet,

Who in the day do mark
Those houses which they plunder in the dark.

Venus is a full square with *Mars*; therefore those that marry Widows must bear with all their bad qualities, and allow her alwaies to carry with her the Inventory of her Goods and the Summ of her Dowry perpetually in her mouth, and alwayes to be arm'd with the praise of the Deceased:

And he who is with such a widow matcht,
He in the marriage noose is finely catcht,

Then may he sing the *hen-peckt* husbands song,

Like a dog with a bottle ty'd close to his tail,
Like a Tory *'n a Bog, or a thief in a Jayl.*

Now *Mars* & *Mercury* are in a friendly Conjunction with *Venus*, which may invite many young people to enter into the marriage-state: and indeed a wife is no *Curse* when she brings the blessing of a *good estate* with her: but to marry a *Town-flurt* with a *painted face*, a *rotten reputation*, & a *brasie fortune*, that man had better go to *hanging* than be so married. But if you will take *my* advice in the choice of a wife, I will give it you freely; and that you may the better keep it in memory, take it *Alphabetically*: Let her be *Amiable, Beautiful, Chast, Delicate, Excellent, Fair, Gracious, Honest, Industrious, Kind, Loving, Merry, Neat, Obedient, Pittiful, Quiet, Rich, Shamefac'd, Temperate, Vertuous, Witty, Youthful,* and *Zealous.*

And those who with these properties are sped,
You shall not need to fear with them to wed.

But that which makes most for our purpose, is that *Venus* is in her *Altitude*, a great sign that Whores will be very impudent, and stand so high upon terms, that poor men . . . so easily purchase the Pox as the *rich*; but let Whores be as dear & as scarce as they will, if that *Rum* be but cheap & plentiful we care not.

A Quart of Rum well burned,
And drank to Bed-ward wholly,
I dare be bold doth cure the Cold,
And purgeth Melancholly.

So much for *Rum*: but the chief matter is to get money to buy it, without which, a wise man is counted a *fool*, and having store of it, the Fool is reckoned a *wise* man: according as the Poet wittily expresseth it:

Whose rich? the wise, whose poor? the foolish man
If I were wise, I should have Riches then.
Whose wise? the rich, & who's a fool? the poor.
If I were rich, I should be wise therefore.

We shall conclude our Predictions with some Observations on St. *Paul's* day.

If St. Pauls *day be fair and clear,*
Then will the Wayes *more* clean *appear*
But if it chance to snow or rain
The Wayes will dirty *be again;*
And if the Winds aloft should be,
Then tumble down will many a Tree
But if there be no wind at all,
The Trees may stand, *and so not* fall.
With Allowance.

FINIS

Of Telescopes.[17]

The Telescope or great Prospective Glass was invented in the beginning of this Age, it is now made 20, 30, and unto 60, or 80 foot long, whereby Objects at great distance are clearly and more distinctly seen and discovered; matters hereafter mentioned, appear but as Objects of 60 or 70 Leagues distant. It hath been observed, that all the Planets and Stars, excepting the Sun are so many *Opaque* and *Dense Bodies*

[17] Henry Newman, *An Almanack . . . for 1691* (Boston). Only known copy, MHS.

without any light whatever, but only what they borrow of the Sun. 2. That every one of the Planets, except the Sun, change their Faces like the Moon; that each of these Planets, except the Sun, have Spots in their Superficies, just as the Moon hath, and of the same kind of blackness; there is discovered new Stars in the Firmament, the which having appeared a certain time, do so decrease in their bigness, that they cannot any longer be discerned and then afterwards, after the revolution of Months, Years or Ages, do appear again as if they were newly come into Being. *This Prospective discovers to us in the Heavens, a far greater number of Stars than we can discern with the naked Eye. It discovers to us in the Pleiades, in a Circle of one degree of Diameter, which encompasseth them, the number of 46 Stars, wheras we can perceive but six, the seventh having disappeared a long time agone.*

Of the Rainbow.[18]

Pliny saith, the Rainbow is made by the Sun, beams striking upon a hollow cloud, when their edge is repelled and beaten back against the Sun & thus ariseth variety of colours by the mixture of clouds, air and fiery light together, but (as he saith) it pretendeth naither fair nor foul weather.

Of Rain.

Of these kind of meteors you may read *Ariist Libro Primo Meteor Logicorum.* cap. 1. *And* 2. But briefly, rain is a cold vapour and earthly humour, raised from the earth and water, into the middle Region of the air, whereby the extremity of cold, it is thickned into the body of a cloud, and after being dissolved, falleth upon the Earth.

Of Hail.

Hail is ingendered of Rain, congealed into ice, freezing the drops presently after the dissolving of the cloud, whereby we have great irregular stones fall on the Earth.

[18] John Tulley, *An Almanack for . . . 1693* (Boston).

Of Snow.

Snow is of the same humour that Hail is, but not grown together so hard. *Pliny*, saith hail sooner melteth then snow, and the hail cometh sooner in the day than in the Night:

Of Frost and Dew.

When in the day time through the faint heat of the Sun, there is a cold & moist vapour drawn up a little from the earth, presently at night it descendeth again upon the earth, and is called dew, and in the Spring or Harvest, it is a sign of fair weather, but if by means of cold it be congeal'd, it is called Frost, and therefore Dews come not so often in hot seasons, neither when winds be up, but after a calm and clear night, Frosts dry up wet and moisture: for when (as *Pliny* saith) the ice is melted, the like quantity of water in proportion is not found.

Of Wind.

Wind is nothing but many Exhalations drawn from the earth, and inforced laterally above the Sun.

Of sudden Blasts.

A windy exhalation being thrown down, & encompassed (as *Pliny* saith) in a thin course of clouds, newly over cast, coming at sometime with such a violence as it bursts and cleaves a Dry cloud in sunder, and makes a storm; of the *Greeks* called *Ecnephias*, but when this cleft is not great, but that the winds be forced to turn round, and roll his descent without Lightning, there is made a whirl-puff, or gust called *Typhon*. That is to say the storm *Ecnephias* sent forth a winding violence, and this wind doth bear many things away with it, changing from place to place but if the hole in the cloud were great, it is called *Turbo*, casting down, and overthrowing all that is next it, *Pliny* saith *Ecnephias* cometh with snow nor no *Typhon* from the South, some say, Vinegar thrown into this wind, breaks the gust.

Of Earthquakes.

Plenty of Winds gotten in the Bowels, holes and Corners of the earth, bursting out of the Earth, and the earth closing again causeth the shaking, or Earthquake, and is a token of ensuing War.

Signs of Earthquakes.

When Waters in Wells or Pits be troubled, and have a bad savour, the long absence of the Winds, strange noises, the obscurity or darkness of the Sun with Clouds, and strangely coloured, *&c.*

Of Thunder, and Lightning.

When an Exhalation, hot and dry, mixt with moisture, is carried up into the middle Region, and there in the body of a Cloud, now these two Contraries being thus shut or pent in one room together, they fall at variance, whereby the water and fire agree not, until they have broken the Prison wherein they were pent, so that fire and water flie out of the cloud, the breaking whereof maketh a noise like the renting of Cloth, which they call Thunder, and the Fire Lightning, first seen, in respect the Light is before the hearing, and of Lightnings there be many sorts.

FINIS

An Account of the Cruelty of the Papists acted upon the Bodies of some of the Godly Martyrs.[19]

1. John Wickleif Parson of *Lutterworth, in Leicestershire,* was a Learned, Pious, Painful Preacher of Gods Word, brought up in the University of *Oxford,* and admired of all for his profound Learning: He stoutly opposed the Pope, and by many undeniable Arguments proved him to be Antichrist. He confuted and condemned his Doctrine about Bulls, Indulgencies, *&c.* for which he was hated and persecuted by the Bishops of those times; but by the favour of

[19] John Tulley, *An Almanack for . . . 1695* (Boston).

King *Edward* the Third (in whose time he lived) and *John* of *Gaunt*, he weathered it out; afterwards in the Reign of *Richard* the Second, he was by the power of his adversaries banished, yet returned he again from Exile, and dyed in peace at *Lutterworth* aforesaid. But in the year 1428. which was forty one years after his Death, his Dead Body was by the Decree of Pope *Martin* the Fifth, and Council of *Sene*, digg'd up and burned, with the Execration of that Fiery Pope.

And thus went out this Lamp of Light,
Who 'gainst the Pope fought a good fight.

The Cruelty of the Papists.

2. *John Hooper* was Student and Graduate in the University of *Oxford*, where he so profited in the knowledge of the Scripture, as made him altogether averse to Popery; the Devil hereupon raised him up many Enemies, so that for his safety he was forced to fly into *France*, from whence he Travelled into *Germany*; but hearing that King *Edward* the Sixth was come to the Crown, he returned into *England*, and was by King *Edward* made first Bishop of *Glocester*, and then of *Worcester*: In which Office he behaved himself so uprightly and inoffensively, that his Enemies had nothing to say against him. In the beginning of Queen *Marys* days, he was sent for by a Pursivant to *London*, and though he had opportunity, and was perswaded by his Friends to fly, yet he refused, saying, *Once I did fly, but now being called to this place and vocation, I am resolved to stay, and to Live and Dye with my Sheep.* By *Winchester* when he came to *London*, he was railed upon and committed to the *Fleet*, where after much hard usage, he was condemned to the Fire, which he patiently endured, refusing a Pardon that was set before him. One of his sayings was this, *There is neither felicity nor adversity of this world that is great, if it be weighed with the Joyes and Pains of the world to come.*

3. *Thomas Cranmer* was by birth of *Lincolnshire*, and brought up in *Jesus* Colledge in *Cambridge*, a Man of a meek

Spirit, and profound Learning. His first rise to Preferment was by reason of a Courtier and his conversing together about the Divorce between King *Henry* the Eighth and *Katherine* his Wife; *Cranmer* maintaining that the readiest way for the King to attain his desire, was no longer to trace the Labyrinths of the Popes proceedings, but directly to prove it unlawful by the Word of God. This being brought to the Kings Ear, *Cranmer* is sent for, and imployed to the most principal Universities in *Europe*, there publickly to maintain the truth of his Assertions, which he did so powerfully, that after his return, he was for his pains rewarded with the Arch-Bishoprick of *Canterbury*, which he quietly possest during the Reigns of King *Henry* 8 and *Edward* 6. but Queen *Mary* coming to Reign (who set up again the *Romish* Idolatry) he was soon after by *Gardiner* the *Spaniel*, and *Bonner* the *Blood hound* brought into trouble, who never left worrying him till they brought him to the Stake, though upon hopes of a Pardon, he subscribed to a Recantation, for which when he came to burn, he thrust that which subscribed first into the fire, so that his hand died Malefactor, and the rest of his Body a Martyr.

4. *George Marsh*, a man eminent for his Piety, Learning and Religion; was one very conversant in the Scripture, by which he attained to a great perfection of knowledge therein, a rare matter in those times when Ignorance was taught to be the Mother of Devotion, and the reading of the Scripture made punishable, because it agreed not with the *Dagon* which the Pope had set up. But he was the more obnoxious to the Papists hatred, in that he taught and instructed others in the Principles of Religion, and shewing how far the Popes Doctrine differ'd from the Word of God. These things could not be long hid, for though it were out of *Bonners* Diocess, it was not beyond the Popes reach, who had his setting Dogs in every corner, by whom this good man was apprehended, who standing stiff in defence of the Truth, was by them condemned to the fire, and burned in as barbarous a manner as cruelty could invent, having a Firkin of pitch, Rozin and Tar, placed in a Frame over his head, which melt-

ing down basted him, whilst the fire beneath roasted him, such cunning Cooks were the Popes Emissaries to make a restorative dish for a languishing Religion.

A Cruelty beyond compare,
And such the Papists mercies are.

5. *John Huss* is supposed to have been born at *Prague* in *Bohemia,* and therein to have had his Education. It hapned whilst he was a Student there, that *Richard* the 2d. King of *England* married *Anne,* Sister to *Wincestaus* King of *Bohemia,* with whom came over many Courtiers, who here did light on the Books of *John Wickleif,* which they carried home into their own Country, which *Huss* had the happiness to peruse, wherein he so profited, that he began zealously to preach and propogate the truth; but coming to touch the Errors of *Rome,* the Fryars muster'd up all their Malice against him, as wherein their profit was concerned, so that he was Excommunicated by Cardinal *Delohunna,* but to no purpose, for the Nobility and Gentry stuck close to him, so that he continued preaching still. But this not prevailing, he was summoned to the Council of *Constance,* to which he went, having the Emperour *Sigishmunds* safe conduct, and the Popes own word, for his going and returning in safety; but they tell us plainly, that Faith is not to be kept with Hereticks, and this *John Huss* found true to his cost, for having him in their power, they condemned him to the fire, which he constantly endured, receiving thereby a Crown of Martyrdom.

6. *Jerome of Prague* was, if not born in that City, in some part of *Bohemia,* he was at first nuzled [*sic*] up in the Romish Superstition, but by reading *Wickleif's* Books, and converse with *John Huss,* he soon rectified his Judgment, and publickly opposed the Doctrine of the Pope, especially that of Purgatory and Prayers for the Dead: Now Purgatory being the Fire which keeps the Popes Kitchen warm, made all the Orders of Friers like a Nest of Hornets with their venemous stings, very busie against him; however, yet he stood unmoveable, till hearing that his dear Friend *John Huss* was in restraint at *Constance,* he hastneth thither,

where he put up the Heads of some Positions, proffering publickly to defend them, and withal moved the Council that he might have leave to come and go in safety; but this being denied him, he sought to make an escape, but in his return was taken, and brought bound to the Council, where being several times baited with railing and opprobrious terms, he was cast into Prison, and 107 Articles Framed against him, but he standing firm in defence of the Truth, was by them condemned to the Fire, and burned at *Constance, June* 1. 1416. his Ashes being cast into the River *of Rhine*.

Those who in Blood their chiefest pleasure have,
Most commonly in Blood roul to their Grave.
Blood will have Blood, and seldom seen we have
That Murtherers go quiet to their Grave.
Thus some do make a sport of Cruelty,
And with delight do practice Villany.
Those who to such a height of Pride *aspire,*
The Devil and not God must be their Sire.

AN ALMANACK.[20]

In Youth let Blood from the Change to the First Quarter; In Middle Age from the first quarter to the Full; In Elder Years from the full to the last quarter; In old Age from the last quarter to the Change: But under the Age of 14. & above the Age of 56 it is not good to Bleed at all. *Again*, in Dog-days it is very hurtful to take Physick at all, unless there be great need; in such a case the disease being desperate, the cure must be adventured. *Purge* when the Moon is in one of these three *Signs, Cancer, Scorpio* or *Pisces,* & it will be sure to work the better; for in a moist sign the humors of the Body are then stirred up & down, and the better purge out, in this case, it cannot be amiss to prepare humors by something that's lexative: let this be done, when the Moon is either in *Gemini, Libra,* or *Aquarius.* Take a Vomit that it may work thoroughly, when the Moon is in *Aries, Taurus* or *Capricorn*; and in letting of Blood as aforesaid beware

[20] John Tulley, *Almanack for . . . 1701* (Boston).

the sign be not in that part of the Body which is let Blood, but rather at a considerable distance therefrom.

To the R E A D E R.[21]

SEing Mr. Clough *finds but one fault in my* Kalendar *for the year past, I think I may venture to present thee with one for the year to come. I shall not here enumerate all the faults in his for* 1703. *but will pass over them with the same rapidity as he has done my reflections (as he calls them) upon the* quondam fraternity; *Esteeming it less worth my time to engage one who has the Vanity to arrogate that to himself which he intirely borrows from others, and the confidence voluntarily to affix his name to a work which a person of the least Ingenuity would be very much asham'd to own, than he doth to contend with one he knows not; and only observe for the one Error he met with in my* Kalendar, *he himself hath found four in his own* Almanack, *and might if he had pleas'd upon a slight enquiry (as well as others) discovered fourscore, and most of them of the first magnitude, and this he will find too true, if he will but examine his* Apoge's, Perige's *the places of the* Planets, (*especially of* Mars, *and of the two Inferiour* Venus *and* Mercury) *and the Solar Eclipse in* November *wherein Mr.* Clough's *Tables of Latitude & Parallaz have once more fail'd him. I remember he told us in his Preface we should find something not usual in his* Almanack, *which (to speak like an* Astrologer) *perhaps was this great number of Errors, but they afforded I believe his* Courteous Reader *and* Kind-Country-men, *but little pleasure or Satisfaction.*

Reader, *I have taken all possible care to avoid mistakes, and hope thou wilt find this Correct.* Farewell.

AN EPHEMERIS.[22]

It is to answer the request of most (if not all) of the Uranical Students in (and about) this Province, that I have

[21] Lover of Astronomy, *Almanack for 1704* (Boston).

[22] Jacob Taylor, *An Ephemeris . . . for 1705* (Philadelphia). This is written by Caleb Pusey.

thrown out these few Calculations of the Planets Motions, for this Year 1705. I could not refuse to serve them thus far; although I incur the scandalous Title of an Almanack-Maker. As for Daniel Leeds, They know there is nothing of this kind to be expected from him; his Magazine is exhausted (John Gadbury's Ephemerides exspired) and for these three Years last past, he has had none to Copy. Yet we cannot say that he has quite forgot the very Names of the Sun Moon & Stars (Wherewith he made such a bluster, while he had their Motions Calculated to his hand, and nothing to do but to transcribe and publish them in his own Name.) for if you look into his Almanack for the last year, (1704) you'll find some of his Pages headed with verses concerning the Configurations of the Planets; and what Mortal could have thought of a wiser way? for altho' it might be some trouble to find the Day and Hour of an Aspect; Yet one would think the laziest Drone living (pretending to these Faculties) might guess within a Month in time, or Thirty or Forty degrees in the Planets Motions. But how much are they Amazed that do but take the pains to Compare our Author's verses with the true Motions of the Planets! when they find them meer fictions, and the Planets in quite a different Order from what he there talks of! His method is the most Monstrous that ever was in the World: For without making any Calculations of the Coelestial Motions, he falls to his Discourse, just as if the Sun the Moon and Stars were obliged to forsake their own Proper Motions, & Dance after the jingling of his Rhymes.

But what a hard shift dos D. L. make to patch up his Almanack, since that beloved Ephemeris expir'd? if he should not set in the Change and full of the Moon and the sign (as they call it) and two or three words about the Eclipses, it would never pass for an ALMANACK; and where (do you think) dos he get his poor stock of furniture? You may know, that about 8 years ago I threw out a little book, called the Eclipses of the Sun and Moon Calculated for 20 Years; wherein was also inserted the New and Full moons. This is of very great use to our Author, for he copies it Exactly every year, (since Gadb. Ephem. exspir'd) Then having the time of the New moon, a man may Reckon on his Fingers ends where the sign will be any day in the Month: but as easy as it is, our Author very often sets it down Notorious false. If my poor little book had not fall'n into his hand, I believe he must have left off his Faculty of Almanack Writing: I am sure I have Reason enough so to think or say, of which I shall give you one Instance; (If I had room I cou'd give you ten)

In the said book there happened an Error in the Tables of the Lunations for the Year 1703. The figure 6 standing (in the First Column of the Table) for the sixth Month (August) was Typographically Misplaced, which made the Tables useless in that Month, to one that had not the Ingenuity to find where the said Figure should have stood: here our Author was forced to Leave his Transcribing Art, and venture at a Piece of computation. Do but look in his Almanack for 1703. in August, You shall see, New Moon 4. day at 4 afternoon. This is above three days too late; then he sets down, First Quarter 12 day: Which should have been the 8th. day. Then he goes to Full Moon, 19 day at 4 1 after noon: Here he hops more than four days from the truth. Then he sets Last Quarter 26. day, Three days false. The next Change he never mentions right nor wrong. . .

FINIS

A Little (for the present) concerning D: Leeds.[23]

Having made a small Beginning the last Year to expose the false, abusive & inartificial Writings of that unparallell'd Plagiary & unreasonable Transcriber, D: Leeds, who hath now for 19 years, with a very large stock of Impudence, filched matter out of other men's Works to furnish his spurious Almanacks; I shall take the pains to proceed a little further in that business: and if but little, 'tis no matter at

[23] Jacob Taylor, *Ephemeris Sideralis. A Mathematical Almanack for . . . 1706* (Philadelphia).

present: there is time to every purpose. He hath indeed a little Company of Abettors, as good-natured as himself; They say he is proficient in the Sidereal Sciences, and (Poor Creatures) think they give a reason for it, viz: He hath for many years wrote Almanacks wherein he has discounted abundance about the Planets & their Aspects, and we do not know what. That's very true, and I think their Argument is an indefatigable proof of his Impudence, but not of his Art; for as much as neither he nor they (nor all the world) can shew us in all his 19 years Almanacks so much as the places of the Planets for one day, not an Aspect; nay, not so much as the Change or Full of the Moon, but what he hath Coppied out of other mens Calculations, altho' he hath (with confidence enough) published them in his own name, but see what a thundering answer he makes to my last year's discourse on this subject, in his postscript to the book entituled, The Great Mystery of Foxcraft he begins with me thus: As to J: T's vipures against me, if it would edify, or be of advantage to mankind, I would confute him. If by vipures against him he means vaunting or insulting over him I deny his Imputation; yet shall not be thereby deterred from exposing his baseness. As to his saying he would confute me, if &c. I think that's indeed a vapour not worth confuting. But hear him further. For 'tis some errors of the Press which he harps most upon, and would make to be mine and he rakes them out of old Almanacks too; when as he knows, I could severely lash him with the same whip from all his (calculated) Almanacks, and his Book too, but I have other fish to fry. I must confess, at this rate he'll make something of his Argument; for when a man hath a fore-head hard enough to give the Lie to all mankind, what need hath he to regard any thing? He may write all manner of Lies & Non-sense without Contradiction, if it be sufficient excuse, to lay the fault on the Printer. I know there are in his Almanacks (as well as in mine) several Errors of the Press, but I scorn to impute any thing to him, that hath the least probability of being such; and 'tis an easy matter (for the most part) to distinguish them from the real Ignorance of the Author; And I challenge him to instance one of these Gross Absurdities of his, which I observed (last year) that can, with the least Umbrage of Reason, be thought an Error of printing. But what doth he mean by Raking old Almanacks? Doth he think that all his false, artless heap of stuff is annihilated as soon as his Almanack is out of date? I wish he would lay aside the frying of his fish so long as to let us have one line of good sense from him. His grudging me the use of his Book (saith he) is like selling me Roast-meat, and then beating me with the spit; but what less can I expect from a Quaker? Here's a nice touch; he is so much accustomed to transcribe other folks Works, that it seems very odd to him to have his waycrost: But let me tell him, that Book was printed in my absence, and there are Errors in it, (some were my own) and for him to Coppy it every year, Errors & all (as he doth) in my Judgment, renders him the most insipid Animal among all living Creatures; But he goes on thus, Gadbury would have scorned to have done so by him, for copying after his Ephemerides several years, in his Book. Here he seems to insinuate that I am a plagiary like himself. The Book, he speaks of is an Account of the Eclipses for 20 years, which did indeed commence 4 years before Gadbury's Ephemerides were expired, and therefore I might have had some help from thence in the making of one fifth part of the said book, if I (like him) could not have gone on without it. But what then must one have done with the other 16 years; but even during those 4 years, there was not one Eclipse above our horizon, of which I did not clearly distinguish my calculation from Gadbury's either by setting down the Minutes of the beginning, or the digits Eclipsed, which were noticed by Gadbury; and this could not be done without a new Operation. And D. L: himself was pleased to observe a great difference between Gadbury's account & mine, in an Eclipse of the moon Anno 1700; yet now would have his Reader think that I coppied after Gadbury; But in defiance of his base Insinuations, I desire all (that please) to compare the said book with Gadbury's Ephemerides, and you may soon determine whether I have plaid the Plagiary, or he the false Insinuator.

But let us hear how he goes on. But in short (saith he) he is welcome to me, to go on with his yearly Calculations; he has (it may be) more leisure than I; and I shall make a shift to write an Almanack (perhaps as true as his) either with his help, or without it. And let him not be grieved that my Almanack sells better than his. Here he seems a little kinder than before; for altho' he'll calculate nothing himself, he is pleased to grant me leave to do it; but this is not the first time that his want of leisure hath been his excuse. Now, is it not an amazing miracle that a man could not squeeze one half an hour in 19 years, to let us see that he could do something beside transcribing? As for his writing with my help, or without it, I do desire him to do the latter, but I believe he will not, for the aforesaid Book is his roast-meat, and he's a hungry Purloiner, and a notable faculty he has is to please himself with his own Conceipt; for having formed a fancy that his Almanack sells better than mine, he has presently another whimsy to clap to it, viz: That I am grieved at it. Such is the Vanity of this Lazy Animal.

To the Reader[24]

I am told that *Jacob Taylor*, the *Philadelphia* Almanack-maker (himself great in Parts and Art) had 5000 of his Almanacks printed last year, but did not sell one quarter of them, notwithstanding his many pretty witty crabbed Names he there bestows on me. But why should I complain, seeing he at last prefers me to be Rhodamanthus; *i.e.* Judge of Hell.

Note. He cannot for his Conscience use Heathenish words in his Almanack, no, not so much as the Names of the Months, yet he can for all his Conscience use this Heathenish word, and more, elsewhere, to spit out his Venom against me.

Well, but if I am Judge of Hell, let him take heed here-

[24] Daniel Leeds, *An Almanack for . . . 1707* (New York).

after of abusing me, as he has done, lest when he comes there to be judged, I should Sentence him to be tormented according to his Deserts.

But behold what an exact Artist he would be! for in his Almanack, 1703, he takes the Longitude of this place to half a minute. Again, Contrary-wise, behold how exact he is in giving us the Southing of the Moon in his last years Almanack: He makes the Moon at every full to be South; for two nights together, at one and the same hour and minute. As you may see, on the 17 day of *January* he makes her South at the same time as on the 18 day. So on the 16 and 17 days of *February*, the same on the 18 & 19 days of *March*; and so of every month at full Moon. Whereas almost every Water-man and every one that can but read knows the moon is ordinarily South 3 quarters of an hour later every night, as well as full as at any other time. Therefore *Jacob* is great indeed if he can stop the Moons Course to make it suit his Tables. Suppose I should set down the time of High-Water to be at the same hour and minute, for two days together, at every full Moon (for so must be if the Moon be South as he tells us) O how would he be elevated to throw fresh Banters out of his Budget against me.

Lastly. I need not here defend my self against his insinuating throughout his Almanack. *That I am Ignorant . . . in Art, only to transcribe, &c. because I* feel 'tis in no Artists power to believe him, no not the *stupid Crew of his own Adherents,* as his term is

So now, to his Quaker Light *I must leave him,*
And pray God, by his Grace may undeceive him,
And of his Pride and Confusion bereave him.

January hath xxxi Days

Thus I've appear'd in print full twenty year,
While others play Bow-peep sometimes appear,
Then disappear. Yet still I keep my station.
Against the Spite of *Momus* I have stood,
And the Censorious Darts of bad and good.

The Preface[25]

Whereas *Jacob Taylor*, in his Almanack 1706 makes the Moon to be South for two Nights together, at the same hour and minite [*sic*], and I have affirmed the contrary. For which, in his last years Almanack, he counts me an Ignoramus, as knowing nothing of Art. Wherefore I desire such Gentlemen, and others, who have Clocks or Watches to observe the Southing of the Moon, as they may by her shadow on a Sun-dial; and if they find her to be south two nights together at the same time of night, either at full or at any other time, I here promise to publish my self a fool to the world in print.

Nay, behold how this wrangling *Taylor* hits himself a Box on the ear, by terming me a fool herein! for in his Almanacks 1702 and 1703. he sets down the Moons Southing (by his tyde table) in the method as I do, and so is a fool by his own argument.

His arguing that the Moon is not south so often in the year as I make her to be; is salatious, and for nothing but Cavil, and therefore not worth further reply; for he makes her South as often as I do, as every Reader may see.

But is not this *Taylor* a lump of deceipt, in that he has all along pretended, he calculated the Planets places himself, and has been vapouring and crowing against me by telling the world, I can do nothing but transcribe from an *Ephemeris*; whenas he has all this while been lazily transcribing from a *German Ephemeris*, that still continues till 1712. And I for want thereof, have been forc'd to be at the pains of Calculations; and this I can prove by divers witnesses, This indeed is very like him, especially considering his Monthly Rhymes last year, which are profane and Atheistical. I'll give one instance thereof from two lines in *December*, where he says,

Created Forms Distinctions. Orders. Rules,
Bones[?] *of Religion make it fit for Fools.*

[25] Daniel Leeds, *The American Almanack for . . . 1708* (New York).

Here he mocks at Religion; for I appeal to all judicious Men whether any sect or Religion can con . . . or be professed without all these, viz. *Reforms*[?] *Distinctions, Orders, and Rules.* And yet these he says makes it fit for fools. So that none but fools profess to be Religious.

I shall now trace him no farther, but must needs conclude, that no Government else in Christendom would suffer such Atheistical Scoffs at Religion to be published, without Just rebuke to the Authors and Printers.

(Poetry for January)

My Dull and heavy Genius, Awake,
Rouse up thy self, and prudent courage take:
Keep to the G . . . thou art Adepted to,
Still serve my Friends, yea and the Country too,
Tho' spiteful Criticks yearly snarll at me,
Advance along, good men will grateful be.

WHat I wrote in my laſt years Almanack, in favour of the *Epiſcopal Church*, which (as is manifeſt from Scripture) is the *only Order of Chriſtians* that Chriſt and his Apoſtles eſtabliſhed in the World, gave offence not only to the *Quakers*, but to other *Diſſenters*; which ſhews thoſe *Diſſenters* to be equally Enemies to the Church, according to their power, with the *Quakers*. But thoſe *Diſſenters* have not the power of doing that miſchief to *Chriſtianity*, as the *Quakers* have, becauſe thoſe *Diſſenters* diſſent not for any *main Principle of Religion*, but chiefly for ſome *Ceremonial part* or other. But the *Quakers*, under pretence of *Owning all*, *Deny all*: They declare our Religion to be *altogether falſe*, as *Edw. Burroughs* in his Epiſtle to *Geo. Fox's Great Myſtery*, ſays, *That they* (the *Quakers*) Deny our whole Religion: And ſays to his Reader, Thou mayeſt eaſily perceive, we Differ in Doctrine and Principles: and the one thou muſt juſtifie, and the other thou muſt condemn, as being one clean Contrary to the other.

Now by this you may perceive, that the former *Quakers* were ſo honeſt as to ſpeak the truth in this Caſe, as their Practice makes appear; but the preſent *Quakers* endeavour by deceit, to hide it. As for inſtance; *C. P.* in his laſt year Almanack, pag. 22. to make us think that they believe in a *Chriſt without them*, brings the *London Quakers* ſmooth Confeſſion, almoſt in the words of our *Creed*, & yet at the ſame time mean not one word of it as all *ſound Chriſtians* mean and underſtand. Nay, the *Quakers* could never yet be brought to print to the world, *That they believe in a Chriſt without them now in Heaven, &c.* for then their Religion would not be *clean Contrary to ours*, as their great Prophet *Burroughs* tells us it is. And therefore their *ſmooth Confeſſions*, like our Creed is but the *Bait* by which they make Proſelytes by deceit, and delude the unwary into the Devils Net. They only Otherways word the matter, as G. W. confeſſes, but intend and mean the ſame as formerly. And C. P. ſays as much, pag. 22. *viz.* That they are the Same in All points of Doctrine as at firſt.

THIS is that *deep Deceit* that I am in Conſcience bound to lay open, as far as God enables me, and is the Duty of every *Chriſtian* ſo to do.

Daniel Leeds, *Almanack for .... 1706* (New York). JCB.

I Have been told, that the Preachers now among the *Quakers*, contrary to their former Books, speak very modestly of *Water-baptism* & the *Supper*. Now this would be a good hearing, were it not a piece of *Quaker sincerity* such as *W. Penn* shews an example of, *Reas. against Rail.* p. 108. where speaking of the outward *Baptism* and *Supper*, *We can testifie (says he) from the same Spirit by which* Paul *renounced Circumcision, that they are to be rejected, as not now required*: Yet the same *W. Penn* in his *Key* printed in 1699. (speaking of *Baptism* & the *Supper*) says, *The People called Qrs. cannot be said to Deny them; that's Too Hard a word; but they leave them off as fulfilled in Christ, &c.*

Here *W. P.* first shews that the *Qrs.* Deny them (or *Reject* them, which is all one) and their Practice also confirms it) and then, in Contradiction to himself, or *Otherwise wording the matter but intending the same*, he again says, *They cannot be said to Deny them*. But I will give an Instance to prove that the *Quakers* do deny Baptism, and that with the same Abhorrence as formerly.

William Atkison, a Neighbour of mine, went off from *Quakerism* with *G. Keith*, but his wife still remained a *Quaker*, & is now dead, who, when she lay on her dying Pillow, was in fear that her Husband would get their Children baptized after her Death; whereupon she called him to her Bed side, to let him know, *That she could not be satisfied unless he would promise her, Not to do it.*

By which it appears that this VVomans *Indignation* against *Baptism* answers to their *former Doctrine*, as face answers face in a Glass. Thus they are taught, Thus they Live, and Thus they Die! But for People to be so taught, as that in their last most serious & Dying thoughts to appear with such *Indignation* against an express Command of Christ, practised by his Apostles and *primitive Christians*, and in all Ages since, till *George FOX*, must needs look, in the eyes of every sober *Christian*, to be most deplorable Doctrine. *Lastly*. Did ever any *Quaker* at any time submit to be baptized with water, and still remain a *Quaker*? No, never. It is Impossible: 'tis as Opposite to *Quakerism* as Christ is to Anti-christ.

I Shall prove from matter of Fact, that the *Quakers* still hold their former Opinion of the Scriptures, notwithstanding their late pretence of owning them of *Divine Authority*.

The aforesaid *William Atkison*, whose wife dyed a *Quaker*, she did at her Death earnestly request her Husband to go again to their Meetings; and this she did in the hearing of some Neighbour *Quakers*, who, after his wifes death, put him in mind of his wifes dying Request, *desiring him to fulfill it, and come again to Meeting*. VVhereupon he knowing they often had no Preacher, but held Silent Meetings (except sometimes reading a *Quaker* Epistle) he Resolved on their invitation, to try them, whether they had indeed that *respect for the Scriptures*, as they of late pretended: He went to their Meeting, and there being no Preacher, he pulled a Bible out of his Pocket, and opening it, fell a reading the 17 and 18 Verses of the 4th Chapter of St. *Luke*. Upon which they presently rose up with one accord, crying out *Confusion, Confusion; Here's Confusion*; and would not endure it to be read, but broke broke up their Meeting in the Hubbub; which was Confusion indeed. *This* the man will testifie; but he believes the *Quakers* of that Meeting called *Mattacopany* dare not deny it.

Now observe, *first*, *This Man* (who had been a Preacher among them) went to the Meeting upon their Invitation. 2dly, They having no Preacher, he could make no more Interruption or Disturbance by reading a Chapter in the Bible, than they by reading a *Quaker*-Book, which they had done a little before. 3dly, His so reading the Scriptures was by the Example of Christ and his Followers as that very *Text*, and many other *Texts* testifie.

Let every *sober Christian* therefore judge of the *Deceit* of these *Quakers* in their late pretence *of esteeming the Scriptures above their own Books*, when their *Practice* tells the contrary. *They* may call to mind how *Geo. Hutchinson* once put their Meeting at *Burlington* into the like Fright by opening a Bible and but offering to Read, which they would not endure, but told him, *It was a token of his Apostacy from the Truth*.

LAst Year I quoted the *Quaker Great Charter* (signed by 15 of their chief men & seconded by *S. Fisher*) *To secure their right and claim to the Government of the Nations, even their Heirship to the uttermost parts of the Earth.* And *That their King* (the Light within) *might command them to fight, &c.* Now the *Quaker-Almanack* in his Reply, p. 12. shews me a piece of *his Sincerity*, for, because I had not quoted more than belongs to the matter, he complains *of words left out*, while he himself not only *leaves out words*, but *leaves out the whole substance of the Quotation*: He is not willing it should be seen; No, they must *still keep it under the Thumb.* But he would have us think, *That their King will not ever make use of them to fight with Carnal Weapons.* No, we hope the *Warnings* that our *Superiours* in *England* have had, will cause them to take care, to keep them from that *at present*; yea, they have taken care, for they have made a Law, *That no Quaker or reputed Qr. shall bear any Office or Place of Trust or Profit in the Government.*

But seeing the *Quaker-Almanack* tells us over and over, *That 'tis not Carnal, but Spiritual Fighting and Weaponing that they mean to use*; and seeing it appears that *W. Penn's* last grant for *Pennsilvania*, dated *August* 1695. was upon this condition, *That he has engaged to secure and defend* Pennsilvania, *and to send* 80 *Souldiers to* N. York. *when required, or find Money to pay them*; therefore they should tell us in their next print, whether these are *spiritual Souldiers* that they mean, or the charge to be paid in *spiritual Money*; & when their hand is in they may, if they please, tell us *That the* 300 l. *which they paid to Governour* Fletcher *for the Souldiers at* Albany, *was spiritual Money too.* This last Grant of *W. P*'s is quoted against the Qrs in the *Snake in the Grass*, p. 237. To which the *Qrs.* reply in their *Switch*, p. 337. but deny not the matter only give the Author some of their sweet Names, as *Scandalous Libiller*, *Insolent*, *Sawcy*, &c. So that this instance about *W. Penn* is undenyable, *That he has engaged to maintain Souldiers*, &c. Whereupon they ought either quit their *pretended Principle*, or disown *W. P.* but they are cross, and will do neither. But they will use their Arts to Sham such Answers as will best perswade their *deluded Followers* to believe, that I (and all that oppose their errors) are *Lyars* & *false Accusers.* This is their only and last Fortification.

SEeing the *Quakers* Almanack will have it, p. 14, *that no Government is so weak or cruel to think the Quakers mean to fight* carnally *or* litterally, *but only and altogether with* Spiritual Weapons. Therefore let them tell us whether those Guns and other Iron Instruments of War were Spiritual Weapons which their Brethren armed themselves with in August, 1704, in *Burlington* County, when a report was, that a party of *French* were near at hand.

This Passage of *Qrs.* taking up Arms being lately printed in the Mystery of Fox-Craft, has touch't them in a sore place; wherefore some leading *Qrs.* have been with some of that Company of armed men, (who were not *Qrs.*) and perswaded them to sign Papers of they know not what, being persons unlearned, and had no Copy of what they signed to. Now this they do in order to print (for Print they must) and publish me a Lyar, for discovering the truth. But in defence of the truth two of the said Persons have, *June* 30. 1705. deposed on Oath, as follows, *viz.*

Whereas D. L. published in print, that when a report was, that a party of French were lurking about Ancocus Creek, the Quakers there about got together, in a Military posture, to meet them, namely, Tho. Bishop, Jos. Indicot, W. Petty, Jacob Lamb, and Richard Are. We under written being sworn upon the holy Evangelists of Almighty God, do depose That the Persons above named, together with us the Deponents, were got together in Arms, with their and our Guns charged, in order to defend our selves and Neighbours. Alexander Bennet, John Bennet. Jur. coram nobis Tho. Revell, Robert Wheeler, Justices.

Thus these two men confess honestly, that they did it for their Defence, and 'tis commendable for them and all men so to do. But these 5 men above-named are *Qrs.* certified to be such under the hands of *Burlington Meeting-Men*, and refuse to bear arms at the command of the Government, or to pay one Penny towards bearing arms to defend against the Enemy; and therefore what they mean by thus acting, and yet refuse to act, who can tell?

WHereas the *Quaker* Almanack stands to it, *That the Qrs. are the same in all points of Doctrine as at first.* So the last Instance of their taking arms, proves it more plain than their hiring men to fight, as the *Philadelphia Quakers* did, to retake a Sloop which some Pyrates had stollen from thence. So that I grant him his Saying, **That they are the same in their Fighting Principle as in Cromwells days.**

To confirm which, I will relate you a pleasant story of their Brother *W. Mead*, who with an Oak Staff (but I cannot think it was a Spiritual Staff) Knock't down and beat 3 High way-men that wanted his Purse; and it being thereupon reported how stoutly *Quakers* could Fight, the *London* Friends took their Friend *Mead* to task about it, who (as I have heard) return'd them this short answer, **Verily, Friends, the Spirit of the Lord came upon me, and I could have fought with seven Men.** Which, it seems, silenced the Friends. For, alas! what can any man say against the **Spirit of the Lord.** *Note*, This echo's back to *FOX*, who boasted, **That one Quaker could cuff with seven Men**, as I quoted last year.

I am informed, that the *Qrs.* in *East-Jersey* are not so zealous as those in *West*, to cheat the Queen of her loyal Subjects, by listing their Sons and Servants under their Monethly-Meeting Banner, by Certificate, but are more willing they should train, and be ready to defend against the Enemy; and that all the *Qrs.* in *Elizabeth-town* do train (and at *Long-Island* several do the same) not with Swords, but with Guns and Hatchets. No matter for that, they may do as much execution with a Hatchet, upon occasion, as with a Sword: they are to be commended; I wish our *Qrs.* here were not *too* proud to learn the like obedience to Government; I am sure they are not too old; for there's not a *Qr.* amongst 'um all, but, on a provoking occasion, will resist and fight: they know that man is not arrived to the perfection of a Beast, that can see his Wife ravished and Children killed, and not do his endeavour to defend and relieve them. Therefore they must not think thus to bore out our Eyes, and call their **Proud Rebellious Spirits** by the Name of **Conscience.**

WHen I was a *Quaker* I never believed it unlawful, but our right & duty to defend our selves; yet I must confess, that when first Coll. *Hamilton* was our Governour, I did (with my fellow-Assembly men) oppose appearing in a posture of Defence, *viz*. *Training*. & I gave my Reasons for it (*not Reason's of Conscience*, but) because *we were poor, and but a few People, and secured by our Neighbours who lived between us & danger: and no forreigner would trouble them selves with us*. And tho' *Time* has made part of these Reasons void, and discovered the weakness and unjustness of the rest, yet I still think the upper part of *West Jersey* more secure than her Neighbours. 'Tis out of the power of my old Friends (the *Quakers*) to make the *Indians* believe they cannot fight; they have seen the contrary from their beginning here; for at the first settling of *Burlington* some *Sweeds* or *Dutch* (who grudg'd the *English* any footing here) had told the *Indians*, *That those were* Quakers *who would not fight, and therefore they might beat or kill them and take their goods* (as some *Indians* after told it) and the *Quakers* having Intelligence, *That the* Indians *designed it one night*, they armed their people and Servants, and put themselves on the *watch & defence* which the *Indians* perceiving, were surprized, and their proceeding stopt; and told it, *That they* (the *Dutch* or *Sweeds*) *had told them lyes, for* Quakers *would fight as well as other People*.

Thus 'tis plain that their refusing to bear Arms at the command of the Government, or performing equivolent, by *paying their Money*, procee's from a *scornful proud ungoverned Spirit*, first infused into them by their *chief Prophets*, who teach *That None have a right to Rule, but They*, who one day expect to have all in their own hands.

But, *Tush*, what is all this to what our *Quakers* of the Council & Assembly of *New-Jersey* can do? They can work a greater Wonder than to Conquer and be Masters of this earthly Globe (if we could believe them) for they have engaged (to Lord *Cornbury*) by the Oath of *Abjuration*, *To defend the Queen against all her Enemies, to the utmost of their Power, and that as the word* [Defend] *is commonly understood too*; and yet at the same time declared, *That they can neither do it in* Person *nor* Estate. This indeed wou'd be the greatest Miracle that ever men did since the world began.

Of Swearing.

W. *Penn* in his Book entituled, *An Account of the Rise and Progress of the People called* Quakers (being his *Preface* to *FOX's* Journal) p. 14 tells us *That the Qts. way of affirming or assuring their Truth, is according to Christ's own form of sound words, by simple and Uncompounded Answers of* YEA & NAY, *without Asseverations, Attestations or Supernatural Vouchers.*

Note, The Qs. Oath, which they call an Attestation, is this, **I A. B. Do declare in the Presence of Almighty God the Witness of the Truth of what I say.**

Now observe, does not every Qr. call this an *Attestation*, and yet *W. Penn* tells us, *The Qts. use no Attestations.* But is not this a Compounded Answer? Compounded with a witness. Yet Mr. *Penn* tells us *They use none in assuring their Truth, but simple and Uncompounded Answers.* Let the Qrs. try their arts to make truth of these two Contraries.

In their *Treatise of Oathes,* signed by *W. Penn, G. Whitehead* & 11 *Quakers* more, p. 17 (speaking of Swearing) *We look upon it* (say they) *to be no less than a presumptuous tempting of God, to summon him as a Witness, not only to our terrene, but trivial business.— — —What! make God, the great God of Heaven and Earth our caution in worldly Controversies, as if we would bind him, to obtain our own ends: It is to make too bold with him.*

Observe, and mark well the words of these *Quakers*: The Oath they call *a summoning God as a Witness.* Now there is no People give their evidence in this form of words of *Summoning him as a Witness,* but the *Quakers.* Our form is to *Call on God to help us,* as they all know. Therefore by their own Doctrine, their form of words is a more full and proper Oath than ours. Some of them being Confounded in reconciling this their *Oath* & *Doctrine,* they now lay all the stress on *Kissing the Book.* So it seems they can *Sign to the Truth of their Evidence,* but cannot *Seal* to the truth of it. This sort of *Quibbling* becomes none but *Jesuites* and *Quakers.* Our kissing the Book is only a sealing with our Lips to the truth which express with our Tougue and Lips.

I Could bring Testimonies from the *Quaker-Books*, too large to recite here, wherein they positively say, *That invoking God as a Witness, calling God to witness, or any ways to imploy or use his sacred Name for security to earthly matters; is an Oath, a proper Oath* [I refer to a Book, called, *Satan disrobed*, p. 38. 39. for Quotations of this kind] Yet because *Quakerism* obliges 'um to unsay every thing they say, when occasion suits, they do say, *Their aforesaid form of words, (which the Law obliges them to use instead of an Oath) is No Oath.* Therefore I will here set the *Testimony* or *Verdict* of a Grand Jury of 22 *Quakers* at *Burlington* Court in *June*, 1705 concerning *M. Levally* who being brought up a *Quaker*, refused to take the common Oath to a debt that she demanded, but took the *Qrs. solemn affirmation* to a false Bill, viz. We of the grand Jury for the County of Burlington do present Mary Levally for taking a false Oath. Signed by Rich. Ridway, Fore-man.

Here you have the judgment of 22 *Quakers* that what is commonly call'd *The Quakers attestation*, is an Oath. Yet that they may be accomplish't *Quakers*, made up of Contradiction, if we ask them man by man, singly, they will tell us *'tis no Oath.*

Their *Angel of Light* has them in the same Lock, in their *giving Honour to God*; for when they *call on the sacred Name of God*, in their *Oath* or *Affirmation*, we desire them to honour him by *taking off their Hats*, as they do when they call on his Name at other times; but they are cross & will not, pretend *Conscience* and cannot; and yet they pretend *Conscience for doing it* at other times. Here is *Conscience for doing*, and *Conscience for not doing* one and the same Act of *honour to God*: And thus they wou'd make a very *Ass* of Conscience.

And yet again at others times they can both *take off their Hats* and take the *common Oath* too: As for example, some *Long Island Qrs.* (Friends in the Unity, Monethly Meeting Members) coming before my Lord *Cornbury* at *New-York* to prove some Wills of their deceased Relations, they took off *their Hats* & came before his Excellency *with their Hats under their Arms*, but pretended *Conscience* they could *not swear*. His Lordship told them *They did not appear to him to be Qrs. and therefore he could not administer the Quakers Test to them.* Whereupon they took the common Oath.

WHereas in the *Mystery of Fox-Craft*, lately published, in the Margent of a Letter of *G. FOX*, among other things [to convince the pretended *sinless Qrs.* that they have sin as well as others] there is these words viz. *Mary A. of Long Island left her Husband to exercise her Talents in* Barbadoes, & *became pregnant in that fruitful Island*, &c.

Now this *Mary A.* is generally taken to be *Mary Andrews*, (tho' *R. Williams* Book names two more *Marys* [Preachers too] that went from those parts to *Barbadoes* about the same time and *that the both Tript*, &c.) But if it be meant *Mary Andrews*, then I say, so far as the words are taken to reflect on her, as being dishonest to her Husband, so far she seems to be wronged thereby; for the matter being thus made publick, has caused her case to be strictly examined, and it is strongly asserted (and for ought I know, truly) *That she did become Pregnant in* Barbadoes, *yet not in such time, but that she might very well be honest to her husband in that particular.* This I thought fit to publish in point of justice, to prevent mistakes; for I would have nothing printed as mine, that might be justly construed to wrong any Person whatsoever.

Not to favour *G. FOX* his Ordinance of *Women Preachers* directly contrary to the Gospel of St. *Paul*, 1 *Cor.* 14. 34. and as contrary to the example of Christ: For how many good Women do we read of, when Christ chose his *Twelve* and his *Seventy Apostles*; yet not one Woman fit for an *Apostle of Christ*; No, Not one Woman did Christ chuse among them all to travel Countries and spread his Gospel as the *Quaker Women Apostles* do, to spread *Their Gospel*. But thus the *Quakers inward Christ* leads them, in Opposition to the Commands & Example of the *Christians Christ* and his *Apostles*; and therefore it is no wonder that this their *inward Master* so often takes off the outward Vizard to pay them a *Shame*. Though 'tis true, a woman is a more fit instrument for a *Quaker-Preacher* than a *Man*, as having a Voice more suitable, and therefore *Women* are commonly more followed by that *poor deluded People*; for the Life of *Quaker Doctrine* (whether Sense or Nonsence) consists in being preached in a *whyneing singing Melancholy Tone*, and a *furious Zeal* which the *Quakers* call the *Power*. This I shall demonstrate from matter of *fact*.

Of Enthusiasm.

I Write from Experirnce, That the life of *Quaker*-Doctrin whether true or false, sence or non sence, is from the Preachers delivering *it* in a fiery Zeal antick Posture, wry face, and a Tone suitable. This I shall demonstrate from *J. Telner* a Dutch-man who [when I was a *Quaker*] preacht at *Burlington* in Dutch, without an Interpreter, and tho' we understood not his Doctrine yet he had such a powerful Testimony (that is, preacht with such fierceness, and a Tone agreeable) that he mightily raised that we called the Life, *viz.* set us generally a weeping & singing, *Hum, hum, ha ha*, I among the rest was bewitcht with this *enthusiasm*; for 'tis no less than spiritual *witch craft* because it is not only contrary to the Gospel of St. *Paul*, 1 *Cor.* 14 but also when the *Qrs.* had the r difference with *G. K.* this man's Principles were found to be *gross & blasphemous*, & that in so witless a manner [he not having the art to hide *it*, *by otherwise wording the matter*] that his brethren, the *Qrs.* were ashamed of him, and would not own his preaching.

The oft remembrance of this mans pow'rful preaching, to the melting the hearts of those who understood not what he said, has been a means [I thank God] to learn me the difference between a false joy and a false peace proceeding from *wild enthusiasm*, & a true joy & true peace, proceeding from & grounded on the sobriety of the *Christian Religion*.

The Book called, *The 3d & last part of the Defence of the Snake in the Grass*, p. 243 shews, that the *Heathen Priests*, the *Brachmans*, the *American Indians* the *Mahometans* the *Regulars* in the Church of *Rome*, yea, & all the vilest & most *pestilent Enthusiasts* in all ages have been & are possest with this *power, peace & transports of joy & refreshments* as well & as much as the *Quakers*, & have set up & gain'd Proselytes on the same score; he also shews that there has been Martyrs in all these cases. The Book is well worth reading.

LAstly, As to *C. Pusey's* doughty Reasons against what I wrote last year in favour of the *Episcopal Church*, he begins, pag. 27. where he says, *'Tis* Judaism and not Christian, *to observe Days, Times, Sabbaths, &c.* Behold! here

here he calls that *Judaism* which themselves practise, and have enforced a Law for: VVe see they observe Days and Times (now) as well as others, and they have made a Law to observe the first Day as Sabbath, and have punished some for not observing it; even this same *Judaism*.

But he goes on as he begins, for p. 29. he would have it to be the *Priests*, and not the *Quaker Preachers* that gratifie Peoples Humors, & please their fancies; yet he knows the *Quakers* [having *itching Ears*, as the Apostle says] commonly leave their home Preachers & run about the Country after all new Preachers (having plenty of them of late) especially after *Women Preachers*, as best pleasing their fancies with their sweet Tones. Did not the Scotch Lad in *Pennsilvania* mightily please their fancies, insomuch that they set him free from his service, because he had got the Tone & knack of Preaching and preached in the Power & Life, and hugely pleased their humors, till he unluckily let the worlds People know how he crept in at the window after the Women, &c. The *Friends* know VVho VVhen & VVhere.

At last, p. 31. C. P. is for running down the Common-Prayer, where his dark Light leads him to conclude, *That for People to know before hand what they must pray for, tends to quenching the spirit.* But this is rank *Quakerism*.

He goes further, and denys, *That Christ left or enjoyned any set form of Prayer.* Now here he must act the *Jesuite* by having some meaning, or otherwise he knows 'tis false.

VVhen the Disciples desired Christ to teach them how to pray, he did not say to them, *Take no thought what ye shall speak, for it shall be given you the same hour* as he did in the case of being brought before Rulers, but he prescribed them a *Form*, and commanded them to use it, *Luke* 11. 2. so that the *Lords Prayer* is a Badge of our Profession, imposed by Christ himself, to be used by those who would be counted his Disciples. But the spirit of Pride leads the *Quakers* above this command of Christ. It would indeed quench the spirit of *Quakerism* to obey this command of the outward Christ; for they obey none. I challenge them to shew wherein they obey so much as one of his Commands, any more than *Jews* do, who deny him. If they cannot do this, how sad is their Condition!

APPENDIX B

An Astronomical Description of the Late COMET.[1]

I. *THis Comet is no sublunary Meteor or sulphureous Exhalation, but a Celestial Luminary, moving in the starry Heavens.*

The Truth hereof may be demonstrated, 1. *By the vast Dimensions of it's body.* Some Comets have been observed by Astronomers to be halfe as big as the *Moon*, some bigger then the *Moon*, yea some bigger then the *Earth*. The exact Dimensions of this Comet, I may not presume to determine, but it seemeth not to be of the smallest size. Now 'tis not easy to imagine how the *Earth* should afford matter for a *Meteor* of such a huge magnitude, except we grant the greater part of the lower World to be turned into an exhalation. 2. *By the smalness of it's Parallax.* The Parallax is the Distance between the *true* place of a *Planet* and the *apparent*. The lower and neerer any Planet is to the Earth, it hath the greater *Parallax*. The Moon's *Parallax* in her *Perige*, is one degree and six minutes. I could not by my Observation discerne that this Comet had any considerable *Parallax*. 3. *By it's large circular motion.* If it had moved in the upper Region of the *Aire*, it might have finished the whole visible *arch of it's Circle* in a few houres: but wee saw it perform it's proper motion with great constancy in a very large *Circle*, such as the aire is not capable of. 4. *By it's long duration and continuance.* Had it been a *Sulphureous Vapor* kindled in the Aire; it might have been consumed in a short time; as other *fiery Meteors* are: but this continued about three months. 5. *By it's Visibility to all Countries and Nations.* We already hear that this *Comet* was seen at *Virginea, Jamaica, St. Martha, Cartagena* and *Barbados*, and no doubt but it was visible to the whole habitable World.

[1] S. Danforth (Cambridge, 1665).

But the highest region of the Aire is accounted not much above fifty English miles from the Earth, and had this *Comet* been no higher, it had been impossible that other *Countries* and *Nations* so far distant, should have beheld it. Whether this *Comet* was created in the beginning of the World together with the rest of the *Stars,* and hath been hidden in the height and profundity of the *Heavens,* and at a certain time descending toward the *Earth,* becomes Visible and Signal to the World, I leave free to after-disquisition.

II. *This Comet is not an Opake Body, like the Moon and other of the Planets, but Transparent and Pellucid, the Sun Shining through it.*

The *Moon* is enlightened on that part onely which is next the *Sun,* and like a looking glasse she reflects the solar *Beames,* which are cast upon her: but the Sun *irradiates the Comet* and *shines through it* as through a *Gemm* and illustrates a long tract in the Heavens beyond it. As the *Moon,* being a thick and dark Body, casts a dark shaddow from the *Sun,* so the *Comet* being a clear and *Diaphanous Body* transmits the light and casts a bright and shining stream from the *Sun*; which alters and varies according to the diverse aspect of the *Sun.*

III. *The Coma or Blazing Stream that issues from the Comet, is no real flame, but the Irradiation and Resplendence of the Sun through the Transparent and Pellucid Body of the Comet.*

A *Comet* is denominated from it's *Coma* or Bushy lock for the Stream hath some resemblance of a lock of hair. Now this Stream is not the *flagrancy of the Comet,* but the *Beames of the Sun* shining through the *Diaphanous* and *Translucid head of the Comet*; as may be argued and demonstrated, 1. *By it's site* and *position* which is alwaies in opposition to the *Sun.* Had it been a natural flame, arising from it's *flagrant head* it would have constantly moved upward, as the flame of a *Lamp* or *Torch*; unless it had broken forth by violence: but this streaming was sometimes *upward,* sometimes somewhat *downward,* sometimes *westward,* sometimes *northward,* sometimes *eastward,* according to the position of the Sun: neither can I imagine that any violence caused it so to move. 2. *By the diverse form and figure of the stream according to the diverse aspect of the Sun.* One while it was like a beard, another while like a taile. 3. *By the diverse dimensions of the Stream.* It was sometimes *longer,* sometimes *shorter,* sometimes *broader,* sometimes *narrower,* according as the *Comet* was neerer or further from the *Earth.* 4. *By the diverse quality and colour of the stream.* It was sometimes *bright* and *radiant,* at other times *obscure, dullish* and *faint,* according to the apparent radiation of the *Sun* and the *Comets* distance from us. 5. *By it's duration.* Had it been a real and natural flame, it is difficult to understand how the head of the *Comet* could have supplied it with food and fuel for so many months together. Obj, *If the Stream be an irradiation of the Sun how comes it to be conspicuous and visible to us?* The Sunbeames passing through the etherial Heavens are not in themselves visible, neither do they terminate our sight. *Answ.* The only reason thereof (that I can yet learn) is the Refraction and Reverberation of the Sunbeames, as they pass through the *Comet's condensed body,* whereby they are so congregated and so neerly united, as that they terminate the sight and become conspicuous in the Heavens. "I have read *of a certain semi-transparent Gemme, calle'd the Heliotrope, that if it be put into faire water, opposed to the beames of the Sun, it doth change it's beames, and by the repercussion of the Aire, seems to shadow the clearness of its rayes, and so induce a sanguineous colour in the Aire, as if the Sun by the interposition of the body of the Moon, did suffer an ecliptick darkness.*"

IV. *This Comet is not a new fixed Star, but a Planetick or Erratick Body, wandring up & down in the etherial firmament under the fixed stars.*

Some learned Astronomers distinguish these more noble and celestial *Phenomenæ* or *Appearances* into *Fixed* and *Erratick.* Several new Stars have appeared which are fixed, *i.e.* they keep the same place in the *Heavens,* and the same distance from the *fixed Stars.* One in *Cassiopeia* Anno

1572. which continued a year and four months. Another in *Antinous*: another in the *Girdle* of *Andromeda,* another in the *Whale,* another in the *Brest of the Swan,* which continued many years. But this *Comet was* 'Αστὴρ πλανήτης (as *Jude* speaks) a *wandring Star,* which kept not the same place in the Heavens, nor the same distance from the fixed Stars.

V. *This Comet appeared first in the Constellation of the Raven, from whence it descended and crossing the Tropick of Capricorn and some part of Hydra, it went southward until it arrived at the main topsaile of the Ship: then it began to return, and going through the belly of Canis major, it again crossed the Tropick of Capricorn, and passing through the middle of the Hare, it crossed the river Eridanus and the Equinoctial, and entred into the mouth of the Whale, and going through his head, it crossed the Ecliptick and so passed up between* Aries *and* Linum *sepientrionale.*

Some took notice of this *Comet* in the beginning of *November,* and indeed it had passed through the middle of the *Asterism* of *Corvus,* (as I gather from it's following motions) before I saw it. *Dec.* 5 early in the morning it seemed to me to be very neer the *Southern Tropick,* about 3 degrees southward of the *Ravens bill* having longit. *Libra* 4. *Dec.* 8 early in the morning I saw it in some part of *Hydra*; in *Virgo* 28. lat. *S.* 30 *gr.* The stream overshadowing a small star in *Hydra,* that was neer. *Dec.* 16. some observed it among the stars that are in the mainmast of *Argo Navis*: where it had longit. *Leo* 23. Lat. *S.* 45. *Dec.* 17. It was seen amongst the *stellae informes,* which are behinde *Canis major*: where it was apprehended to have longit. *Leo.* 2. lat. *S.* 50. *Dec.* 18. The *Comet* came to *Sirius,* i.e. the *great Dog,* and passed through his belly. That night I saw it in *Cancer* 13. lat. *S.* 48. *Dec.* 19. It ascended from *Canis major* and crossing the *southern Tropick* it arrived at *Lepus,* i.e. the *Hare.* That night I saw it pass over the more *northern Star* in the *Hare's hinder legs*: being in *Gemini* 24. lat. *S.* 44. *Dec.* 23. I saw it as I supposed in *Taur.* 14. lat. *S.* 19. *Dec.* 24. I apprehended it to be in the *Equinoctial* which it crossed in the 44*th gr.* entring into the mouth of *Balaena*: having longit. *Taur.*

12. 30. lat. *S.* 17. *Dec.* 25. In *Taur.* 11. 30. lat. *S.* 14. *Dec.* 28, I saw it in a right line between two Stars in the *head of the Whale,* almost in the middle between them: in *Taur.* 4.15. Lat. *S.* 7. 15. *Dec.* 29 I saw it very neer to another Star in the *head of the Whale*: in *Taur.* 3. lat. *S.* 6. *Jan.* 3. It crossed the *Ecliptick in* Aries 28. 30. *Jan.* 16. it came to Aries 26. lat. *N.* 3. *Jan.* 24. Aries 25. lat. *N.* 4. *Jan.* 31. Aries 25. lat. *N.* 5. 30. *Feb.* 4. Aries 25. lat. *N.* 6. 15. Since that I saw it not, nor any man else, that I hear of. If in these observations I have not attained that accurateness which the Reader desires my want of *Astronomical Instruments* may bespeak his indulgence therein.

VI. *The Comet at it's first appearance was* Oriental *and* Matutine, *afterward it became* Occidental *and* Vespertine.

At first it appeared early in the morning before the rising of the Sun, and then every day rose sooner then other (withall changing it's *AZuante* or point of the Compass in it's rising) until it appeared in the evening, as soon as daylight was ended.

VII. This Comet at first moved slowly, then more swiftly till it came to it's Perige: since which time it hath gradually decreased in it's motion: toward the latter end of it's apparition, it hath moved most slowly.

From *Dec.* 5*th* to the 8*th* (which was the time between my first and second observation) the *Comets* apparent motion in it's proper line upon the *Celestial Sphere,* was about 2 degrees & a halfe in a day, one day with another. *Dec.* 17. it was observed by some to move about 13. *degrees. Dec.* 18 it moved 15, or 16 *degrees. Dec.* 19 it moved about 13, *degrees.* [I cannot precisely determine it's *diurnal motion,* especially when it was so exceeding swift, because I know not certainly the hour of the night, when these observations were made.] From *Dec.* 25, to 29 it moved 2 *degrees* & half in a day, one day with another. *Dec.* 29. 2 *degr. Dec.* 30 1 *degr.* & halfe. *Dec.* 31. 1 *degr.* In the beginning of *Jan.* it moved neer 1 *degr.* in a day: but toward the latter end, not one *deg.* in several dayes. From *Jan.* 5*th* to *Feb.* 4*th* according to my observation it gained scarce 7 *deg.*

VIII. This Comet was continually Retrograde in it's motion, onely toward the latter end of it's apparition, it became Stationary.

This *Comet* from the first time, it was taken notice of, until the latter end of *Jan.* in it's proper motion went contrary to the *series* and *order of the signes, viz.* from *Libra* to *Virgo* and so backward to *Aries*: But in the latter end of *January* and in the beginning of *February* it kept in the same *degree of longitude,* onely it altered it's *latitude.*

IX. This Comet hath moved constantly almost in a right line, or in a great Circle, equal to the greatest circle of the celestial Sphere: but towards it's disappearing, it hath deflected a little and become ellipticall.

This may be demonstrated by the *Celestial Globe.* Depress the Southern Pole 61 *degr.* (which is the complement of the *Comet's* greatest declination,) and you may finde almost all the fore-mentioned observations concerning the *Comets* place to fall just upon the *Horizon of the Globe*: but toward the latter end, you shall finde the *Cometicall line* to recede a little from a *true circle.*

X. *The proper Circle of the Comets motion is Eccentrical, i.e. it hath a center diverse from the center of the world.*

This is evident 1 By the *diversity of it's Latitude,* which was sometimes *southern,* and sometimes *northern.* 2 By the inequality of it's *apparent motion,* which was sometimes *swift* and sometimes *slow.* 3 By the diversity of it's *distance* from the earth, which was sometimes *greater,* and sometimes *less.*

XI. This Comet hath ascended in Meridian Altitude *above* 44 *degr. For it's lowest meridian altitude with us, was* 18 *degr. and* 40 *minutes, and it's highest,* 63 *degr. and* 15 *min.*

XII. The Cometical line descended to 29 *degr. of Southern declination.*

XIII. The Comet's Southern Limit of Latitude was 50. *degr.*

XIV. The apparent motion of the Comet was anomalous and unequal, but it's motion in it's proper Orb or Circle, was very neer equal and uniform.

That it's apparent motion was *unequal* and *irregular* is manifest by it's *Velocity* or *swiftnes* one while, it's *mediocrity* another while, and it's *tardity* or *slowness* toward the latter end. The cause of which *anomaly* and *inequality*, was the *Comet's Eccentricity*. That the *Comet's* motion in it's proper orb or circle was very neer equal and uniform, may be demonstrated by the equality of it's *diurnal motion* in equal distances from it's *perige*. For instance, I finde on the 5*th* of December and on the 25*th*, the *Comet* was equally distant from it's *Perige*, and that then it's apparent motion was equal, *viz.* 2 *degrees* and a halfe in a day: and therefore it's true motion in reference to it's own proper center was very neer equal and regular.

XV. *The* Comet *seemed to be in it's* Perige, *or neerest to the Earth, when it was in the belly of* Canis major, *which was sometime on the* 18*th of* December.

The *Perige* is that point of the *Cometical circle* which is neerest to the earth. The *Apoge* is the point farthest distant from the earth. That the *Comet* was in it's *Perige* at the time and in the place aforementioned may be argued. 1 From the *swiftness of it's apparent motion* on that day. All the Planets are slow in their *Apoge* and swift in their *Perige*. This *Comet* was apprehended to move the most swiftly on that day. 3. [*sic*] from the *Equality of it's apparent motion* in equal distances from thence: An instance whereof I gave before. 3 From the *distance of the place assigned*, (*viz.* the middle of the belly of *Sirius*) to the place of the *Comet's* disappearing. In the Cometical line the distance is about 90 *degrees*. Now according to the Theory and doctrine of *Comets*, it was never observed that any *Comet* from the point of it's swiftest motion, ever ran beyond the fourth part of a circle, which is 90 degrees. *N. B.* On the selfe same day (*viz.* the 18*th* of *December*) the Sun was also in his *Perige*.

XVI. *Since* December 5*th, the Comet hath proceeded in it's proper curricle upon the celestial Sphere,* 153. degrees: *and I suppose in all, since it's first apparition,* 180. degrees.

XVII. *The cometical circle seemeth to include and encompass the Earth.*

This may be Argued 1. From the *length* and *greatness* of the visible and apparent *Arch* of the *Cometical circle,* which was very neer to, if not a true *semicircle.* 2. From the *Duration* and long *continuance* of it's *Apparition,* which was about three months.

XVIII. *The true and real magnitude of the* Comet *was constantly one and the same, but it's apparent magnitude was Various and Diverse.*

At it's first appearance it seemed but *small,* at length it appeared far *greater,* sometime it seemed to be very neer halfe as big as the *Moon*: after that it decreased successively, till at last it appeared like a cloudy star. The reason wherof is evident; at it's first appearance it was very high in the Heavens, and therefore it's *diameter* seemed less: afterward it descended lower and neerer to the earth, and then it's *diameter* encreased: at length it went up higher & was removed further from our sight, and then it's *basis* together with the *angle of the optick Cone* was diminished, until at last it disappeared and vanished out of sight.

XIX The true colour and splendor of the Comet was alwayes one and the same, but it's apparent colour was various and diverse.

At first appearance it's colour was *pale and obscure*: afterward *bright and radiant,* at length it grew very *obscure* and *faint* like a cloudy star. In the West Indies it appeared *fiery, red* and *dreadfull.*

XX *The Coma or Stream that came from the head of the Comet, was alwayes cast into that part, which was diametrically opposite to the Sun.*

When the *Comet's irradiation* was from the *Southeast,* it's streaming was toward the *northwest,* when it's *irradiation* was from S.S.E. it's streaming was toward N.N.W: when it's *irradiation* was from the *South*, it's streaming was toward the *north*, when it's *irradiation* was from S.S.W. it's streaming was toward N.N.E. when it's *irradiation* was from the S.W. it's streaming was toward N.E.

XXI. *The Comet in respect of it's stream, hath been of a diverse figure according to the diverse aspect of the Sun.*

Comets in respect of their figure are distinguished into *Barbate*, *Candate* and *Crinite*. A *Comet* is *barbate*, when the stream like a beard, goes before the body of the *Comet*. *Candate*, when the stream like a tail follows the body of y[e] *Comet*. *Crinite* when the stream goes right up into the Heavens and seems like a hairy-lock to be wound up about the *Comet's* head. This *Comet*, while it was *Oriental*, was *Barbate*, the stream going before its body, like a beard. When the *Comet* became *Occidental*, it was *Candate*, the stream following the *Comet's* body like a tail. But it could not be properly *Crinite*, in regard of the greatness of the *Comet's* southern latitude at the time of it's opposition with the Sun.

XXII. The stream hath appeared of a diverse height, breadth and extent, according to the diverse position of the Sun, and the Comet's distance from us.

The stream was not alwaies of the same height in the Heavens with the head of the *Comet*, but sometimes *higher*, and sometimes *lower*. Neither was the *dilation* of the stream alwaies one and the same, but it was sometimes *broader*, and sometimes *narrower*. The *length* and *extent* of the stream was also *diverse*: *Dec*: 8. It was apprehended to be 38 *degr*. long, *Dec*. 17. 20 *degr*. *Dec*. 30. 15 *degr*. *Jan*. 6. 14 *degr*. *Ian*. 25. 7 *degr Ian*. 31. 3 *degr*.

XXIII. *This Comet hath been vertical to all countries, ha lye* [*sic*] *between* 29 *degrees of Southern Latitude and* 15 *degrees of Northern Latitude.*

The Comet is said to be *Vertical* to any people, when the Body of the *Comet* passeth over their heads. This Comet was vertical to the chief *Islands* of the *East Indies*, as also to *Guinea* and to the most of the Southern part of *Africa*: likewise to *Peru*, *Brasilia*, *Guiana*, *Castilia deloro*, *nova*

Andaluzia, and to several of the *Islands* of the *West Indies,* as *Trinidada, Granada, Barbados, Matalina, Dominica* and many other.

XXIV. *The stream which came from the* Comet *hath turned about and pointed toward most countries and Kingdomes in the habitable World.*

XXV. *This* Comet *is not* evaporated *nor* dissolved, *but it is ascended higher toward it's* Apoge *and so departed out of our sight.*

If the Comet be no vapour but a *celestial planetick luminary,* moving constantly in it's *Eccentrick orb,* and if the stream thereof be no real flame, but the *irradiation* of the *Sun* through the Comet's *head,* it will necessarily follow that the Comet is not *consumed, dissipated* or *extinguished,* but rather *ascended* toward it's *Apoge, i.e.* the farthest point distant from the Earth, and so being buried in the *deep abyss* of the Heavens, becomes inconspicuous to us.

XXVI. *This* Comet *hath followed upon a notable Conjunction of the Superiour Planets,* Saturn *and* Jupiter.

Astronomers observe, that *Comets* do many times follow a Conjunction of the *Superior Planets.* The last Year, *October 10th,* was a great Conjunction of *Saturn* and *Iupiter* in the 13*th degr.* of *Sagittarius.*

A Brief *Theological Application* of this strange and notable *Appearance* in the *Heavens.*

I. The *Holy* Scriptures, *which are the* Authentick *and unerring* Canon *of truth, teach us to look at* Comets, *as* Portentous *and* Signal *of great and notable Changes.*

> *Joel* 2. 30, 31. I will shew wonders in the Heavens and in the Earth, Blood and Fire, and Pillars of Smoak. The Sun shall be turned into Darkness, and the Moon into Blood before the great and terrible day of the Lord come.
>
> *Luke* 21. 25. There shall be signes in the Sun, and in the Moon, and in the Stars.
>
> *Acts* 2. 19. 20. I will shew wonders in Heaven above, and signes in the Earth beneath: Blood, and Fire, and

Vapor of Smoak. The Sun shall be turned into Darkness and the Moon into Blood before the great and notable day of the Lord come.

II. *The Histories of former Ages, do abundantly testifie that* Comets *have been many times Heralds of wrath to a secure and impenitent World.*

Take a few Instances.

A little before the *Achaick Warr* (as *Seneca* reports) there appeared a Comet fiery and ruddy, which cast a clear light, whereby the night was enlightened.

Anno Christ: 56. There appeared a Comet. The same Year *Claudius* died, and bloody *Nero* succeeded, who slew his *Mother*, his *Wife* and his *Master Seneca*, and exercised a great deal of cruelty and wickedness.

Anno 323. There were diverse Comets which preceeded the *Pestilent Heresie* of *Arius*.

Anno. 337. A Comet appeared before the death of *Constantine* the great, and innumerable evils followed.

Anno 602. A great Comet appeared, which preceded, if not presaged the slaughter of *Mauritius* the *Emperor*, and the *Supremacy* of the *Bishop of Rome*.

Anno 675, & 676. There appeared a Comet 3 moneths, at which time the *Saracens* greatly afflicted the *Roman Empire*.

Anno. 729 Two Comets appeared, and the same year a great *Plague* invaded the world.

Anno 814. A terrible Comet appeared before the death of *Charles the great*.

Anno 1066. A Comet appeared a long time to the whole World: The same Year *England* was many waies afflicted by *William Duke of Normandy*, and at length subdued.

Anno 1618. There appeared a great Comet: the same year brake forth the *Bloody Wars in Germany*. *Anno* 1652. There appeared a Comet at the beginning of Mr. *Cottons* sickness, and disappeared a few daies after his death. The next year strange and notable changes of state happened in *England*.

'Tis true, some Comets have been thought to presage good to the World, as that in the dayes of *Augustus* before the birth of Christ. [*I intend not that miraculous Star, which appeared to the* Magi.] Another before the death of *Nero*: Another before the reformation by *Wickliffe*: Another before the reformation by *Luther*: but most commonly they are observed to precede, if not portend great Calamities.

Anno 79 Upon a Comet followed horrible *Winds*, an *Earth-quake* and *Pestilence*. When some shewed *Vespasian* this Comet, fearing it might portend his death, he answered merrily that this Prodigie noted not him, but the King of *Parthia*. For saith he, *he nourisheth his hair*, but I am bald. But not long after, Vespasian died.

III. *The Commination of wrath according to Scripture, is to be understood after a conditional manner,* i e. *with an implicite reservation for Gods altering and revoking his threatned dispensation upon repentance intervening.*

> *Jer.* 18. 7, 8. At what Instant I shall speak concerning a nation and concerning a Kingdome, to pluck up and to pull down and to destroy it: if that nation against whom I have pronounced, turn from their Evil, I will repent of the evil that I thought to do unto them.
>
> *Jer.* 36. 3, 7. It may be the house of Judah will hear all the evil, which I purpose to do unto them, that they may return every man from his evil way, that I may forgive their Iniquity and their Sin. It may be they will present their supplication before the Lord, and will returne every one from his evil way: for great is the Anger and the Fury, which the Lord hath pronounced against this People.
>
> *Jonah* 3. 10. And God saw their works that they turned from their evil way, and God repented of the Evil, that he had said that he would do unto them, and he did it not.

IV. *This Blazing Star being in conjunction with diverse other awful Providences and Tokens of Wrath, calls upon us to awake out of security, and to bring forth fruits meet for Repentence.*

A Few Instances of some late awful Providences.

1. *Earth-quakes.* About two years ago *viz. Ian.* 26, & 28. 1662, 63. The foundations of the Earth trembled, and some of our houses rock't like a cradle. 6, or 7 times did the Earth shake under us in the space of 2 or 3 dayes. It was then thought and said, that these *Earth-quakes* might portend the Lords shaking the foundations of our Churches and of our civil state.

2. The late *removal by Death* of some of our eminent *Prophets* and *seers,* who were as eyes unto us in the Wilderness, and the *Charets* [*sic*] of *Israel* and the *Horse-men* thereof. *April.* 5*th,* 1663, That burning and shining Light, who shone in the Church of *Boston,* and gave light to the whole Colony and Country, Mr. *John Norton,* a man eminently accomplished, was taken from us, and translated to an higher Orb. Of whom *New-England* was not worthy.

Iuly 20 1663. That bright and radiant Star, a Star of the first magnitude, Mr. *Samuel Stone,* the strength and glory of *Connecticut,* rested from his labours and sorrows, and fell asleep sweetly and placidly in the Lord. A little before Him, Mr *Iohn Miller* and Mr. *Samuel Newman,* faithful, painful and affectionate Preachers of the Gospel, were also taken from us by death. Thus our Pillars are cut down, our strongest Stakes pluck't up, and our breaches not repaired. Is it a small thing in our eyes, y^t^ our principal Congregations & Head-townes, should be so sadly bereaved, as they are at this day?

3. The sad *Mildew* and *Blasting,* whereby we have been greatly afflicted the *last* Summer, and some of us the Summer before: our principal grain being turned into an husk & rotteness.

4. Severe *Drought* this *last* Summer, which burnt up the Pastures and the latter growth.

5. Early *Frosts,* which smote our *Indian Corn,* and greatly impoverished our latter harvest.

Unto these and some other no less threatning Visitations, is superadded this strange and fearful Appearance in the

Heavens, which is now seconded by a new Appearance this Spring, concomitant to the translation of our Honoured and Aged Governour, Mr. *John Endicot* from hence to a better World: By all which doubtless the Lord calls upon *New-England* to awake and to repent.

To this End Consider.

1. What a jealous eye the Lord hath upon us, observing how we carry and behave our selves at such a time as this. *Ier.* 3. 8. And I saw,

> when for all the causes, whereby backsliding Israel committed Adultery, I had put her away, and given her a bill of Divorce: yet her Treacherous Sister Judah feared not, but went and played the Harlot also.

2. What the Lord expects and looks for from a people so highly favoured and priviledged, and so awfully warned and threatned. *Zeph.* 3. 7.

> I said surely thou wilt fear mee; thou wilt receive Instructions so their dwelling place should not be cut off; howsoever I punished them.

3. How sadly will the Lord Jesus expostulate with us, if we fall asleep in the hour of the Passion and Agony of the Gospel. *Mat.* 26. 40.

> He cometh unto the Disciples and findeth them a sleep, and saith unto *Peter*, what could ye not watch with me one hour? each word is very Emphatical.

4. The danger of being surprized by temptation before we are aware. *Lam.* 1. 9. She

> Remembred not her last end, therefore she came down wonderfully: she had no comforter. *Rev.* 16. 15. Behold I come as a thief. Blessed is he that watcheth and keepeth his garments, lest he walk naked, and they see his shame.

5. The singular blessing reserved for the vigilant and penitent. *Hab*. 3. 16. When I

> heard my belly trembled: my lips quivered at the voice: rottenness entred into my bones: and I trembled in my selfe, that I might rest in the day of trouble. *Luke* 21. 36. Watch ye therefore and pray alwaies, that ye may be accounted worthy to escape all these things that shall come to pass, and to stand before the Son of Man.

To Conclude: God forbid that any of us, should be 'Αστέρες πλανῆται wandring Stars, Eccentrick and Erratick in our motions, as all Seducers and Impostors are: for whom is reserved the blackness of darkness for ever. *Jude*, v. 13. but the Lord grant that we may all become fixed Stars in the new *Jerusalem*, which cometh down from God, observing the Heavenly order prescribed in his holy word, and shining as lights in the midst of a crooked and perverse generation, clearly reflecting that pure and precious light, wherewith we are irradiated by the Sun of Righteousness: and then we may assure ourselves, Christ will still hold us in his right hand, and not suffer us to be cast down from Heaven, but enable us to finish our course with joy, & at length translate us into the Kingdome of the Father, where we shall shine forth as the Sun, and as the brightness of the firmament, and as the Stars forever and ever. *Amen*.

FINIS.

APPENDIX C

OF POETRY, AND OF STYLE[1]

—Cotton Mather

#8. POETRY, whereof we have now even an *Antediluvian Piece* in our Hands, has from the Beginning been in such Request, that I must needs recommend unto you some Acquaintance with it. Though some have had a Soul so *Unmusical*, that they have decried all *Verse*, as being but a meer *Playing* and *Fiddling* upon *Words*; All *Versifying*, as if it were more *Unnatural* than if we should chuse *Dancing* instead of *Walking*; and *Ryme*, as if it were but a sort of *Morisco Dancing* with *Bells*: Yet I cannot wish you a Soul that shall be wholly *Unpoetical*. And Old *Horace* has left us an *Art of Poetry*, which you may do well to bestow a Perusal on. And besides your *Lyrick Hours*, I wish you may so far understand an *Epic Poem*, that the Beauties of an *Homer* and a *Virgil* may be discerned with you. As to the *Moral* Part of *Homer*, 'tis true, and let me not be counted a *Zoilus* for saying so, that by first exhibiting their *Gods* as no better than *Rogues*, he set open the Floodgates for a prodigious Inundation of Wickedness to break in upon the Nations, and was one of the *greatest Apostles* the *Devil* ever had in the World. Among the rest that felt the Ill Impressions of this *Universal Corrupter*, (as Men of the best Sentiments have called him,) One was that overgrown Robber, of execrable Memory, whom we celebrate under the Name of *Alexander the Great*; who by his continual Admiring and Studying of his *Iliad*, and by following that false Model of Heroic Virtue set before him in his *Achilles*, became one of the worst of Men, and at length inflated with the Ridiculous Pride of being himself a *Deity*, exposed him-

[1] From *Manuductio ad Ministerium* (Boston, 1726), pp. 38-47. Although this book was published first in 1726, his ideas on poetry and style were doubtless formulated long before that date.

self to all the Scorn that could belong unto a *Lunatick*. And hence, notwithstanding the Veneration which this Idol has had, yet *Plato* banishes him out of a *Common-Wealth*, the Welfare whereof he was concerned for. Nevertheless, *Custom* or *Conscience* obliges him to bear Testimonies unto many Points of *Morality*. And it is especially observable, That he commonly propounds *Prayer* to Heaven as a most necessary Preface unto all Important Enterprizes; and when the Action comes on too suddenly for a more extended *Supplication*, he yet will not let it come on without an Ejaculation; and he never speaks of any *Supplication* but he brings in a Gracious Answer to it. I have seen a Travesteering *High-Flyer*, not much to our Dishonour, Scoff at *Homer* for this; as making his Actors to be like those whom the English call *Dissenters*. But then, we are so much led into the Knowledge of *Antiquities*, by reading of this *Poet*, and into so many Parts of the *Recondite Learning*, that notwithstanding some little *Nods* in him, not a few Acute Pens besides the old Bishop of *Thessalonica's*, have got a Reputation by regaling us with *Annotations* upon him. Yea, Tho' One can't but smile at the Fancy of *Croese*, who tries with much Ostentation of Erudition, to show, That *Homer* has all along tendred us in a Disguise and Fable, the *History of the Old Testament*, yet many Illustrations of the *sacred Scriptures*, I find are to be fetched from him; who indeed had probably read what was Extant of them in his Days; Particularly, Our *Eighteenth Psalm* is what he has evidently imitated. *Virgil* too, who so much lived upon him, as well as after him, is unaccountably mad upon his *Fate*, which he makes to be he knows not what himself, but Superiour to *Gods* as well as to *Men*, and thro' his whole Composures he so asserts the Doctrine of this Nonsensical Power, as is plainly inconsistent with all Virtue. And what *fatal Mischief* did *Fascinator* do to the *Roman Empire*, when by Deifying one Great Emperor, he taught the Successors to claim the Adoration of *Gods*, while they were perpetrating the Crimes of *Devils*? I will not be a *Carbilius* upon him; nor will I say any thing, how little the *Married State* owes unto One who writes as if he were a *Woman hater*: Nor what his Blunders are about his poor-spirited and inconsistent *Hero*, for which many have taxed him. Nevertheless, 'tis observed, That the Pagans had no *Rules of Manners*, that were more Laudable and Regular than what are to be found in him. And some have said, It is *hardly possible seriously to Read his Works without being more disposed unto Goodness, as well as being agreeably entertained.* Be sure, had *Virgil* writ before *Plato*, his Works had not been any of the *Books prohibited.* But then, This *Poet* also has abundance of Rare *Antiquities* for us: And such Things, as others besides a *Servius*, have imagined that they have instructed and obliged Mankind, by employing all their Days upon. Wherefore if his *Aeneis*, which tho' it were once near twenty times as big as he has left it, yet he has left it unfinished, may not appear so valuable to you, that you may think *Twenty Seven Verses* of the Part that is the most finished in it, worth One and Twenty Hundred Pounds and odd Money, yet his *Georgicks*, which he put his left Hand unto, will furnish you with many things far from Despicable. But after all, when I said, I was willing that the *Beauties* of these *Two Poets*, might become *Visible* to your *Visive Faculty* in *Poetry*, I did not mean, that you should Judge nothing to be Admittable into an *Epic Poem*, which is not Authorised by their Example; but I perfectly concur with One who is inexpressibly more capable to be a Judge of such a Matter than I can be; That it is a *false Critic* who *with a petulant Air, will insult Reason itself, if it presumes to oppose such Authority.*

I proceed now to say, That if (under the Guidance of a *Vida*) you try your young Wings now and then to see what Flights you can make, at least for an *Epigram*, it may a little sharpen your *Sense*, and polish your *Style*, for more important Performances; For this Purpose you are now even overstock'd with *Patterns*, and *Poemata Passim.* You may, like *Nazianzen*, all your Days, make a little *Recreation* of Poetry in the midst of your more painful Studies. Nevertheless, I cannot but advise you, *Withhold thy Throat from*

Thirst. Be not so set upon *Poetry,* as to be always poring on the *Passionate* and *Measured* Pages. Let not what should be *Sauce* rather than *Food* for you, Engross all your Application. Beware of a *Boundless* and *Sickly* Appetite, for the Reading of the *Poems,* which now the *Rickety* Nation swarms withal: And let not the *Circaean* Cup intoxicate you. But especially preserve the Chastity of your Soul from the Dangers you may incur, by a Conversation with *Muses* that are no better than *Harlots*: Among which are others besides *Ovid*'s Epistles, which for their Tendency to excite and foment Impure *Flames,* and cast *Coals* into your *Bosom,* deserve rather to be thrown into the *Fire,* than to be laid before the *Eye* which a *Covenant* should be *made* withal. Indeed, not meerly for the *Impurities* which they convey, but also on some other Accounts, the *Powers of Darkness* have a *Library* among us, whereof the *Poets* have been the most *Numerous* as well as the most *Venemous* Authors. Most of the Modern *Plays,* as well as the *Romances* and *Novels* and *Fictions,* which are a sort of *Poems,* do belong to the *Catalogue* of this cursed Library. The *Plays,* I say, in which there are so many Passages, that have a Tendency to overthrow all *Piety,* that one whose Name is *Bedford,* has extracted near Seven Thousand Instances of them, from the Plays chiefly of but Five Years preceding; and says awfully upon them, *They are National Sins, and therefore call for National Plagues*; *And if GOD should enter into Judgment all the Blood in the Nation would not be able to atone for them.* How much do I wish that such Pestilences, and indeed all those worse than *Egyptian Toads,* (the Spawns of a *Butler,* & a *Brown,* and a *Ward,* and a Company *whose Name is Legion*!) might never crawl into your Chamber! The *unclean Spirits* that *come like Frogs out of the Mouth of the Dragon, and of the Beast*; which *go forth* unto the young People of the *Earth,* and expose them to be dealth withal as the Enemies of GOD, in *the Battle of the Great Day of the Almighty.* As for those wretched *Scribbles* of *Madmen,* My Son, *Touch them not, Taste them not, Handle them not*: Thou wilt *perish* in the *using* of them. They are,

The Dragons whose Contagious Breath Peoples the dark Retreats of Death. To much better Purpose will an Excellent but an Envied *Blackmore* feast you, than those Vile *Rapsodies* (of that *Vinum Daemonum*) which you will find always leave a Taint upon your Mind, and among other ill Effects, will sensibly indispose you to converse with the *Holy Oracles* of GOD your SAVIOUR.

But there is, what I may rather call a *Parenthesis,* than a *Digression,* which this may be not altogether an Improper Place for the introducing of.

(There has been a deal of a do about a STYLE; So much, that I must offer you my Sentiments upon it. There is a *Way of Writing,* wherein the Author endeavours, that the Reader may have *something to the Purpose* in every Paragraph. There is not only a *Vigour* sensible in every *Sentence,* but the Paragraph is embellished with *Profitable References,* even to something beyond what is *directly spoken.* Formal and Painful *Quotations* are not studied; yet all that could be learnt from them is insinuated. The Writer pretends not unto *Reading,* yet he could not have writ as he does if he had not *Read* very much in his Time; and his Composures are not only a *Cloth of Gold,* but also struck with as many *Jewels,* as the Gown of a Russian Embassador. This *Way of Writing* has been decried by many, and is at this Day more than ever so, for the same Reason, that in the old Story, the *Grapes* were decried, *That they were not Ripe.* A Lazy, Ignorant, Conceited Sett of Authors, would perswade the whole Tribe, to lay aside that *Way of Writing,* for the same Reason that one would have perswaded his Brethren to part with the Encumbrance of their *Bushy Tails.* But however *Fashion* and *Humour* may prevail, they must not think that the Club at their *Coffee-House* is, *All the World,* but there will always be those, who will in this Case be governed by *Indisputable Reason*: And who will think, that the real Excellency of a Book will never ly in *saying of little*; That the less one has for his Money in a Book, 'tis really the more Valuable for it; and that the less one is instructed in a Book, and the more of Superfluous *Margin,* and Superficial *Harangue,* and the less of *Substantial Matter* one has in it, the more tis to be accounted of. And if a more Massy *Way of Writing* be never so much disgusted at This Day, a *Better Gust* will come on, as will some other Thing, *quae jam Cecidere.* In the mean time, Nothing appears to me more Impertinent and Ridiculous than the *Modern Way,* (I cannot say, *Rule*; For they have *None*!) of *Criticising.* The Blades that set up for *Criticks,* I know not who constituted or commission'd 'em!—they appear to me, for the most part as *Contemptible,* as they are a *Supercilious* Generation. For indeed no Two of them have the same *Style;* and they are as intollerably Cross grain'd and severe in their Censures upon one another, as they are upon the rest of Mankind. But while each of them, conceitedly enough, sets up for the *Standard of Perfection,* we are entirely at a Loss which *Fire* to follow. Nor can you easily find any one thing wherein they agree for their *Style,* except perhaps a perpetual Care to give us Jejune and Empty Pages, without such *Touches of Erudition* (to speak in the *Style* of an Ingenious Traveller) as may make the Discourses less *Tedious,* and more *Enriching,* to the Mind of him that peruses them. There is much Talk of a *Florid Style,* obtaining among the Pens, that are most in Vogue; but how often would it puzzle one, even with the best Glasses to find the *Flowres*! And if they were to be Chastized for it, it would be with as much of Justice, as *Jerom* was, for being a *Ciceronian.* After all, Every Man will have his own *Style,* which will distinguish him as much as his *Gate*: And if you can attain to that which I have newly described, but always writing so as to give an *Easy Conveyance* unto your *Idea's,* I would not have you by any *Scourging* be driven out of your *Gate,* but if you must confess a *Fault* in it, make a Confession like that of the Lad, unto his Father while he was beating him for his *Versifying.*

However, since every Man will have his own Style, I would pray, that we may learn to treat one another with mutual *Civilities,* and *Condescensions,* and handsomely *indulge* one another in this, as *Gentlemen* do in other Matters.

I wonder what ails People, that they can't let *Cicero* write in the *Style* of *Cicero*, and *Seneca* write in the (much other!) *Style* of *Seneca*; and own that *Both* may please in their *several Ways*.—But I will freely tell you; what has made me consider the *Humourists* that set up for *Criticks upon Style*, as the most *Unregardable Set of Mortals* in the World, is This! Far more Illustrious *Criticks* than any of those to whom I am now bidding Defiance, and no less Men than your *Erasmus*'s, and your *Grotius*'s, have taxed the *Greek Style* of the *New Testament*, with I know not what *Solaecisms* and *Barbarisms*; And, how many *Learne'd Folks* have Obsequiously run away with the Notion! Whereas 'tis an Ignorant and an Insolent *Whimsey*; which they have been guilty of. It may be (and particularly by an Ingenious *Blackwal*, it has been) Demonstrated, That the Gentlemen are mistaken in every one of their pretended Instances; All the Unquestionable *Classicks*, may be brought in, to convince them of their Mistakes. Those Glorious Oracles are as *pure Greek* as ever was written in the World; and so Correct, so Noble, so Sublime in their *Style*, that never any thing under the Cope of Heaven, but the *Old Testament*, has equall'd it.)

[On Slavery][2]

—Samuel Sewall

Quest. *Whether Trading for Negros* i.e. *carrying them out of their own Country into perpetual Slavery, be in it self Unlawful, and especially contrary to the great Law of* CHRISTIANITY?

Answ. Sir, After a mature and serious consideration of the Question proposed, I am for the Affirmative, and cannot see how such a Trade (tho' much used by Christians) can be any way justify'd, and fairly reconciled to the Christian Law. And here, first let me propose my Reasons, and then answer such weak Pleas as use to be made for it.

[2] Published in *The Athenian Oracle*, I, 545-548. Reprinted as Massachusetts Broadside.

1. I take it to be contrary to the great Law of Nature, of doing unto all Men as we would they should do unto us; and which as our Saviour tells us (Mat. 7. 22.) *Is the sum of the Law and the Prophets.* For let us put the case to our selves, and consider what it would be for a Man to be stolen away from his Native Country, and hurryd into perpetual Bondage; Or to have a Child snatch'd from his Embraces, and so us'd: and then see if this Trade and practice can be any way reconciled to this Rule. And surely, they that have the *Gospel,* and yet sin against the very Laws of *Nature*: shall have a severer punishment at the Day of Judgment, than those poor silly Wretches that have only that dim Light to guide them. And perhaps those poor Wretches in Chains, when Death shall make them free; may rise up in Judgment, and condemn those more cruel and unnatural Men that so unjustly deprive them of that Liberty which God and Nature had given them.

2. 'Tis plainly contrary to the Word of God, and forbidden both in the Old Testament, and in the New; See Exod. 21. 16. *He that stealeth a Man and selleth him, or he be found in his hands, he shall be surely put to Death.* The prohibition is general; He that Stealeth any Man whatsoever, without distinction; whether one of their Brothers, or a Stranger; a meer Heathen, or a Pagan: *He shall be surely put to Death*; the punishment is Capital, and good reason for it. For if he that sheddeth Mans blood, by Man shall his blood be shed: surely Liberty is as dear as Life it self. Yea, he that intends to sell a Man into some kind of Bondage; would do him a greater kindness to free him from a miserable Life. And I am well assured, this is the case of some of those poor Wretches, with a witness.

Again, In the New-Testament St. *Paul,* I *Tim.* 1. 10. joyns the Man-stealer with the most horrid and unnatural Sinners; *Murderers of Fathers, and Murderers of Mothers, and Defilers of themselves with Mankind.*

3. Its Practice is a Disgrace to Christianity, and makes the Name of Christ to be blasphem'd amongst the Gentiles, and (in all likelihood) hinders the Propagation of the Chris-

tian Faith in the World. For I am verily perswaded, that if a fair and honest Trade and Commerce had been carried on amongst them; and no violence had been done to their persons: Christianity must have gotten as great footing by this time amongst them, as it has amongst the poor Infidels of *New-England*: Or, at least, they might have been in a great forwardness to receive that holy Doctrine; which now they hate and abominate for the sake of this practice of Christians amongst them.—And Wo be to that person, that shall by any means hinder that blessed design for which Christ came from Heaven; and both Himself, his Apostles, and many Primitive Christians spent their dearest blood to promote; *viz.* to have the Mind and Will of God known unto the World.

But perhaps some may make light of this, and perswade themselves, they have sufficient pleas to vindicate the Practice. I know indeed many times, when a man's Interest lies in the Ballance; a very weak Plea and light Excuse will pass for a weighty Reason: But for my part (who am a person indifferent, and altogether unconcern'd that way) I could never yet receive any Answer or Excuse that could raise in me the least doubt of the Unlawfulness of it.—That which I have heard pleaded for it, is to this Effect; *viz.*

Plea 1. We deny the Charge, we do not Steal them: but make a lawful Purchase of them.

A. Purchase them (for Toyes and Baubles) perhaps you may: but lawfully I am sure you cannot. For they which Sell them do Steal them, or take them away by violence. And you know the Proverb, *The* DEALER *is as bad as the* STEALER. We are they that call our selves Christians, that Encourage them in such Evil Practices. Our Law (in many Cases) looks upon the Accessary as bad as the Thief. I am sure, the Law of God does. *Prov.* 29. 24. *Whoso is Partner with a Thief, hateth his own Soul.* And the holy Psalmist charges it as a great crime, when we see a Thief, to consent with him, *Psal.* 50. 18. The Learned and Pious Bishop *Hall*, in his Decade of Cases of Conscience, *Decade* 1. *Case* 10. *p.* 66. Resolves this Case; That to buy those Goods, which we know, or have just cause to suspect, are stoln or plunder'd; is no better than to make our selves accessary to the Thief; If you do it with an intention to possess them as your own (*i.e.* not return them to the right Owner) For what do you else but *ex post facto*, partake with that Thief which stole them, and encourage him in his leud practices; since according to the old Word, *If there were no* RECEIVERS, *there would be no* THIEVES.

Plea 2. But most of them are taken Prisoners of War, by one petty Prince from another; and sold by the Conqueror.

A. But who are commonly the cause of this War, or what do they commonly fight about, but to gain the Booty of the Field; Slaves to be Sold?—And I am credibly inform'd 'tis usual for the Traders in this unlawful Commodity, to send Presents to some petty Prince among them, to make War with his Neighbouring Prince, to take such Prisoners, and furnish their Cargo: And who then must answer for all this Blood and Injustice?

Plea 3. Those Men are more Heathens than Pagans?

A. Pray, What then? What have we to do with them? Have they not a common Right to those Temporal Blessings, which an indulgent Creator has given them, as well as we? Is Dominion founded in Grace? May a man that is pleas'd to call himself a Christian, under that Notion, wrong or molest such as had not the Happiness to be born in a Christian Country? Did our Lord and Master (tho' the Lord of the whole World) give us any such Example, when in the World? And doth not the Apostle bid us do good unto all Men, and especially to the houshold of Faith? Tho' we ought to be kinder to our Brother Christian; yet surely we ought to do good; or, at least, to do no wrong to meer Pagans and Infidels.

Plea 4. Did not the Jews buy Slaves? How often do we read of the Bond-Servant bought with their Money in the Jewish Law? And may we not do what God's own People did?

A. I answer First, in the general, that the Judical Law of *Moses* (whereof this about Bond-Slaves, is one) is made void, and no Rule, (further than it carries a moral Reason with it) for Christians to walk by; who (as says the Apostle) are not under the Law, but under Grace. But,

2dly. Let us deal with those poor Negros, as the Jews were commanded to do with the Heathen. 1. When they had bought them, they were obliged to bring them up in the true Religion. See *Gen.* 17. 12, 13. God commands *Abraham,* He that is born in thy House, or bought with Money of any Stranger which is not thy seed; such an one must needs be Circumcised, and brought into Covenant with God. 2. Whilst they were in the House, they were to be kind and loving towards them; and tis often repeated, Be kind unto Strangers; for you your selves were Strangers in the land of Egypt.

Plea 5. The Law of our Land allows it.

A. The Law of our Land is so far from allowing it; that if an Infidel be brought into this Kingdom, as soon as he can give an Account of the Christian Faith and desires to be Baptized; any Charitable lawful Minister may do it: and then he is under the same Law with other Christians— As for our Islanders abroad; from whence they came, what carried them thither, and what kind of Christians the most of them are; I need not inform you. 'Tis their great *Diana,* by this Craft they have their Gain. And therefore we can never expect that they should make any private or By-Laws against it. But if the Law be ever so much silent in this Case; He that will do any thing that the Law (which can never provide in all Cases) does not plainly forbid: would be but a bad Subject, and I'm sure, a Worse Christian.

Lastly, They say, They thereby make them, those useless Creatures, to become greatly advantagious to Mankind; bring them into happier Condition: and many of them become good Christians. *&c.*

A. How dare we pretend to order things better than an All-Wise Lawgiver has plainly commanded us? Or think to put those poor Wretches to better Uses, than an all-wise Providence seems as yet, to have design'd them for? If they came freely, what need a Cargo be carried to purchase 'em? What need of Chains, and Bolts, and Fetters? And why do many of those poor Wretches endeavour to starve, or destroy themselves, or leap overboard: If so mighty glad of being carried into perpetual Slavery? Or if they find themselves happier under their Bondage, than in their own Country: What is the reason that when one of their Fellow-Slaves dyes, all the rest sing, and rejoyce, and dance about him; as foolishly concluding he is happily returned to his own Country? And tho' some of them may be admitted to become Christians, 'tis more than the Seller knows, or any way obliges the Purchaser to: Neither can that attone for the rest. And surely, methinks, what as [*sic*] been said, should be enough to convince all such as are not resolved before-hand, that they will not be convinced; or at least, to render the Case extraordinary dubious; and then the safer part is to be chosen, specially in this Case, where (if we are afterward convinced we have done those poor Wretches any wrong) We can never make them Restitution.

A BRIEF RULE To guide the Common-People of New-England[3]

The *Small Pox* (whose nature and cure the *Measels* follow) is a disease in the blood, endeavouring to recover a new form and state.

2. This nature attempts—1. By Separation of the impure from the pure, thrusting it out from the Veins to the Flesh.—2. By driving out the impure from the Flesh to the Skin.

3. The first Separation is done in the first four dayes by a Feaverish boyling (Ebullition) of the Blood, laying down the impurities in the Fleshy parts which kindly effected the Feaverish tumult is calmed.

4. The second Separation from the Flesh to the Skin, or *Superficies* is done through the rest of the time of the disease.

[3] Massachusetts Broadside (Boston, 1677). Subtitle: How to order themselves and theirs in the Small Pocks, or Measels.

5. There are several Errors in ordering these sick ones in both these Operations of Nature which prove very dangerous and commonly deadly either by overmuch hastening Nature beyond its own pace, or in hindering of it from its own vigorous operation.

6. The Separation by Ebullition in the Feaverish heat is over heightned by too much Clothes, too hot a room, hot *Cordials*, as *Diascordium*, *Gascons powder* and such like, for hence come *Phrenzies*, dangerous excessive sweats, or the flowing of the Pocks into one overspreading sore, vulgarly called the Flox.

7. The same seperation is overmuch hindred by preposterous cooling that Feaverish boyling heat, by *blood letting*, *Glysters*, *Vomits*, *purges*, or *cooling medicines*. For though these many times hasten the coming forth of the *Pox*, yet they take away that supply which should keep them out till they are ripe, wherefore they sink in again to the deadly danger of the sick.

8. If a *Phrensie* happen, or through a *Plethorie* (that is fulness of blood) the Circulation of the blood be hindred, and thereupon the whole mass of blood choaked up, then either let blood, Or see that their diet, or medicines be not altogether cooling, but let them in no wise be heating, therefore let him lye no otherwise covered in his bed then he was wont in health: His Chamber not made hot with fire if the weather be temperate, let him drink small Beer only warm'd with a Tost, let him sup up thin *water-gruel*, or *water pottage* made only of Indian Flour and water, instead of *Oat-meal*: Let him eat *boild Apples*: But I would not advise at this time any medicine besides. By this means that excessive *Ebullition* (or boyling of his blood) will by degrees abate, and the Symptoms cease; If not, but the blood be so inraged that it will admit no delay, then either let blood (if Age will bear it) or else give some notably cooling medicine, or refresh him with more free Air.

9. But if the boiling of the blood be weak and dull that there is cause to fear it is not able to work a Separation,

as it's wont to be in such as have been let blood, or are fat, or Flegmatick, or brought low by some other sickness or labour of the (*Gonorrhea*) running of the Reins, or some other Evacuation: In such Cases, *Cordials* must drive them out, or they must dy.

10. In time of driving out the *Pocks* from the Flesh, here care must be had that the *Pustules* keep out in a right measure till they have attain'd their end without going in again, for that is deadly.

11. In this time take heed when the *Pustules* appear whilst not yet ripe, least by too much heat there arise a new *Ebullition* (or Feaverish boyling) for this troubles the driving out, or brings back the separated parts into the blood, or the Fleshy parts overheated are disabled from a right suppuration or lastly the temper of the blood and tone of the Flesh is so perverted that it cannot overcome and digest the matter driven out.

12. Yet on the other hand the breaking out must not be hindred, by exposing the sick unto the cold. The degree of heat must be such as is natural agrees with the temper of the fleshy parts: That which exceeds or falls short is dangerous: Therefore the season of the year, Age of the sick, and their manner of life here require a discreet and different Consideration, requiring the Counsel of an expert Physitian.

13. But if by any error a new *Ebullition* ariseth, the same art must be used to allay it as is before exprest.

14. If the *Pustle's* go in and a flux of the belly follows (for else there is no such danger) then *Cordials* are to be used, yet moderate and not too often for fear of new *Ebullition*.

15. If much spitting (*Ptyalismus*) follow, you may hope all will go well, therefore by no means hinder it: Only with warm small Beer let their mouths be washed.

16. When the *Pustles* are dryed and fallen, purge well, especially if it be in *Autumn*.

17. As soon as this disease therefore appears by its signs, let the sick abstein from Flesh and Wine, and open Air, let

him use small Bear [*sic*] warmed with a Tost for his ordinary drink, and moderately when he desires it. For food use *water-gruel*, *water-pottage*, and other things having no manifest hot quality, easy of digestion, boild Apples, and milk sometimes for change, but the coldness taken off. Let the use of his bed be according to the season of the year, and the multitude of the *Pocks*, or as sound persons are wont: In Summer let him rise according to custome, yet so as to be defended both from heat and cold in Excess, the disease will be the sooner over and less troublesome, for being kept in bed nourisheth the Feaverish heat and makes the *pocks* break out with a painful inflamation.

19. In a colder season, and breaking forth of a multitude of *Pustules*, forcing the sick to keep his bed, let him be covered according to his custome in health, a moderate fire in the winter being kindled in his Chamber, morning and Evening: neither need he keep his Arms alwayes in bed, or ly still in the same place, for fear least he should sweat which is very dangerous especially to youth.

20. Before the fourth day use no medicines to drive out, nor be too strict with the sick; for by how much the more gently the *Pustules* do grow, by so much the fuller and perfecter will the Separation be.

21. On the fourth day a gentle *Cordial* may help once given.

22. From that time a small draught of warm milk (not hot) a little dy'd with *Saffron* may be given morning and evening till the *Pustules* are come to their due greatness and ripeness.

23. When the *Pustules* begin to dry and crust, least the rotten vapours strike inward, which sometimes causeth sudden death; Take morning and evening some temperate *Cordial* as four or five spoonfuls of *Malaga Wine* tinged with a little *Saffron*.

24. When the *Pustules* are dryd and fallen off, purge once and again, especially in the *Autumn Pocks*.

25. Beware of anointing with *Oils*, *Fatts*, *Ointments*,

and such defensives, for keeping the corrupted matter in the *Pustules* from drying up; by the moisture they fret deeper into the Flesh, and so make the more deep Scarrs.

26. The young and lively men that are brought to a plentiful sweat in this sickness, about the eighth day the sweat stops of it self, by no means afterwards to be drawn out again; the sick thereupon feels most troublesome disrest and anguish, and then makes abundance of water and so dyes.

Few young men and strong thus handled escape, except they fall into abundance of spitting or plentiful bleeding at the nose.

27. Signs discovering the Assault at first are beating pain in the head, Forehead, and temples, pain in the back, great sleepiness, glistring of the eyes, shining glimmerings seem before them, itching of them also, with tears flowing of themselves, itching of the Nose, short breath, dry Cough, oft [s]neezing, hoarseness, heat, redness, and sense of pricking over the whole body, terrors in the sleep, sorrow and restlessness, beating of the heart, *Urine* sometimes as in health, sometime filthy from great *Ebullition*, and all this or many of these with a Feaverish distemper.

28. Signs warning of the probable Event. If they break forth easily, quickly, and soon come to ripening, if the Symptomes be gentle, the Feaver mild, and after the breaking forth it abates; If the voice be free, and breathing easie; especially if the Pox be red white distinct, soft few, round, sharp top'd, only without and not in the inward parts; if there be large bleeding at the nose. These signs are hopeful.

29. But such signs are doubtful, when they difficultly appear, when they sink in again, when they are black, blewish, green, hard, all in one, if the Feaver abate not with their breaking forth, if there be Swooning, difficulty of breathing, great thirst, quinsey, great unquietness, and it is very dangerous, if there be ioyn'd with it some other malignant Feaver, called by some the pestilential Pox: the *Spotted Feaver* is oft joyned with it.

30. Deadly Signs if the *Flux* of the *Belly* happen, when

they are broke forth, if the Urine be bloody, or black, or the *Ordure* of that Colour; Or if pure blood be cast out by the Belly or Gumms: These Signs are for the most part deadly.

These things have I written Candid Reader, *not to inform the Learned* Physitian *that hath much more cause to understand what pertains to this disease than I, but to give some light to those that have not such advantages, leaving the difficulty of this disease to the* Physitians *Art, Wisdome, and Faithfulness: for the right managing of them in the whole Course of the disease tends both to the* Patients *safety, and the* Physitians *disired Success in his Administrations: For in vain is the* Physitians *Art imployed, if they are not under a* Regular Regiment. *I am, though no* Physitian, *yet a well wisher to the sick: And therefore intreating the Lord to turn our hearts, and stay his hand, I am*

A Friend, Reader to thy
Welfare,
Thomas Thacher.

21.11.1677/8

BOSTON, Printed and sold by *John Foster.* 1677.

INDEX

Abbay, T., 93f., 105.
Aiken, Conrad, 275.
Almanacs, 32-36, 137 *seq.*, 209f., 281-330 (chronological order): agriculture, 53f., 306ff.; astronomy, 34, 41-51, 281-288, 294f., 304-306, telescope, 47f., 314f.; geography, 289f.; medicine, 65, 321f.; meteorology, 51-53, 291f., 301-304, 307-308, 315-317; religion, 33f., 288f., 292-294, 295-301, 317-321; satire, 308-314, 322-330.
Alsop, George, 13, 14, 15, 18, 85f., 95f., 105, 112f., 128, 272.
Anatomies, 150, 205-207.
Apuleius, *Herbarium*, 207.
Aristotle, 111, 247, 250, 266.
Astronomy and astrology, see almanacs.

Bacon, Francis, 5, 97, 98, 194, 207, 212, 238, 239f.
Bay Psalm Book, 107-110, 115, 127, 272.
Beverly, Robert, *History of Virginia*, 55, 76.
Bible, influence, 240-243.
Biography, 127-131, 168-175, 187 *seq.*
Botany, 55-56.
Boyle, Sir Robert, 40, 205.
Bradford, William, 7, 214; *Journal*, 115; *Dialogue*, 116, 171f.; history, 16, 117, 127; *Memoir of Elder Brewster,* 174; portrait of Lyford, 173f.
Bradstreet, Mrs. Anne, 7, 81, 82, 105, 152-154, 274f., 279, 280.
Brattle, Thomas, witchcraft, 23f.
——————,William, 32, 34f., 238, 240, 294.
Bridge, Thomas, *Jethro's Advice*, 163, 221.
Brigden, Zech., 281.
Browne, Sir Thomas, 5; *Pseudodoxia Epidemica*, 207, 226.
Burton, Robert, 5, *Anatomie of Melancholy*, 205-207; 226.

Calef, Robert, *More Wonders of the Invisible World*, 19n.
Camden, *Britannia*, 211, *History of Elizabeth*, 212.
Castiglione, *The Book of the Courtier*, 217, 222 *seq.*
"Character," The, 158-167, 168 *seq.*, 215, 217n.
Chauncy, Israel, 43, 238.
——————, Nathaniel, 43, 238, 286.
C[heever], S[amuel], 283.
Cicero, 247-257, *passim*, 266.
Clap, Roger, *Memoirs*, 82.
Classical inheritance, 3, 5, 245-262.

Clough, Samuel, 33f., 43, 53, 137, 138, 210.
Colman, Benjamin, *Faith Victorious*, 158, 164f., 244, *Practical Discourses . . . the Ten Virgins*, 158, 160f., 162.
Comet, 46, 331-345.
Cook, Ebenezer, *The Sot-Weed Factor*, 133n.
Cotton, John, *The Bloody Tenent, Washed*, 143; style, 226f., 234-236, 239; *The Way of Life*, preface by William Morton, 97; 266.
Courtesy books, 216-225, *passim.*
Crèvecoeur, St. John de, 104n.
Cudworth, James, 84.
Culpepper, *English Physician*, 65.
Culture, 3 *seq.*; literary influences, 203-225.
Cushman, Robert, 116; *Self-Love*, 157.

Danforth, S., 43, 46; on the comet, 331-345.
Davis, William, *Jesus the Crucified Man*, 98f.
Demosthenes, 247, 252.
Denton, Daniel, *A Brief Description of New York*, 11, 12, 76, 114, 264.
Douglass, Dr., 64n., 67.
Du Bartas, *Divine Weeks and Works*, 274.
Dudley, Joseph, 32, 47.
——————, Thomas, 83, 91.
Dummer, Jeremy, *Discourse on the Holiness of the Sabbath*, I. Mather's preface, 130.
Dunton, John, *Letters from New England*, 88-91.

Earthquakes, 68-70.
Eliot, John, 83.
Elyot, Thomas, *The Governour*, 217-219, 222-225.
Erasmus, *Manual of a Christian Knight*, 218, 219.
Essays to Do Good, i, 180, 194-199, 263.
Exempla, 186, 215-216.

Flint, Josiah, 32, 33, 87, 238, 288.
Foster, John, 43, 205, 291.
Foxe, *Book of Martyrs*, 84, 216.

Gates, Sir Thomas, 272.
Gookin, Daniel, letter to Charles II, 103.

Hale, John, *A Modest Inquiry into . . . Witchcraft*, 19n., 26.
Hammond, John, *Leah and Rachell*, 10n., 113.
Harvard, John, 4.
Harvard College, Laws of, 3, 233, 245.
Hermogenes, 260-261.

Higginson, Francis, *New England's Plantation*, 9-11, 13, 18, 204.
————, John, 26, 116, 118, 127, 128.
History, theory of writing, 111-127; influences, 210-215.
Holme, Captain, *A Short Advertisement*, 10.
Hooke, William, on war, 29ff., 264.
Hooker, Thomas, 84; *Culpable Ignorance*, 157; style, 241-243, 244; *A Survey of the Summe of Church Discipline*, 100f.; *Wilful Hardnesse*, 157.
Horne, Robert, *A Brief Description of the Province of Carolina*, 10n,
Hubbard, William, *The Present State of New England*, 26n., 124f.

Indians, 71-76.
Isador of Seville, *De Natura Rerum*, 207, 209.

Johnson, Thomas H., 277.
Josselyn, John, *New England's Rarities*, 10, 56, 58f., 66f., 71-73, 208f., 271; *Account of Two Voyages*, 76.

Keith, George, An Exhortation . . . Concerning . . . Negroes, 28; Quaker controversy, 139ff.; 210; 306, 327-330.
Kittredge, G. L., *Witchcraft in Old and New England*, 18n.
Knight, Madame Sarah K., 78f., 80, 271.

Lawson, John, *A New Voyage to Carolina*, 59f., 76.
Leeds, Daniel, 33n., 36, *Temple of Wisdom*, 39f., 47f., 240; 53, 65; Quaker controversy 139ff.; 210; 306, 327-330.
Leigh, Edward, "Hints for Travellers," *Three Diatribes*, 204.
Libraries, 4ff.
Livy, on history, 213.
"Lover of Astronomy," 137, 322.
Lucian, on history, 213f.

Machiavelli, 217.
Magnalia, see C. Mather.
Mason, Capt. John, *Some Grounds of War against the Pequots*, 119-124, 127.
Mather, Cotton, 7, 40, 176-199, 208, 236, 239, 265; almanacs, 33, 43, 64n., 295; *Batteries Upon the Kingdom of the Devil*, 28, 157, 159; *Christianus per Ignem*, 191-194; *Decennium Luctuosum*, 181f.; diary 80, 176ff., *Essays to Do Good*, i, 180, 194-199, 263; funeral sermons on Wigglesworth, 167, 249, 259, on Winthrop, 158; *Great Physician*, 180n.; *Magnalia*, 128, 152, 183-190, 228; *Manuductio ad Ministerium*, 110n., 346-352; *Meat Out of the Eater*, 179; meditations, 148f.; *Memorable Providences*, 19n., 20, 21, 26f., 27, 128; *Memoria Wilsoniana*, 157, poetry, criticism, 346-350; *Political*

Fables, 133, 135f., 143, 146; reading, 230n.; smallpox, 64n., 67, 68; "stage player unmasked," 28, 159; style, 184f., 228-232, 244, 271, 272, 350-352; *Things That Young People Should Think Upon*, 28, 158; *Unum Necessarium*, 179; *Winter Meditations*, 190f.; witchcraft, 19-27, *passim*, letter to Richards, 23, 27; *Wonders of the Invisible World*, 19n., 20n., 21f., 24f., 26.
———, Increase, 23, *Cases of Conscience Concerning Witchcraft*, 25f., comet, 46; *Early History of New England*, 125f.; earthquakes, 68-70; *Illustrious Providences*, 19n., 23, 27; preface to Dummer's *Discourse*, 130; to Willard's *Peril of the Times*, 129; *Relations of the Troubles which have hapned in New England*, 119n.
———, Nathaniel, 43, 304.
———, Richard, preface to *The Bay Psalm Book*, 107-110, 272.
———, Samuel, 128, 231f.
Medicine, 64-67, 321, 357-362.
Meditations, 147-154.
Menander, Rhetor, 256-260, *passim*.
Mitchel, Jonathan, 86.
Monardes, *The New Founde World*, 207.
Moodey, Joshua, 20n.
Moray, Sir Robert, 40, 67.
More, Dr. Nicholas, 54, 83.
Morison, Samuel Eliot, 275.
Morrell, William, *Nova Anglia*, 104.
Morton, Charles, 20n., 26n., 37-39, 40f., 90f., *The Spirit of Man*, 149f., 245-255, *passim*; *Whence came the Stork*, 60-63, 272.
———, Nathaniel, *New England's Memorial*, 116, 117, 118f., 127, 128, 203n., 208.
———, Thomas, *New England Canaan*, 13n., 272.
———, William, preface to Cotton's *The Way of Life*, 97, 240.
"Mourt, G.," 115, 116.
Murdock, Kenneth, 18n., on C. Mather's reading, 230n.

Natural histories, 207-209.
New England's Crisis, 102f.
Newman, H., 43, 44, 46, 314.
Nowell, Alexander, 43, 238.

Oakes, Urian, preface to I. Mather's *Divine Right of Infant Baptism*, 100.
Ovid, 84, 237, 273.

Pain, Philip, 273.
Pascall, Thomas, 83.

Pemberton, Ebenezer, *Divine Original and Dignity of Government*, 220f.; funeral sermon on Willard, 168; *Souldier Defended and Directed*, 162f.; 215.
Penn, William, 10, 18, 114, 264.
Personal records, 78-91.
Pliny, *Natural History*, 5, 207, 208, 209, 315.
Poetry, 271-280.
Polybius, on history, 213.
Pory, John, 83.
Prefaces, dedications, *etc.*, 92-131; familiar spirit, 93-96; didactic spirit, 96-101; critical estimates: apology, 102-104; poetry, 105-110; history, 111-127; literary biography, 127-131.
Prince, Thomas, 117, 119.
Purchas His Pilgrimes, 203.
Pusey, Caleb, 142.

Quaker controveries, 133, 137, 139, 142.
Quarles, 218.
Quintilian, 247-260, *passim.*

Raleigh, Sir Walter, *History of the World*, 211, 274.
Reading, of colonists, 3 *seq.*; see C. Mather.
Rich, Richard, *Newes from Virginia*, preface on poetry, 105f., 272, 273.
Rogers, John, *Sixty Memorials*, 152.
R[ussell], Daniel, 289, 301.

Sandys, George, 7, 106, 273.
Satire, 132-146, see almanacs.
Science, 37-77, 204-209.
Sermon, 155-167.
Sewall, Samuel, diary, 78-80, 84f., 87, 91; on slavery, 28, 352-357; 236, 264.
Shakespeare, William, *The Tempest*, 273.
Shepard, Thomas, 82; letter to his son, 88, 240, 250, 252f.; *Theses Sabbaticae*, 233.
Sherman, John, 33, 292.
——————, Stuart, 1n., 132n.
Slavery, 28f.; 352-357.
Smallpox, 64n., 65, 67, 357-362.
Smith, George G., *Elizabethan Critical Essays*, 101.
——————, Capt. John i, 1, 8, 10, 15; "A note for men that haue great spirits, and smal meanes, 15, 18; 55, 71, 93-95, 96, 112, 118, 126, 128, 263, 264, 265.
Stanford, Donald, 277.

Stoddard, Solomon, *Gods Frown in the Death of Useful Men*, 165.
Stone, Samuel, *A Congregational Church*, 128.
Style, 126-127, 226-244; see C. Mather.

Taylor, Jacob, 41f., 43; Quaker controversy, 139ff.; 210, 322-327.
————, Edward, 37, 277-279, 280.
Thacher, Thomas, on smallpox, 65, 116, 118, 357-362.
Thomas, Gabriel, 114f.
Travel, 8 *seq.*, 203f.
Travis, Daniel, 44.
Tulley, John, 33, 49f., 51f., 53, 65, 137, 208, 210, 307, 308-314, 315, 317-321.

Usher, John, bookseller, 6.

Wadsworth, Benjamin, *Considerations to Prevent Murmuring*, 158; *Good Soldiers a Great Blessing*, 30n.; *King William Lamented in America*, 166, 169, 258.
Ward, Nathaniel, *Simple Cobler of Aggawam*, 30f., 105, 133-135, 143, 146 264, 272.
Wendell, Barrett, *Cotton Mather*, 18n.
W[hittemore], N., 137, 138f., 210.
Wigglesworth, Michael, 26n., 81, 82, 259, *Day of Doom*, 107; 167, 186, 215, 249, 275-277, 278, 279.
Willard, Samuel, 20n., 26n., 90, 215, 239; *Brief Meditations*, 150f.; *Character of a Good Ruler*, 103f., 162, 220-222; *Child's Portion*, preface, 97f.; *Fiery Trial*, 155; *Peril of the Times Displayed*, 28n., 129; *Truly Blessed Man*, 158, 162.
Williams, Roger, 133, *Bloody Tenent of Persecution*, 143f.; . . . *Yet More Bloody*, 143; *George Fox Digg'd Out of His Burrowes*, 143; *Key Unto the Language of America*, 73-76, 82n., 118; style, 234-236, 239, 243f., 253, 265, 266, 272.
————, William, 52, 303.
Winslow, Edward, *A Short Story . . . of the Antinomians*, 100; *Journal*, 115.
Winthrop, John, "little speech on liberty," 28; 81, 82.
————, ————, Jr., basket-fish, 63f., 68, 265; letter to his son, 87.
Witchcraft, 18-27.
Wood, William, *New England's Prospect*, 10, 12, 13, 15, 18, 54f., 57, 68, 71, 118, 128, 204, 237f., 264, 265, 271.
Woodbridge, John, 105.
W[ooley], C., *A Two Years Journal in New York*, 76.
Wright, Thomas Goddard, *Literary Culture in Early New England*, 4 *seq.*, 211n.

Zoology, ornithology, etc., 57-64.